The Active Writer

THE ACTIVE WRITER

MICHAEL J. FRISBIE
DOUGLAS CHICKERING
SUSAN S. FRISBIE
ARTHUR W. HALL
JO KEROES
MELANIE SPERLING

With the Assistance of
PATRICIA TOLLEFSON

MACMILLAN PUBLISHING CO., INC.
New York

COLLIER MACMILLAN PUBLISHERS
London

To Bill Robinson

Macmillan Publishing Co., Inc.
866 Third Avenue, New York, New York 10022

Collier Macmillan Canada, Ltd.

"The Movers" by Russell Lynes on pp. 51–53 is reprinted from *The Domesticated Americans* by Russell Lynes. Copyright © 1957, 1963 by Russell Lynes. Reprinted by permission of Harper & Row, Publishers, Inc.

"Marrying Absurd" by Joan Didion, pp. 68–70, is reprinted from *Slouching Towards Bethlehem* by Joan Didion. Copyright © 1969 by Joan Didion. Reprinted by permission of Farrar, Straus and Giroux, Inc.

"Being a Boy" by Julius Lester, pp. 72–75, is reprinted from *MS Magazine*, July 1973, pp. 112–113.

"Shame" by Dick Gregory, pp. 77–80, is reprinted from *Nigger* by Dick Gregory with Robert Lipsyte. Copyright © 1964 by Dick Gregory Enterprises, Inc. Reprinted by permission of the publisher, E. P. Dutton.

"Farewell" by Roger Angell, pp. 83–84, is reprinted from *The Summer Game* by Roger Angell. Copyright © 1968 by Roger Angell. Reprinted by permission of Viking Penguin Inc.

Library of Congress Cataloging in Publication Data

Main entry under title:

The Active Writer

    Includes index.
    1. English language—Rhetoric. I. Frisbie,
Michael J.
PE1408.R28   808'.042   81-6028
ISBN 0-02-339520-6   AACR2

Printing: 4 5 6 7 8   Year: 5 6 7 8 9

ISBN 0-02-339520-6

Preface

Students (and teachers) sometimes find it hard to think of the writing done in a composition class as "real." Paragraphs and essays too often seem only exercises to show that a student has mastered some particular concept, like how to use the semicolon or how to compare and contrast.

But stop and think for a moment.

The very thoughts that you just stopped and thought were formed with words, phrases, and sentences: the clarity of your thoughts depends on the clarity of the words, phrases, and sentences expressing them.

The process of putting any words down on paper, then, reflects the mysterious and highly individual process of thought. And while it's true that our innermost thoughts may be more complex or eloquent than the 500 words in an English paper, our minds are judged and sharpened by our writing.

This isn't a book about how to think. It's not even a guide to writing like a professional.

But it does offer you choices—

choices among words, so that you can pick the one that says exactly what you're thinking

choices among sentences, so that you can create rhythms that match your voice

choices among methods of development, so that you can construct, or perhaps reconstruct, the arguments, experiences, and insights that lead to the point of your paper

choices among the many ways to join and separate ideas, so that you can make your reader see the connections you've forged in your mind

choices among essay forms, so that the structure of your paper suits your purpose and topic

choices among the sometimes treacherous array of mechanical and grammatical constructions, so that you'll spell the right word the right way

We'd be lying if we promised that learning to write better will make you a better thinker. But we'd also be lying if we said that it can't. If you can see writing for this class as a chance to sharpen your thoughts and your ability to form them, to think about things that interest you and to figure out *why* they interest you, to gain control over the way other people understand you—you'll be doing yourself a greater service than this textbook, or any other, can.

Acknowledgments

We would like to thank the staff at Macmillan, including John Travis, our Production Editor, who coordinated the complex transition from manuscript to finished book. We are especially grateful to D. Anthony English, Executive Editor at Macmillan, for his confidence in this project, as well as for his advice and wit, both of which gave us sustenance. We also thank our students, some of whose work appears in these ages, and all of whom made us better teachers.

A NOTE TO THE STUDENT

While *The Active Writer* is designed to be used as a textbook, you needn't wait for your instructor to assign a specific section before you can use the book to advantage. We'd suggest that you take a few minutes to leaf through the text, to get a general idea of what it covers. Even on this initial pass, you might notice a few topics that have given you trouble in the past; if so, it wouldn't hurt to get a jump on them now by at least skimming those portions.

Whether you're reading on your own or as part of an assignment, always try to read as actively as possible (when we're not complaining that writing is becoming a lost art, English teachers are usually worrying about the decline and fall of careful reading). As you move through a passage, ask yourself questions to see whether you fully understand what you've read. Look carefully at the examples and see how they illustrate the explanation that precedes or follows them. As the course progresses, find examples in your own papers of the principles discussed in the book. Pay particular attention to the exercises, which you should always do on paper, not just in your head; if an exercise proves troublesome, reread the explanation in the text, then try the exercise again. Use the index and the Usage Manual to clarify points and to help you benefit from your instructor's comments on your papers: if the discussion of fragments in the text doesn't seem clear enough, check the corresponding entry in the Usage Manual; if your instructor suggests that you might need to define your terms more fully or that you need a stronger thesis statement, look up "definition" and "thesis statements" in the index and check out the appropriate sections of the book.

One of our main messages in this text is that you should make conscious and active choices in your writing. You'll find the book itself more useful if you approach it attentively and actively as well.

If you find the idea of even beginning any sort of writing project distressing, it may help to know that most writers, even professionals, feel some anxiety when they face a blank page. But if writing can be frightening, it can also be exhilarating. The British novelist V. Sackville-West used to say that while she hated writing, she loved having written. Often the pleasure you take in completing an activity is proportional to the effort you put into it: the joy of mentally wrestling with a subject and getting the results on paper is much like the pleasure of winning a hard-fought athletic match. It can be exciting to discover, through writing, precisely what you think and feel about a subject; it can be rewarding to impart your thoughts clearly and interestingly to someone else.

Later in the book, we discuss some particular ways to get started on longer assignments. For now, we'll offer some general suggestions that may make the process of getting started on any assignment less difficult.

Often, just getting the first words down—any first words—is the hardest step. It might help, then, to just jot down a couple of notes on the topic. This not only gets the first words down on paper, thereby breaking the verbal ice, but also starts your creative energies flowing. Research shows that we do our most creative thinking about a problem when we work with it for a time and then get away from it. So if you write just a few lines on a topic, you've started your assignment and earned the luxury of just thinking about it for a while.

If you feel overwhelmed by an assignment, it may help to remember the story of the man who was told he had to eat an entire elephant. When he asked how he could ever manage such a task, the answer was, "One bite at a time." So break your writing down into bite-size pieces. Having made your initial notes, you can set them aside until tomorrow (providing, of course, that you're not writing in class). Then you can go over your notes, arranging your points into a provisional outline. Next, after a suitable and well-earned break, you'll do a rough draft, without worrying too much about how each sentence is phrased. Next, you can polish your draft, adding transitions, filling in details, eliminating padding, checking punctuation, looking up words you're not sure how to spell. Finally, you read the finished draft aloud, improve it where necessary, and write up the final version. You can find a real measure of satisfaction, and calm, in setting up and following a workable schedule.

Even when you're writing in class, make a list of the steps you'll follow in writing your paper. Just knowing that you don't have to create a piece of writing in one motion can help allay your anxiety. As you jot down your ideas, as you write up an outline, as you move through your first draft—check off each task, looking ahead only to the next one, not to the sometimes intimidating process of writing the whole paper.

Sometimes, though, it's hard to get started at all. Here are some ideas that may help when you're really stuck:

1. If you can't bear the thought of putting in a solid hour or two on an assignment, promise yourself that you can stop after half an hour or even fifteen minutes. Then take a break (if you still feel like stopping after fifteen minutes), and schedule another mini-session for yourself.

2. Put your thoughts down on three-by-five cards or scraps of paper as they occur to you; you might want to carry a pocket note-book with you, so you can make notes whenever inspiration strikes. After you've accumulated some notes, go through them, looking for relationships among your ideas and putting related scraps into the same pile. This should help you arrive at what you want to say, and even the order in which you want to say it.

3. Don't feel you have to begin writing at the beginning of your paper. Write any part that seems clear in your mind, whole paragraphs or even individual sentences. You may have an easier time filling in the rest once you have something down.

4. If possible (not in class, unfortunately), talk your ideas out, either to a friend or to yourself, perhaps into a tape recorder. Once you've got an idea out in speech, it may easily make the transition to paper.

5. When the ideas just won't flow, stop fighting it for a while.

Again, we want to stress that no essay or paragraph springs full-grown from the writer's pen or typewriter. Each is built one step at a time, at a different pace and in a different order for each writer. If you break your task down into steps that seem reasonable to you, you're more likely to end up with a piece of writing that will please both you and your readers.

Contents

The Active Writer

Some General (and Specific) Principles

There's an important difference between writing just for yourself—taking class notes, keeping a diary, jotting down a shopping list—and writing for other people. If no one else can decipher your notes, or make sense of the entry "pick up stuff for Friday" on your shopping list, it doesn't matter. But if your letters, job applications, and papers for school are not as clear to the people reading them as they are to you, you've got a problem: the friend reading your letter is confused, the employer is reluctant to hire you, and your teacher may give you a low grade.

Most of the writing you do for others, particularly in college, must do more than just make sense. *It must also make a point of some kind.* In other words, it must explain or defend an idea. (A play-by-play account of a football game or a description of your morning routine makes sense, but it doesn't, in itself, have a point.) You can usually make your point clear only if you support it with specific evidence and explanation. Writing for college involves a constant interplay between your *general ideas* and the *specific details* necessary to make them understandable and believable.

To achieve the blend of the general and specific that is usually necessary in a piece of writing, you can begin working in a couple of

1

ways. You can start with a general observation and then hunt up the evidence to support it. Or you can first gather information on the topic you're writing about and then see what conclusions you can draw.

Working from the General to the Specific

If you work from the general to the specific, you have the advantage of beginning with at least a tentative idea of what you want to say. You then need only select the specifics that enable you to make your point clearly and convincingly.

We use this same general-to-specific approach in other kinds of situations—in planning a meal, for instance. If you knew you were having company, you'd probably first decide what to serve them and then assemble the specific ingredients. If you wanted to have spaghetti, salad, French bread, and fresh fruit, you'd review what you needed for each course, check to see what was already around the house, and then go buy the rest. While shopping, you might find that lettuce was high in price and low in quality this week or that the stores were out of French bread. In that case, you might want to revise your menu.

You might work in more or less the same way if you were writing a paper for your English class. Assume you were asked to write about television. First, you'd decide what you wanted to say on the subject. Realizing that most critics see TV as a mindless medium geared to a dimwitted norm, you could decide to write a paper whose point was that TV is dumb. This probably wouldn't interest your readers, however, since they would have heard that point before. And, just as important, writing such a paper wouldn't interest you very much either.

After pondering the matter for a while, you realize that deep down you think television is okay: it's relaxing, it's free, it's occasionally entertaining and almost never demanding. So you decide to write a paper praising TV the way it is, asserting that America needs a low-level form of entertainment for people to turn to.

Having chosen your general point, you then need to back that point up. It's not enough to write, "I think television is fine the way it is." That's only vaguely clear, it's not at all interesting, and most teachers won't accept a paper that short. So you draw on your own experiences with television, recalling the many times you've arrived home exhausted, seeking comfort from the friendly tube. You realize that for all the talk of television's being aimed at a single common denominator, it actually caters to quite a diverse audience, from fans of roller derby to opera buffs, from people who like only movies from the thirties and forties to those who watch only the news. You remember seeing an article in last week's *Time* indicating that 82 per cent of those polled wouldn't change the programming coming into their homes. Integrating these facts with your general point, and maybe revising the general point to fit the facts, you write a paper that is clear to the reader and less dreary for you than a rote recitation of the arguments against TV that everyone has heard and just about memorized.

Other kinds of "real world" writing work on the same general-to-specific principle. Most people writing in response to newspaper editorials *first* react to the newspaper's position and *then* recall or find the facts necessary to support their rebuttal. If this book's authors read an editorial attacking college English teachers, we would of course instantly disagree with the writer. As we calmed down, we would need to think of or look for evidence to show the editorial writer and the readers of the newspaper that college English teachers are generally doing a heroic and splendid job. If your landload dropped by to tell you that he was raising your rent, presumably—unless you're saintlike in your fairness or independently wealthy—you wouldn't sit down and weigh the landlord's needs against the tenants' before deciding on your attitude toward the rent raise. You'd probably react immediately against your landlord's proposal. If you decided to write him in protest, you would then need to come up with enough facts to change the landlord's mind.

EXERCISE 1

A. Each of the general statements below is followed by details, only *some* of which support the statement. Put a checkmark by the valid details and be prepared to explain your choices.

Example:

General statement: Over a decade after the group disbanded, the Beatles' work is still worthy of admiration.

Details: Songs such as "Eleanor Rigby," "She's Leaving Home," and "Rocky Raccoon" are like short stories in miniature. √
The Beatles sold more records than any other rock group.
The lyrics of some of their songs have been compared to classical poetry. √
Many of their songs were recorded by other groups and individuals.
Their records still sell well.
No other group has equalled the imagination and restraint with which the Beatles incorporated musical influences from outside rock and roll, including sitars, string quartets, and British music hall ditties. √

(Only the specifics checked support the general idea that the Beatles' work is to be admired.)

1. *General statement:* Alcoholics Anonymous and Gamblers Anonymous are effective because they give their members vital support in coping with difficult problems.

Details: People draw comfort from knowing that others have similar problems.

Alcoholism and compulsive gambling are diseases.

The "buddy system" is an essential part of such programs; each member has at least one other member to call on.

The group provides counselling to new members.

Members who backslide and take a drink aren't expelled from the group.

Gambling can ruin a person's family life just as drinking can.

Now there are dieters anonymous groups for overweight people and similar groups for child abusers.

2. *General statement:* Dolphins seem to have an extraordinary ability to form sonic images of objects and organisms in their environment.

Details: A dolphin can pick out a foreign object 30 feet away from it amid a school of shrimp by making a simple clicking noise. It senses the object by monitoring the echoes the noise creates.

Regardless of the proportions or composition of an object, a dolphin can, on request, distinguish a particular quality of a distant object—for example, a cylindrical shape.

Dolphins can dive to 1,700 feet below the surface of the water without suffering any ill effects.

At depths below 750 feet dolphins do not suffer from the bends, as humans would, because their ribcage collapses, driving all air from their lungs and thus preventing nitrogen from being absorbed into the bloodstream.

3. *General statement:* A balanced vegetarian diet can meet all of your nutritional needs without the health dangers of a diet containing red meat.

Details: You can get animal protein from milk products as well as meat.

Meat provides protein but so do vegetables.

Red meat contains an unhealthy excess of fat.

Animals must be slaughtered in order for humans to eat meat.

Cholesterol, found in quantity in red meats, has been linked to heart disease.

With rising food costs, vegetarianism is becoming increasingly popular.

Leather products could be made from synthetic materials like vinyl instead of animal hides.

Both meat and vegetables purchased in stores are often contaminated, but while it's possible to wash the pesticides off the vegetables, it's not possible to get rid of the hormones and steroids in the meat.

Because animals are higher on the food chain than plants, it takes more energy to produce meats than vegetables.

4. Decide which of the details above support the following different generalization:

Vegetarianism offers several economic advantages.

B. Supply three supporting details for each of the following general statements.

1. Strength of character requires self-discipline and the willingness to do things that may be distasteful.
2. Filmmakers may try to incorporate serious issues into films intended to entertain mass audiences.
3. Many magazine ads insult readers' intelligence.

C. Write one of your own generalizations and give three supporting points for it.

Working from the Specific to the General

You can also approach a writing assignment from the other direction—by moving from the specific facts to a general conclusion, deciding what point you want to make only after you've sifted through some information.

To see how this principle works in another context, imagine that you and a friend come home some evening after the stores are closed and decide to fix dinner. It would be inefficient and perhaps disappointing to decide what to make until you saw what ingredients were in the house. Looking in the cupboard, you find a box of raisin bran, half a package of spaghetti, a can of condensed milk, tomato paste, an assortment of spices, cooking oil, some graham crackers, two bananas, and some grapes. In the refrigerator you see a bottle of 7-Up, a carton of cottage cheese, lettuce and tomatoes, salad dressing, and, in the freezer, some ground beef, frozen fish, ice cream, and an unidentified mass wrapped in foil. After thinking awhile about how you might put these ingredients together, you decide to fix spaghetti, salad, and French bread, perhaps finishing off the bananas and grapes as you work. You obviously would have been foolish to try to use everything in the house to make a meal, but by assembling your supplies selectively, you could make an acceptable dinner.

In writing your paper on television, you might prefer to mull the topic over before deciding what you want to say, maybe taking some time out to watch TV. You think about sitting in front of the set for eight hours straight last Saturday, watching a tennis match, a Humphrey Bogart movie, and three situation comedies. You remember the mass media class you took last semester, in which most other students admitted that they and their families watched and enjoyed a fair amount of television. In looking over last Sunday's paper, you find an article suggesting that television induces alpha waves in viewers, putting them in a passive, tranquil frame of mind. According to the article, TV is therefore not a good medium for intellectual discussions, serious drama, or anything else mentally taxing. You also remember reading that TV was actually invented back in the 1920s, though not put into commercial use for some time. As you think over these seemingly unrelated facts, you discover a common thread through most of them: people, yourself included, seem to like TV pretty much the way it is. You decide to make that the point of your paper. You won't get to use all of the facts you thought of (for this paper it doesn't make any difference that TV was invented in the 1920s) and you may have to find some new evidence to flesh out your essay. But by working from specific facts toward a general conclusion, you've ended up with a paper like the one generated by the writer who worked from the general to the specific.

You'll find that you also use this specific-to-general approach in preparing writing that you do outside school. Suppose you check into a hotel on your vacation. Even though you have a confirmed reservation, the desk clerk tells you that no rooms are available. After a tedious exchange with the desk clerk and the hotel manager, you are finally given a room smaller than the one you had reserved. You find that the shower drips noisily and incessantly, the heater doesn't work, and the control knobs on the TV are missing. After an uncomfortable night on a rocky mattress, you call downstairs to order some coffee. An hour later, room service arrives with someone else's scrambled eggs. When you check out, two days earlier than you had originally planned, the desk clerk responds to your complaints with a weary, "I'm not sure what you expect *me* to do. Perhaps you had better stay elsewhere in the future."

If you decided to write a letter to the hotel manager or to the president of the conglomerate that owns the hotel, it would be because the *specifics* of the experience led you *to* the *general* conclusion that there was something to complain about. In other words, you didn't walk into the hotel presuming that you would find cause for complaint; that sorry fact became evident only as the irritations piled up.

When you begin working on a writing assignment, neither the general-to-specific nor the specific-to-general approach is necessarily better than the other. You may prefer to work from the general to the specific when you're writing in class or discussing an issue you already feel strongly about. On the other hand, you may find it easier to work from the specific to the general when you have the luxury of time for research and thought or when you're not yet sure exactly what you want to write about. As we've mentioned, the approach you take will not necessarily affect the organization or content of the writing itself. The following paragraph, for instance, could have come from an essay written by someone who began by working in either direction:

> If you subscribe to *The New Yorker,* like Woody Allen movies, read the books on the best seller list, or take adult education classes in astronomy (or astrology), people will admire your active interest in the world around you. You'll also win their praise if you go to museums, attend city council meetings, play bridge, or bake your own bread. But if you timidly suggest that you watch and, even worse, enjoy television, you'll be scorned. It *is* permissible to keep a small, malfunctioning black-and-white set in the closet and to drag it out for National Geographic specials about Africa and British soap operas on Public Television. But anyone with even a touch of couth does not watch talk shows, situation comedies, reruns of *Dragnet,* or the local news. Such fare, the argument runs, does not tap your intellectual and physical reserves, does not put you in touch with your society. Nonsense. *The New Yorker's* "Talk of the Town" is just as trivial as most talk shows; it takes about as much mental and physical exertion to watch *Star Trek* as it does to attend an astrology class; playing along with *The Million Dollar Last Chance Quiz* jostles the brain as much as a couple of hands of bridge; most local news shows aren't any more banal than most local newspapers; you can discharge your civic responsibility by watching *Meet the Press* on Sunday afternoon as well as you can by sitting through the city council meeting on Wednesday night. In short, watching television is no better and no worse than the kinds of activities that win admiration—and television watchers are unlikely to be self-righteous.

The following exercise will give you some practice working from specific details to general conclusions.

EXERCISE 2

A. You awaken suddenly to the sound of an electric alarm clock. The clock says eight. At the same time the grandfather clock in the hall chimes once, indicating half past the hour. Without seeing the hall clock, you go out to get the paper, the headlines of which indicate there was a half-hour power failure during the night. From this evidence you conclude (choose one):

1. The time is 8:30 and the grandfather clock has the correct time.
2. The time is 8 o'clock and the grandfather clock is off by half an hour one way or the other.
3. The time is 7:30 and your alarm clock is fast.

B. Imagine you're a detective just called to the scene of a crime, a two-story suburban home. Here's what you find:

The fully clothed body is on a bed in an upper bedroom.
A revolver is in the right hand.
There is a bullet hole through the victim's white shirt just at heart level.
The bullet is found on the bed beneath the victim. Microscopic examination shows traces of a white chalky substance on the bullet.
The leather on the victim's shoes is bent away and separated from the shoe at the back part of the heel.
There are two parallel black lines on the linoleum floor in the dining room.
The fingerprints of the victim's daughter are found on the silverware downstairs.
The dining room walls are made of sheetrock.
The victim has a callus on the right side of the middle finger of his left hand.
The dining room table is set for two.

Facts you know about the victim:

Doctors recently told the victim he was terminally ill.
The victim had a sizable life insurance policy payable to his daughter.

Pick one of the following conclusions and write an analysis of the facts to support it. One might seem a more obvious choice than the others, but you could make a case for any one of them with a careful, clever analysis of the facts.

1. To avoid the slow death his doctor had predicted, the victim committed suicide in his bedroom.
2. The victim was murdered, perhaps by his daughter.

3. Anticipating the thoroughness and cleverness of the police investigation, the victim committed suicide but tried to make it look like murder, planting enough clues to suggest that he really didn't shoot himself in his bedroom.

C. Which one of generalizations 1–3 below follows logically from the following details?

Details: More and more families continue to move from the cities to suburban communities.

Violence continues to be a problem in urban schools.

Students in inner-city schools are the victims of gunshots and knifings in hallways and bathrooms.

Urban teachers don't feel safe in their classrooms.

Teachers in metropolitan high schools have had the tires on their cars slashed and have received threats.

Teachers in urban areas can't teach subject matter because they're busy enforcing discipline.

Urban students feel they are receiving inadequate preparation for future employment.

Generalizations:

1. The high school curriculum is changing according to pupil demands.
2. Schools in cities face problems so serious that they make education difficult and endanger students and teachers.
3. It's hard to be a teacher these days, but even harder to be a student.

In the next section we give you a list of details and ask you to provide a conclusion which fits the details.

D. With the following information at your disposal, come to your own conclusion about medical research.

You read an article in the newspaper that cites evidence that a particular red dye causes cancer.

Several weeks later you read another article that discloses certain inconsistencies in the evidence. The dye was tested on rats, and one of the researchers apparently mixed up rats that didn't receive the dye with those that did.

You read another article that cites evidence that eggs contribute to heart disease and hardening of the arteries because they contain cholesterol.

Six months later you read an article that states that eggs also contain sizable amounts of lecithin, a substance that breaks cholesterol down. From this new evidence some scientists have concluded that eggs do not contribute to arterial problems.

Several years after the initial finding that cigarettes contribute directly to lung cancer, you read an article confirming this information. The incidence of lung cancer was much higher in a group of smokers than in a nonsmoking group.

Often students feel that, regardless of which approach they're taking, they can't find enough evidence to form or back up a general point. Whether you're getting support for an assertion you've already come up with, or assembling information to help you form a generalization, it's important to consider the wealth of experience and evidence you have at hand. Your own experience includes much more than what's happened to you or the things you've done. It's also books and magazines you've read, conversations you've had, and classes you've attended, as well as plays and movies, radio and TV programs, and the connections you make among all of these.

2

The Paragraph

Why Start with Paragraphs?

You may feel that being asked to study paragraphs at this point in your education is like being told to review your multiplication tables in the middle of a trigonometry course. But paragraphs are more complex and more important than they may at first appear, whether in isolation or as parts of a full-length composition. The same skills that go into a strong paragraph go into a strong essay: you need to zero in on a central point and support it thoroughly, convincingly, and interestingly.

Why Paragraphs at All?

Basically, the paragraph is a convenience for both the reader and the writer. Consider your reaction to opening a book with page after page of nearly solid print; you probably feel like closing it before you've even begun to read. A page of printed material with several paragraph breaks, on the other hand, looks more inviting and accessible.

And it is. Besides giving the reader an occasional rest, paragraph indentations are a mental convenience. Since paragraphs usually contain one main idea and the details needed to support it, *a paragraph break signals a new idea, or a new facet of an old one.* Because of this principle, teachers of speed reading often suggest that their students "preread" a textbook assignment by reading only the first and last paragraphs and the first sentence of every paragraph in between. In doing so, they will get a good general sense of what the material is about and have a framework for all the secondary details when they go back and read the section through.

THE TOPIC SENTENCE

This "prereading" method works, of course, because of the *topic sentence*. While you could probably come up with a definition of the term, something like "the sentence that expresses the main idea of the paragraph," consider how often you consciously write a topic sentence. You may not be completely aware of how much a carefully worded topic sentence can help or how badly the absence of one can hurt. To begin with, let's look at what can happen without one.

Lost in a Maze

Many weak paragraphs simply don't have a point. (Or to put it another way, perhaps they have too many.) Without a clear topic sentence, these paragraphs fail to concentrate on a single idea, wandering instead through several tangentially related points. Good luck in finding your way out of this one:

> Dr. Michael Dean, known as the world's foremost hypnotist, is an amazing man. He performs psychic judo on the subjects he works with. He believes that a hypnotic trance can be defined as a state of attentive responsive concentration, a definition that goes against many people's idea that hypnosis puts a person to sleep. In fact, quite the opposite is true. The subject is awake and focused. Hypnotizing someone is not any kind of a magical trick. It is not something a hypnotist does to a person; a person does it to himself. This is not to suggest, however, that in unpracticed hands hypnosis cannot be risky. It is nothing to fool around with.

As you can see, the student who wrote this paragraph does not lack for ideas. She has several that could be worked into an essay on hypnosis. But what single idea did she really want to discuss? Is this paragraph supposed to be about Dr. Dean's amazing talents, the true nature of hypnosis, or the possible dangers of trying hypnosis without training and experience? The writer probably wasn't sure either, because she didn't decide on a main idea and write it out in a topic sentence. So she instead hit randomly at several aspects of her topic, rather like a trapped bee flinging itself all over a windowpane.

The Way Out

In contrast to the paragraph on hypnosis, the following two paragraphs were written by students who had decided what they wanted to say. After reading each paragraph through, go back and underline the sentence that expresses its controlling idea.

1. My friend Gladys is what you might call a Miss Know-It-All. If you want to know the exact time the sun rises and sets, ask Gladys. If you want to know exactly how long it takes to boil an egg, ask Gladys. If my watch is five minutes faster than hers, she'll say, "Ooh, girl, your watch is fast. I know my watch is right because I set it every morning by calling the time." Little does she know that each morning I set my watch the same way. Every time I give her some facts about something, she always says, "I know." To put it lightly, it makes me want to reach in and pull the vocal cords out of her throat. Once I told Gladys that the reason my mother's car is soft blue is that it's her favorite color. Gladys said, "I know." There was no way she could have known what my mother's favorite color is because we've never discussed it. Why do I associate with such a person? I really don't know.

2. A glance at *TV Guide* might make the casual observer think television had gone realistic. But despite *Family* and *One Day at a Time,* some shows still with us in reruns portray the "typical teenager" as superhuman. Many television teenagers are blessed with extraordinary abilities. Greg Brady of *The Brady Bunch* not only is an honor student, but is also on the varsity football and basketball teams. Greg's sister Marsha is a budding ballerina, has been student body president of her junior high school, and was valedictorian of her class. Together the six Brady kids have formed a successful singing group. On another channel we can see *The Partridge Family,* with five musically talented children who play different instruments and sing when they aren't running campaigns for school offices. On Sunday nights Nancy Drew and the Hardy Boys track down hardened criminals, solving cases that have baffled the police for months. But these talents aren't as unbelievable as the overabundance of time these teenagers have to cram all these activities into. Even though they attend school all day, they rarely have homework. I spend most of my time after school and before bed slaving over the books, while they have hours to hang out at the pizza parlor or ice cream shop, where they keep their slender

bodies thin and their clear complexions pimple-free. Or they can debate about what shoes to wear to school tomorrow, talk on the phone for hours, or just hang around the kitchen. I'm amused but irritated by the way each of these perfect adolescents, portrayed by performers in their twenties, somehow manages to live the lives of fifteen real teenagers.

The first sentence in Paragraph 1 and the second in Paragraph 2 are the *topic sentences,* general statements supported by the more specific sentences that follow.

Your Contract with Your Reader

In expressing a general idea and limiting the discussion of a paragraph, a topic sentence establishes a *contract* between the writer and the reader. When you write a topic sentence, you are promising that you will stick to the idea it expresses and do your best to substantiate it.

In the first paragraph the writer fulfills her contract by demonstrating that Gladys is indeed that irritating type, the know-it-all. In the body of the paragraph she presents the details that prove the point: Gladys' insistence that only she knows the correct time or the proper way to boil an egg, her constant "I know" response to any remark, and her apparently psychic knowledge of people's favorite colors.

In the second paragraph, the writer promises to show that TV is unrealistic in its depiction of what supposedly average teenagers are like. She fulfills her contract by offering several specific examples that do in fact make TV teenagers appear superhuman. The method is a bit more complex here, since there are two subpoints to the main idea, but under each the writer presents specific examples and details to substantiate the topic sentence:

Topic sentence: Some shows portray the typical teenager as superhuman.

    I. TV teenagers are blessed with extraordinary abilities.
       A. Greg Brady—honor student and star athlete
       B. Marsha Brady—ballerina, school president, and valedictorian
       C. Six Brady kids' singing group
       D. *The Partridge Family*—all musically talented
       E. Nancy Drew and The Hardy Boys—able to solve cases the police can't
   II. Teenagers have an overabundance of time.
       A. No homework
       B. Time for pizza parlors and ice cream shops
       C. Time to decide on shoes, talk, hang around the kitchen

Concluding sentence: I'm amused but irritated by the way each of these perfect adolescents . . . somehow manages to live the lives of fifteen real teenagers.

You might think of a well-structured topic sentence as having two parts, the *subject* and the *key words,* which *name* and *limit* what you're going to discuss. For instance, in Paragraph 1 above, the subject is *Gladys* and the key words are *Know-It-All.* Therefore, the rest of the sentences in the paragraph relate to Gladys and her infuriating habit of being conversant with anything and everything. By using the topic sentence as a self-check, the writer would be able to recognize when she'd left the path and begun discussing Gladys' messy room, for example. Similarly, in Paragraph 2 the subject is *the typical teenager,* and the key word is *superhuman.* Thus the writer would know she was off the track if she started writing about literally superhuman adults like the Incredible Hulk or about the way many detective shows often portray teenagers as mindless junkies.

A Couple of Cautions

Since the topic sentence expresses the main point of an entire paragraph, it will probably be the broadest, or most general, statement in it. This is useful information, because it warns you against laying out a topic sentence that is too narrow. It's easy to imagine what might happen if you used "The waxed paper rested on the kitchen table" as a topic sentence. It would leave you with nothing to "prove," nowhere to go, and thus no contract to fulfill with the reader. So make sure your topic sentence leaves you something to discuss.

We need to warn you, though, against framing a topic sentence so general that it could not be well-supported in a twenty-page paper, let alone a paragraph. The overly broad topic sentence is just as difficult to work with as the overly narrow one. Imagine, for instance, the burden of fulfilling in one paragraph a contract which reads: "Technology represents the greatest disaster that has ever befallen America." Finding the path between the topic sentence that is too broad and the one that's too narrow takes time and practice, but it repays the effort, since the good topic sentence can guide you in writing the remainder of the paragraph.

Topic Sentence Checklist

Now that you know what topic sentences consist of, here are some questions that will help you test the effectiveness of your own.

1. Does the topic sentence tell the reader what the entire paragraph will be about?

2. Is the topic sentence the broadest statement in the paragraph?
3. Does the topic sentence make an assertion that requires further explanation, raises questions, or demands proof?
4. Does the topic sentence both name and limit the subject at hand?
5. Is the topic sentence narrow enough to be covered in one paragraph but broad enough to be developed?
6. Does the topic sentence make a promise you can stick to?

EXERCISE 1

Some of the sentences in the following list would work well as topic sentences while others are too broad or too narrow. Decide which category each sentence falls into, marking it "OK," "TB" (too broad), or "TN" (too narrow). (You'll notice that even though some of the sentences are too narrow, they might be effective as introductory sentences in descriptive or narrative paragraphs.)

1. Writing is important.
2. During his presidency, Lyndon Johnson sponsored legislation that clearly improved existing civil rights laws.
3. The movie *Gone with the Wind* starred Vivien Leigh as Scarlett O'Hara and Clark Gable as Rhett Butler.
4. In recent years I've been doing some thinking about guns.
5. Too often we resort to clichés instead of finding our own words to express our thoughts and feelings.
6. Surfing at Ocean Beach in San Francisco is one of the most soul-satisfying experiences I know of.
7. In this mechanistic world we live in, love is the key to happiness.
8. The home plate umpire has the most difficult job on the baseball field.
9. My Uncle Seymour was picked up in a raid on a massage parlor.
10. My father has a terrible temper.
11. Every politician is looking out for himself.
12. There is now evidence to suggest that plants respond to human emotions.
13. My boyfriend always honks his horn when he comes to pick me up.
14. The general lack of morality in our country today is simply appalling.
15. The speed of light is 186,000 miles per second.

EXERCISE 2

Taking each of the sentences you've marked as "too broad" or "too narrow," write a workable topic sentence for a paragraph on the same general subject, as we've done in the examples below:

Example:

Original: My boyfriend always honks his horn when he comes to pick me up.
Revision: My boyfriend's manners are atrocious.
Original: Every politician is looking out for himself.
Revision: In the debate last Tuesday among congressional candidates, Joe Bingster appeared to be a politician who was only looking out for himself, caring about neither his party nor his constituents.

EXERCISE 3

Write a topic sentence for each of the subject areas below. Remember to *limit* as well as name the subject.

1. Getting revenge
2. People who bore their friends
3. Cooking
4. Nuclear energy
5. Grades
6. Consumer protection
7. Sex education
8. Computer registration in college
9. Employment opportunities for women
10. Competition
11. Television coverage of sporting events
12. Mental health

EXERCISE 4

Write a paragraph of at least 125 words focusing on one significant characteristic of a person or place. Your topic sentence should name that characteristic ("My ninth-grade English teacher, Mrs. Hotchkiss, was the most nervous woman I've ever met"; "The truck-stop's kitchen was filthy"), and the rest of the paragraph should consist of specific details supporting the topic sentence. Make sure the body of your paragraph fulfills the contract the topic sentence commits you to. Use the checklist on pages 15–16 to check your finished product.

DEVELOPING YOUR PARAGRAPHS

Put simply, *development* means getting specific, offering details and examples to drive a point home. While the topic sentence orients your readers, it is the details that persuade and interest them. Your readers won't be able to picture the furniture in your apartment, for instance, if you say the decor includes a variety of styles and leave it at that. You need to mention the rickety bookshelf, the rocking chair, the art déco lamp in the shape of a ballerina, the early-Goodwill coffee table, and the electric-blue shag carpet donated by your well-meaning but color-blind Uncle Lloyd.

Nor is it enough, in a persuasive paragraph, to say that television encourages children to be passive. You need to say much more. Point out, for instance, that children spend sunny Saturday mornings sitting goggle-eyed in darkened rooms watching cartoons instead of roller-skating or playing soccer outside. Mention that the average child spends many more hours watching television than doing homework, or that research shows that many young children accept anything they hear on TV as absolute fact, often unable to distinguish between reality and fantasy.

Details do more than lead readers to accept your point; they also get them involved with what you're saying. Notice in your own reading how your interest picks up when a writer becomes specific. For instance, compare the following two statements:

> The professor bored his students.

> As the professor droned through his lecture notes, his students dozed, doodled, or wrote letters home to Mom.

Certainly the second sentence carries more weight and is more interesting and accurate. In place of the fairly abstract phrase "bored his students," which encompasses several possibilities, we have been provided with a whole scene we can readily imagine. Notice too that the sentence has gone from five words to eighteen, more than three times what we started with; if you're convinced that you can't possibly turn out a full-length essay, try getting more specific about your subject.

But one word of caution: don't confuse *development* with *wordiness.* In an essay on the miseries of dorm life, for example, the student who is trying only to get to 500 words (counting words per line and totaling them in the margins) will write, "The food that is prepared by the cooks in the cafeteria at the dormitory on this campus where I eat every day is somewhat less than appetizing to my taste" when all he means is, "I find dorm food revolting." The way to reach that miraculous 500th word (or whatever you've been assigned) is not to use thirty words when five would convey the idea more clearly, but to go into greater detail about your subject. To back up your assertion that food in your dorm is revolting, for instance, you can draw on a host of specific examples only too familiar to you: the rubbery fried eggs, the rusted lettuce lying limply on egg-smeared plates, the anemic Jell-O and the mud-colored hamburger patties in half-congealed fat. Before you know it, you will have produced the requisite number of words. What's more important, you will have *shown* your readers what you're talking about, thus making them more inclined to accept your opinion.

EXERCISE 5

Before you move on to develop whole essays, a little practice writing sentences that are specific will help you get the idea of what we mean by development. Try rewriting the general sentences that follow, as we rewrote the sentence about the boring lecturer. Rewrite them in specific terms, making sure that what you've added contains real substance and isn't simply padding.

Example:

Original: Handmade ornaments added a distinctive touch to the Christmas tree.

Revision: Handmade ornaments, everything from threaded popcorn to wooden soldiers with golf tees for noses, added a distinctive touch to the Christmas tree.

Original: I hate losing at tennis to a smug opponent.

Revision: I burn with resentment when my tennis opponent hits a perfect passing shot down my backhand alley and then patronizingly says, "Nice try!" as I nearly dislocate my shoulder trying to return it.

1. My sister gets along well with all kinds of people.
2. The high school gymnasium looked dilapidated.
3. Ralph is obnoxious at parties.
4. We all need recreation after work.
5. Family gatherings can be quite unpleasant.
6. Learning to play a musical instrument is satisfying.
7. The flowers in the park were pretty.
8. To succeed in politics nowadays, a person must make compromises.
9. A knowledge of physiology is very useful.
10. Movies have come a long way.

When you rephrased these sentences, you probably had to struggle at times, partly because you weren't working with your own ideas, but mostly because it can be much harder to think of specific sentences than general ones.

Details, Details

Being specific forces you to strain after the concrete realities underlying a general impression or concept. Good writers work until
they've gotten the necessary details down, if not on the first draft,
then on the second, third, or fourth. For instance, in a paragraph
describing a strict elementary school teacher, it would be easy to
come up with something like the following:

> My sixth-grade class was very regimented. The teacher, Miss
> Marlow, was awfully strict and even looked like a tyrant. She made
> us do all sorts of things the other teachers didn't, really piling on the
> work. And we didn't dare misbehave because she was always watch-
> ing us. For these reasons, it was rare for anyone to act up in her
> class.

As it happens, the student who actually wrote about Miss
Marlow knew how to develop, how to keep going. Look at the
difference:

> Miss Marlow's sixth-grade class was as regimented as an Eastern
> military academy. With her tall, erect carriage, her clicking heels, and
> the blackboard pointer always held at her side, she walked the length
> of her silent class like the Master at Arms of an English warship. We
> were not to mumble; we were to "enunciate." No one spoke without
> raising his hand and one always stood to address the class. Unlike the
> other teachers, who sat at the front of the classroom, Miss Marlow
> located her desk at the rear. From this vantage point she might watch
> us as we worked silently on sentence diagramming and arithmetic
> exercises, and it was impossible for us to know whether or not at
> any given moment her gaze was fixed at the back of our dear little
> ears. It was considered a singular act of daring to pass a note or
> shoot a spit wad during one of these work periods. Even so much as
> a furtive glance to the rear was apt to be met with swift denuncia-
> tion. "You must apply yourself, Mary."

The details make this paragraph work: Miss Marlow's clicking
heels and the sentence diagramming, for instance. Rather than saying
"We didn't dare misbehave," the writer shows us specific misbehavior,
like passing notes and shooting spit wads. The general idea of the
paragraph *could* have been conveyed in a few simple sentences, as it
is in the first version. But readers would never have been able to picture Miss Marlow's posture, her walk, her mannerisms, or her unique
ways of controlling the class. So stop yourself from stopping, and cultivate the habit of going on, adding details to complete your picture.
Somewhere in your head you probably do have a whole picture,

a whole set of images and ideas associated with the thought you're trying to express. And the only way to get the details of that private picture into your readers' heads, short of ESP, is to write them down. If details don't spring to mind automatically when you're writing (and to most people, even many professional writers, they don't), make lists ahead of time. That's where the following exercise comes in.

EXERCISE 6

Suppose that for one reason or another it is appropriate for you to write paragraphs on the topics and ideas in this exercise. For each one, list in phrase form at least five (and if you're feeling generous, a few more) details you might include. Be as specific as possible. By asking yourself questions, you can often tell your readers more clearly and directly what you've discovered about your subject. If you're delving for details about your first boss, for instance, you might first surface with "a real character." A good start, but ask yourself leading questions: What do you mean by "character"? Was he a friendly character? A mean or peculiar one? What were his idiosyncrasies, his habits, his mannerisms? What were his distinctive physical traits and how did they harmonize or contrast with his personality? How did others react to him? This process should help you make your entries as specific as those in the example that follows.

Example: *The contents of a cluttered drawer*

slightly blurred photographs of my family's 1970 trip to Yosemite National Park
two 10¢ coupons for Scott Family Tissue that expired on December 31, 1979
four ballpoint pens that have run dry
several eraserless pencil stubs, chewed almost beyond recognition
a mostly dried-up tube of rubber cement
a Phillips screwdriver
one bent blue thumb tack

1. Things you have always wanted to do
2. Your idea of a delicious meal
3. Good manners
4. Childhood memories of summer
5. Benefits of reading
6. Humiliating moments in your life
7. Problems in your community
8. Distinctive physical characteristics or mannerisms of famous people

9. Boring tasks
10. Satisfactions of working
11. Landmarks in your town
12. Frustrations of being a college student
13. We'll leave this one to you. Now that you've got the idea, make up your own category and list specifics under it.

EXERCISE 7

Choose one of the preceding categories and write a paragraph using the details on your list. Remember to include a topic sentence that turns your list of details into a paragraph with a point. For instance, a topic sentence for the example about the drawer might be: "The contents of my cluttered kitchen drawer reveal that I'm reluctant to let go of anything."

PARAGRAPH PITFALLS

Writing well can never be an automatic process. As much as we'd like to hand you a few simple formulas that would guarantee success, we can't, because in the end there's no substitute for thinking. If you want to write an "A" paragraph, the best advice we can give you is to think carefully about what you want to say before you get too far into the writing. But even if we can't anticipate every problem you may face, we can alert you to the most common traps we've seen our students fall into. If you can avoid these pitfalls, you'll probably be turning out successful paragraphs, and at the same time you'll be sharpening your ability to think your way through a topic, a skill that will help when we move on to the essay.

Speed Kills

Probably the greatest mistake you can make is to jot down any old topic sentence in a spirit of "Well, let's get this over with" and then to dash off the rest of the paragraph, never looking back. Once you have a topic sentence, examine it critically to make sure it says what you really mean. Then check back occasionally as you continue the paragraph to make sure you haven't deviated from your original idea. If you do discover that you have gone off the track, you have a choice: scrap the irrelevant material or change your topic sentence to reflect the new direction your paragraph has taken.

If you work carefully, keeping the relationship between your topic sentence and your list of supporting details in mind, you probably won't write a paragraph that falls into any of the following categories.

THE HEADLESS PARAGRAPH

Sometimes the individual details in a paragraph are potentially interesting, but we can't be sure exactly what the writer wanted to say because there is no topic sentence. The following paragraph reads smoothly and contains a lot of information, but what would you say is the main point the writer wants to make?

> Out of habit we set the alarm for the same hour each morning and turn out the light at almost the same time each night. We read the same columnists every day in the same newspapers and rely on the same TV shows for our entertainment, even watching reruns of our favorite programs once the regular season is over. We spend our free time getting together with the same small group of friends we have known for years. We eat the same menus week after week, macaroni and cheese on Tuesday nights and fried chicken on Saturdays. Even when we dine out, we go to the same places, ordering prime rib at the fancy restaurant we patronize twice a year, and choosing the old standby #3 Combination Plate whenever we visit the Mexican restaurant around the corner. And on the first of August, we head for the same campground where we have been spending our two-week vacations for the last ten summers.

These are fine examples, but what do they all add up to? Did the writer want to use those examples to illustrate how locked into routines we are? Perhaps the topic sentence was supposed to be something like "Afraid to try anything new, we unimaginatively live out our lives in the same monotonous patterns." Note, however, that the writer may have had something quite different in mind. The examples could equally well support a topic sentence such as "In a world that requires us to adjust to ever-accelerating rates of change, we find order and meaning in the familiar, making comfortable rituals of the few things still under our control." The paragraph could support either of these ideas; but without a guiding topic sentence, the reader is left with a page full of examples and no context to place them in.

THE LOST SHEEP PARAGRAPH

Sometimes a paragraph begins with a perfectly workable topic sentence that the paragraph begins to develop. But halfway through, the writer seems to have forgotten the controlling idea and lost the way. See whether you can find where the following paragraph begins to wander.

> In some of the things that I like to do, I have become close to expert, but there is always room for improvement. I have been sewing most of my clothes for almost six years now and am happy with the

results, but I would like to learn more techniques for finishing seams, zippers, and buttonholes by hand. Even though I have taken jazz dancing for four years, there is so much for me to improve on. Often I feel stiff, and I'm still learning how to relax while moving across the floor. Since I have been taking jazz dancing, I have more rhythm and style when I do regular dancing. I like to watch other people dance, which is another way for me to learn new ways of moving. If I were to design an ideal house, I would be sure to include a dance studio which I would want to decorate myself, decorating being another of my favorite pastimes. I would also do a lot of drawing, mostly pictures of different scenes of nature, and especially of my favorite animal, the lion. I hope I can continue all these interests and have time for them in the years to come.

Right—the paragraph starts to stray with the sentence that begins "Since I have been taking jazz dancing. . . . " It's easy to guess how this writer got distracted: thinking about her jazz dancing classes made her realize how they have helped her dancing in general, which in turn made her begin daydreaming about a dance studio in her ideal house. We can understand what might have happened to the writer, but it's still an unsuccessful paragraph, despite its good start.

THE PARAGRAPH WITH A SPLIT PERSONALITY

Sometimes a paragraph fails because its topic sentence commits the writer to proving *two* points. Like someone attempting to do homework and watch TV at the same time, the writer winds up doing justice to neither. The student who wrote the following paragraph began with the workable idea that cooking with natural foods can take extra time. But she felt that to be fair, she should also say that it was worth the trouble. She thus wound up moving back and forth between the two ideas, splitting her attention between them. The resulting paragraph is understandably disjointed:

Cooking with natural foods can be time-consuming, but worth the effort. Purchasing the proper ingredients—whole grains, organically grown produce, and meats—is a process that often means having to shop at specialty shops or health food stores. But the time seems well-spent when I sit down to a healthy, organic meal I've prepared myself. I get slightly dizzy, though, when I have to convert standard recipes to substitute heavy flours and whole grains; there are also tricky adjustments to be made when honey is used instead of white sugar. Although I'm glad not to be filling my stomach with TV dinners, avoiding processed foods means spending more time in the kitchen cooking meals from scratch and learning how to season foods with herbs and spices by trial and error. Still, I enjoy the time

I spend preparing natural foods, and have more respect for what I'm putting into my body.

A simple technique will often solve the problem of the paragraph divided against itself. Briefly acknowledge the secondary idea, and then go on to make the point you wish to emphasize. This writer would have had an easier time if she had simply revised her topic sentence to read, "Although cooking with natural foods is definitely worth the effort, it can be quite time-consuming." That natural foods are good for you would become a "given" in the paragraph, and the writer could devote her energy to showing that it takes time to make granola from scratch or convert a standard recipe for carrot cake.

THE TOP-HEAVY PARAGRAPH

Occasionally, the problem is one of proportion. The writer spends a great deal of time introducing the topic sentence but then rushes through the rest of the paragraph, skimping on the supporting details. For example, the writer of the potentially excellent paragraph that follows stuffed it with introductory remarks, but stopped too soon, using only one sentence to back up his central assertion, that there is another side to the town he is writing about.

> Sausalito is a town that nurtures artistic talent and is never hesitant to display the work of local favorites in colorful and stunning shows at which the price tags are equally stunning. This "display case" vision of Sausalito is what most people see while passing through. But Sausalito is not all art shows. There is another side of town where the Winnebago Motor Home Club variety of visitor seldom ventures, an area inhabited by an elusive and curious host of characters. The other side is Gate Five Road, where rats and people make their homes under the cement outcroppings and broken remains of old munitions warehouses, where winos and weirdos stagger around derelict buildings.

This paragraph isn't so much top-heavy as bottom-light. While the three introductory sentences do help set up the contrast between "most people's idea of Sausalito" and "the other side of town," the paragraph is out of balance in its present form. Three introductory sentences in a five-sentence paragraph are like a thirty-minute overture to a twenty-minute production.

When you find that your introduction is too long for the paragraph you've written, step back and look at it critically. If, as in the example we've just considered, the introduction does help prepare for your real topic, go into more detail about your actual subject. But if you're only stalling for time in those first few sentences, get rid of them and come more quickly to the point. In either case, you need to shift the proportion.

The Hasty Generalization—or On the Road to Nowhere

We now consider a more subtle kind of pitfall: the illogical topic sentence. Once you've written a possible topic sentence, you need to consider what it asks you to do, and whether you (or even an army of professionals) can possibly pull it off. Suppose you begin with the statement "Competition is harmful." At first glance, it seems to fulfill many of the requirements for a good topic sentence: it states an arguable opinion, it can be developed in the sentences that follow, and it deals with a topic you have some views on. Relieved at getting something on paper, you proceed.

But one of two disasters is likely to occur when you've begun with this kind of topic sentence. It is so general, commits you to doing so much more than is possible, that you may end up writing more generalizations to "support" it. You go on to say that competition makes people cutthroat and that the American system (whatever that is) forces us to compete for material goods. Before you know it, you've made several such general assertions, leaving yourself with an impossible amount to prove.

Or, remembering that a paragraph should offer specific support for its topic sentence, you attempt to prove your point by giving one or two concrete examples. You describe how your little brother was hurt by getting the lowest grade on an arithmetic test in his fourth grade class. Too quickly you conclude that making people take tests and compete against each other is inhumane and counterproductive. Knowing of your brother's experience, you have formulated a generalization based on a very small sample—one experience, in fact. An attentive instructor will pounce on the paragraph, writing "Logic?" or "Insufficient evidence" in the margin.

If you find yourself in this kind of trouble, take another look at the topic sentence that flowed so smoothly from your pen. A statement like "Competition is harmful" proves troublesome because it consists of only a few words, none of them limited in any way. While some children in the fourth grade may wither under the pressure of competition, it doesn't follow that *all* competition is *always* harmful to *everybody.* You don't have to throw out the whole topic, but you do need to work further on the topic sentence until you've turned it into an assertion you can prove.

It is sometimes useful to work backwards from the specific details you want to include in your paragraph to the general statement of the topic sentence. Prepare for the story you're going to tell about your little brother by making the topic sentence relate to his situation: "Competition in the elementary school classroom can be harmful." Notice here how you've limited your claims, reducing "competition" to "competition in the elementary school classroom" and changing "is" to "can be." To give your reader an exact idea of what you mean and at the same time help direct the rest of the paragraph, you can be more specific about *why* you see this form of competition as harmful: "it may endanger a child's self-esteem." And to be on the safe side, since a reader can always think of exceptions to your argument (the Nobel prizewinner whose lifelong interest in science began when he won first prize at a long-ago science fair), you might begin your topic sentence by conceding the possible benefits of competition: "Although it sometimes motivates students to do their best work. . . ." Look at the difference:

> Competition is harmful.

> Although it sometimes motivates students to do their best work, competition in the elementary school classroom may endanger a child's self-esteem.

At first reading, absolute statements often sound strong and convincing. Notice the superficial allure of the following:

> Male students learn more from female teachers than do female students.

If you look closely, you'll realize assertions like this cannot be proved because they contain unqualified terms. For instance,

> *All* male students (*regardless of character, ability, or effort?*) learn more (*What is "more"? How can you measure it?*) from female teachers (*any female teacher, regardless of her ability?*) than do female students (*any female student, regardless of character, ability, or effort?*)

If the first version of a topic sentence seems too sweeping, revise it to fit the circumstances you're familiar with, as we rewrote the topic sentence about competition.

EXERCISE 8

Below are several "headless" paragraphs—paragraphs whose topic sentences are missing. After reviewing the section on headless paragraphs on page 23, write a topic sentence for each paragraph, taking care that the "head" is general enough to sum up the paragraph's main points, yet specific enough to be appropriate to the "body."

A. _____

_____

Each morning she would flutter into the classroom late, with her excuses of forgetting to set her alarm, misplacing her keys, or running out of gas on the way to school. Nor could she make it to class with the materials needed for the day. She would forget yesterday's corrected papers, today's quiz, or tomorrow's assignment. At school she would forget where she had put the brushes, paint, pencils, or construction paper. One never knew what Miss Sullivan would forget next. Would it be what she had been saying, what project to turn to after lunch, where she had put the chalk and eraser, or who she was?

B. _____

_____

We've all read news stories about elderly people who have been forced to live on a diet of tuna products intended for cats. Frequently our senior citizens can't keep up with the property taxes on the homes they have owned for years and are forced to move to apartments in low-rent, high-crime sections of town. Many of these apartments are in buildings that are dilapidated, infested by rats and insects, and unsafe in case of fire. And all too often, such places not only house the elderly but attract the criminals who prey on them. With barely enough money for food and housing, the elderly can seldom afford adequate health care or even the luxury of a once-a-month visit to the movies.

C. _____

_____

Before the drought, residents kept their lawns green by watering them so frequently and with so little regard for the amount of water they were using that thousands of gallons ran into the street and disappeared into the nearest sewer. People washed their cars once a week, and if they wasted water in the process, they didn't care or even notice. They assumed that a daily shower was a necessity; after all, cleanliness was next to godliness. If asked to turn off the water in their sinks while washing dishes, shaving, or brushing their teeth, or to avoid flushing their toilets, they would have felt put upon and complained bitterly about being deprived of the minimal decencies of life.

D. (This one is a little tougher. Here you have two related paragraphs, sections from a larger essay about conditions in state mental hospitals. Write a topic sentence for each. When writing the second "head," remember that it needs to link the paragraphs as well as serve as a topic sentence for its own material.)

In some of the hospitals, up to one-half of the toilets don't function. In addition, because many patients have never been toilet-trained the floors and walls have years' worth of excrement ground into them. The resulting stench has made more than one visitor nauseated, and it's not difficult to imagine what effect the permanent odor has on the inmates and staff. Frequently, the buildings themselves are in disrepair, lacking adequate heating and ventilation. There are gaping holes in some roofs that admit the rain and snow in winter, and flies and other insects in summer. The problem is intensified by old and worn-out supplies and equipment. The blankets and sheets are thin and ragged, providing inadequate warmth in cold weather, and in the summer there are no fans or air conditioners to keep the fetid air moving and counter the stifling heat.

On the average, state mental hospitals have 350 people over capacity. Beds are squeezed into every available space, corridors and even small closets included. Some rooms are so crammed with beds and patients that it is impossible for the staff to cross them without walking on the mattresses. Meal times present special problems. Patients hardly have time to finish their food before their bowls are cleared away and another group of patients comes in to eat. For those who cannot feed themselves, including infants, the problem is still more severe. Attendants may have only two or three minutes per person because hundreds must be fed in a very short time. It is not uncommon for inmates to inhale food and come down with lung infections, which are sometimes fatal. And there are never enough attendants to watch people (much less interact with them); as a result, accidents and fights occur constantly, patients are often covered with cuts and bruises, and an unnecessary atmosphere of fear can pervade a ward.

EXERCISE 9

At some point in the following paragraph, the writer goes off the track and forgets his topic sentence. First mark the spot at which the paragraph jumps its rails and then rewrite the paragraph from that point, making sure that what you add contributes to the controlling idea.

People are reading less these days not because they dislike the printed word, but because it's so much easier to be informed and entertained through other media. In the past, if we wanted to keep up with current events, we had to spend at least half an hour a day with the newspaper. Now, we can hear the highlights of the news on the car radio and see the newsworthy people and events themselves on television: it's not nearly as interesting to sift through the facts about the electrical fire in a building the city inspector had just deemed safe as it is to see the orange and yellow flames against the billowing gray smoke on the six o'clock news. For relaxation, people used to read novels and short stories in magazines, but now they can go to the movies or stay home and watch TV. A lot of people, of course, prefer not to leave the comfort of their living rooms to take a chance on a film that may be a disappointment and will certainly be an expense. By the time you figure in the cost of buying the theatre tickets, parking, paying the babysitter, and getting popcorn, you're much better off sending the kids upstairs to bed, getting a beer from the refrigerator, and settling back to watch *Casablanca* for the eighteenth time.

EXERCISE 10

The writer below made the mistake of trying to deal with more than one controlling idea in the same paragraph. Decide which of the two ideas you want to develop. Then rewrite the paragraph accordingly, adding appropriate details.

Barry Burnett, my boss at Hamburger Haven, is fanatical about cleanliness, and he can be unexpectedly generous. For instance, we were all startled to find an extra $50 in our pay envelopes last Christmas, even though we knew business had not been particularly good lately. But such acts are the exception rather than the rule; usually he's after us to polish the chrome around the stove until we can see our reflections in it or to pick up discarded gum and cigarette wrappers in the parking lot. When I got sick last fall, he kindly gave me a day off without docking my pay, although as a part-time patty-frier I am not entitled to sick leave. Probably he was afraid my flu was catching;

if anyone so much as sneezes, Barry whips out a can of Lysol disinfectant and sprays it into the air. He insists that tables be wiped the second they are vacated, and if we miss even one crumb, old "Flashlight Burnett" will be on it in no time. He has his car washed twice a week and polishes his shoes every day before work and again at lunchtime. On holidays, though, he always has balloons for all the children who come in, and they think he's second cousin to Santa Claus.

EXERCISE 11

The following topic sentences are unworkable for one reason or another. Explain as clearly as you can what's wrong with the reasoning behind each. Then rewrite five of them, correcting the problem so that you could write a strong paragraph supporting the new topic sentence. Note that some simply need qualifying words while others require complete revision. The example sentence contains undefined terms and is far too absolute to be provable. What does modern education consist of? Is all modern education irrelevant to everyone in every way?

Example:

Original: Modern education is irrelevant.
Revision: Many of the courses I've taken in college seem to have nothing to do with my daily life.

1. New housing is poorly constructed.
2. Automobiles are unnecessary in metropolitan areas.
3. You can't lose in real estate.
4. All generalizations are false.
5. If slang is allowed, it will cause the collapse of American society as we know it.
6. People who are well-educated and refined prefer classical music above all other musical forms.
7. From the story of Helen Keller, we can see that anyone can learn just as well as the next person.
8. As the past two thousand years of Western history have demonstrated, the nuclear family provides the only secure framework in which to raise children successfully.

3

Methods of Paragraph Development

An anthropology final exam once consisted of the essay question "What is the best way to conduct field work?" One student's entire response, for which the instructor commended him, was: "In whatever way works."

We might give the same answer to the question "What is the best way to develop a paragraph?" But unless you've already had enough experience to know what works in particular writing situations, this kind of answer is too concise to be very helpful. This chapter exposes you to the kinds of development most commonly found in good writing and gives you practice in working with some of them.

From reading the last chapter, you know what a good paragraph consists of: a carefully phrased central assertion plus several sentences of specific support. Yet a paper whose paragraphs all used the same approach would be boring to write and even more boring to read. As a writer, you have a choice of strategies. This chapter shows you some of these choices, some of the different methods for making your paragraphs full and interesting. For simplicity's sake, we present each method of development separately, but you should understand that a writer often uses a combination of methods to develop a given paragraph. The idea is not to be a slave to any particular form of development, but to use whatever is necessary to make your ideas as particular and tangible as possible.

DESCRIPTIVE DETAILS

In the last chapter, we talked about details as an effective way to extend your paragraphs, to expand upon the main ideas expressed in your topic sentences. A topic sentence *tells* readers what you have in mind, but the details and examples *show* them. The sentence "My next-door neighbor always seems nervous," for instance, means little until you describe your neighbor's twitching eye, trembling hands, and staccato, humorless laugh—*descriptive details* which serve as examples of his extreme nervousness. Similarly, in the student paragraph that follows, the writer has used precise details to evoke the mood which permeates his San Francisco neighborhood.

> The church of Mission Dolores stands mutely viewing the life and death and stages in between that transpire in its shadows. On windy days, I walk beneath the Mission, step across the gutters littered with crushed Coors cans and leaves from last autumn, pick my way across the car-choked street, and climb the stairs to my apartment. I go to the living room window and look across at the stained glass rose window of the church and wonder what it looks like from inside. Thirty feet below the window, four girls in Notre Dame school uniforms, with grey skirts too short for their knobby knees and green heels too high, totter along, laughing boisterously at a joke heard only by themselves. The children who live downstairs and cry at night because their father beats them are below me on the sidewalk, playing hopscotch and other games which they make up. Across the street, against the chalky walls of the church, leans a wino just come back from hell, or at least from purgatory, in a tattered knee-length coat and pants more wrinkled and unkempt than his face, his eyes watching a brown-frocked priest pass. A hearse backs out from Korski-Roche Mortuary on the corner and pulls into the thoroughfare with a string of black limousines and somber Chryslers in tow. Farther up the block, a jackhammer slams in jagged tempo and the sound comes to me ricocheted off the thick walls of the church. Maternal and majestic, Mission Dolores squats, poised to listen and to look.

On first reading, it may not be apparent how carefully the writer has selected the details he includes; as you reread the paragraph, notice how well these details illustrate "life and death and stages in between."

EXAMPLES

In writing for a composition class, of course, you're usually not just describing something: you're trying to make a point. Probably the most common way to convince a reader is to offer examples, but even here you have choices. Although the following three paragraphs are all developed by examples, each uses a different kind, chosen for a different effect.

Multiple Examples

We've all experienced the frustration of trying to get at a product encased in a package that even Superman would have trouble opening. The writer of the next paragraph reviews this experience and shows us how universal these difficulties really are, by using not just one but several examples to support his contention that American packaging seems to be designed to confound the average consumer. From the fragile egg carton to the cumbersome bags of fertilizer, his illustrations show us that one very effective way of proving a point is to demonstrate it in several ways, using *multiple examples.* This paragraph is lively and fun to read not only because the student's ironic tone suits his subject perfectly, but because he has taken the time to be detailed and concrete.

> I keep having this nightmare. I'm on an island with nothing to eat but canned corned beef. I turn the key and the little metal strip starts getting narrower. I turn it more and more slowly and it gets narrower and narrower and—snap! This isn't so bad as nightmares go. The only trouble is, the same thing happens when I'm awake. To a layman, the philosophy of packaging is a mystery. Light bulbs and eggs are enclosed in some of the flimsiest cardboard modern science can produce. You can crush an egg carton by putting your mail on it, but a steel chisel comes protected by shatterproof plastic. The plastic-bubble-on-cardboard package is popular for this sort of purchase, but don't waste your time on the plastic—you can't dent it. Try to hack or peel away the cardboard from the back. And don't throw away any of those curled-up scraps; they contain the instructions and the guarantee. The sporting instinct of the American people is the greatest friend packagers have. If they can't improve a product, they make it harder to get at. Take something as simple as a bag. I'm talking about the big ones that hold things like dog food and lawn conditioner and come fastened across the top with some braided string. A note is attached saying that if you will pull the red string or the green string, the whole top will open like magic. If you believe this, you will believe anything. Your best bet is to put the bag in a wash tub and cut it in half like a watermelon. Boxes present

another challenge. The powdered sugar and macaroni people favor the thumbnail opening. At the top of the package is a semicircle with simulated perforations around the edge. Underneath they have printed a little joke: "Press thumbnail here." Unless you have the thumbnail of Fu Manchu, all you're going to do is cave in the side of the box. Where is it all going to end? The time may come when our cities with their tall buildings and broad avenues will be empty. Our fur-clad descendants will be crouched over fires, gnawing on roots and bones, while the fruits of our civilization lie all about them—only a thumbnail away.

Extended Example

Even when you use multiple examples in a paragraph, you must develop each one, so that the reader gets more than just a sketchy list of evidence to support your topic sentence. Full development is especially important when you're building your paragraph on just one *extended example.* In the following paragraph, therefore, the writer doesn't simply tell us that Jewish women created their own language, but explains why, giving us the particulars that make the topic sentence plausible. Without belaboring it, the writer gives a single, fully developed illustration that helps us to understand her point.

Disadvantaged groups often respond to their plight by using a language only they understand and share. In this way they give themselves a sense of power, excluding those who have excluded them. For instance, it used to be that Jews—particularly women, who were charged with most of the tasks that required interaction with the dominant, non-Jewish society—would respond to daily indignities with imaginative curses that their tormentors could not understand. Whenever a bureaucrat or merchant would treat them rudely, the women deflected this abuse with a curse. They would mutter, *"Ub a finster yur"* ("Have a dark year") or *"Gue schvolen zolst de veren"* ("You should only swell up") or *"Zolst nor nemen a measa meshena"* ("You should only have a bitter ending") or *"A bitter shu of deer"* ("A bitter hour on you"). In this way, they were able to invoke forces more powerful than those of the everyday world that the majority of society seemed to control.

Anecdote

An *anecdote*—a brief story—is a particular kind of extended example. Because anecdotes have a built-in narrative organization, they can be fairly easy to write and quite interesting to read. You do need to make sure, however, that your anecdote has a point and sticks to it. The writer of the next paragraph uses a story from his own teenage years to argue against lowering the drinking age. Although the anecdote is fairly detailed, the writer never strays from his purpose, which is to show the sometimes irresponsibly brash behavior of teenagers with access to alcohol.

> I believe the drinking age should not be lowered to 18, not because of the obvious reasons, such as the crap parents give their kids about not being mature enough to drink at 18, but because of ecological reasons. I believe that lowering the drinking age to 18 would further pollute our highways, parks, and other recreational areas with the by-products of the drinking culture. To illustrate just some of the pollution that can be produced from just one beer party, I'll recount one of my own youthful encounters with liquor. It all started early one Saturday evening about eight or ten years ago when my two friends and I decided to look up our local liquor dealer, a college student who had just turned 21, and see how much beer we could buy for $6.39, which was all we could cough up after putting two dollars' worth of gas and two quarts of oil in my '56 Ford. A couple of hours later found us out near the coast on some old back road, finishing off the last of the malt liquor and starting in on the Schlitz. As we finished each bottle, we'd just heave it out on the road. As the bottle hit the pavement and broke into a million pieces, we'd let loose with a roar of laughter. We couldn't have cared less that we were polluting a state highway, and, in this particular instance, the road we were breaking our bottles on was the entrance to a state beach. We made flying saucers out of the cardboard bottle holders and sailed them at the bridge abutments as they flashed by. After a few miles of twisting coast road, I heard some muffled mutterings from the back seat that sounded like "Hurry up and pull over, man." I stomped on the brakes just in time. My buddy jumped out and proceeded to throw up all the excess beer in his stomach. The yellowish, foul-smelling liquid dripped down the roadside sign and left a temporary scar on the road. What would it cost to clean up the mess we had made? How many tires would that broken glass puncture before the highway crew cleaned it up or swept it off the roadway? When I drive down the coast these days and see empty Schlitz cans and broken Ripple bottles along the roadside, I reflect back to that Saturday night and the vomit dripping off the sign.

Hypothetical Example

An example does not have to be literally true to be effective. In the following paragraph, for instance, the writer discusses the effects of a hypothetical (imaginary) shortage to illustrate her point that Americans tend to panic in certain kinds of crises. As this paragraph shows, a *hypothetical example* is a good way to synthesize. Rather than make her point by discussing separately our reactions to the real or alleged shortages of sugar, gasoline, coffee, and toilet paper in recent years, she uses a single hypothetical crisis to reinforce what readers remember from their own actual experience.

> People in the United States tend to panic when they believe a crisis is approaching. If there were flash floods in South America and all the cocoa beans were destroyed, the public's reaction would be devastating. Shoppers would rush to supermarkets everywhere to buy chocolate products in solid, liquid, or powdered form. Hoarders would purchase as much as they could and thus cause the prices to rise. Consumers would raise their picket signs and voices in protest against the high cost of chocolate. Smugglers and black marketeers would attempt to cater to the public's "need" for this product in short supply. Eventually only government regulation—or the American people's fascination with a new crisis—would curb the panic generated by the shortage.

CAUTIONS

Whatever kind of example you use, make sure it actually supports your topic sentence and does not just add colorful but irrelevant information. For instance, in writing about the financial problems sapping American cities, you'd have little cause to talk about your trip to the top of the World Trade Center, even if you could paint the view in words of dizzying clarity. Anecdotes can add an important human touch, but make sure that your favorite story about Aunt Florence, Harry Truman, or Chairman Mao clearly illustrates the point your paragraph makes.

If you rely on a single extended example to develop a topic sentence, show that the example you've picked is representative. The fact that you (or your sister, or someone on the six o'clock news) got unfairly cited for speeding, for instance, would not convincingly support a topic sentence which asserted that police in general or even traffic police in particular are inept.

You should be equally careful when using hypothetical examples; they can be convenient ways of synthesizing experience but they must be clearly tied to the "real" world. Just as an isolated dispute over a traffic ticket wouldn't show that most traffic police don't do their jobs well, the fanciful antics of a hypothetical policeman whom you might describe careening onto traffic islands, giving speeding tickets to ambulances, and ticketing fire hydrants rather than the cars parked next to them wouldn't prove your point either.

OUTSIDE SOURCES

Sometimes your own experience and observations or those of your acquaintances won't serve as adequate evidence to back up the point you want to prove. If you want to write about our antiquated penal system, for instance, and neither you nor anyone you know has ever been inside a jail, the material you could gather from personal sources would hardly be sufficient. However, the opinions of a professor of criminology or the cover story in last week's *Time* on the state of our prisons would serve you well. So instead of developing a half-baked argument or panicking because you know little about a subject, head for the library. At times you'll need to turn to someone well-informed about your subject or to some source of accurate statistics to help you develop your paper, as the writers of the next two paragraphs have done.

Reference to Authority

The writer of this paragraph presents a case for changing the treatment given to newborn babies. Notice how she uses *authorities* on child psychology to back up her initial assertion.

> It seems only right that we give our children a loving welcome into the world. Now, it appears, this idea has the backing of science as well as of our sense of morality. According to Jill Waterman and Charles Spezzano, psychologists at the John F. Kennedy Child Development Center, the first sixty minutes of life, when a child receives his first impressions of the world around him, is the very time this welcome should take place. They feel that the traditional hospital delivery procedure, with its emphasis on sterility, minimizes mother-infant contact and thus ignores the baby's psychological needs. The atmosphere is not right, they say, for an emotional bond to develop between mother and child when an efficient hospital staff removes the baby to a plastic bassinet and the mother to her room, neither to see the other again for hours. Instead, mothers should be allowed to cuddle their infants, to look at them and talk to them—in other words, to show them love. The room should be quiet, the lights low, and the temperature equal to that in the uterus. This environment, say Spezzano and Waterman, can give a child the proper welcome, a "head start on a happy, secure childhood."

When you quote people as authorities, be sure of their qualifications on the issue you're discussing and be careful to represent them accurately. Television ads notwithstanding, celebrity does not equal expertise. Tennis players don't know any more about shampoo than the rest of us; a corporation president doesn't necessarily know anything about water resources; a retired general running for senator might not be qualified to speak on economics.

Facts and Figures

The writer of the next paragraph doesn't overpower us with seemingly endless lists of facts for their own sake, but rather uses them appropriately and effectively to make his point, which is in fact a comment on statistics themselves. *Facts and figures* can persuade, but like other kinds of details, they must be clear and relevant. (The fact that the gross national product may have risen for three consecutive years while unemployment also rose doesn't prove that rising unemployment causes a higher GNP. Similarly, the fact that several state legislatures have not ratified a constitutional amendment proves nothing about the merits of the bill.)

Football statistics don't always tell the true story. Although a list of impersonal game statistics could probably give someone reading them a general idea of what the game was like, they very rarely, if ever, let the reader in on the twisted ankles, the black eyes, or even the hot, smelly tackle laid out on the sideline after having had the air knocked out of him by a brick wall wearing a uniform. In black and white, a 3.7-yard-per-carry average of a fullback or a 48 per cent passing completion statistic doesn't sound that impressive. But if the average sports fan stopped for a moment to consider that the slithering quarterback completed those 48 out of 100 passes underneath a hailstorm of bulging triceps and hairy armpits, he would be quite impressed. After all, only 22 per cent of all pro quarterbacks complete more than 50 per cent of their passes. Even in college ball, statistics can be misleading. In the past four games, San Francisco State's fullback averaged 3.6 yards per carry and caught 82 per cent of all passes thrown to him. What the statistics don't tell is that he was actually a mule, little by little trudging up a steep mountain slope while pulling the whole offensive team behind him. He carried the ball 32 times in one game, and with every snap from center it became harder to burst through that endless sea of blood-and-sweat-soaked jerseys. These figures become even more impressive when you realize that only a small percentage of high school players actually get the highly prized opportunity to become a statistic in college football.

ANALOGY

By comparing the writing process to something entirely different, the student who wrote the paragraph below was able to clarify the difficulties she encountered as a writer. This kind of comparison, which sustains a connection between two apparently different things, is called an *analogy*. This is an especially interesting strategy of development because it allows the writer as well as the reader to make new connections between the familiar and the unfamiliar, to see the abstract in terms of the concrete.

> I have always found writing a lot like trying to catch frogs with my bare hands. Even if I'm agile enough to get the jump on a subject, it often slips through my fingers and escapes. I blame part of my problem on the nature of words themselves, which, like a lidless jar, won't keep the ideas I'm trying to capture from wriggling away. Because words are abstractions, I can use them only to describe, to approximate an experience; I can't actually re-create that experience. If I used a string of adjectives a page long, I couldn't make you feel what I feel when I hold that squirming, slimy, terrified little piece of protoplasm, that frog, in my hands. The most I can hope for when I write, "The frog, trying to escape, wriggled in my hands," is that you have had an experience similar to mine and that my words evoke the memory of that experience. Yet sometimes I have found that in trying to hold onto the frog and not let it go, I squeezed it so hard that I killed it. In my writing, too, I find that by describing too minutely and defining too carefully, sometimes I squeeze all the life out of my subject. I did this to my poetry several years ago. While trying to crystallize my experience, and trying to remove each false word, I found my poems shrinking smaller and smaller until they disappeared. I found myself without a good picture of my frog, without even a bad picture of my frog, and with poems that had croaked.

DEFINITION

Before you can discuss something clearly, you will sometimes have to define the terms of your discussion. Although we most often think of definition as a technique used in a limited way to give a word's literal meaning, as in a dictionary, good writers also use definition to explore ideas and to advance their arguments. The following paragraph, from an article on disaster movies in the *Times Literary Supplement*, defines its subject early in the essay:

> The term "disaster movie" needs some definition: though never a true generic label like "Western" or "horror movie," it was nevertheless in fairly current use and endowed for a time with a definite if imprecise meaning by the cinema-going public. Someone going to see a disaster movie knew by and large what she or he was going to get.

Irwin Allen, producer of *The Poseidon Adventure,* pointed to some of the essential characteristics of that meaning in a 1972 interview with *Hollywood Reporter,* the American film industry's main trade paper: "We have a perfect set-up of a group of people who have never met before and who are thrown together in terrible circumstances. In the first six minutes, 1,400 people are killed and only the stars survive."

—Nick Roddick

EXERCISE 1

For each of the following topic sentences a method of development is suggested. Be prepared to discuss how you might write a paragraph based on each, using the strategy provided. In addition, select one of the topic sentences and write a paragraph for it, using the method given.

1. With few exceptions, neither private nor public colleges are attracting the number of students they used to. (*facts and figures*)
2. The configuration of the atom in many ways resembles the structure of the solar system. (*analogy*)
3. The President is a fierce competitor even outside politics. (*anecdote*)
4. According to some fans of the comic strip "Peanuts," Lucy is not a cantankerous brat, but a liberated woman. (*multiple example*)
5. Parental influence is greatest during a child's first six years. (*reference to authority*)
6. Pro football often brings out the (worst/best) in a spectator. (*hypothetical example*)
7. Etiquette is more than just rigid adherence to an arbitrary code of behavior. (*definition*)
8. The very things technology has created for our convenience are now threatening to destroy us. (*extended example*)

As you've seen, some topic sentences seem to lend themselves quite clearly to particular methods of development. But good writers still recognize that a topic sentence can often be developed in several ways. Each of the following paragraphs uses a different method to develop the same topic sentence.

Extended example:

Though most of us are just beginning to realize it, anthropologists have known for years that man is just as susceptible to the powerful reactions brought on by overcrowding as the rest of the animal king-dom is. It came as no great surprise to the anthropologists, then, that at the end of World War II there were residents of Berlin who reacted violently to enforced overcrowding. For the first week after Allied authorities had ordered those in a heavily bombed section of the city to share their homes with their neighbors, social amenities were scru-pulously observed. But midway into the second week, once amiable acquaintances had begun killing each other for bathroom privileges.

Reference to authority:

Though most of us are just beginning to realize it, anthropologists have known for years that man is just as susceptible to the powerful reactions brought on by overcrowding as the rest of the animal king-dom is. According to Edward Hall, a respected anthropologist, modern urban man is exhibiting all the symptoms of overcrowding usually associated with animals. During a recent intensive study of people living and working in downtown Manhattan, he discovered that most of them had tremendously swollen adrenal glands, and he found a high incidence of arterial disease and heart attack, the same symptoms that killed half a herd of deer confined on a small island in the Chesapeake Bay. Massively swollen adrenal glands, Hall says, are the result of continued stress over long periods. When an animal is put under enormous tension, as it is in overcrowded conditions, its adrenal glands respond by pumping large amounts of adrenalin into his system. If the overcrowding, and therefore the stress, continue indefinitely, the gland just keeps pumping and expanding to handle the extra load, in effect running the biological machine at red line hour after hour, day after day . . . until something in the machine, like the heart, simply gives way.

Facts and figures:

Though most of us are just beginning to realize it, anthropologists have known for years that man is just as susceptible to the powerful reactions brought on by overcrowding as the rest of the animal king-dom is. There is no doubt that animals respond adversely to over-crowding. Four hundred wild Norway rats, given all the food and shelter they need, cannot survive on a quarter acre of land. They just die off. In 1959, half a herd of Sika deer living on an island one mile square in the Chesapeake Bay died for no apparent reason. When the population had thinned, however, the herd suddenly stabilized and showed signs of improved health. Anthropologists were dismayed to discover that the same symptoms and diseases prevalent in the ani-mals, chiefly tremendously swollen adrenal glands and a high inci-dence of heart attack, were also common among people living in overcrowded environments.

Definition:

Though most of us are just beginning to realize it, anthropologists have known for years that man is just as susceptible to the powerful reactions brought on by overcrowding as the rest of the animal kingdom is. When you and I talk of overcrowding, we usually mean specific crowds in specific, isolated situations: the lines in front of the box office at the current hit movie, or the number of glistening, apparently lifeless brown bodies we stumble over to find a patch of sand at the beach. But when anthropologists talk of overcrowding, they are talking of the constant and inescapable violation of our private space, of subways so full that the doors can't close, of buses poisoned with cigarette smoke, of people and machines and the stench of gas fumes in traffic jams, of the claustrophobic cubicles we live and work in. Anthropologists are talking about the kind of continual overcrowding in both our public and private lives that is killing us—not so slowly, and very methodically.

EXERCISE 2

A. Which method or methods could you use to develop a paragraph that began with each of the following topic sentences? Be able to explain your choice.

Example:

Leopold Stokowski was one of the most lovable men in modern symphonic music. (This statement could be more easily and effectively developed through anecdote than through statistics.)

1. Many Americans think they are living in a democracy, yet have little understanding of what a "democracy" is.
2. A freshman trying to cope with computerized registration is like a person playing chess without knowing the proper moves.
3. While the number of available teaching jobs in the U.S. continues to decline, the number of qualified applicants continues to increase.
4. Americans seem unwilling to make sacrifices in an energy crisis unless it directly affects their lives.
5. My history professor may be a brilliant person, but he is so disorganized that I find it difficult to learn from him.
6. According to scientists, air pollution is threatening to destroy not only human life but the natural food chain as well.
7. Much of twentieth-century American culture is relentlessly youth-oriented.

B. Write a paragraph developing one of the topic sentences above.

LEVELS OF GENERALIZATION

"Needs to be more conscientious" says the note your boss has written at the bottom of your recent performance review, on which you got a good numerical rating. You're disappointed, of course, but you also become increasingly irritated as you look over the form and find no other notes, only check marks and numbers. You approach your boss and ask him to let you know more specifically how you need to improve. The next day he returns your review with an additional comment: "Has problems managing time." Well, you think, that's a start, but exactly when and how have you gone wrong? Have you been starting tasks and not finishing them? Do routine jobs take you too long? Concealing your exasperation, you go in to see your boss, who finally tells you that you don't always get to work right on time and that you sometimes don't follow up on things promptly enough. Asked for an example of the last point, he recalls that you didn't return an important call yesterday and that you once left a letter unanswered for a week. Though still disappointed, you at least now understand clearly what your boss had in mind. He would have been more helpful, however, had he anticipated your questions and given you from the start all the information you needed.

As you kept after your boss, you forced him to make his general remarks increasingly specific, and this is just how dialogues of various kinds—magazine interviews, conversations between friends, exchanges of letters—tend to work: the film director says that she likes some of her movies better than others, so the interviewer asks her to name a couple of her favorites; your friend tells you that he had a close call on the way to work, and you immediately ask him what happened; your second cousin from Tombstone, Arizona, writes to tell you that she'll be out your way sometime this summer, and you write back to find out more precisely when she'll be arriving (perhaps so you can arrange to be out of town).

In your exchange with your boss, you were finally satisfied only when you had both his general reaction *and* his specific explanations. As you asked questions, his responses grew more exact, moving from the general to the specific. To visualize this process, let's take your boss's responses and rank them, from "1" for the most general to "4" for the most specific:

   (1) Needs to be more conscientious
    (2) Has problems managing time
     (3) Doesn't always get to work on time
     (3) Sometimes doesn't follow up on things
      (4) Didn't return phone call
      (4) Left letter unanswered

These rankings are called *levels of generalization,* which indicate the range between the specific and the general.

Naturally, you don't usually have the chance to converse with your readers, to let them ask you questions so that you can then frame specific answers. You must do what your boss in the example should have done: anticipate what your readers need to know and supply that information. As you know from reading the earlier sections, it's not enough to make a very general statement like "I am opposed to pass-fail grading." You could hold that opinion for a variety of quite different reasons. You might feel that only letter grades can motivate you to do your best; you might think that pass-fail grading doesn't weed less serious students out of our colleges and universities; you might even believe that all evaluations of student work, including pass-fail grades, should be eliminated. Even if you had given one of these reasons, you would need to get still more specific and show how you came to your conclusion. If you say you're opposed to pass-fail grading because you work well only when you're inspired, or threatened, by letter grades, you need to recount the specific experiences that taught you that lesson. The levels of generalization in your paragraph, from the quite general statement that you're opposed to pass-fail grading, to the less general explanation that letter grades bring out your best work, to the specific facts behind that conclusion, reflect the actual thought and experiences that led to your observation about grades.

EXERCISE 3

In order to use levels of generalization effectively in your writing, you'll need to be able to spot them, to distinguish different levels within a particular context. This exercise gives you some practice with words and phrases before you tackle the more difficult job of working with levels of generalization in a paragraph.

Rank the words or phrases in the following lists, giving "1" to the most general and "5" to the most specific. (Note: there may be more than one item on a given level.)

Example:

    2   4   5   3   1
scented liquid; French perfume; Chanel #5; perfume; fragrance;
    5
Arpège;

1. actors; performers; Robert Redford; movie actors; Paul Newman; movie stars

2. roses; natural beauty; beauty; daffodils; flowers; tulips; sunshine; Niagara Falls; Peace rose; waterfalls
3. household convenience; top-loading automatic; electrical appliance; dishwasher; timesaver; washing machine
4. saunter; move; amble; walk slowly; travel on foot; drive; walk
5. food; filet mignon; meat; hamburger patty; lima beans; greasy French fries; potatoes; vegetables; cooked potatoes
6. sport; mixed doubles; five-card draw; card game; activity; poker; tennis; doubles; bridge
7. vertebrates; Alaskan Huskies; biped; Woody Allen; dogs; animals; quadruped; man; cat; Siamese cats

---

In the exercise you just finished, you were working only on identifying levels of generalization. To show you how a writer can actually use levels in a well-written, cohesive paragraph, we have taken a passage presented earlier as an illustration of good development and have charted it for levels of generalization. The principle of levels of generalization probably seems familiar to you because it works like a traditional outline, which is the form we've decided to use here:

I. Though most of us are just beginning to realize it, anthropologists have known for years that man is just as susceptible to the powerful reactions brought on by overcrowding as the rest of the animal kingdom is.

A. It came as no great surprise to the anthropologists, then, that at the end of World War II there were residents of Berlin who reacted violently to enforced overcrowding.

1. For the first week after Allied authorities had ordered those in a heavily bombed section of the city to share their homes with their neighbors, social amenities were scrupulously observed.

2. But midway into the second week, once-amiable acquaintances began killing each other for bathroom privileges.

The most general statement in that paragraph is the assertion in the topic sentence that "man is just as susceptible to the powerful reactions brought on by overcrowding as the rest of the animal kingdom is." As though the writer had anticipated the request to narrow the abstractions *man* and *powerful reactions* into something more specific, he has in effect responded, "Some people in Berlin reacted violently." This invites yet another question: "Can you be more specific about how they reacted?" and the next two sentences tell of particular reactions.

Of course you won't always want to write paragraphs in which the levels of generalization descend in a regular order. This could get boring for both you and your readers and wouldn't always be appropriate anyway. A well-written paragraph developed by multiple example might look like this when outlined:

I. Topic sentence
  A. Example
  B. Example
  C. Example
  D. Example

And the introductory paragraph of an essay might be very general and look like this:

  I. Introductory sentence
 II. Introductory sentence
   A. Example
III. Thesis statement

But good writers most often produce paragraphs with several levels because what they have to say usually demands that they show their readers the relationship between general ideas and specific evidence, leading smoothly from one thought to the next.

EXERCISE 4

This exercise lets you try your hand at writing your own sentences at different levels of generalization. We've given you some fairly general sentences, from which you are to write some more specific ones, making sure that you follow the levels we've indicated.

Example:

I. Students today often seem uninterested in political issues and personalities.
  A. On our own campus, most students know little about national politics.
    1. A recent survey of our student body indicated that only 60 per cent knew who the senators from our state are and only 38 per cent could name the representative from their congressional district.
    2. Of students responding to the same poll, fewer than a third could name more than one member of the President's cabinet.
  B. Students here are apathetic even about campus politics.
    1. In the last campus election, only 23 per cent of the student

body bothered to vote, despite the fact that the polls were open from 7 a.m. to 10 p.m. for three days.

1. I. Having a garden isn't always a bed of roses.
   A.
      1.

2. I. Food in restaurants usually tastes better than the stuff my mother prepares at home.
   A.
      1.
      2.
   B.
      1.
      2.

3. I. Many men and women are confused by society's changing notions of what is "masculine" and what is "feminine."
   A.
      1.
   B.
      1.

4. I. Students often have a hard time finding a good part-time job while attending college.
   A.
      1.
   B.
      1.
         a.

EXERCISE 5

Now that you've worked with individual words, looked at someone else's paragraph, and written some warm-up sentences, it's time to solo. In this exercise we've provided the first and last sentences to three potential paragraphs, but nothing in between. Choose one pair, and fill in the specifics we've neglected to supply, moving through different levels of generalization as you write. Pay particular attention to how the paragraph ends so that when you add detail, you will move smoothly toward the conclusion, making sure it doesn't creep up on you unexpectedly.

Example

First sentence: The afternoon soap operas portray women as passive, inept, and subservient.

Last sentence: It is as if they are somehow being punished for being women and therefore weak, as if they somehow deserve the diasters that always befall them.

Paragraph: The afternoon soap operas portray women as passive, inept, and subservient. All women and girls who engage in premarital or extramarital sex even once, through seduction, stupidity, or rape, will end up pregnant. Even independent women of the highest professional stature, who should presumably be able to call upon their charm, prestige, and intelligence, manage to get themselves in the most muddled messes, from which only strong, brave, intelligent males can extricate them. These characters are raped, divorced, abandoned, misunderstood, given drugs, and attacked by mysterious diseases, and more females than males go mad, have brain tumors, and die. It is as if they are somehow being punished for being women and therefore weak, as if they somehow deserve the disasters that always befall them.

1. *First sentence:* Americans tend to live for the moment, never thinking about the future.

   Last sentence: With each puff he takes on his morning cigarette, the American smoker is one step closer to sealing his own fate.

2. *First sentence:* With advancing technology, we have become more and more obsessed with "instantness."

   Last sentence: Every night the corner singles' bar is filled with people in search of a three-hour relationship.

3. *First sentence:* People who are always helping others may really be motivated by selfishness.

   Last sentence: They may not care so much about being helpful as they do about winning the fleeting praise of others.

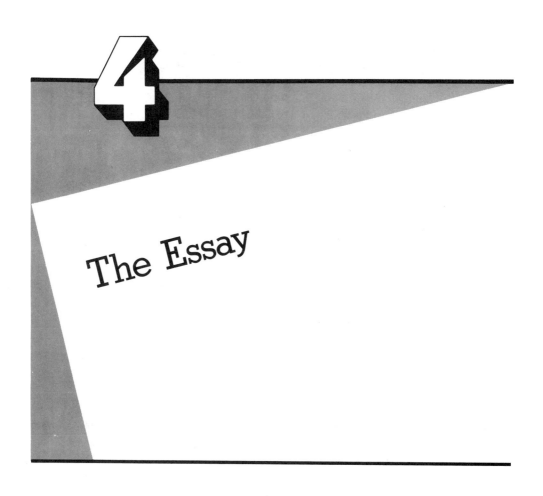

The Essay

Students often approach essay assignments with only a vague sense of exactly what is expected of them. If they knew more clearly what an essay was supposed to look and sound like, many of our students have told us, they might have an easier time producing one.

This chapter clears up some common misconceptions about essays and gives you some important principles to bear in mind when you write one. Although we'll be dealing mainly with essays for English courses, you'll find that you can apply most of what we say to writing for your other courses and even to writing outside school.

A Sample Essay

To begin with, let's look at an essay. We ask that you read it *twice*, first just to get a general sense of what the author is saying, then again to see how the different paragraphs in the essay work together.

THE MOVERS

On a winter afternoon in 1842, Charles Dickens, who had a marked talent for setting the teeth of Americans on edge, took a train from

Boston, a city of which he had generally approved, to Worcester, a matter of fifty odd miles. There was a quality about the landscape that he saw from the windows of the train that surprised and amused him. "All the buildings," he wrote in his *American Notes*, "looked as if they had been built and painted that morning and could be taken down on Monday with very little trouble." Dickens, of course, was used to stone houses in the English landscape, houses that looked as though they were as permanent as the hills about them. A New England village where "every house is the whitest of white" and where "the clean cardboard colonnades had no more perspective than a bridge on a Chinese tea cup" made him wonder if Americans ever intended to settle down. Not only did the houses look impermanent; they looked unprivate. ". . . those slightly built wooden dwellings," he noted, "behind which the sun was setting with a brilliant lustre, could be so looked through and through, that the idea of any inhabitant being able to hide himself from the public gaze, or have any secrets from the public eye, was not entertainable for a moment."

One of the reasons why Mr. Dickens got under the skin of so many Americans was that his observations were so frequently and so uncomfortably accurate. It was easy enough to explain, of course, that Americans built of wood rather than of stone because wood was so cheap and so available, but that did not explain either the disregard for privacy or why, as Dickens noted of the suburbs around Boston, American houses looked to be "sprinkled and dropped about in all directions, without seeming to have any root at all in the ground." Indeed, it appeared to him as though "the whole affair could be taken up piecemeal like a child's toy, and crammed into a little box." It was something more than white clapboards that gave America a here-today-gone-tomorrow look. It was more than just the newness of the houses and the fresh white paint, the meadows, "rank, and rough, and wild." It was something in the American character that, though Dickens did not define it, he seemed to discern: a restlessness, an urge to move on, a sense of there being unlimited space to be used or wasted, an unwillingness, in spite of all protestations to the contrary, to put down permanent roots.

The truth of the matter is that ours is a society as mobile as wheels, ambition, almost unlimited expanses of land, and an itch to sample the grass in the next pasture can make us. To move is as natural to the American as maintaining roots is to the European. Our restlessness and mobility are in our metaphors. In England a man *stands* for Parliament; in America he *runs* for the Senate. The American prides himself on his "get up and go." We think of progress as "covering ground" and we admire the man who "makes it under his own steam." The bright young man of promise is "a young man who's going places." The failure in our society is the man (or the institution, for that matter) who "stands still." The most famous exhortation in the American vernacular is "Go west, young man." We sing: "Where do we go from here, boys? Where do we go from here?" and "Don't Fence Me In," "How You Gonna Keep 'em Down on the Farm?" and "It's a Long, Long Trail."

There is more truth than humor for the American in the aphorism "Home is where you hang your hat." It is part of our mythology, rather than of our history or of our longest memories, that the American homestead is the symbol of family continuity and stability and the stronghold of democratic institutions. We associate the homestead with the virtues of family unity and solidarity, the sacrifices that the family makes for its members, the peace and reassurance of the hearth, and the sharing of pleasures and tragedies. No legend, no nostalgia, is without some basis in fact, but enduring homesteads have been few in our history compared with the vast number of transitory homes, pickings-up and puttings-down, homes that were expected to be only stepping stones to something better. Our romanticized notion of the homestead reflects actuality about as accurately as a cheerful Currier and Ives print reflects nineteenth-century life on a farm. Americans are nomadic.

It is not possible to understand the relationship between the American and his house, which he is more likely to regard as a piece of equipment than as an institution, without considering the conflict that has been in progress for more than a century and a half between foot-loose Americans and those who have tried to get them to settle down and put permanent roots into the community. Some of the pressures that have kept us moving have been practical ones, some have been romantic. Sometimes our motives have been greed, sometimes escape, sometimes hope, sometimes despair, and sometimes merely the restlessness of boredom or loneliness. We have moved in order to avoid the snapping of an economic trap sprung by a failing industry or worn-out soil; we have moved because someone a long way off needed our skills and because nobody at home any longer did. We have moved because the character of neighborhoods changed and we no longer felt at home in them. We have moved because of divorce or because our children had been fledged. We have moved because of our social aspirations or because of our loss or gain in financial status. We have moved for the fun of it, because we got tired of the view from the terrace, because of another child in the family, or because we wanted a house with a picture window. We have moved for no reason at all, except for the sake of moving.

—Russell Lynes

Essays are not random collections of facts and observations; like paragraphs, *they need to be unified around a central point.* Probably the first thing you should ask yourself when you finish reading an essay is "What has this author tried to show me?" For the essay you've just read, your answer will probably be something close to this: "Russell Lynes has tried to show that ours is a mobile society, whose restlessness is part of our history. He shows that Americans keep moving for both practical and romantic reasons." Once you've accurately summed up on essay's main points, you've identified the thesis—what the writer believes and is trying to convince his or her readers of. In many essays you'll find a sentence or two, called a *thesis statement,* that sums up the essay's main point much as a topic sentence sums up the main point of a paragraph. The nearest thing to a thesis statement in Lynes' essay comes at the beginning of the third paragraph: "The truth of the matter is that ours is a society as mobile as wheels, ambition, almost unlimited expanses of land, and an itch to sample the grass in the next pasture can make us."

If Lynes doesn't come to his main point until the beginning of Paragraph 3, what has he been doing until then? And how does the material in those introductory paragraphs relate to the essay as a whole? Lynes introduces his topic by quoting rather extensively from Charles Dickens' *American Notes,* and he has several reasons for doing so. First, Dickens' comments about American houses lend weight to Lynes' argument that we are a nation of movers. By quoting from notes made 140 years ago, Lynes shows that our mobility is no recent development but something deeply ingrained in our national character. Note too that Lynes hasn't picked just anyone to quote; Charles Dickens is well-known for the sharpness with which he depicted the contemporary English social scene in his nineteenth-century novels. By quoting a writer of Dickens' stature, Lynes leads us to take his own ideas seriously. Finally, the quotations from *American Notes* inject some added interest into the essay by letting us see what an articulate and observant foreign tourist found to comment on more than a century ago. While no two introductions are exactly alike, Lynes does what any writer tries to do in an introduction: to give background that prepares for the essay's thesis, while capturing the reader's interest.

Once Lynes has introduced his topic and given us his thesis, he uses the rest of his essay to support his contention that Americans are a mobile people. First he shows how our restlessness is reflected in expressions that permeate our language. In Paragraph 4, he considers the familiar image of the American homestead where a family has lived for generations and dismisses it as merely a comfortable myth. Finally, in Paragraph 5, he goes into the reasons Americans have moved and keep moving, cataloguing both the practical and the romantic concerns that have kept us "on the go." Good writers usually support a thesis in more than one way; that's why we gave you practice with different kinds of paragraph development in the last chapter.

In a successful essay each sentence flows logically and smoothly into the next. Careful writers cushion their readers against jarring shifts of subject matter by providing *transitions* between paragraphs and even between sentences within paragraphs. For instance, take the first sentence in Paragraph 4: "There is more truth than humor for the American in the aphorism 'Home is where you hang your hat.'" It provides continuity by reminding us of the songs and sayings about mobility mentioned in the last paragraph. At the same time, it prepares us to accept Lynes' next point, that the American homestead is a myth.

Finally, an essay doesn't just bump to a halt: it ends smoothly, giving the reader a sense of completion. Having illustrated that we are a mobile society about as thoroughly as is possible in a piece of this length, Lynes brings his essay quietly to rest with the notion that sometimes we "have moved for no reason at all, except for the sake of moving." Notice that without just restating his thesis, a process that would be tedious and unnecessary in such a short essay, Lynes concludes by bringing us back to a central point.

Essay Checklist

You'll have an easier time putting together your own essays if you remember that every essay should include the following:

- a unifying thesis—an idea that holds the essay together much as a topic sentence unifies a paragraph
- an organized presentation of details and examples to illustrate the essay's thesis
- an introduction designed to interest readers and lead them to accept your thesis
- a conclusion that brings the essay smoothly to rest, giving readers a sense of completion
- smooth transitions between sentences and paragraphs

In the coming pages we'll be offering you help with each of these. But first, a little more on the *definition* of an essay.

The Essay: Definition and Distinctions

Obviously every essay you write isn't going to be just like "The Movers." Essays not only cover different topics but take different forms, depending on the author's purpose. But any essay you write should fit the working definition devised by composition expert Frederick Crews, of the University of California at Berkeley.

- An essay is a fairly brief piece of non-fiction that tries to make a point in an interesting way.

For our purposes, "fairly brief" means between two and ten typed, double-spaced pages. If the paper is much shorter than 500 words, or two pages, it usually lacks the scope or depth to be an effective essay.

An essay is not fictional. The reader presumes that the content of the essay is true. When you stray from the strict truth in your examples, you need to make it clear that you're being hypothetical (see Chapter 3).

An essay "tries to make a point." That point is usually summed up for the reader in the form of a *thesis statement,* which may be presented immediately in the first paragraph or may appear elsewhere in the essay. Just as crucial as the thesis is its development and support. Even though you may state your main point clearly, it won't stick unless you develop and support it convincingly.

An essay tries to make its point "in an interesting way." This blanket phrase covers everything from the way you first hook the reader, to the examples you choose to keep the reader reading, to the variety of your sentences, to the ways you make your voice come through. (Much of this text is concerned with these ways to make your writing interesting as well as correct.)

Keep in mind this definition of an essay. It's a useful guide to what it is you're supposed to produce when a teacher asks you to "write an essay for next week. . . ."

THE FOUR MODES OF THE ESSAY

With a working definition of the essay in mind, we can now consider in some detail the four main *modes* (or forms) of the essay (which have come down to us from classical Greek rhetoric):

- Description
- Narration
- Argument or persuasion
- Exposition

Your college writing assignments will usually require a *blend* of these modes, but for convenience we will discuss them one at a time. The different modes help you achieve different purposes, and they have different effects on your readers.

Description

As the name implies, a descriptive essay is one consisting mainly of detailed descriptions of something, someone, or some place, but always to a purpose. You might, for example, describe the baseball field in your home town. In a description like this, your purpose is usually to recreate the atmosphere for readers who have never been there, to stimulate their senses and evoke a place they've never seen. Outside the English class, you might use description extensively in a term paper about the daily routines of the Coastal and the Plains Indians. In this case, your purpose might be to show how routines differed and thus reflected the tribes' different values.

Knowing the power of description, professional writers often use it to help them make their points. For example, in her essay "Marrying Absurd" (page 68), Joan Didion relies heavily on descriptive details to help her show the superficiality of the Las Vegas "marriage industry." Description alone, though, won't usually make a point. Good writers most often use it to enhance their thesis, not to replace other ways of supporting it.

Narration

A narrative is a story about a person or event. A narrative *essay* tells a story in order to make a point, so it's important to make sure you have a clear point to make and don't simply get caught up in telling the story. In a narrative, your purpose might be to relate a key occurrence that changed the way you view the world, your social responsibilities, your bicycle, or any other subject.

A good example of a narrative essay is Dick Gregory's "Shame" (page 77), in which Gregory tells a couple of stories to illustrate his thesis about the nature of shame, both the kind that others make us feel and the kind that wells up from our own conscience.

Narratives have the effect of sweeping readers into the story, of creating momentum and taking readers out of themselves; this helps make them more receptive to the content of your essay.

Argument or Persuasion*

For most purposes, an argumentative or persuasive essay is one that seeks to win neutral or opposed readers over to its view of a subject. You might want to argue, for instance, that we must use economic incentives rather than political pressure to woo the mineral-rich nations of Africa. Or you might try to persuade a skeptical public that

---

*For a more detailed discussion of argument and persuasion, see pages 114–117 in the next chapter.

the benefits of solar energy can be realized in the fairly near future, contrary to the claims of many advocates of nuclear power.

You find examples of argument everywhere around you, from the daily editorial in your newspaper to the 60-second "It's My Turn" slot on the radio.

The argumentative or persuasive essay tries to change readers' thoughts or feelings. For example, the student essay "Corporate Power?" (page 75) tries to persuade us that corporations aren't as powerful as we've been led to believe. Such an essay gets readers to think, forces them to question not only your ideas but their own. In short, the argumentative or persuasive essay engages the intellect or rouses the emotions.

Exposition

In an expository essay, you explain or examine a subject for the purpose of informing your readers. Perhaps you might make the point that anti-pollution regulations have become increasingly complex in recent years. Or you might want to investigate the natural imagery in the latest Ingmar Bergman film or in a Shakespeare comedy. A bit broader than the other three categories, exposition encompasses much of the writing you will be doing for your English composition classes.

The primary effect of exposition is to enlighten your readers about something, whether it is how a solar home heating unit works, or how a piece of literature is structured. The student essay "I Have an Audience" (page 80) explains the persuasive techniques used in Martin Luther King's most famous speech.

Bear in mind that you won't encounter too many examples of "pure" descriptive, narrative, argumentative, or expository essays. The main point for you to take away from this discussion is that you have a choice about the form your essay takes. Whether you choose description, narration, argumentation, or exposition will depend on your overall purpose. For example, you might decide that before you can hit your readers with a strong proposal urging expanded foreign aid to Africa, you need to soften them up with a brief *narrative* about a starving family in Uganda. Or perhaps you might think that a detailed *description* of living conditions in Chad or Angola will convince readers. Or maybe you can best *persuade* by *explaining* the ecological changes Africa is facing due to drought, expanding desert regions, and shrinking croplands, all of which necessitate help from the U.S. The persuasive writer keeps the essay's purpose firmly in mind and then chooses the approach(es) that will serve that purpose best.

MATTER AND MANNER

It's been said that a good essay gives readers a sense of both the topic and the writer. So when you write an essay, whether it's a report, a personal narrative, or something in between, you are doing more than telling readers about your subject. You are also telling them about yourself, revealing your attitudes and feelings as well as your sensitivity and common sense.

From *what* you write, your readers learn about the *topic* of your essay, acquiring information, confronting arguments, seeing the connections you make between facts and ideas. From *how* you write, your readers get some sense of the *person* behind the page. The words you choose, the tone you take, your purpose in writing, the assumptions you make about your readers, and the courtesies you extend them all contribute to your readers' picture of you.

Naturally, the choices you make about the matter, or substance, of an essay are conscious. You wouldn't pick a thesis statement out of a hat or string sentences together at random. Less obviously, but just as importantly, the manner of your writing should reflect deliberate decisions as well.

If you gloss over technical information in an essay because you know your readers share your specialized background, they will see you as their colleague. If you choose only arguments that appeal to reason, dispassionate readers will see you as level-headed. If you adopt an appropriately dramatic tone in an essay on a volatile subject, readers will see you as a dramatic, interesting person, at least in regard to the issue you're writing about.

If, on the other hand, you step falsely or carelessly in presenting yourself, readers may see you as less than admirable and interesting. If you neglect to provide necessary technical information to general readers, you'll seem rude. If you take a calm and reasonable approach to an issue that your readers feel intensely about, they may see you as cold. If you adopt a dramatic, flamboyant tone in discussing a fairly routine procedure, like assembling a terrarium, they may think you're a bit unbalanced.

You must therefore carefully consider a number of elements besides just your topic. The student who wrote the passage below seemed not at all concerned about the manner of her presentation. Her concern was only for her information, and this one-sidedness shows:

> There are three characteristics that I have found make a good teacher. They are the following: being organized in class, keeping current on the subject, and caring about each student. In this paper, I am going to explain these characteristics, which are important for all people who want to be teachers to consider.

The student was no doubt making responsible statements that she could support concretely. But the flatness of her tone, the routine nature of her material, and her lack of effort to actively involve her reader all suggest a pretty predictable, lifeless essay written by someone either unaware of or indifferent to the importance of the writer's manner.

The writer of the following paragraph erred, in some ways, in the opposite direction. His tone is inappropriately bouncy for what his real topic sentence (underlined) finally turns out to be; he also drags in background information that the reader (his English teacher) is already aware of and that, in any event, is irrelevant to the essay:

> For a while there, it looked like we were going to get a bunch of "demons of the deep" movies: first there was the blood-curdling, blood-letting *Jaws,* then the low-budget fakery of *Orca the Killer Whale,* then the embarrassingly exploitative *Jaws II.* Of course, all these movies share a common ancestor in Melville's classic tome *Moby Dick,* which we all had to slog through in high school. (*Moby Dick* was also a movie, with granite-jawed Gregory Peck playing Ahab, the captain who's paranoid about the great white whale.) Melville, who lived to a ripe old seventy-two, but not long enough to see the films his leviathan spawned, tends to equate justice and revenge in *Moby Dick,* as I hope to show in this paper.

As we've said, good writers consider more than just the topic of their essays. In planning, writing, and revising your papers, you should keep in mind the following four areas:

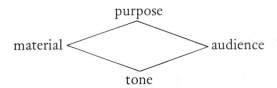

Purpose

You write all the time, and for many different reasons. Sometimes your purposes are obvious. In a diary, for example, your purpose might be to pour out your feelings about your latest love affair; in a letter to a department store it might be to get a refund on a poorly made sweater; in a note to a friend, it might be to show concern, to express gratitude, or simply to entertain. Whatever the case, you try to present yourself in a manner appropriate to your purpose. (If your complaint to the department store seems no more than an outpouring of feelings and not a reasoned request for action, your grievance won't be taken seriously.) Though seldom confused about purpose when writing for personal ends outside the classroom, students are often stumped about purpose when it comes to a class assignment.

Your most basic purpose in an essay is *to involve your readers in your material so that they seriously consider what you have to say.* Through your examples, your thesis, your style, your argument, you keep your readers' attention as they move through your paper.

Even though you'll always want to involve your readers, you'll also have other purposes, depending on the nature of the assignment. Sometimes instructors will have made it easy for you to figure out these "classroom" aims or purposes by having implicitly built them into the assignment. For example:

- They might want you to show that you've thought independently about a topic: "Given the political and social atmosphere of the 1950s, evolve a theory to explain the rebellion of the 1960s."
- Or they might want you to show that you can make connections between a topic you've studied and a topic not covered in class: "Relate a Marx Brothers film to Freud's views on comedy."
- Sometimes all an instructor wants is simple proof that you've understood a certain body of material: "Explain the three key differences between cultural and physical anthropology."

Although it's important to follow what your instructor wants you to demonstrate in a particular assignment, nothing shows up more obviously than an essay written merely to get the assignment over with, rather than to interest and involve the reader.

Audience

A neurosurgeon writing to different audiences about the newest techniques in brain surgery will address the readers of *The New England Journal of Medicine* in language and detail much more technical than he uses for the readers of *Newsweek.* In order to engage his audience, he has to consider what that audience is like, bearing in mind what they know already and what their attitude toward the subject is likely to be. The readers of the *Journal* will find a technical discussion both more accessible and more interesting than would *Newsweek* readers, who probably would want only a general, nontechnical overview.

When you write for your own ends, you probably always take your audience into account, altering your writing according to who's receiving it. You know, for example, that your stay-at-home cousin is unfamiliar with Chicago, so in a postcard to him you not only mention that you rode on the "el" but tell him what it is, defining it as an elevated railway. You would leave that definition out of a postcard to your well-travelled aunt, however.

You should show this same consideration for your audience

when you write essays, for which your "audience" is usually your instructor. If you don't provide information he or she needs (your English instructor may not know the difference between a light photomicrograph and an electron scanning photomicrograph) or if you hit your instructor over the head with the obvious (no need to mention, for instance, that the book you're writing about is "the novel that was assigned last week for this course"), you're going to lose your reader's interest, and your writing will lose much of its effect.

Know-Your-Audience Checklist

When considering whom you're writing for, you might ask yourself these questions:

- What do my readers already know?
- How much background information do they need?
- If my readers' attitudes are different from mine, which argument or details will be likely to convince them to see things my way or to understand my point? If their attitudes are like mine, how can I best keep their interest?
- If the assignment is open-ended, will the topic I create hold readers' attention and match their interests? Am I overly enthusiastic, for example, about a personal experience that few other people would want to know about?

Tone

When we speak, our words carry any number of messages just because of the tone our voices assume. Take, for example, the words "Come here." Whispered, barked in anger, sung seductively, or stated flatly, the same phrase does more than convey its literal sense; it also tells us something in each different case about the speaker, his purpose, and his relationship with his listener, helping to reveal his *attitude* toward the situation. With different people, or even with the same people in different situations, we all modulate our tone of voice to fit the circumstances.

In writing, as in speaking, the right tone should emerge if you pay attention to your audience and your purpose. For tone in writing conveys your attitude just as your speaking tone does. But when you don't have sound waves working for you, you can regulate tone only with word choice, the structure and length of sentences, and the information you choose to relay. The conscious writer uses all three to advantage.

Inexperienced writers often have a difficult time with tone, perhaps because they've been misled about how they should or shouldn't "sound" on paper. As we'll see in Chapter 10, the words we choose and the ways we arrange them create a wide range of literal meanings and more subtle implications. Our words may unintentionally make us sound stuffy and stilted when we're trying to sound serious or may add a flippant cast to a piece we're merely trying to make informal.

Your essays should sound as though you were comfortable in writing them. We hope you learn to cringe at writing that is:

hysterical or fist pounding ("You must remove the curse of white bread from your daily diet. Your very life may depend on it!")

overly reliant on slang ("The bozos in national office these days are the pits.")

inflated or pompous ("The perspicacity evinced by the novelist in this opus is nonpareil, especially vis-à-vis the meager offerings of his oft-touted, though distinctly inferior, contemporaries.")

flowery ("As the glinting glimmer of the fading sun played peek-a-boo through the gentle glade, we set off for home, our hearts abrim with the richness of our golden afternoon.")

Unless its purpose dictates an unusual tone, a college essay usually strikes a middle ground that still allows the writer's own personality to come through.

Testing for Tone in Your Own Writing

One way to test for appropriate tone in your own writing is to *listen* to what you've written, reading aloud to yourself or to a friend. In this way you can more easily answer some important questions about your essay's tone:

- Am I conveying my information with some style, or is the essay too dry, like a report?
- Am I using style just for its own sake, or does it help to get my meaning across?
- Have I used slang? If so, is it appropriate to the subject?
- Am I being pompous or flowery—in other words, unnatural and stiff?
- Is my tone appropriate to the subject: light when the subject is light, serious when the subject is serious?

Material

The way you communicate in an essay is determined by a final element working in conjunction with purpose, audience, and tone, and that's the material itself.

NATURE OF THE MATERIAL

Some material almost automatically lends itself to being treated in a certain way: seriously, poetically, humorously, whimsically, mysteriously, "academically." For example, a lighthearted tone would probably be most appropriate for an essay drawn from an informal survey of the dating preferences of the varsity football team. Treated humorously, such a survey could help make an admittedly overstated point about "male personality types." Treated with scholarly rigor and infused with a no-nonsense, impersonal tone, such an essay would be dull and incongruous. Material taken from interviews with the family of a murder victim, on the other hand, would naturally have to be treated seriously, serving a purpose more profound than entertainment.

AVAILABILITY OF MATERIAL

As we'll see in our discussion of various types of assignments, the approach you take to an essay is sometimes limited by the material available to you. If you remember a compelling article on the subject you're writing about but can't remember where you saw the article, or if you would like to quote statistics but don't have time to get to the library, you'll obviously have to find or generate other material.

SUITABILITY OF MATERIAL

Most often, your choice of material will depend on the interplay between your audience, your purpose, and the tone you adopt.

If you were writing on gun control and wished to construct a concise case against gun control laws, you might choose a constitutional argument, whose simple essence would be that the Bill of Rights flatly guarantees that "the right of the people to keep and bear arms shall not be infringed."

If you wanted to argue against gun control by hitting its proponents with a strong emotional appeal, you could cite examples of homeowners or shopkeepers whose property and livelihood were preserved through their use of firearms.

If you wished to write a fairly lengthy, scholarly paper informing readers about the various attempts to control guns in the past, you would build your essay on the examples culled during your necessarily extensive research.

If you were to write a satirical paper in favor of gun control, you'd need to pepper your essay with examples that make readers laugh rather than blanch or cringe. Truly violent, horrible anecdotes about people inadvertantly killing or injuring others would hardly be appropriate.

If arguing for gun control to an unsympathetic audience, you'd need to cite the most objective statistics and sources you could find to counteract the opinions of your readers.

A FINAL WORD

Since purpose, tone, audience, and material are connected, any change in one area may require a change in the rest. If you decide to change the tone of an essay, you may have to modify your purpose and pick new examples. If you can't find the material you'd planned on using, the tone and purpose of the paper may change. If your audience turns out to be different from the one you'd expected, you may need to reconsider your tone, purpose, and material.

The constant message of this book has been that you should make your choices carefully and consciously. *Choose* your material and tone deliberately; consider your purpose and audience thoughtfully. Your efforts will yield a stronger essay, and your readers will get a stronger, more positive sense of you as a writer.

EXERCISE : Practice with Purpose, Audience, Tone, and Material

For this exercise, imagine that you have been the victim of an injustice. An instructor (you choose the course) has given you a failing final grade, not because you did unacceptable work, but because he took a dislike to you based on _____ (you choose the reason: perhaps your race, sex, age, or some other factor over which you have no control, and that shouldn't affect your grade in any case).

Your assignment is to produce *three* distinct pieces of writing, each directed at a different audience:

1. A letter to the dean of your school, making a request of some sort.
2. A letter to a friend.
3. A short essay about discrimination in the classroom, one which uses your own experience *and other evidence* to support your point.

In writing these letters and the short essay, keep the following in mind:

1. Who your *audience* is.
2. What your *purpose* is (what you want to get and what you want your writing to *do*).
3. How your writing should *sound*, given your audience and purpose.
4. What points you want to make, how much time and space you

should devote to various points, what you want to touch on only lightly, what you want to ignore, etc.

Note: This is a rather long assignment, in that each piece of writing should be at least 250–300 words long. Be sure to allow enough time to treat each well.

A SAMPLER

So you can see how the ideas in this chapter work in practice, we've chosen a few essays, some by professionals, some by students. You'll find them diverse in topic and in style, ranging from a fairly theoretical discussion of communities and solitude to highly personal narratives about adventure and shame.

As you read these essays, consider the following questions:

- What is the writer's thesis?
- How does the writer lead up to the thesis? What kind of background information does he or she provide? How does the writer try to get and hold my interest?
- How does the writer match the tone of the essay to its subject?
- What kinds of evidence and examples does the writer use? Are they effective?
- Which of the four modes—description, narration, argument or persuasion, or exposition—does this essay fall into? Does it seem to fit more than one mode?
- Which of the methods of paragraph development discussed in the last chapter does the writer use?
- What assumptions does the writer seem to make about his or her readers?
- Is there anything unusual about the form of the essay?
- Why did the writer choose this form?
- How does the essay conclude? Does the writer seem to leave a key issue closed or open?
- What sense do you get of the writer's voice, of his or her individual personality and sensibilities?

This last question is perhaps the most important, for no good essay reflects only an allegiance to the rules and customs of good writing, with the commas in the right place, the arguments dutifully developed, and the sentences suitably varied. While good writing does most often adhere to these conventions, it also provides a unique glimpse into another mind, with a different set of values and experiences, and a different style, from our own.

RIDING THE BULL

I was traveling through Utah when I stumbled across a local rodeo in one of the small towns. It was a warm, pleasant Sunday, and the rodeo looked like a friendly event, with neighbors getting together to compete, relax, swill beer, swap stories, and show off their livestock. It looked like a good way to pass time; so I decided to stay.

The corral was a permanent structure, the site of many such rodeos. The announcer sat above the paddocks at the far end of the arena, and the loudspeaker blared out the events and the names of the contestants, interspersed with a colorful running commentary on the antics of the riders. I ambled up to a buxom, Western-clad blonde, and stood talking to her while the bull riding began. I said that it looked like a snap and she suggested that I give it a try.

For one second, I wasn't sure how the cowboys would feel about it; perhaps it was the cynicism of the lifetime city-dweller that made me wonder, for a moment, whether these men would take offense at an arrogant city-slicker taking on a proud and pioneering tradition. But the thought passed quickly, and I was eager to test my skill. I walked over towards the announcer, who stood as the maestro of a symphony of men and animals coming together in a surging, synergistic cadence. I told him that I wanted to ride the bulls.

He motioned me to the fence around the bull pen, where a man was running bulls into a chute. He agreed to set up the next bull for me, and while I was waiting, I sat on the fence and lit up a Marlboro. Suddenly I felt myself getting caught up in the role, just like the man in the cigarette commercial: the cowboy, the Western archetype, the image of American masculinity par excellence—the sort of guy who holds up his socks with thumbtacks and can hit a spittoon at ten feet, upwind. So here I was, about to make my play in the arena, ready to throw myself into the primeval struggle of man against beast, noting the fact that it was a short run, if necessary, to the safety of the fence. This was going to be my chance to link up with destiny, my proving ground, and I was determined to put on a good show.

I took my place above the bull in the chute. A thin rope was passed through his legs and over his shoulder, making a circle. I closed my hand under it, my knuckles white with straining, and gave the signal. The side of the chute fell open and we burst into the arena. The bull spun wildly to the left, and an exuberant shout tore from my throat. I was aware of nothing but the raw, muscled power of the beast pounding me with sledgehammer force. He bucked and my hat flew off. I began to slide and realized that I would be under his belly in another second, which was an experience I thought I could pass up. The buzzer sounded and I sprang off sideways, tracing a perfect trajectory into the dirt. For effect, I remained lying for a minute in the soft, pungent earth, but then I thought better of it (the stench was getting to me), and pulled myself to my feet. I walked slowly over to my hat and dusted it off with bravado. The crowd cheered wildly.

As I made my way from the arena, I was overcome with a sense of my own worth. I had almost literally taken the bull by the horns, stayed on the requisite number of seconds, and had lived to tell about it (and accept my ovation). As a kid, I had always been "the Indian"; now I was all my cowboy heroes rolled into one: Tom Mix, Gene Autry, Singing Sandy, Roy Rogers, Andy Devine, and the toughest of them all, Gabby Hayes.

The rodeo is the last vestige of the life of the Old West; what the cowboy did as a job, the rodeo preserves as a contest. There is a thrill that goes hand in hand with the danger of rodeo sports; you could be killed or maimed at any time. There is the excitement of competition and the exhilaration of pitting oneself against the brute strength of an animal. When I rode the bull, I tapped into a vein of history, even though I was simply playing at the sort of work that had, in the Old West, been a routine and necessary part of survival. In that space of time, I shed my urban persona and found a new respect for the people that preserve these old skills and traditions in rodeo.

—Student Essay

MARRYING ABSURD

To be married in Las Vegas, Clark County, Nevada, a bride must swear that she is eighteen or has parental permission and a bride-groom that he is twenty-one or has parental permission. Someone must put up five dollars for the license. (On Sundays and holidays, fifteen dollars. The Clark County Courthouse issues marriage licenses at any time of the day or night except between noon and one in the afternoon, between eight and nine in the evening, and between four and five in the morning.) Nothing else is required. The State of Nevada, alone among these United States, demands neither a pre-marital blood test nor a waiting period before or after the issuance of a marriage license. Driving in across the Mojave from Los Angeles, one sees the signs way out on the desert, looming up from that moonscape of rattlesnakes and mesquite, even before the Las Vegas lights appear like a mirage on the horizon: "GETTING MARRIED? Free License Information First Strip Exit." Perhaps the Las Vegas wedding industry achieved its peak operational efficiency between 9:00 p.m. and midnight of August 26, 1965, an otherwise unremarkable Thursday which happened to be, by Presidential order, the last day on which anyone could improve his draft status merely by getting married. One hundred and seventy-one couples were pronounced man and wife in the name of Clark County and the State of Nevada that night, sixty-seven of them by a single justice of the peace, Mr. James A. Brennan. Mr. Brennan did one wedding at the Dunes and the other sixty-six in his office, and charged each couple eight dollars. One bride lent her veil to six others. "I got it down from five to three minutes," Mr. Brennan said later of his feat. "I could've married them *en masse,* but they're people, not cattle. People expect more when they get married."

What people who get married in Las Vegas actually do expect—what, in the largest sense, their "expectations" are—strikes one as a curious and self-contradictory business. Las Vegas is the most extreme and allegorical of American settlements, bizarre and beautiful in its venality and in its devotion to immediate gratification, a place the tone of which is set by mobsters and call girls and ladies' room attendants with amyl nitrite poppers in their uniform pockets. Almost everyone notes that there is no "time" in Las Vegas, no night and no day and no past and no future (no Las Vegas casino, however, has taken the obliteration of the ordinary time sense quite so far as Harold's Club in Reno, which for a while issued, at odd intervals in the day and night, mimeographed "bulletins" carrying news from the world outside); neither is there any logical sense of where one is. One is standing on a highway in the middle of a vast hostile desert looking at an eighty-foot sign which blinks "STAR-DUST" or "CAESAR'S PALACE." Yes, but what does that explain? This geographical implausibility reinforces the sense that what happens there has no connection with "real" life; Nevada cities like Reno and Carson are ranch towns, Western towns, places behind which there is some historical imperative. But Las Vegas seems to exist only in the eye of the beholder. All of which makes it an extraordinarily stimulating and interesting place, but an odd one in which to want to wear a candlelight satin Priscilla of Boston wedding dress with Chantilly lace insets, tapered sleeves and a detachable modified train.

And yet the Las Vegas wedding business seems to appeal to precisely that impulse. "Sincere and Dignified Since 1954," one wedding chapel advertises. There are nineteen such wedding chapels in Las Vegas, intensely competitive, each offering better, faster, and, by implication, more sincere services than the next: Our Photos Best Anywhere, Your Wedding on A Phonograph Record, Candlelight with Your Ceremony, Honeymoon Accommodations, Free Transportation from Your Motel to Courthouse to Chapel and Return to Motel, Religious or Civil Ceremonies, Dressing Rooms, Flowers, Rings, Announcements, Witnesses Available, and Ample Parking. All of these services, like most others in Las Vegas (sauna baths, payroll-check cashing, chinchilla coats for sale or rent) are offered twenty-four hours a day, seven days a week, presumably on the premise that marriage, like craps, is a game to be played when the table seems hot.

But what strikes one most about the Strip chapels, with their wishing wells and stained-glass paper windows and their artificial bouvardia, is that so much of their business is by no means a matter of simple convenience, of late-night liaisons between show girls and baby Crosbys. Of course there is some of that. (One night about eleven o'clock in Las Vegas I watched a bride in an orange minidress and masses of flame-colored hair stumble from a Strip chapel on the arm of her bridegroom, who looked the part of the expendable nephew in movies like *Miami Syndicate.* "I gotta get the kids," the bride whimpered. "I gotta pick up the sitter, I gotta get to the midnight show." "What you gotta get," the bridegroom said, opening the door of a Cadillac Coupe de Ville and watching her crumple on the seat, "is sober.") But Las Vegas seems to offer something other than "convenience"; it is merchandising "niceness," the facsimile of proper ritual, to children who do not know how else to find it, how to make the arrangements, how to do it "right." All day and evening long on the Strip, one sees actual wedding parties, waiting under the harsh lights at a crosswalk, standing uneasily in the parking lot of the Frontier while the photographer hired by The Little Church of the West ("Wedding Place of the Stars") certifies the occasion, takes the picture: the bride in a veil and white satin pumps, the bridegroom usually in a white dinner jacket, and even an attendant or two, a sister or a best friend in hot-pink *peau de soie,* a flirtation veil, a carnation nosegay. "When I Fall in Love It Will Be Forever," the organist plays, and then a few bars of *Lohengrin.* The mother cries; the stepfather, awkward in his role, invites the chapel hostess to join them for a drink at the Sands. The hostess declines with a professional smile; she has already transferred her interest to the group waiting outside. One bride out, another in, and again the sign goes up on the chapel door: "One moment please—Wedding."

I sat next to one such wedding party in a Strip restaurant the last time I was in Las Vegas. The marriage had just taken place; the bride still wore her dress, the mother her corsage. A bored waiter poured out a few swallows of pink champagne ("on the house") for everyone but the bride, who was too young to be served. "You'll need something with more kick than that," the bride's father said with heavy jocularity to his new son-in-law; the ritual jokes about the wedding night had a certain Panglossian character, since the bride was clearly several months pregnant. Another round of pink champagne, this time not on the house, and the bride began to cry. "It was just as nice," she sobbed, "as I hoped and dreamed it would be."

—Joan Didion

WE ARE NOT ALONE

We are not alone. Whether a man lives in the country or in the city, he cannot attain perfect solitude for any prolonged period of time, and although there have been notable exceptions to this, we seem to be rather compelled to be companionate creatures. For most of us, this is the way we prefer to live; humans, like so many other species from lions to bees, being more effective and content when living in a group, whether it is a hunting band of ten or twelve, or a city of 1.2 million.

Amazingly enough, we as a species have spent less than one per cent of our time on earth living in groups large enough to be considered anything other than familial. In fact, urban living is so new to us that I am sure we should expect it to affect us in some very peculiar ways, many of which I doubt we comprehend or even notice.

Life in a small town, though, is not so different from life in a familial group, for each person has a recognized place and purpose, and life tends to follow a structured, well-ordered routine. Generally, too, each person has ample private space, for a brief walk will bring one to fields or forest where it is possible to be alone. Solitude seems to me as necessary as companionship, for it enables one to sort through the varied data acquired in contact with others, to derive conclusions and solutions which are personally satisfying, and thus to retain a sense of self.

But in a city, we are never alone, except when locked in our rooms, and many city-dwellers don't even have the relative luxury of a private room. We are subjected to a constant influx of data, and it is often nearly impossible for us to attain the space and quiet necessary for suitable assimilation. The only solution: establish defenses against this influx, and these defenses, I believe, are something quite new for us.

A stranger encountered by a small hunting band must have been cause for intense excitement, and a newcomer in a small town is subject to the scrutiny of the curious townspeople, who try to discover everything they can about the new person. But we are surrounded by strangers in the city, where any curiosity we might naturally feel is ruthlessly suppressed as rude at best, and possibly quite dangerous.

We are usually taught as children that it is rude to stare at others, even though some of the people we see in the city are so unusual as to be fascinating to someone free of this inhibition. We take offense at being stared at by others, and a personal query is apt to be met with an abrupt reply, which will soon deter those still inclined to ask personal questions of strangers. We defend "our" space jealously, rattling papers and fidgeting if someone sits too close on the bus, walking rapidly with head down if we sense someone approaching us on the street, turning if someone we don't know or don't like the looks of appears to require our assistance.

Yet we pay a price for this protection of our limited ability to accept contact with others. Our defenses are too effective, causing us to feel isolated; nameless entities in a crowd. We have to circumvent this problem if we are to feel comfortable, and the way we do it interests me quite a lot. We establish small communities within our cities, communities quite analogous to small towns, except that membership in a small town is usually an accident of birth or marriage, while membership in a community in a city is deliberate, based on similarities of interest. Having established these communities, we again feel "at home," having certain places, restaurants, bars, shops, which we patronize regularly and where we are recognized as individuals. We have our friends, the other people in our community, and it is they who help us form our sense of ourselves and our world. Thus we limit the scope of our day-to-day lives, allowing ourselves to function in an impossibly complex and claustrophobic urban environment by creating our own more nurturing communities within it.

—Student Essay

BEING A BOY

As boys go, I wasn't much. I mean, I tried to be a boy and spent many childhood hours pummeling my hardly formed ego with failure at cowboys and Indians, baseball, football, lying, and sneaking out of the house. When our neighborhood gang raided a neighbor's pear tree, I was the only one who got sick from the purloined fruit. I also failed at setting fire to our garage, an art at which any five-year-old boy should be adept. I was, however, the neighborhood champion at getting beat up. "That Julius can take it, man," the boys used to say, almost in admiration, after I emerged from another battle, tears brimming in my eyes but refusing to fall.

My efforts at being a boy earned me a pair of scarred knees that are a record of a childhood spent falling from bicycles, trees, the tops of fences, and porch steps; of tripping as I ran (generally from a fight), walked, or simply tried to remain upright on windy days.

I tried to believe my parents when they told me I was a boy, but I could find no objective proof for such an assertion. Each morning during the summer, as I cuddled up in the quiet of a corner with a book, my mother would push me out the back door and into the yard. And throughout the day as my blood was let as if I were a patient of 17th-century medicine, I thought of the girls sitting in the shade of porches, playing with their dolls, toy refrigerators and stoves.

There was the life, I thought! No constant pressure to prove oneself. No necessity always to be competing. While I humiliated myself on football and baseball fields, the girls stood on the sidelines laughing at me, because they didn't have to do anything except be girls. The rising of each sun brought me to the starting line of yet another day's Olympic decathlon, with no hope of ever winning even a bronze medal.

Through no fault of my own I reached adolescence. While the pressure to prove myself on the athletic field lessened, the overall situation got worse—because now I had to prove myself with girls. Just how I was supposed to go about doing this was beyond me, especially because, at the age of 14, I was four foot nine and weighed 78 pounds. (I think there may have been one 10-year-old girl in the neighborhood smaller than I.) Nonetheless, duty called, and with my ninth-grade gym-class jockstrap flapping between my legs, off I went.

To get a girlfriend, though, a boy had to have some asset beyond the fact that he was alive. I wasn't handsome like Bill McCord, who had girls after him like a cop-killer has policemen. I wasn't ugly like Romeo Jones, but at least the girls noticed him: "That ol' ugly boy better stay 'way from me!" I was just there, like a vase your grandmother gives you at Christmas that you don't like or dislike, can't get rid of, and don't know what to do with. More than ever I wished I were a girl. Boys were the ones who had to take the initiative and all the responsibility. (I hate responsibility so much that if my heart didn't beat of itself, I would now be a dim memory.)

It was the boy who had to ask the girl for a date, a frightening enough prospect until it occurred to me that she might say no! That meant risking my ego, which was about as substantial as a toilet-paper raincoat in the African rainy season. But I had to thrust that ego forward to be judged, accepted, or rejected by some girl. It wasn't fair! Who was she to sit back like a queen with the power to create joy by her consent or destruction by her denial? It wasn't fair—but that's the way it was.

But if (God forbid!) she should say Yes, then my problem would begin in earnest, because I was the one who said where we would go (and waited in terror for her approval of my choice). I was the one who picked her up at her house where I was inspected by her parents as if I were a possible carrier of syphilis (which I didn't think one could get from masturbating, but then again, Jesus was born of a virgin, so what did I know?). Once we were on our way, it was I who had to pay the bus fare, the price of the movie tickets, and whatever she decided to stuff her stomach with afterward. (And the smallest girls are all stomach.) Finally, the girl was taken home where once again I was inspected (the father looking covertly at my fly and the mother examining the girl's hair). The evening was over and the girl had done nothing except honor me with her presence. All the work had been mine.

Imagining this procedure over and over was more than enough: I was a sophomore in college before I had my first date.

I wasn't a total failure in high school, though, for occasionally I would go to a party, determined to salvage my self-esteem. The parties usually took place in somebody's darkened basement. There was generally a surreptitious wine bottle or two being passed furtively among the boys, and a record player with an insatiable appetite for Johnny Mathis records. Boys gathered on one side of the room and girls on the other. There were always a few boys and girls who'd come to the party for the sole purpose of grinding away their sexual frustrations to Johnny Mathis's falsetto, and they would begin dancing to their own music before the record player was plugged in. It took a little longer for others to get started, but no one matched my talent for standing by the punch bowl. For hours, I would try to make my legs do what they had been doing without effort since I was nine months old, but for some reason they would show all the symptoms of paralysis on those evenings.

After several hours of wondering whether I was going to die ("Julius Lester, a sixteen-year-old, died at a party last night, a half-eaten Ritz cracker in one hand and a potato chip dipped in pimiento-cheese spread in the other. Cause of death: failure to be a boy"), I would push my way to the other side of the room where the girls sat like a hanging jury. I would pass by the girl I wanted to dance with. If I was going to be refused, let it be by someone I didn't particularly like. Unfortunately, there weren't many in that category. I had more crushes than I had pimples.

Finally, through what surely could only have been the direct intervention of the Almighty, I would find myself on the dance floor with a girl. And none of my prior agony could compare to the thought of actually dancing. But there I was and I had to dance with her. Social custom decreed that I was supposed to lead, because I was the boy. Why? I'd wonder. Let her lead. Girls were better dancers anyway. It didn't matter. She stood there waiting for me to take charge. She wouldn't have been worse off if she'd waited for me to turn white.

But, reciting "Invictus" to myself, I placed my arms around her, being careful to keep my armpits closed because, somehow, I had managed to overwhelm a half jar of deodorant and a good-size bottle of cologne. With sweaty armpits, "Invictus," and legs afflicted again with polio, I took her in my arms, careful not to hold her so far away that she would think I didn't like her, but equally careful not to hold her so close that she could feel the catastrophe which had befallen me the instant I touched her hand. My penis, totally disobeying the lecture I'd given it before we left home, was as rigid as Governor Wallace's jaw would be if I asked for his daughter's hand in marriage.

God, how I envied girls at that moment. Wherever *it* was on them, it didn't dangle between their legs like an elephant's trunk. No wonder boys talked about nothing but sex. That thing was always there. Every time we went to the john, there *it* was, twitching around like a fat little worm on a fishing hook. When we took baths, it floated in the water like a lazy fish and God forbid we should touch it! It sprang to life like lightning leaping from a cloud. I wished I could cut it off, or at least keep it tucked between my legs, as if it were a tail that had been mistakenly attached to the wrong end. But I was helpless. It was there, with a life and mind of its own, having no other function than to embarrass me.

Fortunately, the girls I danced with were discreet and pretended that they felt nothing unusual rubbing against them as we danced. But I was always convinced that the next day they were all calling up all their friends to exclaim: "Guess what, girl? Julius Lester got one! I ain't lyin'!"

Now, of course, I know that it was as difficult being a girl as it was a boy, if not more so. While I stood paralyzed at one end of a dance floor trying to find the courage to ask a girl for a dance, most of the girls waited in terror at the other, afraid that no one, not even I, would ask them. And while I resented having to ask a girl for a date, wasn't it also horrible to be the one who waited for the phone to ring? And how many of those girls who laughed at me making a fool of myself on the baseball diamond would have gladly given up their places on the sidelines for mine on the field?

No, it wasn't easy for any of us, girls and boys, as we forced our beautiful, free-flowing child-selves into those narrow, constricting cubicles labeled *female* and *male.* I tried, but I wasn't good at being a boy. Now, I'm glad, knowing that a man is nothing but the figment of a penis's imagination, and any man should want to be something more than that.

—Julius Lester

CORPORATE POWER?

"Corporations are those massive structures of organized economic and political power that decide where Americans shall live, what they shall eat, where they will work, and how they will die. . . . In this country corporate power has had an unchallenged pre-eminence over government."

—Alan Wolfe in the *Saturday Review*

An interesting contrast to Wolfe's view is provided by a survey of U.S. opinion leaders reported recently [1980] by *U.S. News and World Report.* The opinion leaders were asked to name the five people "you think exercise—through position, power, ability, or wealth— the most influence in national decision making." Of the persons designated by this poll as the ten "most influential," seven are elected or appointed government officials, and one, Rosalynn Carter, the wife of a government official. Only one, David Rockefeller, who ranked fifth, is in private enterprise. The final person in the top ten was Walter Cronkite, who ranked eighth, a representative of the Fourth Estate (news media).

Of the twenty next "most influential Americans," ten are connected with government and four with the news media. Of the remaining six, one heads a trade union (13th), two head major corporations (25th and 29th), one heads a bank (30th), and two are private citizens who fall into none of these categories (22nd and 28th).

Not much sign there of a country run by big business; rather, by big Washington—the home base of most of the top 30.

The anti-big-business group will dismiss this evidence as a facade, as window dressing. These are the puppets, they will say. The strings are really being pulled behind the scenes by "corporate power," especially by multi-national corporations.

That contention has some merit, but it cannot explain a top corporate income-tax rate of 46 per cent. It cannot explain the enactment of a so-called "windfall profits tax" on petroleum products estimated to total $227 billion in the next decade, against the concerted opposition of the multinational oil companies. And this list can be extended indefinitely.

Corporations do exert power, and too much power. However, they typically exert that power by their ability to influence government rather than through the marketplace. The Chrysler Corporation could never, through the market, have forced workers who earn less than most Chrysler employees to pony up funds to bail it out of financial difficulties, and, incidentally, pay those high wages. Yet that is just what it has succeeded in doing through government. The U.S. Steel Corporation could never, through the market, have forced buyers of its steel to pay more than the price at which Japanese or other foreign steel was available. Yet that is just what it did through the now abandoned "trigger price" system enforced by the U.S. Treasury, and what it is trying to get the government to do on a still larger scale.

Airline fares were kept high and service limited, not through the market but through the Civil Aeronautics Board, as has been demonstrated since the partial deregulation of air travel. The trucking industry imposes billions of dollars of extra cost each year on all of us, not through the market but through the Interstate Commerce Commission. Opposition to the deregulation of trucking comes not from the trucking industry's customers or potential competition but from big business, big labor, and the trucking firms themselves.

The Big Business Day protesters, recently organized by Ralph Nader, are barking up the wrong tree. With few exceptions, big business—or small business for that matter—can exercise arbitrary power over the rest of us only when it can form an alliance with government, whether Federal or local. The protesters would do far more to promote their ostensible objections by urging complete free trade abroad, and a wider measure of free enterprise at home, rather than by asking for another dose of government intervention.

—Student Essay

SHAME

I never learned hate at home, or shame. I had to go to school for that. I was about seven years old when I got my first big lesson. I was in love with a little girl named Helene Tucker, a light-complected little girl with pigtails and nice manners. She was always clean and she was smart in school. I think I went to school then mostly to look at her. I brushed my hair and even got me a little old handkerchief. It was a lady's handkerchief, but I didn't want Helene to see me wipe my nose on my hand. The pipes were frozen again, there was no water in the house, but I washed my socks and shirt every night. I'd get a pot, and go over to Mister Ben's grocery store, and stick my pot down into his soda machine. Scoop out some chopped ice. By evening the ice melted to water for washing. I got sick a lot that winter because the fire would go out at night before the clothes were dry. In the morning I'd put them on, wet or dry, because they were the only clothes I had.

Everybody's got a Helene Tucker, a symbol of everything you want. I loved her for her goodness, her cleanness, her popularity. She'd walk down my street and my brothers and sisters would yell, "Here comes Helene," and I'd rub my tennis sneakers on the back of my pants and wish my hair wasn't so nappy and the white folks' shirt fit me better. I'd run out on the street. If I knew my place and didn't come too close, she'd wink at me and say hello. That was a good feeling. Sometimes I'd follow her all the way home, and shovel the snow off her walk and try to make friends with her Momma and her aunts. I'd drop money on her stoop late at night on my way back from shining shoes in the taverns. And she had a Daddy, and he had a good job. He was a paper hanger.

I guess I would have gotten over Helene by summertime, but something happened in that classroom that made her face hang in front of me for the next twenty-two years. When I played the drums in high school it was for Helene and when I broke track records in college it was for Helene and when I started standing behind microphones and heard applause I wished Helene could hear it, too. It wasn't until I was twenty-nine years old and married and making money that I finally got her out of my system. Helene was sitting in that classroom when I learned to be ashamed of myself.

It was on a Thursday. I was sitting in the back of the room, in a seat with a chalk circle around it. The idiot's seat, the troublemaker's seat.

The teacher thought I was stupid. Couldn't spell, couldn't read, couldn't do arithmetic. Just stupid. Teachers were never interested in finding out that you couldn't concentrate because you were so hungry, because you hadn't had any breakfast. All you could think about was noontime, would it ever come? Maybe you could sneak into the cloakroom and steal a bite of some kid's lunch out of a coat pocket. A bite of something. Paste. You can't really make a meal of paste, or put it on bread for a sandwich, but sometimes I'd scoop a few spoonfuls out of the big paste jar in the back of the room. Pregnant people get strange tastes. I was pregnant with poverty. Pregnant with dirt and pregnant with smells that made people turn away, pregnant with cold and pregnant with shoes that were never bought for me, pregnant with five other people in my bed and no Daddy in the next room, and pregnant with hunger. Paste doesn't taste too bad when you're hungry.

The teacher thought I was a troublemaker. All she saw from the front of the room was a little black boy who squirmed in his idiot's seat and made noises and poked the kids around him. I guess she couldn't see a kid who made noises because he wanted someone to know he was there.

It was on a Thursday, the day before the Negro payday. The eagle always flew on Friday. The teacher was asking each student how much his father would give to the Community Chest. On Friday night, each kid would get the money from his father, and on Monday he would bring it to the school. I decided I was going to buy me a Daddy right then. I had money in my pocket from shining shoes and selling papers, and whatever Helene Tucker pledged for her Daddy I was going to top it. And I'd hand the money right in, I wasn't going to wait until Monday to buy me a Daddy.

I was shaking, scared to death. The teacher opened her book and started calling out names alphabetically.

"Helene Tucker?"

"My Daddy said he'd give two dollars and fifty cents."

"That's very nice, Helene. Very, very nice indeed."

That made me feel pretty good. It wouldn't take too much to top that. I had almost three dollars in dimes and quarters in my pocket. I stuck my hand in my pocket and held onto the money, waiting for her to call my name. But the teacher closed her book after she called everybody else in the class.

I stood up and raised my hand.

"What is it now?"

"You forgot me."

She turned toward the blackboard. "I don't have time to be playing with you, Richard."

"My Daddy said he'd . . ."

"Sit down, Richard, you're disturbing the class."

"My Daddy said he'd give . . . fifteen dollars."

She turned around and looked mad. "We are collecting this money for you and your kind, Richard Gregory. If your Daddy can give fifteen dollars you have no business being on relief."

"I got it right now, I got it right now, my Daddy gave it to me to turn in today, my Daddy said . . ."

"And furthermore," she said, looking right at me, her nostrils getting big and her lips getting thin and her eyes opening wide. "We know you don't have a Daddy."

Helene Tucker turned around, her eyes full of tears. She felt sorry for me. Then I couldn't see her too well because I was crying, too.

"Sit down, Richard."

And I always thought the teacher kind of liked me. She always picked me to wash the blackboard on Friday, after school. That was a big thrill, it made me feel important. If I didn't wash it, come Monday the school might not function right.

"Where are you going, Richard?"

I walked out of school that day, and for a long time I didn't go back very often. There was shame there.

Now there was shame everywhere. It seemed like the whole world had been inside that classroom, everyone had heard what the teacher had said, everyone had turned around and felt sorry for me. There was shame in going to the Worthy Boys Annual Christmas Dinner for you and your kind, because everybody knew what a worthy boy was. Why couldn't they just call it the Boys Annual Dinner, why'd they have to give it a name? There was shame in wearing the brown and orange and white plaid mackinaw the welfare gave to 3,000 boys. Why'd it have to be the same for everybody so when you walked down the street the people could see you were on relief? It was a nice warm mackinaw and it had a hood, and my Momma beat me and called me a little rat when she found out I stuffed it in the bottom of a pail full of garbage way over on Cottage Street. There was shame in running over to Mister Ben's at the end of the day and asking for his rotten peaches, there was shame in asking Mrs. Simmons for a spoonful of sugar, there was shame in running out to meet the relief truck. I hated that truck, full of food for you and your kind. I ran into the house and hid when it came. And then I started to sneak through alleys, to take the long way home so the people going into White's Eat Shop wouldn't see me. Yeah, the whole world heard the teacher that day, we all know you don't have a Daddy.

It lasted for a while, this kind of numbness. I spent a lot of time feeling sorry for myself. And then one day I met this wino in a restaurant. I'd been out hustling all day, shining shoes, selling newspapers, and I had googobs of money in my pocket. Bought me a bowl of chili for fifteen cents, and a cheeseburger for fifteen cents, and a Pepsi for five cents, and a piece of chocolate cake for ten cents. That was a good meal. I was eating when this old wino came in. I love winos because they never hurt anyone but themselves.

The old wino sat down at the counter and ordered twenty-six cents worth of food. He ate it like he really enjoyed it. When the owner, Mister Williams, asked him to pay the check, the old wino didn't lie or go through his pocket like he suddenly found a hole.

He just said: "Don't have no money."

The owner yelled: "Why in hell you come in here and eat my food if you don't have no money? That food cost me money."

Mister Williams jumped over the counter and knocked the wino off his stool and beat him over the head with a pop bottle. Then he stepped back and watched the wino bleed. Then he kicked him. And he kicked him again.

I looked at the wino with blood all over his face and I went over. "Leave him alone, Mister Williams. I'll pay the twenty-six cents."

The wino got up, slowly, pulling himself up to the stool, then up to the counter, holding on for a minute until his legs stopped shaking so bad. He looked at me with pure hate. "Keep your twenty-six cents. You don't have to pay now, not now. I just finished paying for it."

He started to walk out, and as he passed me, he reached down and touched my shoulder. "Thanks, sonny, but it's too late now. Why didn't you pay it before?"

I was pretty sick about that. I waited too long to help another man.

—Dick Gregory

I HAVE AN AUDIENCE

In the midst of the turbulent 1960s, a decade in American history torn by violent racial struggles, Martin Luther King emerged to lead one of America's most significant civil rights movements—the struggle for the rights of Negroes. Even though his assassination prevented him from achieving his ultimate goal, the complete acceptance of Negroes as equals in America, King successfully managed to change the traditionally bigoted social view of the position of

Negroes in a society run by Caucasians. Although he might equally be remembered for his tactics of non-violent civil disobedience, King's most influential tool for implementing these changes was his speaking ability. His "I Have a Dream" speech, the embodiment of King's ideas on racial equality, was most effective in its rhetoric. Using many tactics of persuasion, including propaganda techniques and poetic devices, King attempted to achieve his goal: Caucasian awareness of racial discrimination.

The content of King's speech stemmed from his classifications of American people. First of all, there were the egalitarians, most of whom were either his followers or members of America's liberal-minded intelligentsia. Obviously he had no need to persuade those who had already committed themselves to the cause. On the other end of the spectrum were the traditionalists. These predominantly Caucasian, race-conscious militants were intractable in their thinking about racial equality. King knew a not so small miracle would have been needed to break their close-mindedness concerning this social reform. Therefore, the third group, the undecided, was the target of King's speech. This faction, also predominantly Caucasian, was still unsure of the position of Negroes in America, but was equally unsure of the traditionalists' standpoint on this issue. Knowing that this group could be swayed either way in their thinking, King, in desperate need of non-Negro support, directed the tactics of persuasion in this speech at the undecided.

First of all, King's mention of Abraham Lincoln in the opening of his speech is an "appeal to a *white* authority," aimed at the Caucasian listeners. Such phrases as "five score" and "all men are created equal" caused the people gathered to think of one of America's most respected presidents. King could have expressed the same ideas with quotes by Booker T. Washington or Frederick Douglass but knew that these names, although famous, could not produce the same effect as the name Lincoln. King realized that the Caucasian listeners would have less difficulty understanding the Negro struggle if they could follow a respected Caucasian's belief in the same cause. Lincoln was this unique person who both historically supported the Negroes' viewpoints, and still stood out as worthy of respect in the minds of the Caucasian population. Conversely, if King were speaking exclusively to a Negro audience, he would have been more inclined to use a B. T. Washington quote while still employing the "appeal to authority" technique.

King appeals to authority again with his allusion to the United States Constitution. The architects of the Constitution, all of whom were white Anglo-Saxon Protestants (WASPS), are men still held in the highest esteem by a majority of Americans. These men explicitly stated that *all* men, which implicitly includes Negro-Americans, are guaranteed the unalienable rights of life, liberty, and the pursuit of happiness. This phrase is unquestionably the foundation of the American Constitution. Americans historically have believed that the foundation of the Constitution should not be altered. In 1978, when Governor Jerry Brown addressed both houses of Congress and stated that the contemporary problems in America called for a restructuring of the Constitution, he was virtually dragged away from the podium. By grounding the Negro cause in this staunch belief in the righteousness of America's founding document, King was viewed by the Caucasian listeners as a man, an American, who was simply following the principles of the Constitution as so many of their forefathers had done in the past. The use of the Constitution as a respected symbol of America persuades Caucasian listeners to believe that the constitutional rights of *Americans,* and not Negroes, are being infringed upon.

King's metaphorical comparison of the Negro social reform movement and a bounced check is also an attempt to present Negro insurgency in terms Caucasian-Americans could understand. Even until the 1960s, the use of checks as a substitute for currency was a typically Caucasian practice. In general, Negroes at this time were still on the "high-risk" listings. Thus, they were denied the opportunity to use such a payment system. If King were directing his speech at an all-Negro audience, the impact of this metaphor would be insignificant. But considering the fact that King was trying to make the biggest impact on the Caucasians, this metaphor was very effective. Caucasians themselves knew how upset they become when given a check only to later discover that the check is a worthless piece of paper because of "insufficient funds." Conversely, if King metaphorically compared a Negro-American to a calf at a rodeo that attempts to run away from its captors, but is eventually caught and tied up helplessly, the image produced by this comparison would not be clearly visualized by his Caucasian audience. Especially during the 1960s, Negroes knew what it was like to be rounded up like cattle; but Caucasians never experienced such wide-scale persecution. Thus, a comparison only understood by Negroes would be very difficult for the undecided Caucasians to comprehend.

Persuasive speakers, like persuasive writers, take their audiences into account when organizing a speech. Concerned with the effect of the speech on his audience, Martin Luther King scrutinized his listeners, and, consequently, chose propaganda techniques and metaphorical comparisons that truly reflected the viewpoints of his undecided audience. Persuading these listeners to think of the Negro struggle as an *American* struggle, Martin Luther King intelligently used all his power as a speaker to shift popular American skepticism about the Negro cause to his side of the podium. "I Have a Dream" would not have taken on any definite shape if King had not first said to himself, "I have an audience!"

—Student Essay

FAREWELL

The Polo Grounds went under last week, and I had no wish to journey up and watch the first fierce blows of ball and hammer. The newspaper and television obituaries were properly melancholy but almost entirely journalistic, being devoted to the celebrated names and happenings attached to the old ballfield: John McGraw, Christy Mathewson, Mel Ott; Carl Hubbell's five strikeouts, Bobby Thomson's homer, Willie Mays' catch, Casey Stengel's sad torment. Curiously, these historic recollections played little part in my own feeling of sadness and loss, for they had to do with events, and events on a sporting field are so brief that they belong almost instantly to the past. Today's fielding gem, last week's shutout, last season's winning streak have their true existence in record books and in memory, and even the youngest and brightest rookie of the new season is hurrying at almost inconceivable speed toward his plaque at Cooperstown and his faded, dated photograph behind a hundred bars. Mel Ott's cow-tailed swing, Sal Maglie's scowl, Leo Durocher's pacings in the third-base coach's box are portraits that have long been fixed in my own interior permanent collection, and the fall of the Polo Grounds will barely joggle them. What does depress me about the decease of the bony, misshapen old playground is the attendant irrevocable deprivation of habit—the amputation of so many private, repeated, and easily renewable small familiarities. The things I liked best about the Polo Grounds were sights and emotions so inconsequential that they will surely slide out of my recollection. A flight of pigeons flashing out of the barn-shadow of the upper stands, wheeling past the right-field foul pole, and disappearing above the inert, heat-heavy flags on the roof. The steepness of the ramp descending from the Speedway toward the upper-stand gates, which pushed your toes into your shoe tips as you approached the park, tasting sweet anticipation and getting out your change to buy a program. The unmistakable, final *"Plock!"* of a line drive hitting the green wooden barrier above the stands in deep left field. The gentle, rockerlike swing of the loop of rusty chain you rested your arm upon in a box seat, and the heat of the sun-warmed iron coming through your shirtsleeve under your elbow. At a night game, the moon rising out of the scoreboard like a spongy, day-old orange balloon and then whitening over the waves of noise and the slow, shifting clouds of floodlit cigarette smoke. All these I mourn, for their loss constitutes the death of still another neighborhood—a small landscape of distinctive and reassuring familiarity. Demolition and alteration are a painful city commonplace, but as our surroundings become more undistinguished and indistinguishable, we sense, at last, that we may not possess the scorecards and record books to help us remember who we are and what we have seen and loved.

—Roger Angell

5

Planning Your Essays

There is no formula for success in writing an essay, and even professional writers don't agree on the best way to approach their craft. Some plunge straight into a first draft, writing before they know for sure what they want to say. Others don't like to write until they've mapped out a complete outline right down to the *a*'s and *b*'s under the *1*'s and *2*'s. Some writers prefer to gather material only after they've decided on an overall plan; others begin doing research right away and use their findings to help them decide what to say. Some write in bits and pieces, splicing them together into a finished draft; others get uncomfortable unless they write straight through from beginning to end, finishing and editing each paragraph before moving on to the next. And these are only the extremes: most writers probably use a combination of methods. They may, for instance, begin with a general plan, write awhile, go back to refine their notes, write some more, and then outline what they've written to make sure it all fits together.

So although we can make recommendations, your approach to an assignment will depend on your temperament, how easily you write, and what's worked best for you in the past. But there *are* certain steps nearly all writers go through at some stage in planning a writing project, even if they don't all perform them in the same order or spend the same proportion of their time on them. These steps include

- Finding a topic (if you haven't been given one)
- Deciding on a thesis
- Collecting evidence
- Organizing

In this chapter, we'll talk about each step, in an order that seems logical to us. If you haven't yet evolved your own style for tackling an assignment, or if you want to try our way to see if there is anything in it for you, you can work through the steps in the order we give them. But even if you'd rather take these steps in a different order, you will be able to apply them to your own way of working.

FINDING A TOPIC

Suppose your English instructor assigns an essay but leaves the topic entirely up to you. While some students welcome the chance to write on their own subjects, many find this freedom more inhibiting than being asked to write on an assigned topic. Either they can't think of anything worth writing about, or they can think of so many possibilities that the choice is overwhelming. In this section you'll find some ideas to help you out when you need an essay topic but the perfect choice doesn't spring to mind.

First consider whether the assignment offers any general guidelines, and, if so, make sure you understand what they are. Very seldom will you be told simply to write "anything you want"; even with an open topic, your instructor probably has certain expectations. Think of the four modes of the essay we mentioned earlier: are you being asked to describe something? tell a story? provide information about something? take a stand of some kind?

"Write about what you know," teachers have been encouraging writers for generations, and it's usually good advice. If you base your essay on something you're familiar with, you're likely to be able to develop your ideas more fully and concretely. Think back over your experiences during the past month or so. Do they suggest anything you might write about? Have you seen anything unusual, read anything that especially moved or interested you, met anyone who made you think about something in a new way? Even a boring chemistry lecture might get you thinking about some of the techniques that can make the difference between good and bad instruction.

As we noted in the last chapter, most essays must do more than just describe your experience; you long ago moved beyond the kind of "essay" that told only "What I Did on My Summer Vacation." That doesn't mean, though, that you can't still use your own experiences to develop an *idea* of some kind. For instance, if you spent last summer working on a conservation project at a state park, you may have come to some conclusions about how Americans regard (or disregard) the environment. If you had a job typing correspondence for a law firm, you might be able to inform your readers of some of the ways television courtroom dramas distort the prosaic reality of a typical day at a law office.

Think of what has especially delighted or disgusted or angered you recently, and why. A woman who wrote an essay in *Newsweek* began by describing the sudden wave of pleasure she felt at hearing the sound of a hand-pushed lawn mower in a neighbor's yard. Her essay went on to argue that our growing reliance on technology (power lawn mowers, for instance) has robbed us of much of the connection we used to feel with our work and our world.

Listen to the people around you, to what they are saying to each other. A conversation overheard in a supermarket line or at a bus stop might give you an idea. Turn on the TV and flip a few channels, or thumb through a newspaper or magazine. One of our students recently wrote an excellent essay pointing out that advertisers do us a disservice by bombarding us with images and expectations life cannot possibly measure up to; she got the idea while reading through the latest issue of *Cosmopolitan.* If you encounter an opinion you disagree with strongly, you may well have a topic right there, whether the opinion is expressed in an editorial about energy problems, a columnist's suggestions for getting rid of the vice squad, or even Dear Abby's advice to a 17-year-old girl considering moving in with her boyfriend. There are even possible topics on the weather page. For example, since suffering a frightening two-year drought during the middle 1970s, many of us in the San Francisco Bay Area have become sensitive to the way people fatuously refer to rainy weather as "bad." That in itself might not make an essay, but it could lead you to realize that many "inconveniences," like rainy weather, are in fact necessities that we should appreciate; that realization could be the basis for a good essay.

If you're still stuck for an idea, try looking around you. Your room is full of things to write about: houseplants, clothes, music, textbooks, furniture, photographs, television. . . . Look out the window. Take a walk, especially somewhere you're not used to going. Ask your family and friends what's happening in their lives. Had any good arguments lately? What were they about? What were the deeper issues involved?

In trying to help students at a loss for something to write about, one of us developed the following method, almost guaranteed to suggest possibilities. Take any general category—say "transportation."

Then figure out some way to subdivide it. For instance, transportation can be divided into transportation by air, by land, and by water.

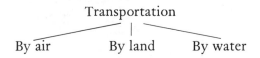

Take a look at your breakdown. Does it suggest anything you might write about? If not, divide your new categories further. Air transportation, for instance, could be divided into airplanes, helicopters, and hang-gliders. After you've thought up specific forms of transportation for each of the other categories, your chart might look like this:

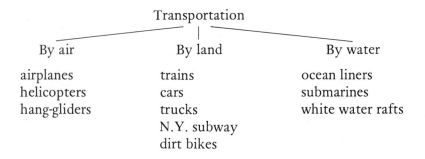

By air	By land	By water
airplanes	trains	ocean liners
helicopters	cars	submarines
hang-gliders	trucks	white water rafts
	N.Y. subway	
	dirt bikes	

Take a look at what you have now. Does it give you any ideas? For instance, free-associating to the chart above, you might be reminded of an enjoyable train trip you took two years ago and write an essay detailing the advantages of travel by train. Or you might notice that most of the items you've come up with are designed to move people and goods from one place to another, but a few—hang-gliders, dirt bikes, and white-water rafts—are not. So you could write an essay showing that we use some modes of transportation not as a means to "get anywhere" but for less practical, more personal, reasons. On the other hand, your new breakdown of categories might suggest nothing at all. In that case, you can either subdivide your categories again or scrap "transportation" and begin with a new general category, like "sports" or "professions" or "nations."

EXERCISE 1

Thinking back over where you've been, the conversations you've had, and some of the things you've seen, heard, or read during the past few weeks, write three essay topics.

EXERCISE 2

Look through a magazine or newspaper and write two essay topics based on your reactions to things you find there.

EXERCISE 3

Take a general category of your own and break it down, as we did with transportation. Use the results to come up with an essay topic.

FROM TOPIC TO THESIS: DECIDING WHERE YOU'RE GOING

Students will sometimes tell us that they're having trouble getting started on an essay. They've thought about the topic, but when they try to get their ideas down, they either go blank or find the essay heading off in several different directions.

For instance, a student may decide to write on "the importance of privacy," a promising subject but not, as you know from the last chapter, a thesis. Asked what he wants to say *about* the importance of privacy, the student may refer to notes in which he's written the following points: privacy is important and elusive, the government seems to know too much about us, computers threaten our privacy, some people don't like to spend time alone because they don't realize the potential benefits of privacy, and different cultures place different values on privacy.

With such a diverse list, it's no wonder the student can't get started: he's trying to cover too much, to discuss a number of different ideas with no specific common denominator. Instead of trying to tackle all the areas he's thought of, he'd be better off narrowing his subject to one point, like the benefits of spending time alone.

Even then he won't know how to proceed until he's decided what he wants to say *about* these benefits. The essay could wander off in three or four different directions, unless the writer commits himself to a single unifying idea. He'll also have an easier time getting started if he writes out a provisional *thesis statement,* a sentence summing up what he intends to say about the topic. For instance, after giving considerable thought to the topic, the student might write, "Spending some time, even half an hour, alone each day can help you see yourself more clearly than you could if you spent all your time with other people." This unifying idea paves the way for an essay that can explain and illustrate the self-insight that solitude makes possible.

The plight of the student we've just considered is not unusual.

Too often writers make the mistake of assuming their planning is over once they've decided on a subject: travel, inflation, death. Like nearly all general subjects, these are far too broad for the scope of a short essay; they need to be pared down to manageable topics. "Travel" could become "Greyhound buses"; "Inflation" could be reduced to "The Economic and Psychological Effects of Inflation on Middle-Class Families" "Death" could be scaled down to "Children's Attitudes Toward Death." In turn, each of these topics needs to be molded into a thesis statement:

> Travel by Greyhound can expose you to an endless variety of people you would rather not meet.
>
> If it continues, runaway inflation will require us to redefine our idea of the middle-class American family.
>
> Children are sometimes better able to confront death than their elders are.

What Will a Thesis Statement Do for Me?

Even a trial thesis statement will help you in several respects. First, it's a way of making sure that you know where you're going, that you've thought through what you want to say. It puts limits on your topic, helping you see what you need to cover and what you should leave out. When readers come upon your thesis statement in an essay, it lets them know what to expect from the paper (and if the reader happens to be your English teacher, it provides a basis for judging how well you've achieved what you set out to do). Some thesis statements even give you a basic outline for your paper. For instance, it shouldn't be too much trouble to organize a paper whose thesis statement is, "Although the election of a President every four years presents certain problems, it also helps keep politics and government vigorous." You'd probably start by looking briefly at the problems and then proceed to a fuller discussion of the benefits.

How Do I Get a Thesis Statement?

On blessed rare occasions, you may already know what you want to say about a subject. You may have strong views on the subject, you may have read enough about it to be able to discuss it well, or you may have even had a recent flash that's given you a new way of looking at your topic. Usually, though, you'll have to take a few wrong turns before you arrive at a thesis. People who write fairly easily sometimes get to a thesis simply by writing until they've reached one ("How do I know what I think until I see what I've said?" asks one of E. M. Forster's characters). This method can lead you to ideas you wouldn't have come to otherwise, but it is time-consuming, and you may have to throw away a major part of what you've written, always a painful act. We've probably all had the experience at some time or another of getting to the end of a paper only to realize, too late, "*That's* what I should have written about."

A more efficient method of finding out what you want to say, if you're short on time or hate to throw out major portions of a first draft, is to brainstorm on paper. Begin by randomly jotting down different possible approaches to the topic and different ideas about it. Don't reject anything that comes to mind as too stupid or difficult; the whole point of brainstorming is to free your creative powers by turning off the critical part of your brain. Even if an idea is completely untenable, it may be a link in the chain that leads you to one that will work.

Talking to someone about the topic is another good method, especially if you keep a note pad handy to write down your best ideas before they evaporate. If you find yourself staring vacantly into space and thinking about everything besides the assignment you're supposed to be working on, try setting a timer for 15 minutes and writing continuously for that time about your subject, not worrying about spelling, punctuation, or style, or even about whether you could logically defend what you're saying. Often a possible thesis for an essay will emerge. The most important thing is to get going. And once you know what you want to say about a topic, much of your anxiety about an assignment will probably disappear.

When you have a thesis statement down on paper, don't make the mistake of feeling you've committed yourself to it for life, or even for the time it takes you to write your paper. You won't know for sure if you have a good thesis until you've worked with it for a while. Often you'll have to go back and change your thesis to reflect the shape the essay takes as you write it, but one of the pleasures of writing is that you can change your mind so often. Look upon your thesis statement as a hypothesis: if the essay you write turns out different from what you'd expected, you will need to change your thesis just as you would change your hypothesis in a scientific experiment if your data failed to substantiate it.

How Do I Know If My Thesis Is Any Good?

If you think back over what you've already learned about topic sentences, you'll be a long way toward understanding what makes a good thesis. The thesis statement is to the essay what the topic sentence is to the paragraph. If you're mathematically inclined, think of the last sentence as a formula:

$$\frac{\text{Topic sentence}}{\text{Paragraph}} \quad : \quad \frac{\text{Thesis statement}}{\text{Essay}}$$

THESIS STATEMENT CHECKLIST

Like the good topic sentence, a successful thesis

- gives you something to prove, back up, develop
- sums up what you're going to say
- is neither too broad nor too narrow for the scope of the assignment
- does more than state a well-known fact—usually makes an arguable assertion of some kind
- establishes a contract between you and your readers. They can expect that you'll support this thesis convincingly and interestingly, and that you will not be bothering them with extraneous information

Bearing these criteria in mind, decide what is wrong with each of the following as potential thesis statements:

1. Richard M. Nixon was the first President of the United States to resign from that office.
2. An examination of the benefits of penicillin.
3. In this essay, I am going to talk about the problems faced by ex-prisoners in returning to society.
4. Have you ever wondered why most people read so much more slowly than they need to?
5. Unemployment is a serious problem in today's world.

1. Simply a statement of fact; that Nixon was the first President to resign is a matter of historical record. The writer has nothing to prove or support.
2. Not even a sentence; it's only a title. The writer has apparently not decided what to say about the benefits of penicillin.
3. Not a thesis; it's a sentence, all right, but like (2), it does nothing more than state the topic. What is the writer going to say *about* these problems? The topic is also too broad for most short essays; the writer would probably do better to confine the discussion to a particular problem ex-prisoners face.
4. A question, and probably a good way of getting an essay on speed-reading off the ground. But since it doesn't *state* anything, it can't be a thesis.
5. Expresses a point almost no one would disagree with; it doesn't state an assertion that needs to be argued. An effective thesis on the problems of unemployment would have to state something beyond the obvious: why tell people what they already know?

The sentence is also too broad and marred by the vagueness of the phrase "in today's world." (That catch-all phrase, along with the equally fuzzy "in today's society," should probably be stricken from your vocabulary.)

Do I Have to Include a Thesis Statement?

Professional writers in particular often omit an explicit thesis statement, instead making their unifying idea clear through a careful arrangement of their points and examples. But until you get the hang of writing essays, you will probably do best to include a thesis statement, so that you *and* your readers know exactly what you're trying to show in a particular writing assignment. (Martha Graham has said about dance that "You learn a discipline in order to forget it"; the same holds true for writing. Once you've mastered the basics, you can begin experimenting with variations.)

Even if you decide not to include a thesis statement, make sure you still have an underlying *thesis* that you could state in one or two sentences. Then read your paper critically to make sure this thesis will come across unmistakably to the reader; you will have to organize your essay with particular care if it doesn't have a thesis statement.

The Dead-End Thesis

Deciding on your thesis is nothing to rush through. A thesis nonchalantly jotted down may seem fine at first and only later prove illogical, too broad to develop, or too obvious to bother writing about. This would be a good time to review our earlier discussion of the over-general or illogical topic sentence (p. 26) since, as we've said, a thesis statement is really a topic sentence for a whole essay.

In particular, beware of writing a thesis stating something that your reader (and everyone else) already knows. In their efforts to be reasonable and play it safe, we've seen students come up with thesis statements like "Studying is one of the most important aids to learning." Would anyone think studying was *not* an important aid to learning? There's nothing wrong with writing on the topic of studying if you have some little-known tip to give or a philosophy about what makes for successful studying; you might even write an essay arguing (either humorously or seriously) that studying is often *not* an effective aid to learning. But don't waste your readers' time as well as your own by pointing out something no one would disagree with.

Some other "theses" that will earn you nothing but an instructor's resounding yawn:

Movie stars often have little privacy.

Nuns live lives of great dedication and self-sacrifice.

The best parents are those who care about their children's happiness and welfare.

Owning a car is convenient but potentially expensive.

Try to pick a slant on your topic that is often overlooked—perhaps that nuns are often highly skilled in some surprising areas, or that parents' good intentions will not guarantee a child's happiness unless the parents also provide certain specific stimuli, both physical and psychological. Get your readers involved in your ideas, instead of making them turn to the end of the paper to see how much more there is to get through.

Beware too of the kind of thesis that will lead to nothing but a "laundry list." For instance, one of us recently got a competently written paper whose whole point was that "There are many different sports, something for every taste." The paper predictably and drearily went on to devote a paragraph to each of the major sports—football, basketball, baseball, tennis, soccer, and golf—pointing out the attractions of each. The student was probably propping one eye open by the time she got to the end, and the instructor *certainly* was.

Forming a Thesis on a Reading Assignment

Many students find it particularly difficult to write papers about something they've read, a type of essay assigned in many college classes besides English. Asked something specific ("Do you agree with Freud's basic view of the unconscious in *Civilization and Its Discontents*?" or "Does the play *Death of a Salesman* still have something important to say to Americans thirty years after it was originally produced?"), most students can produce a decent essay. But if a class is asked merely to respond to something they've read, over half the essays turned in will probably be poorly organized, underdeveloped, and unfocused. Many students turn in high-schoolish book reports or random reactions to several of the author's points. Once again, the secret of doing better lies in limiting your material and coming up with an interesting and workable approach—in other words, a good thesis.

First, remember that you don't have to tell everything that's in the book you're discussing. If the whole class has read it, you can assume the instructor knows it as well as or better than you do. If you're bringing in material from the outside, you may have to spend a paragraph or two summarizing the work, but that should serve only as a lead-in to your essay. Secondly, limit your essay to a particular central aspect of what you've read. You might even try making up your own essay question and answering it. For instance, asked to write a paper on *Pride and Prejudice,* you might decide to confine yourself to a discussion of a minor character, Miss Bingley. The question you set for yourself could be "What does Miss Bingley, a fairly unimportant character, contribute to the novel as a whole?" Your answer—that is, your thesis—might be: "By acting as a foil for some of the more important characters in *Pride and Prejudice,* Miss Bingley helps Austen show that surface appearances and social background are of far less importance than character and intelligence."

What if I Have No Opinion?

Students often complain that they haven't done well on an essay because they "couldn't relate to the topic." Certainly when a writing assignment is open, you'll usually do best to choose a topic you care about; you're likely to enjoy writing the paper more and have an easier time coming up with convincing support for your thesis. But don't assume that you can't write a good paper on an assigned topic you have no particular opinion about.

If you find yourself in such a predicament, think for a moment. Maybe you don't have an opinion on the topic because you've never been asked to consider it before. If you still find yourself immobilized, try manufacturing an opinion and see how you can best support it. You might even try taking two or more sheets of paper, writing a different opinion at the top of each one, and then listing possible supporting evidence below. You can then choose the view you find you can back up most specifically, logically, and interestingly.

It may seem insincere to advocate a position you don't really believe in, but it can be an excellent intellectual exercise, if only to help you discover what you *do* think, and to help you appreciate other people's points of view. When you put your name on a paper, you're certifying only that it's your own work, not that you'll endorse the view presented for the rest of your life.

A Final Caution

It's also possible for a thesis statement to be *too* specific. For instance, a student who knew quite a bit about film once decided to write about how actors and actresses are often chosen to receive Academy Awards for the wrong reasons. Trying to be as explicit as possible, he wrote this thesis: "Actors appear often to have received Oscars on the basis of sympathy, politics, lucky timing, popularity, or old age rather than acting merit." The problem was that he gave the whole show away. All he could do then was to go on to illustrate each of the reasons in his thesis statement, and his readers knew exactly what to expect. The writer would have done better to leave his thesis statement a bit more interestingly general: "Actors appear often to have won Oscars for reasons unrelated to their acting ability.'' The direction of the paper would still be clear, but there would be more of an incentive to read on.

Summary

You may have an easier time remembering what a thesis is supposed to be if you think about the derivation of the word. Like *theory* and *theme,* it comes from the Greek word for ''believe.'' Your thesis, then, states what you believe about your topic, or at least the position you're taking on it. Unless you know what you believe (or are claiming to believe) and unless you can write it down in one or two sentences, you're probably not ready to get very far into the writing of your essay. But once you've got a workable, carefully thought-out thesis, you'll find the next steps—organizing and writing your paper— much easier.

EXERCISE 4

Take four of the following subjects and boil each down to two topics that might work for a 500-word essay. Then write two workable thesis statements for each topic.

Example: MUSIC

Topics: Broadway musicals
       Folk-rock

Thesis statements:
During the last decade, Broadway musicals have become much more realistic.

For many reasons, *Oklahoma!* represents a turning point in the history of Broadway musicals.

Folk-rock, a listless hybrid of rock and roll and traditional folk music, was popular in the 1960s and 1970s not because it was innovative and powerful, as is sometimes claimed, but because it was safe and unthreatening.

Some of the most talented singers/songwriters of the folk-rock boom have made a successful stylistic transition to the more general field of mainstream popular music.

1. Politics
2. Recreation
3. Illness
4. The 1950s
5. Agriculture

6. Photography
7. The Middle East
8. Cooking
9. The English Language
10. Business

COLLECTING EVIDENCE

If you're like most writers, you may feel so relieved at having decided on a thesis that you immediately whip out a piece of paper and begin to scrawl out your rough draft with only the most general idea of how you'll *develop* your main point. As we've said before, that's fine if you like writing your way into your ideas and are willing to spend lots of time revising. But most students simply don't have time for that. You can still add examples or make changes as they occur to you during the writing, but you'll almost certainly write with more confidence and a better sense of direction if you map out a provisional organization in advance.

Before you can organize your material, you need to find it. A good way to start is to take a piece of paper and list everything you can think of that might help you make your point. Spend some time doing this. It's good to train yourself as a writer to think harder and reach beyond the obvious choices to the ones more difficult to find but more convincing and compelling. "Not the first," F. Scott Fitzgerald used to tell his friend Sheilah Graham when she asked him to give her writing lessons; by that, he meant that the first ideas that come to us are often not the best. If you take the trouble to think up eight possible ways to support an idea, you can then choose the best four or five, and your paper will be stronger than if you had simply grabbed the first ideas you thought of. (You might be interested to know that writers who produce advertising copy typically spend four times as long researching and planning their copy as they spend writing it.)

Nor should you feel you have to stop with the ideas drawn from your own thinking and experience. If you have the time, you may want to go to the library and do some extra reading on the subject; libraries aren't just for term papers. If you can't find what you're looking for, ask a reference librarian to help you. Try talking to your friends or your family about the topic, too. Not only will they sometimes be able to give you good suggestions, but the very act of discussing your subject with someone may give you an idea you wouldn't have thought of otherwise.

You should anticipate two questions from your reader throughout the writing process: "Can you give me an example?" and "So what?" If you remember the first, you'll think in terms of offering concrete evidence that will help convince your reader. And if you're able to answer the second question, you'll be sure your examples really *are* to the point.

If your support still feels less substantial than you think it should be, go back and review the methods of paragraph development discussed in Chapter 3. For easy reference, here they are again:

- descriptive details
- multiple examples
- extended example
- anecdote
- hypothetical example
- reference to authority
- facts and figures
- analogy
- definition

If after a reasonable effort, you find you're having trouble coming up with supporting ideas, it may be time to consider changing your thesis. It may simply be that your thesis is unprovable, or that getting the evidence necessary to prove it may take more time and effort than you're willing to expend. Or sometimes, in listing your evidence, you'll discover you actually have more support for a thesis different from the one you started with.

If you're still pretty sure you want to stick with your original thesis, here are some leading questions to help you generate more material:

- Why do I believe X?
- If someone told me I was crazy to think X, how would I try to defend myself?
- When did I first start believing X? What were some of the things that formed or changed my opinion?

As you jot down your answers to these questions, you'll probably wind up with some material you can use in your paper.

You can also make up specific questions related to your particular topic. For instance, if you were writing on "The Benefits of Spending Time Alone," you could ask yourself some questions like these:

What happens to me when I don't spend enough time alone?

What are some good experiences I've had lately while I've been alone?

How does spending some time alone help me to understand others?

What have I learned through spending time alone? What issues have become clarified? What important decisions have I made?

You might find it helpful to write each question at the top of a separate note card or slip of paper, listing the answers that occur to you beneath. Once you have several such slips, begin reading through them, adding new ideas as they occur to you. Shuffling the slips and reading through them in a different order may help you see new relationships among your ideas. You should find these notes useful when you go on to organize your material (the advantage of having them on separate slips is that you can experiment with different orders until you find the one you like). Another benefit of all this preliminary effort is that you may find that parts of what you've written are good enough to use in your first draft. Without even realizing it, you may have some of your writing out of the way.

EXERCISE 5

Pick five of the following thesis statements and list at least four pieces of supporting evidence for each. For each statement you choose, try to go beyond the obvious forms of support.

Example:

Thesis statement: In many ways, it is more difficult to be an adolescent today than it was ten or twenty years ago.

Evidence:
   a. The economy is in such precarious condition that many adolescents feel justifiably concerned about their futures.
   b. Many 18-year-olds can no longer afford to go to college and live away from home.
   c. Standards of sexual behavior are far less firm than they used to be, so today's teenagers frequently feel pressured to enter sexual relationships before they are ready for them.
   d. Since Watergate, it is harder to believe in the institutions of government; adolescents today cannot share the idealism of earlier generations.

1. The producers of many movies today seem much more interested in making a quick buck than in giving audiences anything to think about or even in supplying them with quality entertainment.
2. Americans are healthier today than ever before.
3. The daily life of a student is filled with conflicts.
4. Gardening can be an effective and relatively inexpensive form of therapy.
5. Baseball is probably the world's most boring sport.
6. Nuclear power plants are dangerous and should be prohibited.
7. Americans as a whole today have too little regard for the importance of family life.
8. Inflation, the energy shortage, and international tensions to the contrary, perhaps optimism about the future is justified.

ORGANIZATION

We would all like to think that there is one right way to arrange a paper, because once we discovered and mastered it, we'd be in permanent control of a difficult part of the writing process. The truth, at once liberating and troubling, is that there are almost as many ways to organize a topic or paper as there are people to do the organizing.

"To organize" means to arrange into a *structured* and *functional* whole. Most of the writing we do, inside or outside school, needs to be organized in some way. We arrange a piece of writing—a shopping list, a letter home, a diary entry, class notes, a recipe—in a form (or structure) that reflects its purpose (or function). We may group the items in the shopping list so that related commodities are together, all the meat first, then all the produce, and so on, or so that the essentials are first, followed by the items we can do without if we run out of money. A letter home might begin with pleasantries and move on to the difficulties of school, culminating in the most important point: our need for money. Class notes will probably be organized to make the main points most prominent, with relevant details beneath them. In each case, the way we arrange the writing is determined by what we want that particular piece to do: to aid us in our shopping, to elicit money from our parents, or to jar our memories as we study.

In writing an essay, you should also create a structure that reflects that essay's particular function. Every time you write, you need to make a conscious, reasoned decision about how to arrange your paper. Although there is no substitute for the sometimes difficult process of thinking clearly about how to organize a paper, in the pages that follow we suggest some general methods of organization that you may find useful for certain purposes.

Why Organize?

In an informal experiment, an instructor took fifteen playing cards from a standard deck and listed them on the blackboard in the same order in which he drew them. He asked the class to memorize the list in the order presented and gave them four minutes to do so. The average student could recall only 6.91. The student who remembered the most could get only ten.

The instructor then shuffled the deck and drew another fifteen cards, but this time he listed them on the board by suit (putting all the spades in one column, all the hearts in another, and so on). The students were given the same amount of time to memorize the list. This time, their average recall shot up to 14.2, with the student who recalled the fewest cards remembering 12 and most remembering all 15.

This experiment tells us something about the way the human mind works. We have an easier time dealing with details, whether they're playing cards or examples of an idea, when they are grouped in some meaningful way. If you want your readers to see the relationships among your ideas, you need to group them so that they don't come across as a random list, like the fifteen cards jotted down on the blackboard at the beginning of the experiment.

There's another important reason for organizing. Educational research has repeatedly shown that the only way people can learn anything new is by relating it to what they've already been told. If you're showing your younger brother how to do an algebra problem, you won't succeed in teaching him anything unless you start with what he already knows and then build from there, taking the problem one step at a time. The same holds true when you're trying to present a point in an essay. Your readers probably won't be able to stay with you unless you take the trouble to guide them through the paper in an organized fashion, each part of the essay building on what's gone before.

Grouping*—The Key to Organization

Our ability to think depends in large part on our ability to group related ideas together. If asked in a contest to list as many domesticated animals as possible, you probably wouldn't randomly spew out "goldfish," "donkey," "Irish setter," "hermit crab," "macaw," and "guinea pig." You'd find it more efficient and natural to list your animals in groups, perhaps mentioning all the farm animals you could think of first, then moving on to house pets, a category that you could in turn break down in a number of ways—dogs, cats, birds, etc. This system, of course, isn't rigid. Even though you'd gone on to the category of "rodents kept as house pets," you could still go back and add "goat" to your earlier farm list.

You can use this same process of grouping in a much more sophisticated way when you plan the structure of your essays. To begin, you write down the main points. You decide what certain points have in common and group them into a category, writing down a heading for it. Finally, you look closely at each category, to see that each has enough examples or specifics and that these examples are appropriate. Thus, this process often requires that you move back and forth, thinking, grouping, writing, regrouping, rethinking, and so on.

*The process we refer to as "grouping" is often called *division, classification,* or *analysis.*

After you have grouped the items on your list into appropriate categories, you're ready to move onto the next step: deciding on the *order* you'll present your categories in. The following "orders" are some of the most common ways writers have of organizing their material. Remember that the order you choose should reflect your purpose in writing.

The Natural Orders

ORDER OF SPACE

Function: To describe the appearance of something, someone, or some place.
Structure: Directional.

When you're describing something, you'll most often present your subject in some order based on direction, moving from top to bottom, left to right, clockwise, etc., following the path the readers' eyes might take if they could see what you're describing.

You might decide to break away from the expected order and present pieces out of sequence for special emphasis or effect. For instance, in a student essay on a swim club, the description moved carefully from the people crowded around the vending machines, to the listless, greased sunbathers lying on the deck, to the children chasing each other through the maze of active and passive bodies. Only at the end of the paper did the writer move to the middle of his scene, the swimming pool itself, the ostensible main attraction and the one spot that was virtually empty.

EXERCISE 6: Space

A. Using the advice in this section as a guideline, rearrange the sequence of sentences in the following paragraph. While there is no one correct order, your revision should reflect the effort you would make in an essay to assist your reader. (Note: assume that the first, second, and last sentences should stay where they are.)

Whatever magic the Beatles may have possessed did not emanate from a flamboyant stage presence. Compared with the smoke bombs, lasers, levitation, fire-breathing, and generally melodramatic flailing about of today's bands, the Beatles were as staid as a string quartet. Next to Paul McCartney was George Harrison, who usually kept his head bent intently over his guitar as he studiously and precisely picked out the chords, fills, and melodic leads necessary to the Beatles' controlled and structured sound. To the far left of the stage stood Paul McCartney, the most gregarious and mobile of this generally inert lot. At the far right, legs bowed, eyes squinting into the lights, thin lips almost sneering, stood John Lennon. Above and behind his guitar-playing cohorts sat drummer Ringo Starr, bashing away good-naturedly, tilting his head speculatively, every so often breaking into a grin that transformed his dour, so-homely-that-he's-almost-cute face. Like McCartney, Lennon would occasionally move with the music, flexing his widely spaced knees; unlike McCartney, he rarely left his spot in front of the microphone. Besides flashing his cherubic smile, McCartney would bounce in time to the music, perhaps taking a controlled little hop or two backwards or casually dipping the neck of his violin-like Hofner bass. In spite of—or perhaps because of—the subtlety and poise of their stage presence, the Beatles were as riveting in person as they were on record.

ORDER OF TIME

Function: To relate a sequence of events.
Structure: Chronological.

If you are writing about an experience or event, something that happened "through time," you can relate the events in the order in which they occurred, starting at the beginning and moving to the end. The student essay "Riding the Bull" in Chapter 4 essentially follows this organization. Again, for special effect, you can break up what we think of as the "natural" sequence of events and start in the middle or the end and work back to the beginning. This "flashback" technique is common in literature and film.

EXERCISE 7: *Time*

A. Think of a sequence of events in your own life that ended in some significant way, perhaps surprisingly, disappointingly, happily, dramatically, instructively, or inspiringly. Make a chronological list of the steps in that sequence. This may not be as easy as it sounds, for you have to make several important decisions as you construct and revise your list: How far back in time should you begin? How many steps in the sequence do you need to list? Have you left out anything important, or included anything irrelevant? Would your list form the basis for an interesting, cohesive essay or paragraph?

B. Using the "flashback" technique mentioned in this section, consider how you might start a paper on this sequence of events by beginning with the "significant ending" and then working backwards. Would this be an effective organization for your paper?

The Logical Orders

ORDER OF IMPORTANCE

Function: To rank points in terms of significance.
Structure: Usually moving from least important to most important.

Once you have several subpoints to back up and explain your thesis, you need to decide on the order in which you'll present them. To make the biggest impression on your reader, you will usually save the most important and interesting point for last, probably devoting the most space to it as well. In some circumstances (say, if you thought the reader might not read your whole paper, or if you were writing in class and were afraid you might run out of time), you might do the reverse and begin with your most compelling point and then move on to secondary ones.

If you were writing an essay to explain why you've returned to school after an absence of several years, you could list your reasons more or less at random. But your paper would probably have more impact if you saved the most decisive reason for last, giving it the bulk of your attention and underscoring it with the most thorough development.

EXERCISE 8: Order of Importance

Take two of the following topics (or substitute one or two topics of your own) and list the points you might include if you were writing an essay on both. Then arrange your list in order of importance, beginning with minor points and building up to the most significant ones.

1. benefits you've found in attending college thus far

2. things you'd like to change at your college if you had the power

3. reasons you'd like _____ (fill in the politician of your choice) to be the next president of the United States

4. reasons you consider _____ the most enjoyable sport to watch

ORDER OF STEPS (ALSO CALLED "PROCESS ANALYSIS")

> *Function:*   To explain how something is done or how it happens.
> *Structure:*   Chronological, with the process clearly broken down into steps.

If you have ever explained how to change a tire or how to make an apple pie, you have done a process analysis. This task is sometimes given to students working on their writing skills because it gives them a chance to discover how to move methodically from one important step to the next, omitting nothing essential. Later you can move on and apply the same skills to taking apart an *idea* step by step.

If you were writing a paper about Hitler's rise to power, you could break the process down into several key steps: his formation of small but ardent groups of supporters bitter about Germany's defeat in World War I; the writing of *Mein Kampf,* Hitler's detailed blueprint for his takeover; the burning of the *Reichstag* as an excuse to suspend individual rights; his assumption of the title and power of *Führer.*

EXERCISE 9: Order of Steps

Pick a process that you're familiar with and write a fairly detailed outline for an essay describing that process. (You need not write the essay itself.) Be sure that you've covered the process in the most useful order; that you've defined any necessary technical terms; that you've included all necessary steps; that you've left out irrelevant and therefore distracting information. To avoid coming up with the obvious, please don't outline a recipe or a routine automotive procedure (like changing a tire).

ORDER OF CAUSE AND EFFECT (ALSO CALLED "CAUSAL ANALYSIS")

> *Function:*   To explain why something happens or to show what the results of something will be.
> *Structure:*   Depending on your purpose, first present the effects, and then discuss the causes *or* first present the causes, and then discuss the potential effects.

When you take an idea apart, you are often analyzing the cause-effect relationship between the parts. For example, if asked to analyze the public transportation system in your area, you might explore the problems now plaguing riders. You might decide, after some research and thought, that the system is inefficient (effect) because it was poorly designed and inadequately funded (causes). The two "causes" would, in turn, require further breaking down and explaining. You might also organize your paper in the other direction, first discussing the slipshod design of the system and the inadequate funding provided for it (causes), then proceeding to the effect the shortcomings produced.

EXERCISE 10: Cause/Effect

A. For each of the following, suggest a possible cause *and* a possible effect.

Possible cause		Possible effect
Example:		
a recession forces lay-offs in major industries	unemployment rises	rate of inflation slows
1.	you dislike reading	
2.	Congressional funding for the space program is cut off	
3.	surprisingly, college seems easier than high school in some ways	
4.	Americans are less interested in "health foods" than they were 10 years ago	
5.	a movie that you expected to be interesting turned out to be boring	
6.	on some days, everything seems to go wrong	
7.	people seem apathetic even about	

issues that affect
them directly

8.   some styles—like
                         button-down shirts—
                         seem to endure longer
                         than others—like the
                         collarless shirts popu-
                         lar in the late 1970s

B. Use one of these cause/effect sequences as the basis for a paragraph. You'll need to decide whether to begin with the effect and then trace the causes or to relate the causes first and then end with their effect. Be sure that your paragraph fits the criteria we've established elsewhere for good paragraph development: it should, for example, have a topic sentence, be well-developed, and be reasonably cohesive.

Categorizing

Function: To show how separate points relate to each other and to
              the topic itself.
Structure: Related elements are grouped under a common heading.

We said earlier that nearly all organization involves the process of grouping like elements under appropriate headings. (Sometimes the form your essay takes will be based entirely on the groups you come up with.) For example, suppose you were asked to discuss the advantages of attending a parochial school. You would probably begin by making a list of the benefits, in whatever order they occurred to you. Looking at the list, you might realize that you could *group* the benefits into three *categories:* academic, social, and religious. Once you set these categories up, you could go back to find additional examples to fill them in further.

To tackle a more ambitious project in grouping, suppose your teacher has asked you to write an essay based on an exercise in Chapter 2, p. 21. There, you were asked in a development exercise to come up with a list of "humiliating moments."

Since we don't have your list and need one for the purposes of illustration, we devised the following collection of humiliating moments.

1. Knocking your glass of red wine over and soaking the tablecloth in a fancy restaurant.

2. Getting so drenched in the rain that your friends can see through your clothes.
3. Coming into a dark house and suddenly hearing everyone yell, "Surprise! Happy Birthday!"
4. Leaving your take-home final on the bus and being unable to turn it in before the deadline.
5. Being stuck with a flat tire in the middle lane of the freeway during rush hour.
6. Giving the valedictorian's address at your high school graduation.
7. Having the wind blow your skirt up over your head while you and a date are taking a walk.

This list would probably be worth an "A" on the exercise, but it needs to be *structured* quite a bit more to become an essay. The first step would be to examine the items on your list and decide whether any of them are related. In other words, you need to group the items into categories. Given our list, you might decide that some of the items involve clumsiness, some relate to being embarrassed in front of the opposite sex, some involve forgetfulness, and some concern suddenly being the center of attention of a large group of people. The key word in each phrase could serve as a *category heading:*

Clumsiness: (1) Knocking over a glass of red wine and soaking the tablecloth.
Sexual embarrassment:
(2) Getting so drenched in the rain that your friends can see through your clothes.
(7) Having the wind blow your skirt up over your head.
Forgetfulness:
(4) Leaving your take-home final on the bus.
Unexpected attention in front of large group:
(3) Coming home to surprise party.
(5) Flat tire on freeway at rush hour.
(6) Giving valedictorian's address at graduation.

Once you've got your list organized this far, you can see that item 6 (giving the valedictorian's address at graduation) doesn't fit. While perhaps a humiliating experience, it doesn't belong here because the category deals with *unexpected* public attention, and a valedictorian knows in advance that he or she will face a large audience. Thus, item 6 must be omitted, and a new example substituted, if you feel it is necessary.

Going in the opposite direction, you might also notice that the category of Clumsiness has only one example to support it. You face a decision here. Should you rule out this category completely?

Should you keep it and include an additional example? Or should you develop the incident so fully that one example is enough to support your point?

One way to decide would be to turn to your thesis. If you have chosen to concentrate on humiliating moments involving your body, you obviously don't want to give up the category of Clumsiness. But if you are still in the preliminary stages of this essay and haven't settled on a thesis, looking at your categories might help you decide what your main point is. With one exception, Forgetfulness, the list does deal with situations in which people notice your body. You might therefore form a thesis something like the following:

> I feel relatively confident about my mental abilities and am usually able to hold my own or bluff my way through most intellectual situations. But I am apt to feel humiliated any time my actions or my mere physical presence draws attention to me.

With this thesis linking the categories and giving the whole essay a point, it is easy to see that the one irrelevant category of Forgetfulness has to go, and that at least one more example under Clumsiness is necessary.

Let's move on to a less personal topic. Suppose you read a magazine interview with Governor Jerry Brown of California, which you feel might form the basis for an essay. Reading through the interview, you cull the following main points and simply put them down in list order:

1. Abandon nuclear power.
2. Balance the budget.
3. Develop public transportation systems.
4. He jogs every day.
5. Limit the growth of personal income.
6. Restrain traditional government spending for social programs.
7. Clean up the environment.
8. Push affirmative action.
9. Develop alternative energy sources.
10. Cut taxes.
11. Move toward a new spirit of sacrifice and commitment.
12. Limit the U.S. mission in the world.
13. He doesn't eat junk food any more.
14. The President of the U.S. can't do everything by himself.
15. Invest in space.

Once again, you can't just take this random list and write up the essay. To structure a paper on this subject, you'd need to group the points. Looking back at the list, you might notice that most of what Brown talked about had to do with how America should deal with the problems facing her today. Certain key words stand out: those like "president," "taxes," "budget," and "government spending" having to do with *government;* and those like "energy," "public transportation," and "space" having to do with *technology and resources.* This fact can in turn lead you to develop two broad categories with the following headings: "New expectations about government" and "New expectations about technology and resources." Now you're ready to realign your random list, grouping items under the appropriate headings.

I. **New expectations about government**
   A. Balance budget
   B. Restrain government programs
   C. Push affirmative action
   D. Cut taxes
   E. Limit U.S. mission in world
   F. Don't expect President to accomplish everything by himself

II. **New expectations about technology and resources**
   A. Abandon nuclear power
   B. Develop public transportation systems
   C. Clean up the environment
   D. Develop alternative energy sources; don't depend on just one source
   E. Invest in space

Points left over:
   1. Brown jogs every day
   2. Limit the growth of personal income
   3. Move toward a new spirit of sacrifice and commitment
   4. Brown doesn't eat junk food any more

Clearly, the next task is to decide what to do with the points that don't seem to fit into the two large categories of "government" and "technology and resources." As in the previous example, you may decide that some or all the points are irrelevant. Since points 1 and 4 have to do only with Jerry Brown's personal habits, you might reasonably conclude that they don't belong in this essay, which is about national policy, not one man. The two remaining points, 2 and 3, do seem connected in some way, however. Here is where a sort of intellectual "leap" comes in: you might see that without a new spirit of sacrifice and commitment accompanied by a limit on the growth of personal income, the entire program wouldn't work. You might find that the seemingly unconnected points are actually the culminating idea of the paper.

It might also occur to you to do some rearranging within the two large categories, perhaps further grouping within the groups. Looking again at category II, for instance, you might decide that A and D are closely related and should be treated together. Likewise, B, C, and E could all be subgrouped under the heading "Investing in productive technologies of the future." You could turn to category I and also tighten its structure, making it easier for the reader, and for you, to see the connections between your points.

And what about a thesis reflecting this new, well-structured progression of thought? You know from reading the article that Jerry Brown is committed to a "policy of limits" which recognizes the restrictions on resources, national priorities, and personal ambition that we must learn to live with. After some work you might come up with a thesis like the following:

> America faces mounting environmental problems, a dwindling supply of resources, and an accelerating loss of economic and political power in the world. To deal with these restrictions effectively, Jerry Brown believes that we may need to adopt a national "policy of limits" that tempers our actions and expectations. This strategy will work, however, only if individuals are willing to make long-range personal commitments and sacrifices.

This thesis statement and the transitional sentences before and after it encompass the three groupings that you had derived from your first list.

As this extended example indicates, grouping is a useful concept because it can help you deal with almost any topic, whether personal or objective. It helps you gain insight into how ideas are connected, and it helps you present those new connections clearly.

EXERCISE 11

Make a list of at least ten details under one of the following headings. Then organize your list into appropriate categories. You may find that some of your details don't fit within a category; if so, you can either discard them or add other details to create a new category. (You might like to review our example of the essay on humiliating experiences, pp. 107–109.)

a. things you like about your job (or things you dislike)
b. advantages of renting an apartment over living in a dorm (or the other way around)
c. main problems you think we face as a nation in the rest of the 1980s
d. performances you've found most memorable in films you've seen
e. qualities that make for a good supervisor or instructor

Comparison and Contrast

> *Function:* To show how two or more things or ideas are alike, or
> different, or both.
> *Structure:* Compare or contrast point by point or block by block.

Many assignments call for you to analyze how things are alike, or how they are different, or how they are alike in some ways but different in others. For instance, your sociology professor may ask you to contrast information in the textbook with information you've acquired on your own. Or your English teacher may ask you to compare the attitudes of one character in a novel to those of another. Or your biology final may require you to analyze two ways of performing the same experiment and to show how the approaches are fundamentally similar even though they differ in some minor ways.

Essentially there are three (fairly obvious) types of essay in which you need to use your ability to compare or contrast: the essay of comparison, in which you analyze similarities; the essay of contrast, devoted to differences; the essay of comparison *and* contrast, dealing fairly equally with both similarities and differences.

The two most common structures for comparison-contrast essays are arrangement of material either point by point or block by block. If you're comparing or contrasting *point by point,* you tackle each area of similarity or difference one by one. For instance, in our earlier example about your English class, you could devote one paragraph to showing how the characters had similar attitudes toward money, another to their attitudes toward their families, a third to their attitudes toward their communities. Your point might be that even though these characters were superficially unalike, in education, social class, and occupation, their basic values were surprisingly similar.

If you were taking the *block by block* approach to the same assignment, you could make the same point by spending a few paragraphs exploring one character's attitudes toward money, his family, and the community, and then taking the next paragraph to discuss the other character's attitudes toward the same things. Your final paragraph could again summarize and analyze the similarity in attitudes implied in the rest of the essay.

Suppose you were writing an essay on backpacking in which your point was that different types of trails offer different sorts of challenges and rewards, and that one should therefore choose a trail that best matches one's purpose and experience. To illustrate this advice concretely, you might contrast two trails in different areas of the same national park.

An extremely general outline for a *point by point* presentation of this essay might look like this:

Paragraph 1: Introduction and thesis statement.
Paragraph 2: Contrast steepness, length, and difficulty of trails.
Paragraph 3: Contrast camping facilities on trails.
Paragraph 4: Contrast popularity of trails.
Paragraph 5: Contrast wildlife and scenery on trails.
Paragraph 6: Conclude by stressing the different attractions and drawbacks of each trail for hikers with different purposes and experience.

If you chose to organize the same essay *block by block,* the outline would look different:

Paragraph 1: Introduction and thesis statement.
Paragraph 2: Steepness, length, and difficulty of first trail.
Paragraph 3: Camping facilities and popularity of first trail.
Paragraph 4: Wildlife and scenery on first trail.
Paragraph 5: Steepness, length, and difficulty of second trail.
Paragraph 6: Camping facilities and popularity of second trail.
Paragraph 7: Wildlife and scenery on second trail.
Paragraph 8: Conclude by summarizing different attractions and drawbacks of each trail for hikers with different purposes and experience.

Although this block-by-block method of organization can be more difficult for both the writer and the reader because information from the first half of the essay must be kept in mind through the second half, both methods can work well providing you have made a conscious choice and faithfully followed the pattern you've chosen.

It's important also to consider the weight you want to give to the points in an essay that both compares and contrasts. For example, a writer may want to merely mention the similarities between the outcomes of the Korean conflict and the Vietnam war and then go on to concentrate on the differences. But if she outlines the similarities in such detail that she unintentionally devotes two-thirds of the paper to this comparison and leaves little room for what was supposed to be the main thrust of her paper, her readers will naturally miss the point.

Remember also that the fact that two things *can* be compared or contrasted doesn't necessarily mean they *should* be. Like all essays, those of comparison or contrast must have a clear, interesting point. Comparing the skylines of New York and Philadelphia, for instance, is worthwhile only if this comparison yields some point beyond the quantitative and obvious; the assertion that both cities have lots of big buildings but that New York has more of them is hardly a legitimate thesis. By the same token, contrasting your kindergarten teacher's facial features with those of your physiology professor would be foolish, but comparing their abilities to motivate students could be an interesting basis for an essay.

EXERCISE 12

Pick two siblings you know (a brother/brother, sister/sister or sister/brother pair)—you can be one of the siblings, if you wish. For each pair consider the following (make brief notes for each category):

a. appearance (what does this person look like?)

b. disposition (what is this person's temperament like? what kind of mood is he or she usually in?)

c. interests (what does this person like to do? what are his or her hobbies, for instance?)

Having done this, prepare two outlines for a comparison/contrast essay about these two siblings. For the first outline, assume that the essay will be organized point by point. For the second, arrange the outline block by block. Given the specific characteristics you came up with for your siblings, which organization seems the most natural and the least disruptive and confusing?

Persuasion

Function: To convince readers of your stand on a debatable issue.

Structure: Usually present the other side's arguments and expose their weaknesses, either one at a time or in a group. Then continue with a strong defense of your own position.

An assignment you may run into frequently in composition classes is the *argumentative* or *persuasive* essay, so named because you argue for a certain opinion on a controversial issue and try to persuade your reader to adopt your views.* For instance, you may be asked to take a stand on the morality of abortion, a ballot proposition, or the legalization of marijuana. Your topic doesn't have to be a burning issue; you might, for instance, write an essay arguing that it's more fun to "follow your nose" on a vacation than to map out a specific itinerary and make reservations in advance. Or you might try to persuade readers that liberal arts students should be required

---

*Teachers of classical rhetoric often distinguish between argument and persuasion. According to some definitions, an argumentative essay seeks only to establish the truth, while a persuasive essay attempts to change readers' minds or to convince them to take a particular course of action. Another distinction sometimes made is that the argumentative essay appeals only to reason, but a persuasive essay can appeal to the emotions as well. The two terms are so closely related, however, that for our purposes we treat them together.

to take at least a semester of college math. But whatever you're arguing for or against, the persuasive essay calls for clear thinking, solid support for your views, and a clear organization to help readers follow your argument.

Because you will be judged on how well you defend your position, you need to make sure you've *thoroughly* thought through what you're saying and gathered the most convincing evidence you can lay your hands on.

Don't make the mistake of trying to gear your views to what you imagine your instructor thinks about the topic. Your guess might be wrong; and, in any case, no responsible teacher would grade you down for your opinion, providing you've presented your case well. You'll probably write most convincingly if you take the position you believe in, whatever the instructor's views. If you have no real opinion on the topic, take the stand you feel you can best defend.

Luckily, once you know what position you're going to take and how you plan to defend it, a persuasive paper is fairly easy to organize. Although there are many possible variations, the persuasive essay is usually organized in one of two general ways.

Method 1: Start with the "case for the opposition." You can sum up the most important arguments usually advanced by those who take the opposite stand on the issue, and then refute them, explaining your reasons for believing as you do. Or you can tackle the other side's arguments one at a time, dispensing with each as you bring it up. (Sometimes you may need to concede that certain of the other side's arguments may be valid, but you will still emphasize that, on balance, yours are stronger.) Continue the essay with the "case for the defense," presenting the arguments for *your* position.

Method 2: Ignore the opposite side. Just proceed with a straightforward explanation of your position.

Let's take an issue hotly debated in recent years, the question of whether school boards should have the right to fire openly homosexual teachers. You decide to take the position that they should not.

If you're using Method 1, you might write a paragraph or two summing up the most common reasons people give for wanting gay teachers fired: that they may serve as "role models" and influence youngsters to become homosexual, that they may molest their students, that homosexuality is irreligious, and that soon there will be "quotas" requiring school districts to hire a certain percentage of gay teachers. Or you might dispense with the overall summary of the opposition's views, and decide instead to refute each argument as you bring it up.

In either case, you would proceed to tackle each of these arguments in turn. In one paragraph, you could state that there is no evidence youths can be "recruited" to homosexuality by an influential adult, quoting from authorities on child development who claim children's sexuality is already determined by the time they start school. In the next paragraph, you could undercut the argument that gay teachers may molest their students by referring to statistics indicating that the overwhelming majority of child molesters are heterosexuals; you can also cite current laws that already protect children from sexual advances by their teachers.

Because it connects with people's deepest beliefs, the religious argument is somewhat harder to dispel, but there are ways you can do it. Remember to consider your audience: saying the Bible is rubbish would only alienate a religious reader, but you could quote from a few of the religious leaders who have recently recommended that homosexuality be accepted as compatible with the teachings of their churches. Perhaps most convincingly, you could argue that our Constitution separates church and state, making it clear that holders of certain religious views cannot dictate laws for the general population. Finally, you can point out that the question of "quotas" is a false issue, for gay teachers are not asking for affirmative action, but only for equal treatment under the law. Having dispensed with the "case for the opposition," you then go on to present your other arguments against making homosexuality grounds for dismissal.

If you decide not to deal directly with the opposition's case at all, you'll concentrate instead on presenting your own case as convincingly as possible (Method 2). For instance, an essay on the topic we've just looked at could simply argue that what teachers do during their off-duty hours has nothing to do with their ability to teach; that a law permitting school boards to fire homosexuals would leave teachers open to slanderous attacks by disgruntled students; that trying cases would waste tax dollars and the school board's time; and, most important, that if any group in a democracy is denied its civil rights, everyone is threatened. The only danger with this method (most useful when you're short of time or space) is that if your readers don't happen to share your views already, they may still be left believing their own arguments. That's why writers of persuasive essays usually spend at least part of their papers rebutting the beliefs skeptical readers are likely to hold.

Appealing to Emotion

Most of the arguments we've mentioned so far in our example about firing homosexual teachers have been appeals to reason. In appealing to your readers on *intellectual* grounds, you can assume you share certain common reference points, because whatever their personal views, readers will find it difficult to argue with statistics, quotations from authorities, or the United States Constitution.

You can also appeal to readers' emotions, trying to arouse their sympathies or to make them indignant enough to move to your side. But emotional appeals need careful consideration, for they can backfire. It's been said that you can change people's minds, but not their feelings. For instance, asking readers to put themselves in the place of a fifth-grade teacher who would have to live in terror that her Lesbianism might be discovered would work well with readers already sympathetic to your cause. But someone convinced that homosexuals are sinful would probably reply, "Good—she *should* be squirming." For this kind of audience (and if you don't know your audience's views, it's always wise to assume they're unfriendly), a better emotional appeal would be to point out how difficult it is to find teachers who are able to work effectively with inner-city children. Go on to paint a picture of a gifted young teacher able to inspire her inner-city pupils, giving them a sense of pride in their schoolwork for the first time in their young lives. Should these students, you ask, be denied the chance of working with this fine teacher merely because she happens to be gay? Having agreed with your initial premise that good teachers in inner-city schools are rare, your readers should have trouble answering "yes."

Used sparingly and effectively, emotional appeals can be a valuable ally in winning support for your cause. But before we turn you loose to go and write your own persuasive papers, we need to pass on a couple of cautions about using "emotional evidence."

- Don't let your emotions substitute for thought.
- Always remember your audience. Don't make the mistake of assuming that what moves you will necessarily affect others. Try to put yourself in the place of skeptical readers, and be cagey about what might sway them.
- Don't make your examples too extreme. If you do, you may lose credibility.

(You might also want to review the entry on "Logic Errors" on pages 337–344 of the Usage Manual.)

EXERCISE 13

Pick one of the topics below and take a stand on it. Once you've decided on your position, (1) write down the strongest arguments you can think of to defend it; (2) make a list of ways in which opponents of your stand might argue against your view; (3) figure out how you could counter each of their arguments; (4) write an outline for a paper attempting to persuade a reader to adopt your views, using one of the methods of organization we mention on p. 115.

Possible Topics

a. outlawing smoking in public places
b. living together before marriage
c. making women register for the draft if men are required to do so
d. holding elementary school students with deficient skills back for a year instead of promoting them to the next grade
e. setting the legal drinking age at 18
f. instituting wage/price controls to curb inflation

A Final Word on Organization

You've now been introduced to some of the major forms of organization, which people have used for centuries to help them give structure to their ideas. (Aristotle wrote about most of them over 2,300 years ago.) You'll probably use all of these methods at one time or another. But don't get the idea that you should try to cram everything you write into one of these structures, as the legendary innkeeper Procrustes was said to have stretched or cut off the legs of his victims so that they would exactly fit the length of his bed. *The ideal organization grows naturally out of the material and purpose for the essay.*

You'll nearly always find it useful to make an outline at some stage of the writing process, before you begin to write, when your ideas suddenly come unglued in the middle of a draft, or even when you've finished your first draft and want to make sure your essay holds together. Don't be put off by feeling you have to duplicate the beautiful outlines you've seen in textbooks; often an informal outline that simply shows how your essay will move from paragraph to paragraph will be sufficient.

An outline helps you map out your ideas in far less time than it would take you to write them all out. Outlines are also useful because they help you keep track of the relationships between sections of your essay as you write. But your outline shouldn't ever become a straitjacket; feel free to change it as you write. We also suggest writing on only one side of a page so that you can cut up your first draft and tape it back together in different orders to see which organization best fits your purpose. You could also write your first draft on every second or third line of notebook paper, leaving room for additions in between the lines you've used.

SOME VARIABLES

We've now taken you through the four basic steps involved in creating an essay from scratch: finding a topic, deciding on a thesis, collecting evidence, and organizing your material. Although the *order* in which you go through these steps will vary from essay to essay (you might, for instance, collect most of your evidence before deciding on a thesis, or you might choose a method of organization before you have all your evidence), our advice so far can apply to almost any writing assignment.

In this last part of the chapter, we come to some variables, those factors that may change from assignment to assignment. For instance, are you writing in class or at home? What kind of assignment have you been given? These also influence the choices you make as a writer.

In-Class Assignments

Many students find in-class writing assignments the most difficult and frustrating kind of writing they must do for college. Required to produce a reasonably complete essay in an unreasonably short time, some students freeze and find themselves unable to write anything at all. Others complete the assignment, but never feel particularly good about what they've done, no matter how many times they're forced to write in class. We can suggest some ways to make the task less threatening.

First, it may help to think of the things you *don't* have to worry about when you write in class, for in many ways the pressure is off, rather than on. In fact, you may be demanding more of yourself than an in-class assignment really calls for. You can be pretty sure, for instance, that when you write in class you don't have to produce a glittering, polished piece of prose, stunning in its originality. More likely, the purpose of an in-class assignment is to get you to apply techniques and principles you have learned, such as those writing strategies you've covered in a composition class, or to give you the opportunity to synthesize ideas that have been covered in class lectures or discussions. Suppose your nineteenth-century American history instructor took seven class hours to cover the Civil War period, devoting two sessions to the social, three to the political, and two to the economic causes of the War. When he asks you to discuss the causes of the Civil War on your midterm exam, he doesn't expect a radical reinterpretation of the facts. Instead, he expects that you can sift through the many causes he's covered and develop a well-supported case for the ones you select.

In response to the Civil War question, you may develop the thesis that the causes of the War, far from being separate, were in fact closely related, so that slavery was at once an economic, a social, and a political issue. While this conclusion may not startle a historian with its originality, it is a departure from the typical—though perfectly acceptable—"there was social cause, a political cause, and an economic cause of the Civil War." This more unified approach may also give you a fresh perspective on material that was unconnected until you wrote about it.

It also helps to remember that just as instructors do not expect you to write a polished essay in class, they also realize that your in-class response isn't necessarily your final word on the subject. You don't have to worry too much, then, about advancing a position that you might not hold if you were given more time to consider it.

Finally, despite the fact that an in-class assignment must be written "on the spot" within a time limit, you don't have to worry about coming to the task completely unprepared, for it *is* possible to get ready at home for in-class assignments. As preparation for an essay in an English composition class, you can review the papers you've already written, checking your instructor's comments to see what your strong points and problems have been. On the paper you wrote last time, were you commended for good, logical organization but urged to be more specific, for instance? If so, then you'll want to keep those comments in mind as you write in class. To prepare for in-class writing in other courses, you can go over your class notes, review any assigned texts, and think carefully about what's been discussed in class. This kind of thorough review can even give you a pretty good idea of the topic you may be asked to write on. It also helps to take notes as you review, even when you can't bring them to class with you; just the act of writing things down can help you to organize and retain information.

With these general guidelines in mind, you might consider the suggestions that follow the next time you're faced with an in-class essay assignment.

First, read the topic carefully, without trying to think of the only possible "right answer," or even the best and most thoughtful response you could come up with if you had plenty of time. Think instead of an answer or position you can defend without having to spend hours to come up with a strategy.

Once you have a statement of that position, write it down and stop for a minute. One of the biggest causes of in-class writing jitters is the mistaken opinion that if you have an hour to write, you must write for an hour. In fact, a poll of our students revealed that those who had the most trouble writing in class tended to be the ones who had not done outlines at all or had written only sketchy ones. Some of these same students wrote detailed outlines for out-of-class assignments, yet felt that they had no time on an in-class essay to do the same. When you are pressed for time on an in-class assignment, it is especially important to take a few minutes to draft a brief outline for your essay, with your thesis statement, your main ideas, and the material you'll use to support those ideas. You can then use your outline to guide your response as the pressure of time increases.

As you plot your outline, keep in mind that even when you haven't come up with a particularly original thesis, you can still try to think of your own fresh support for familiar ideas. The thesis that Americans tend to be materialistic is scarcely novel, but you could still enliven an essay on that subject with well-chosen examples. Perhaps you've dared to cross the threshold of the opulent stores on Rodeo Drive in Beverly Hills, or leafed through a Neiman-Marcus catalogue, or done some thinking about the obsolescent products that seem to wear out just so that we'll have an excuse to buy something new. In any case, the specific support you provide for your thesis can help your reader see the familiar in a new way.

Once you begin writing, you may find that ideas for particular parts of the paper begin to occur to you. Add these to your outline in the appropriate sections; they can jog your memory and help to fill out your thoughts, much as an artist's pencil sketch helps him conceive a finished painting. You can also make notes in the margins of the paper about changes you want to make when you're done writing. You may realize a sentence is jumbled before you've even finished writing it, or notice that a statement needs another example to support it even though you can't think of one at the moment. Rather than interrupt the flow of your ideas, make notes reminding yourself to go back to repair the sentence or add an example later on. Sometimes ideas occur to you as you write, but you may not know exactly where in the essay they belong. If you jot these ideas down, you can go back to find the right place to fit them in. (And it's perfectly all right to make additions to your essay in the margins or even on a separate piece of paper.)

Finally, plan to leave at least ten per cent of your allotted time for proofreading: for going back to that sentence you wanted to fix, for adding the example you wanted to include, for checking to see that you've been reasonably clear, orderly, and coherent. If you've double-spaced your essay, you'll be able to insert corrections that are easy for your instructor to read. Necessary at any time, proofreading is especially important when you've written in a hurry.

While they don't expect miracles, teachers do expect to be able to decipher your handwriting. The important thing, though, is not to waste time copying over your entire essay to make it "neat," but rather to proofread carefully so that you submit a paper that is the best you can do under difficult circumstances.

The Out-of-Class Essay

Of course, any paper you write should reflect your best effort under the circumstances. As we saw in the preceding section, when you write in class your goals and your instructor's expectations may be tempered by the time pressures you face. But when you're writing an essay outside of class, you *do* have time—time to think a topic through, to work on ideas you might have neither the opportunity nor the presence of mind to consider in class.

If you're writing about a personal topic, you can make sure that you've developed a thesis with some substance, that you're making a point that will really interest both you and your reader. You can search your memory for the freshest, most compelling examples to support your thesis.

If you're writing on a less personal topic, you can take the time to look over notes, pull books off your shelf, go to the library, and ask questions as you organize and substantiate a paper that does more than skim the surface of your topic.

Regardless of the topic, an out-of-class paper should be mechanically and grammatically clean: there's little excuse for typographical errors, misspelled words, misplaced apostrophes, and other distractions. The paper should also reflect considerable planning, thought, and revision. You shouldn't write an out-of-class paper as you would write one in class, using the first reasonable thesis that comes to mind and hastily assembling merely adequate support.

Out-of-class writing frees you from some of the compromises you may have to make in class. You're freer to reject ideas and start over, to explore more than the obvious implications of a subject, to make sure you have sufficient evidence to support your thesis.

U-Turns in Dead-End Alleys

When you're writing an essay, you may occasionally try an approach that proves to be unworkable as you develop it. When you run into such a dead end in class, you may have to struggle on as best you can, making minor modifications in the paper as you write. But outside of class, you can go back to the beginning and start over, literally or figuratively tossing your old approach aside and taking a new tack.

Stop Me If You've Heard This One

One of the best ways to lose your readers' attention is to bore them with the obvious. Your papers will be more interesting for both you and your readers if you work from the hypothetical premise that your instructor will read them only if they're truly interesting. You'll thus be spared the rote drudgery of grinding out trivial papers, and your instructor will be intrigued by your essays and grateful for your thoughtfulness.

When you're writing outside of class, you have both time and mobility, so there's no excuse for a paper with an unoriginal thesis backed by equally predictable examples. You should take the time to find a fresh approach to your subject and to think up, remember, or look for interesting examples. Both the premise and the development of the following passage are hackneyed. Despite the paragraph's relative fluency, it makes obvious points in an obvious way:

> As the seasons change, so do our moods. The first robin and the appearance of flowers mark the beginning of spring, and our spirits are filled with life and hope. Overcome by "spring fever," we enjoy walking through the lovely fields, maybe smiling for no apparent reason. As the heat of summer settles in, everything seems to stand still, and we slow down too. It's all we can do to walk lazily down to the pool and lie in the sun. The briskness of fall gets things moving again, as leaves fall from trees and the air takes on the unmistakable bite of autumn. We find ourselves moving more briskly now, forgetting the slowness of summer. When winter comes, nature seems to turn inward. Our thoughts turn inward too, as we sit, perhaps before the fire with a favorite book or friend, looking out at the snow or rain.

Oh, Really?

Occasionally, a student will pursue a thesis that is indefensible—for that particular student in that particular writing situation. Sometimes the thesis is inherently unworkable: "All policemen should also be licensed psychiatrists," "We would be better off if we ran our country according to the rules of the Bible," "The next hundred years hold few surprises." Sometimes the thesis itself might seem all right, as in the following example, but the writer may support it in such a bizarre or unconvincing way that the paper is literally incredible.

See if you can put your finger on what's wrong with the following paragraphs.

> Birds are smarter than most people think. Even though a parakeet may spend hours cocking its head at its reflection in its little mirror, it is still listening to everything that goes on around it. Most animals can sleep in the sun (cats love to stretch out by a warm window, for example), but pet birds can sleep only if you cover their cages. This is because they are so alert and inquisitive that they need to be shielded from all distractions; the slightest motion in the room or snatch of conversation is apt to set them off, chirping and hopping about, eager to join in the discussion or participate in the activity.
>
> Birds in the wild are no less astute. They have such good memories

and plan ahead so well that herons and egrets, for instance, will pick an ideal spot for a nest and return to the same nest year after year. Anyone who has taken a walk in the woods knows that birds talk to each other, exchanging complex information through a series of different calls, arranged in an infinite variety of patterns. Wild birds will also fly over any intruder, carefully assessing him while keeping a safe distance; only after they've determined who the intruder is and whether he has any business in their domain will they either perch or fly off to warn others of their species.

The point the writer is trying to make here is not just obscure, it's impossible for him to prove. He gets into trouble as he pushes ahead into one suspect observation after another, expecting the reader to believe, for instance, that a parakeet is smart because it goes to sleep only when you cover its cage or that herons are intelligent enough to plan their return to the same nesting spot year after year. The way to avoid this kind of problem is to pick a thesis that you can find some rational evidence to support.

TYPES OF ESSAY TOPICS

The approach you take to an assignment will often be shaped by the nature of the assignment itself. Some topics are worded so precisely that they leave you little choice in how you organize your paper. Consider the following, for instance:

> After briefly defining "topic sentence" and "thesis statement," show how they are significantly different as well as alike, using examples from the papers you have written for this course.

Buried not very deeply in that topic is the structure of the essay you would write in response to it. First, you would have to define "topic sentence" and "thesis statement"; then you would need to point out their significant differences and similarities. The topic even dictates the kinds of examples: they must be drawn from your own work.

For the sake of convenience, we've arbitrarily divided into three categories the kinds of essay topics you're apt to encounter. We concocted these categories not so you can spend time deciding which slot a given essay topic fits into, but so you can get in the habit of considering what a topic asks you to do as well as what it's already done for you.

TYPE 1 TOPICS

> List at least three major results of inflation, and suggest ways in which the public and private sectors might cope with each.

>Describe a nonacademic lesson an elementary school teacher taught you. Show how that lesson was useful at the time and how it remains useful in the present.
>
>Compare major league baseball today with baseball in the 1950s, taking into account the players' salaries, the fans' dedication to the sport, and the coverage baseball gets in the print and electronic media.

These *Type 1 topics,* like the one about topic sentences and thesis statements, *limit the subject and provide a great deal of direction,* telling you not only what to write about, in pretty specific terms, but suggesting in what order you might want to consider the components of the topic. Especially when you're writing under the pressure of time, Type 1 topics can be a blessing because they lift from you the burden of narrowing your topic and sketching out the rough organization of the paper.

Look over the sample topics under Type 1. What exactly does each ask you to do? Does the topic suggest a sequence of presentation? Does the topic presume that you have or can get certain information?

Note, for instance, that the second topic asks you to discuss a useful *nonacademic lesson,* presumably ruling out any papers about arithmetic or spelling. The third topic does indeed suggest an order of presentation: in comparing baseball today with the sport in the fifties, you could first discuss players' salaries, then the fans, then the media. The first topic presumes that you know something about the results of inflation; if you're writing outside of class, you might need to get some information from the library before finishing your paper.

Type 1 topics are frequently used by instructors testing to see whether you have specific information or can analyze something in a particular way. Because the topics dictate a fairly predictable response, Type 1 essays are less likely to be scintillating and innovative than papers written on other kinds of topics. But as long as you make your essay as interesting as you can, given the constraints of the assignment, and as long as you stick to the subject, the instructor can't legitimately fault you for producing a fairly direct, unflashy piece.

For most other types of assignment, for example, it's usually not a very good idea to write a paper with an arbitrary three- or four-part thesis statement ("Opera combines the arts of music, drama, and painting") and a paragraph on each of those three or four points. Such papers are predictable, and while their organization is generally clear enough, it can also be boring.

But when you're *given* a topic like the first or third topic listed under "Type 1," you needn't worry too much that your essay will seem arbitrarily organized. The instructor may want to be able to scan your paper to see whether you've listed three major results of inflation (and you really need to do more than just "list" them, of course). You're helping the instructor by making the thesis statement and the organization of the paper explicit, and you're saving yourself the trouble of tinkering with the basic structure of the paper. It's a good idea to list your main points in the thesis statement of this kind of in-class paper, incidentally, so that the instructor can spot your main ideas even if you don't get a chance to finish the essay.

TYPE 2 TOPICS

> Evaluate the grading system at your college.
> Discuss your early experiences with mathematics.
> Propose a comprehensive energy program for your state.

Type 2 topics limit the subject you'll be writing about, *but* they *don't offer* the *direction and* implicit *organization* of Type 1 topics. From the first topic above, for instance, you know *what* to write about: the grading system at your school. But unlike the Type 1 topic about inflation, the grading topic provides no direction for your essay, leaving you to figure out what specific areas to discuss and in what order to take them up.

In planning a Type 2 essay, then, you need to spend some time mapping out your general strategy. Pick one of the topics in the Type 2 list and consider how you would organize an essay in response to it. Would you organize the paper chronologically, perhaps showing how your energy plan could be phased in gradually, tracing its development step by step? Would you arrange ideas in ascending order of importance, beginning with the relatively minor inconveniences created by your school's grading system, moving on to more substantive complaints and concluding with your most telling criticism? Would you group related ideas together, so that paragraphs treating the same general subject would follow each other, showing in one paragraph how your parents sparked your interest in mathematics and in the next paragraph how your first-grade teacher reinforced and expanded that interest? Would you discuss all the positive points (of your school's grading system, your experiences with math, or your proposed energy plan) and then the shortcomings?

Since Type 2 topics don't answer these questions for you, you can structure your essay in any way that seems useful. But before you hand in such a paper done outside class, you should make sure that you have a conscious, considered *approach* for your essay. And before you begin a paper in class, you should at least sketch out an approach for this kind of topic.

TYPE 3 TOPICS

> Inflation.
> The importance of goals.
> Mediocrity.

As you can see, *Type 3 topics neither limit the subject* for you *nor provide direction* for your essay. In one way this is a real plus: you're not bound by the specific subject or sequence that your instructor wants you to stick to. You don't have to list at least three major results of inflation and suggest ways in which the public and private sectors might cope with each. Instead, you could write about the bargains that are still available despite inflation or explain how inflation has affected older people on fixed, already low incomes. As long as your essay falls within the general range of the topic, you've met the assignment.

But remember the difference between writing *about* a general subject and writing about a specific area *within* that subject. As we've mentioned before, you can't expect to write a cohesive essay *about* anything as vague as "mediocrity" or "the importance of goals." You need to somehow boil Type 3 topics down to manageable proportions. Given "mediocrity" as a topic, you could write about mediocre presidential candidates, past and present; you could decry the standard of mediocrity that teachers seem willing to accept from their students (or that students seem willing to accept from their teachers); you could try to explain why the music on AM radio hovers around such a predictably mediocre common denominator.

If you're writing outside of class about a Type 3 topic, you can afford to experiment, to begin and discard drafts as you search for the facet of the topic that most intrigues you and provides the most substance for an essay. You might start to write about mediocre AM music, only to be reminded halfway through your paper of the indistinguishable, frantically friendly AM disc jockeys. So you decide to write about them instead. After beginning *that* paper, you might change your mind again and decide to write about the kinds of mediocre products that these disc jockeys push on their listeners between records, jovial inanities, and time and weather checks.

If you're writing under the pressure of time, though, Type 3 topics impose the greatest obligation to plan your essay thoroughly before you begin writing. Before you begin to write any in-class Type 3 essay, be sure that you have limited the topic and have come up with at least a provisional thesis statement. The beauty of Type 3 topics is that they allow you latitude; the danger is that you might wander too aimlessly within their wide boundaries.

EXERCISE 14

As we've seen in this section, your approach to an essay depends on a number of variables: the topic, the amount of time you have, whether you're writing inside or outside class, the kinds of research you might have to do.

For each of the topics below, consider how you would approach the assignment. What would you have to do before you could start writing? How might you have to narrow the scope of the topic? To what extent would you need to consider the wishes and prejudices of your audience? How would you organize the paper? What kinds of information could you include? What might your thesis statement be? Be prepared to discuss your approach for each topic. You should make notes to help you organize your thoughts and make them specific.

For some of the topics, we've suggested a few things to consider. After you've thought the topic through on your own, you might want to review the italicized suggestions.

A–1. You're asked to write an essay in class on "The Women's Movement." Your paper is to be around 500 words, and you'll have an hour to complete it. The class has not been discussing this topic, and you may not use any references in writing your paper.

(Because you're writing in class under the pressure of time, you need to make a fairly good outline before you begin. As part of that out-lining process, you'll obviously need to narrow and direct the topic, since "The Women's Movement" is far too general a subject for this or any essay. Since you won't have access to outside information, you'll need to draw on information you can remember offhand or on your personal experience. Because efficiency is important here, you should be more concerned with writing a cohesive essay that responds to some facet of the topic than with writing the best, most original piece you're capable of under ideal conditions.)

A–2. Assume the situation is the same, except that you're writing outside class.

(You obviously have more time to decide on an approach; you're also expected to do a better job. You'll still need to narrow the topic so that you can deal with it in 500 words. And, since you may still not consult references, you'll need to rely again on your own knowledge and experience.)

A–3. Assume that you're assigned a 500-word essay, to be done outside class and turned in a week later, on "The History of the Women's Movement in America." You are encouraged to do research in preparing your paper.

(A key to success in this assignment is your ability to pick the major *events to cover in such a brief overview.)*

A-4. You're asked to write a 1,000-word essay in class on the following: "Describe an incident that changed your attitude towards the women's movement. Consider whether that change was permanent or temporary and describe how that change manifested itself in your personal life as well as in school."

A-5. You're asked to write on the same topic as in A-4. Your teacher is an outspoken advocate of feminism.

B-1. You're asked to write a 1,000-word essay outside class on "The Importance of Writing." Nothing is said one way or the other about your being able to use outside sources.

B-2. You're asked to write a 500-word in-class essay on the following question: "How might the skills you acquire in a college composition class help you in your other college work?" You have an hour and a half to complete the paper. During the past week your composition instructor has discussed three or four specific ways in which the course can help you in your other classes.

B-3. The same as B-2, except that you're writing outside class and have a week to complete the assignment.

B-4. You're asked to write a paper outside class on the difference between spoken and written English in both formal and informal situations. The paper is to be 2,500 words and you have a month to work on it. In the course of the semester, the instructor has occasionally bemoaned the fact that students don't seem to know how to write a proper research paper any more, with correct footnotes and bibliographies.

B-5. You're asked to write a 300-word paper on your greatest fears about writing for college. The paper will be reproduced and distributed to the other members of your class, anonymously if you so request. You're asked to write the paper at home, but to spend no more than an hour on it. The instructor will grade it on a Credit/No Credit basis.

6

Building the Beginning, Strengthening the Middle, Tying Up the End

We have placed this chapter after discussions of paragraphs, development, the essay, and organization so you'll be experienced in composing the major sections of your essays—the thesis and its support—before you face introductions and conclusions, which many writers find particularly troublesome. In this chapter we demonstrate some common ways of beginning and ending essays, and also consider **unity** (linking the parts) as well as **revising** (rewriting to fine tune your papers).

INTRODUCTIONS

Beginning an essay is a little like beginning a conversation. Before you come to your point, you need to establish a rapport and to put the person you're talking with in the mood to listen to you and consider what you have to say. But such a comparison won't stretch too far. For unlike the obligatory "And how's the family?" that precedes the statement of one's real business, the introductory paragraph does more than grease the wheels of social communication. An essay's introduction should

- ease your readers into the subject
- capture your readers' interest and move them forward into the entire essay
- prepare for the thesis statement (and perhaps even state it)

At times, an introductory paragraph performs other services as well, such as

- setting the tone of a piece
- establishing a common ground between you and your readers
- providing essential background information
- acknowledging your readers' existence and letting them know that you are aware of their position, even if you disagree with it
- establishing your credentials and character

If you keep in mind what you learned in previous chapters about making things easier for your readers, you will have less trouble thinking through the purposes of your introductory paragraphs.

Some Sample Introductions

The following sample introductions illustrate the approaches most commonly taken to the problem of getting started, of "hooking" readers while informing them of the essay's basic point and direction. You will notice that while some introductory paragraphs include a thesis, others do not. No rule decrees that you *must* include your thesis in your introduction, although many students and instructors have found that certain problems with clarity and organization disappear when the thesis is deliberately positioned at the end of the first paragraph.

DESCRIPTION

Most of the dead animals you see on highways near the cities are dogs, a few cats. Out in the countryside, the forms and coloring of the dead are strange; these are the wild creatures. Seen from a car window they appear as fragments, evoking memories of woodchucks, badgers, skunks, voles, snakes, sometimes the mysterious wreckage of a deer.

It is always a queer shock, part a sudden upwelling of grief, part unaccountable amazement. It is simply astounding to see an animal dead on a highway. The outrage is more than just the location; it is the impropriety of such visible death, anywhere. You do not expect to see dead animals in the open. It is the nature of animals to die alone, off somewhere, hidden. It is wrong to see them lying out on the highway; it is wrong to see them anywhere.

Everything in the world dies, but we only know about it as a kind of abstraction . . .

—Lewis Thomas, "Death in the Open," *The Lives of a Cell,*
The Viking Press, 1974

Cigarette ads rarely try to sell the actual cigarettes themselves. Instead, they offer masculinity, or femininity, or youth, or—in the case of a recent magazine ad that methodically blurs the line between people and product—good looks and charm. The ad pictures a man and woman in their early twenties who have just finished playing tennis and are relaxing outside on a warm, sunny day. His eyes are set on the reader, and her eyes are set on him. The Vantage cigarette the man is about to smoke is white and gold, a color scheme carried through the picture of this couple. He has a white towel draped casually around his neck, and both people are wearing gold shirts that match the gold at the end of the cigarette. The woman is lighting her companion's cigarette with a gold lighter, and this same color appears in the background of the ad. In a foreground corner is a picture of a pack of Vantages with a multicolored bulls-eye. This target symbol has been superimposed over the picture of the couple, centered on the spot where the lighter meets the cigarette. A brief block of copy describes Vantage as though it were a place and not a cigarette: "where great taste and low tar meet."

—Student Essay, "Analysis of an Ad"

ANECDOTE OR NARRATION

I was walking, when the first Cyprus crisis was at its height, among the narrow byways that hug the Athens Acropolis, when three or four very small boys came round a corner and asked me where I belonged, naming one country after another. Having exhausted all they could think of, they looked at me with horror when I said, "Anglia," English. The eldest reached for a stone and they all in chorus cried, "Kyprus." Not knowing any Greek with which to argue, I took the first historic name that came into my mind and said, "Pericles." The classic bond held. "Themistocles," one little boy responded, and I added "Alcibiades" for good measure. The little group instantly adopted me and shepherded me through all the dangers of their fellows, just out from school. This is years ago now, and I had forgotten the episode until I happened to read the single word *Anglia* in a notebook of that day and the whole picture with its fierce gay little figures and the Acropolis hanging above them came back into my mind. The notebook, with its single word, had saved it from total oblivion.

A pen and a notebook and a reasonable amount of discrimination will change a journey from a mere annual into a perennial, its pleasures and pains renewable at will.

—Freya Stark, "On Travelling with a Notebook,"
The Zodiac Arch, Murray, 1968

EXAMPLE

Broken homes are "trees without roots."

Meat markets are "great flesh parlors."

Outsiders looking for thrills are "toys on a fairy lake."

This is the colorful, private speech of the children of America's ghettos, a "hidden language" of haunted phrases and striking subtlety. It is a language little known in the world outside, but for many it is more meaningful, more facile and more developed than the language of standard English.

—John M. Brewer, "Ghetto Children Know What They're Talking
About," © 1966 The New York Times Publishing Co.

The girl on TV has just learned that her lover has found another woman. She sits at the supper table staring dumbly ahead.

"Ruthie," her mother says, "you haven't touched your supper. What's the matter?"

"Nothing, Mamma," she says tonelessly, "I guess I'm just not hungry."

This is probably the most unshakable conviction to be found on TV: A girl who is suffering from unrequited love just isn't hungry.

This is balderdash. In my younger days I frequently went out with girls who had just been jilted by somebody or other, and they ate like wolves.

I guess that's what bothers me most about TV dramas—not the major improbabilities, but the fact that they're so out of touch with reality in small matters. I have no trouble accepting a hero who stows away on a rocket or escapes from a burning sampan, but how can you identify with a man who can always find a place to park his car?

—Will Stanton, "Real Girls Ask for Mint Frappes,"
© 1967 Curtis Publishing Co., Inc.

REFERENCE OR QUOTATION

Ben Franklin encapsulated his world, shooting the pellets into an oft-quoted Almanack ("Three may keep a secret, if two of them are dead"). La Rochefoucauld is still read in French history courses

("Who lives without folly is not so wise as he thinks"). Aesop distilled experience through metaphor ("Do not count your chickens before they are hatched"), inspiring countless imitations that are, as the saying goes, the sincerest form of flattery. Clearly the tradition of the one-line sentiment is well established. Yet something about aphorisms and admonitions running bumper to bumper in commute-hour traffic illuminates a contemporary question—how are we talking, how are we listening, and does anyone care what the words mean? When you stop to think about it, have you ever actually heard someone honk because he loves Jesus?

—Student Essay

DEFINITION

There is hardly a language to describe him, or even a set of social statistics. Just names: racist-bigot-redneck-ethnic-Irish-Italian-Pole-Hunkie-Yahoo. The lower middle class. A blank. The man under whose hat lies the great American desert. Who watches the tube, plays the horses, and keeps the niggers out of his union and his neighborhood. Who might vote for Wallace (but didn't). Who cheers when the cops beat up on demonstrators. Who is free, white and twenty-one, has a job, a home, a family, and is up to his eyeballs in credit. In the guise of the working class—or the American yeoman or John Smith—he was once the hero of the civics books, the man that Andrew Jackson called "the bone and sinew of the country." Now he is "the forgotten man," perhaps the most alienated person in America.

—Peter Schrag, "The Forgotten American," *Harper's,*
August 1969

DIRECT ADDRESS—INVOLVING THE READER DIRECTLY

It's Friday afternoon, and you have almost survived another week of classes. You are just looking forward dreamily to the weekend when the English instructor says: "For Monday you will turn in a five-hundred-word composition on college football."

Well, that puts a good hole in the weekend. You don't have any strong views on college football one way or the other. You get rather excited during the season and go to all the home games and find it rather more fun than not. On the other hand, the class has been reading Robert Hutchins in the anthology and perhaps Shaw's "Eighty-Yard Run," and from the class discussions you have got the idea that the instructor thinks college football is for the birds. You are no fool. You can figure out which side to take.

—Paul Roberts, "How to Say Nothing in Five Hundred Words,"
Understanding English, Harper & Row, 1956

ATTENTION GETTER

> This is a true story. Although much of it has the ring of fiction, of doomsday novels and disaster movies, it is real. If you lived in Los Angeles in 1975, you lived through the nation's first full-scale peacetime nuclear alert.
>
> And that's not even the frightening part . . .
>
> —Michael Singer and David Weir, "Nuclear Nightmare: Your Worst Fears are True," *New West,* December 3, 1979

THE INTRODUCTION THAT RESISTS CLASSIFICATION

Some introductory paragraphs simply can't be neatly categorized. They instead rely on a variety of devices that interest readers and make them want to keep reading, continue listening to this particular voice. The following is an example of such an introduction:

> I am of two minds about this country's present convulsions. My heart is in the highlands with the hellers. But my head tells me . . . It's an old head, mine, without much wool on the top of it in the place where the wool ought to grow. Let me tell you what it is like to be old in the United States of America at the tail end of the nineteen sixties.
>
> —Milton Mayer, "The Children's Crusade," *The Center Magazine,* September 1969

This introduction isn't as artless as it might seem at first glance. Writing at the time of the student rebellions in the late 1960s, Mayer has taken considerable care to woo his audience, young and old. The echo of the old Scottish song—"My heart's in the highlands, my heart is not here/My heart's in the highlands, a-chasing the deer"—reminds us that Mayer remembers what is like to be young and vital, pursuing a goal with vigor and joy, even though he is no longer eighteen or even thirty-two. Most of us recognize the familiar heart/head split, our feelings pulling us in one direction, our thoughts pulling us in another. And he awakens our empathy with his reference to growing bald, a classic sign of aging. Mayer is careful not to overplay this last point, because he wants our empathetic attention, not pity. So he refers humorously to his "wool." And he increases his chances of getting and holding our interest by quickly moving on to his point: "Let me tell you what it is like to be old" at a particular historical moment. The last sentence, of course, draws us in, makes us want to listen to what Mayer has to say. It's almost as if Mayer and his reader were sitting in a train station swapping stories.

Introductions to Avoid

OVER-KILL

Sometimes writers try too hard, strain too far in their attempt to involve the reader. The resulting introduction is often cutesy or even misleading. One of us remembers, for instance, being temporarily fascinated by what seemed to be a very sultry opening that ran something like this:

> The warm tropical night caressed her cheek as she delicately slipped one leg from beneath the blanket, at the same time softly stroking her companion's face and whispering, "Are you ready, dear? I'm so anxious to get started."

As it turned out, this article in a national magazine was about how to photograph wild animals at night in a Kenya game preserve. This isn't an introduction but a come-on, and a shoddy one at that.

Talking about the tendency to over-kill, educator Wayne Booth in his article "The Rhetorical Stance" refers to a college freshman who began every essay with a swear word, because his "high school teacher had taught him always to catch the reader's attention." As Booth goes on to say, even such a firmly established principle needs to be used sensibly.

A final, and very common, species of over-kill introduction is the exaggerated opening. Here the writer may be so caught up in the material that he or she makes extreme claims for it, or may have simply succumbed to the habit of overstatement. The typical exaggerated introduction looks like this:

> If you want to find yourself, spend a week in a national park. It's an experience you will remember forever, because it will change your life totally and permanently.

Writers who produce such introductions may mistakenly think that if they whip themselves up into a frenzy, their readers will become similarly aroused.

But the purpose of the introduction is to tell your readers what to expect. And if you build them up to expect something of cosmic significance, and then give them material that is of no more than normal interest, they will be disappointed. Essays have to be interesting, not profound, so don't feel you must exaggerate your claims in order to get attention.

THE YAWN REACTION

At the opposite end of the spectrum from the over-kill introduction is the Ho-Hum beginning. This graceless and often unconsidered opening is an introductory paragraph only in the sense that it comes first.

> Everybody loves convenience. Even when we could walk we drive our cars. Microwave ovens are increasingly popular for cooking our food, and we also wear clothes that don't need ironing. Many people think time-saving devices free us for more important things, but I think they just make us really lazy. The worst example of an unnecessary time-saving device is the electric can opener.

This introduction is boring because the three examples are of things everyone has heard about—frequently. The writer doesn't refute the opposition, just mentions it in passing. And the last sentence gives no hint of any fresh approach the writer may have in mind. All we know is that the essay will be about the evils of electric can openers. Ho hum.

AVOID THE OBVIOUS

Even after you have virtuously made up your mind to interest your readers and prepare them for the rest of the essay, you're not finished. You still have a couple of decisions to make. First, you must decide how much background information readers need in order to understand the general point of your essay, drawing that notoriously fine line between just enough background information to insure clarity, and too much information, which can make an introduction obvious, irrelevant, or dull. While nothing will discourage readers faster than being forced to face a totally foreign topic without the aid of some general background, the kind of background provided in the first paragraph of the following introduction does nothing to ease readers into the essay.

> Language is essential to every society as a system of communication. Every culture has a spoken language, and most cultures have a written one. Without language, people would find it difficult to communicate at all. In a sense, it is misleading to speak of a culture having a language. Many societies have several: China has many dialects, Canada is a bilingual nation, and South Africans use several languages in different situations and classes. The United States is indeed a melting pot, with the diversity of languages that implies. Each group of immigrants brought with them their own linguistic tradition. Although English is America's official language, it is not the only language used in America.

> Black English is just one of the many languages or dialects found in America. Speakers of Black English—like American speakers of Italian, Dutch, or Japanese—deserve neither praise nor condemnation. To say that Black English is worse than so-called standard English is as absurd as to say that Portuguese is worse than Spanish. Yet to acknowledge that Black English is legitimate is not to imply that speakers of Black English have no need to learn standard English. On the contrary, Black Americans—like Italian Americans, Dutch Americans, and Japanese Americans—need to be fluent in the common language of business, science, and education: standard English.

When you try to decide how much background information is "enough," the test is not whether what you've said is true. (The statements in the first paragraph above are true.) Nor is it only whether the material could conceivably interest someone. If this were to be an essay on the problems faced by multilingual societies, the first paragraph might provide a useful and necessary introduction. The real test is whether you can eliminate most or all of the information without any loss of meaning or effectiveness. Since this is really an essay about how important it is for speakers of Black English to learn standard English, the first paragraph can be omitted completely. The essay now begins more relevantly and forcefully.

In short, one way to liven up a slow, dull start to an essay is simply to cut your first few sentences, or even your first paragraph or so, especially if you wrote them just to get the paper started. With a little editing, you can often find the place where the essay *really* begins, and where your audience would much prefer to start reading.

When You Write about Literature

We wish we could specify exactly how much background information is enough in every case, but that's clearly impossible; you must be sensitive to your audience's needs. There is one area, however, in which we can offer a few guidelines, thanks to long-standing conventions regarding papers on literature.

When you write a paper about a piece of writing—be it an essay, novel, play, poem, or short story—your opening paragraph should mention the author and title of the work you're discussing. For example, you might begin such a paper by writing:

> *After the Fall,* Arthur Miller's autobiographical drama, develops the theme of . . .

Or

> Samuel Taylor Coleridge's "The Rime of the Ancient Mariner" has always fascinated readers with its macabre images of . . .

Or

> In some of his essays, "Marrakech" for instance, George Orwell relies primarily on . . .

As you grow more skillful with practice, you will undoubtedly find still smoother ways to announce your topic to your reader—but remember to do that announcing.

Sometimes students will complain that it seems silly to tell the "reader," who is clearly the instructor, what book is under discussion since it was the instructor who assigned the material in the first place. Such students will often begin an essay with something like:

> In our discussion of the novel last week, I was offended by my classmates' insistence that Hemingway is a great writer.

While the teacher and even other students with good memories might recall what book "last week's" discussion was about, no one else would. In fact, even the author of such an introduction might later be hard pressed to pinpoint which book he was analyzing. You might look upon this "convention" of immediately identifying author and title as a way to help you remember two years from now what you are writing and thinking about today.

UNITY

Unity is really a pretty simple principle: just as every sentence in a paragraph contributes to the main idea of that paragraph, each paragraph contributes to the main idea of the essay.

For an essay to be effective, all the supporting ideas need to be connected in some way, with individual paragraphs moving so smoothly from one to the other that the connections you have in your mind are as clear to your reader as they are to you. Experienced writers unify their prose in a variety of ways; in this section we'll introduce you to some of their techniques.

For the sake of discussion, we can divide the concept of unity in essay writing into two complementary parts:

- unity within an individual paragraph
- unity sustained from one paragraph to the next

Unity Within the Paragraph: Continuity of Key Words

Perhaps the best way to insure unity within a paragraph is to keep in mind that a paragraph usually develops a single idea. Once you know what you want to convey, you can maintain unity by concentrating on that main idea and its various implications. One way to make your paragraphs unified, and to keep yourself on the subject, is to choose key words that consistently refer to some aspect of the paragraph's topic. Consider the following paragraph from Joan Didion's essay "Where the Kissing Never Stops," about Joan Baez and her Institute for the Study of Nonviolence:

> The school itself is an old whitewashed adobe house quite far out among the yellow hills and dusty scrub oaks of the Upper Carmel Valley. Oleanders support a torn wire fence around the school, and there is no sign, no identification at all. The adobe was a one-room country school until 1950; after that it was occupied in turn by the So Help Me Hannah Poison Oak Remedy Laboratory and by a small shotgun-shell manufacturing business, two enterprises which apparently did not present the threat to property values that Miss Baez does. She bought the place in the fall of 1965, after the County Planning Commission told her that zoning prohibited her from running the school in her house, which is on a ten-acre piece a few miles away. Miss Baez is the vice president of the Institute, and its sponsor; the $120 fee paid by each student for each six-week session includes lodging, at an apartment house in Pacific Grove, and does not meet the school's expenses. Miss Baez not only has a $40,000 investment in the school property but is responsible as well for the salary of Ira Sandperl, who is the president of the Institute, the leader of the discussions, and in fact the *éminence grise* of the entire project. "You might think we're starting in a very small way," Ira Sandperl says. "Sometimes the smallest things can change the course of history. Look at the Benedictine order."
> —*Slouching Towards Bethlehem,* Dell Publishing Co., Inc., 1968

In this paragraph we have underlined the words that refer to either Joan Baez or her school. You'll note that these key words, which reflect the paragraph's subject, appear throughout the paragraph, keeping the reader on the subject. (Note also that in the last few lines, Ira Sandperl's name appears, acting as a transition into the next paragraph, which is about Joan Baez's relationship with him.)

In this student passage comparing the artistic abilities of children and chimpanzees, the writer uses the same principle—continuity of key words—to both integrate and develop her paragraph, discussing the progression that the chimp and the child make as they grow older.

> At age two, both a human child and a chimpanzee are ready to explore the world of representational art. After both have found that tapping a pencil to a blank sheet of paper produces not only sound

but a visual product, their interest in drawing begins. They both gain momentum in their bold scribbling, the chimp to a greater degree because of his rapidly developing muscular system. At age three, they begin to simplify the confused scribbling, making outlines of geometric shapes—circles, squares, and the like. The child and the chimp both cut their circles with crosses and divide their squares diagonally. At this point, the chimp is making fan patterns and is marking the inside of the circle. But the chimp's art will never reach the heights that the child's will. The chimp will not add details to his circle in the form of hair, eyes, and ears. This stage is the precursor to the earliest representation produced by the typical child. The chimp grows, but his pictures do not.

If you go through this paragraph and underline the words that refer to the child, the chimpanzee, or art, you'll see that these key words help hold the paragraph together and make it easy for the writer to progress smoothly in her discussion.

EXERCISE 1: Continuity of Key Words

Using our discussion as a guide, rewrite the following paragraph, making it more unified by providing the continuity that it lacks. (You'll probably find this exercise easier if you identify the subjects of clauses—which should usually be key words in any paragraph—before you begin revising.)

Many of us tend to be careless with words we should reserve for special uses. A lot of people toss around the words "friend" and "love," for example, but we may not stop to think what these words ought to mean. Someone may say he "loves" Chevrolet Monzas, meaning really that he finds them stylish and fun to drive. We hear people say they "loved" *Star Wars,* though they probably mean more precisely that they found it entertaining and perhaps visually spectacular. Similarly, you should not refer to a business acquaintance or someone who sits next to you in class as a "friend." Certain words, like rare, mint-condition coins, lose their value when they are thoughtlessly and ubiquitously circulated.

Transitions Within the Paragraph

While continuity of key words keeps you and your readers on the subject, transitions help you make the connection between one idea and another. In a good paragraph, one sentence sets the stage for the next, establishing one point as it prepares for what follows.

Transitions can be anything from a one-word statement of contrast like "however" to long clauses that tie a new point to a previous one. Notice that the following passage employs the full range of transitions along with the consistent use of key words to keep the paragraph unified:

> How can we corrupt an honest person? Conversely, how can we get a person to be *more* honest? One way is to capitalize on the dissonance that results from making a difficult decision. Suppose you are a college student enrolled in a biology course. Your grade will hinge on the final exam that you are now taking. The key question on the exam involves some material that you know fairly well—but, because of anxiety, you draw a blank. You are sitting there in a nervous sweat. You look up and, lo and behold, you happen to be sitting behind a woman who is the smartest person in the class (who also happens, fortunately, to be the person with the most legible handwriting in the class). You glance down and you notice that she is just completing her answer to the crucial question. You know that you could easily read her answer if you chose to. What do you do? Your conscience tells you that it's wrong to cheat—and yet, if you don't cheat, you are certain to get a poor grade. You wrestle with your conscience. Regardless of whether you decide to cheat or not to cheat, you are doomed to experience dissonance. If you cheat, your cognition "I am a decent moral person" is dissonant with your cognition "I have just committed an immoral act." If you decide to resist temptation, your cognition "I want to get a good grade" is dissonant with your cognition "I could have acted in such a way that would have insured that I got a good grade, but I chose not to."
>
> —Elliot Aronson, *The Social Animal,* 2nd edition
> W.H. Freeman and Company, 1976

After finding as many transitions in the previous passage as you can, check the annotated version below, in which we've briefly labelled most of them:

CONTRASTS TWO KEY QUESTIONS — How can we corrupt an honest person? (Conversely,) how can we — REFERENCE TO PREVIOUS TWO SENTENCES

INTENSIFIES WORD FROM PREVIOUS SENTENCE — get a person to be (more) honest? (One way) is to capitalize on the dissonance that results from making a difficult decision. (Suppose) — SHIFT TO SECOND PERSON - YOU / SUPPOSE - THUS INVOLVING READER. SETS UP HYPOTHETICAL EXAMPLE

REPEATS "EXAM" ADDS KEY INFORMATION — you are a college student enrolled in a biology course. Your (grade) will hinge on the final (exam) that you are now taking. The key question on the exam involves some material that you know fairly well—

CONTRAST BETWEEN CLAUSES — (but,) because of anxiety, you draw a blank. You are sitting there in — REFERS TO "BIOLOGY COURSE" FROM PREVIOUS SENTENCE

a nervous sweat. You (look up) and, lo and behold, you happen to be sitting behind a woman who is the smartest person in the class (who — REPEATED CONSTRUCTION WITH VARIATION

ADDS KEY INFORMATION — (also) happens, fortunately, to be the person with the most legible handwriting in the class). You (glance down) and you notice that she is just completing her answer to the crucial question. You know that you could easily read her answer if you chose to. What do you do? Your conscience tells you that it's wrong to cheat—and yet, if you don't cheat, you are certain to get a poor grade. You wrestle with your conscience. Regardless of whether you decide to cheat or not to cheat, you are doomed to experience dissonance. If you cheat, your cognition "I am a decent moral person" is dissonant with your cognition "I have just committed an immoral act." If you decide to resist temptation, your cognition "I want to get a good grade" is dissonant with your cognition "I could have acted in such a way that would have insured that I got a good grade, but I chose not to."

[Marginal annotations:]
RHETORICAL QUESTION BASED ON INFORMATION PRESENTED SO FAR AND INTRODUCING REST OF PARAGRAPH
RECAPS PREVIOUS TWO SENTENCES
CONTRAST BETWEEN CLAUSES
INTRODUCES EXAMPLES OF "DISSONANCE"
REFERS TO ONE RECAPPED OPTION
REFERS TO OTHER RECAPPED OPTION

In most cases transitions are essential to good sense. Without them, movement from one idea to the other often seems disjointed. Notice, for example, the way the first paragraph below reads in comparison with the second.

> The leadership of a political party may not always follow the wishes of the party members. California's Republican leaders seem adamant about retaining a winner-take-all primary. Rank and file Republicans in that state oppose the concept. The leaders have blocked every attempt to abolish the practice. They insist that a winner-take-all primary is the fairest method of selecting candidates. California Republicans now have the only winner-take-all primary in the nation.

> The leadership of a political party may not always follow the wishes of the party members. The California Republican primary is a case in point. California's Republican leaders seem adamant about retaining a winner-take-all primary, even though rank and file Republicans in that state oppose the concept. So far, the leaders have blocked every attempt to abolish the practice. They insist, in their defense, that a winner-take-all primary is the fairest method of selecting candidates. Interestingly—but perhaps not surprisingly—California Republicans now have the only winner-take-all primary in the nation.

After reading the first paragraph, perhaps you can eventually fit together the writer's thoughts. But it might take some effort. Part of what good writing does, and what transitions do, is to help the reader avoid having to make this effort.

In addition to smoothing out the movement from one sentence to another, transitions can add to the writer's meaning. When we read in the second paragraph, "Interestingly—but not surprisingly—California Republicans now have the only winner-take-all primary in the nation," we come away with a much more complete sense of the writer's message, and an appreciation for his cynicism.

Beyond the one-word forms, transitions can be as varied as your imagination and the demands of your writing. "To the naive observer, this is somewhat startling . . ." for example is not a standard transitional phrase like "on the other hand." Yet certain standard forms do occur in good writing, and the following list, while not exhaustive, will help you pick an appropriate transition to serve your purpose.*

Transition Words

TRANSITIONS OF CONTRAST

however

nevertheless

on the other hand

despite the fact that

but

yet

still

though

TRANSITIONS OF TIME

meanwhile

at first

finally

subsequently

initially

to begin with

then

next

afterwards

before

until

TRANSITIONS OF ADDITION

furthermore

in addition

moreover

further

also

and

another

at the same time

beyond

*For a more complete discussion of one-word transitions, see Transitional Expressions, page 213.

TRANSITIONS OF RESULT

as a result
consequently
therefore
accordingly
thus

TRANSITIONS OF EMPHASIS

more/most important
significantly

EXERCISE 2: Transitions Within the Paragraph

Necessary transitions are missing from the following paragraph. Rewrite it, adding transitions that make the paragraph clearer and smoother. You may want to make changes, additions, or deletions.

Many families seem to find it difficult to get by unless they have two incomes. They feel they need two wage earners, or one wage earner holding down two jobs. The family may believe that it can't make ends meet. This feeling may stem from the inflated state of the economy and the increasing cost of goods and services. Gasoline has nearly tripled in price in the past decade, and fewer and fewer families can afford even modest homes. Many families feel that one income is not enough to provide even basic necessities. The two-income family may reflect greed rather than need. The price of gasoline, homes, and food has skyrocketed. Sales of home computers, hot-dog cookers, campers, electronic games, roller skates, and designer clothes have risen. These items are hardly necessities. They seem to be the indulgences of people who have more money than they know what to do with. Are most two-income families barely getting by? Are they accumulating money and products out of a need to consume rather than to survive?

Transitions Between Paragraphs

In order to help your readers grasp the unified scheme of your essay, you must consider the movement of thought between one paragraph and another. This movement is, of course, just an extension of the clear and logical transitions you should provide within a paragraph (see "Transitions Within the Paragraph," in the previous section).

Once again, we are talking about providing your readers with transitions that allow *them* to see how you move your ideas along, and that help *you* to unfold your subject clearly. Like transitions between sentences, transitions between paragraphs can be categorized:

- repetition of key words and phrases
- parallel sentence structure
- transitional words and phrases ("Let me explain," "As was stated above," "Another reason . . .," "Nevertheless," etc.)
- explicit reference to specific material given already
- implicit reference to specific material given already

Take a look at the following excerpt from an essay by politician Shirley Chisholm, "I'd Rather Be Black than Female." In each paragraph after the first, we've underlined the introductory segments, which provide transitions from the paragraphs that precede them.

I'D RATHER BE BLACK THAN FEMALE

[1] If I said that being black is a greater handicap than being a woman, probably no one would question me. Why? Because "we all know" there is prejudice against black people in America. That there is a prejudice against women is an idea that still strikes nearly all men—and, I am afraid, most women—as bizarre.

[2] Prejudice against blacks was invisible to most white Americans for many years. When blacks finally started to "mention" it, with sit-ins, boycotts, and freedom rides, Americans were incredulous. "Who, us?" they asked in injured tones. "We're prejudiced?" It was the start of a long, painful re-education for white America. It will take years for whites—including those who think of themselves as liberals—to discover and eliminate the racist attitudes they all actually have.

[3] How much harder will it be to eliminate the prejudice against women? I am sure it will be a longer struggle. Part of the problem is that women in America are much more brainwashed and content with their roles as second-class citizens than blacks ever were.

[4] Let me explain. I have been active in politics for more than twenty years. For all but the last six, I have done the work—all the tedious details that make the difference between victory and defeat on election day—while men reaped the rewards, which is almost invariably the lot of women in politics.

[5] It is still women—about three million volunteers—who do most of this work in the American political world. The best any of them can hope for is the honor of being district or county vice-chairman, a kind of separate-but-equal position with which a

woman is rewarded for years of faithful envelope stuffing and card-party organizing. In such a job, she gets a number of free trips to state and sometimes national meetings and conventions, where her role is supposed to be to vote the way her male chairman votes.

[6] When I tried to break out of that role in 1963 and run for the New York State Assembly seat from Brooklyn's Bedford-Stuyvesant, the resistance was bitter. From the start of that campaign, I faced undisguised hostility because of my sex.

—McCall's, August 1970

This is what the underlined segments do:

PARAGRAPH 2:

"Prejudice against blacks was invisible to most whites for many years." This sentence echoes a key phrase of Paragraph 1, "there is prejudice against black people in America." It also expands implicitly on the idea in Paragraph 1 that prejudice against women is invisible to most people.

PARAGRAPH 3:

"How much harder will it be to eliminate the prejudice against women?" By setting up a comparison ("harder"), this sentence refers to the difficulty of eliminating racist attitudes described in Paragraph 2 and also allows Chisholm to open up the topic at the heart of her essay: sexism against women.

PARAGRAPH 4:

"Let me explain." With this transitional clause, Chisholm tells her readers that she will be explaining her statement that women in America are "brainwashed and content with their roles as second-class citizens."

PARAGRAPH 5:

"It is still women—about three million volunteers—who do most of this work in the American political world." Here Chisholm quantitatively reinforces the key idea of Paragraph 4, that it has always been the lot of women in politics to do the "work." Here she brings this idea up to the present. Notice also that she repeats the key words "women," "politics (political world)," and "work."

PARAGRAPH 6:

"When I tried to break out of that role in 1963 . . ." Notice the explicit reference ("that role") to the clause in Paragraph 5, "where her role is supposed to be to vote the way her male chairman votes." Chisholm's repetition of the word "role" (rather than the substitution of a synonym) provides a further link to the paragraph above.

Chisholm does no more than other writers who are conscious of their material and considerate of their readers: she moves reasonably and clearly from idea to idea, from paragraph to paragraph.

We have illustrated a few ways in which one writer chose to guide her readers, but these aren't the only choices you have to guide yours. We can give you a further sense of the range available to you with an illustration:

Suppose that you're angered by what strikes you as irresponsible reporting in the press—lurid stories of crime and disasters; the premature disclosure of information in sensitive situations like criminal trials and international crises; and a casual, sometimes sloppy handling of facts. You decide to write an essay advocating self-restraint by the press, introducing your paper with a paragraph that acknowledges your opposition:

> No one would deny that the First Amendment guarantee of freedom of the press provides essential protection for our democracy. The press must be free—free to expose corruption and incompetence in government, to record the promise and threat of advancing science, to give us the facts we need to make political, social, and economic decisions wisely. Whether imposed by government fiat or brandished by pressure groups, any external threat to freedom of the press endangers all the other guarantees in the Bill of Rights and the rest of the Constitution.

Now look at a few ways you might lead in to your next paragraph:

subordinate clause	Because the press generally is free from outside restraint, it must be willing to restrain itself.
conjunction	So the press must be willing to limit its own freedom, exercising the power that neither government nor special interests should interfere with.
phrase	Given this freedom, the press must be willing to exercise self-restraint.
sentence	Yet freedom from outside interference does not give the press license to behave irresponsibly.

You could probably come up with many more examples than these, depending upon the connections between ideas that you had in mind. What we want to stress is that you don't have to rely on formulas to get you and your readers through your essays. If you credit yourself as an interesting guide, you'll avoid falling into traps like this:

Thesis:	In this essay I am going to tell you about three X's.
Paragraph One:	The *first* X is . . .
Paragraph Two:	The *second* X is . . .
Paragraph Three:	The *third* X is . . .
Concluding Paragraph:	*Thus* I have presented the three main X's . . . ("transitions" italicized)

These "transitions" fail to show *how* your ideas are connected. If you find yourself resorting to transitions like these, perhaps you should check to make sure that your ideas *are* in fact connected in some logical, coherent way, rather than just sharing the same page.

As with all good essay writers, it is part of *your* function to provide your readers with a path worth following as you take them through your essay, carefully and interestingly leading them in one end, and, with as much care and interest, leading them out the other.

EXERCISE 3: Transitions Between Paragraphs

In the following excerpts from essays, we have dropped the transitions between paragraphs. Where we've left a blank, try adding a word, phrase, or sentence to bridge the gap between the two paragraphs.

1. Some words are what we call "colorful." By this we mean that they are calculated to produce a picture or induce an emotion. They are dressy instead of plain, specific instead of general, loud instead of soft. Thus, in place of "Her heart beat," we may write, "Her heart *pounded, throbbed, fluttered, danced.*" Instead of "He sat in his chair," we may say, "He *lounged, sprawled, coiled.*" Instead of "It was hot," we may say, "It was *blistering, sultry, muggy, suffocating, steamy, wilting.*"

   _____, it should not be supposed that the fancy word is always better. Often it is as well to write "Her heart beat" or "It was hot" if that is all it did or all it was. Ages differ in how they like their prose. The nineteenth century liked it rich and smoky. The twentieth has usually preferred it lean and cool. The twentieth-century writer, like all writers, is forever seeking the exact word, but he is wary of sounding feverish. He tends to pitch it low, to understate it, to throw it away. He knows that if he gets too colorful, the audience is likely to giggle.

—Paul Roberts, "How To Say Nothing in 500 Words,"
Understanding English, Harper & Row, 1956.

2. Roses are unbelievably tough and long-suffering. In one hurricane, climbing roses on Long Island were covered with salt water yet went on to bloom better than ever the next summer. A terrific New Year's Day ice storm in New Jersey broke many frozen canes yet made little difference to June bloom. Once in August a huge tree fell on a client's bushes, completely smashing two dozen roses. We trimmed the plants near the ground level and by October every bush had sent up new canes and most were in bloom.

_____

_____, roses provide the longest possible blooming season. In the suburban New York area hybrid teas provide bloom for about six months and by choosing a few early–blooming species such as *Rosa primula* or *R. hugonis,* which sometimes start in April, the season can be lengthened to nearly eight months. I have cut buds of Else Poulen in early December and once I took sprays of Orange Triumph to brighten evergreens at a Christmas Greens show. Long after chrysanthemums are black with frost there is color in the rose garden.

—Cynthia Westcott, *Anyone Can Grow Roses,*
Macmillan, 1965

3. A few months ago, I went to dinner at the house of a woman who had just been through a weekend of *est* (Erhard Seminar Training), the latest and most popular new therapeutic enthusiasm. The training is designed to provide its participants with a new sense of fulfillment and competence, and it seemed to have worked with my hostess, for she assured me that her life had radically changed, that she felt different about herself, that she was happier and more efficient, and that she kept her house much cleaner than before.

_____

_____, but in the course of the evening she also added that because of the training she now understood: (1) that the individual will is all-powerful and totally determines one's fate; (2) that she felt neither guilt nor shame about anyone's fate and that those who were poor and hungry must have wished it on themselves; (3) that the North Vietnamese must have wanted to be bombed, or else it could not have happened to them; (4) that a friend of hers who had been raped and murdered in San Francisco was to be pitied for having willed it to occur; (5) that in her weekend at *est* she had attained full enlightenment; (6) that she was God; (7) that whatever one thought to be true was true beyond all argument; (8) that I was also God, and that my ideas were also true, but not as true as hers because I had not had the training; and (9) that my use of logic to criticize her beliefs was unfair, because reason was "irrational," though she could not tell me why.

—Peter Marin, "The New Narcissism,"
Harper's Magazine, October 1975

4. Two very different conceptions of human life are struggling for mastery of the world. In the West we see man's greatness in the individual life. A great society for us is one which is composed of individuals who, as far as is humanly possible, are happy, free, and creative. We do not think that individuals should be alike. We conceive society as like an orchestra, in which the different performers have different parts to play and different instruments upon which to perform, and in which cooperation results from a conscious common purpose. We believe that each individual should have his proper pride. He should have his personal conscience and his personal aims, which he should be free to develop except where they can be shown to cause injury to others. We attach importance to the diminution of suffering and poverty, to the increase of knowledge, and the production of beauty and art. The State for us is a convenience, not an object of worship.

The Russian Government _____.

The individual is thought of no importance: he is expendable. What is important is the State, which is regarded as something almost divine and having a welfare of its own not consisting in the welfare of citizens. This view, which Marx took over from Hegel, is fundamentally opposed to the Christian ethic, which in the West is accepted by free-thinkers as much as by Christians. In the Soviet world human dignity counts for nothing.

—Bertrand Russell, "If We Are to Survive
This Dark Time—," © 1961 George Allen and Unwin, Ltd.

5. In jail I learned much that I could never have learned isolated in the ivory tower that was my home town. Rapists, killers, drunks and juvenile delinquents were all to be found there, and they gave lectures endlessly on a wide variety of curricula. I learned how to hot-wire a car, jimmy a door, brew potato mash and chew marigold seeds. More important than these skills, which I have, thankfully, never been called upon to use, I learned about life. Not the success-oriented, structured life that one plans, and is planned for

one—but a life of poverty, no education, hopelessness, and an end-less cycle of crime and punishment.

For instance, I learned how easy it is to get along with all kinds of people if one only listens—and how willing people are to tell you their life-stories (even if they're only 50 per cent true) if you have a sympathetic ear. Most importantly, I learned about freedom, a concept I knew abstractly but had always taken for granted. Never again will that be the case. In jail the only light at the end of the tunnel is the thought of freedom; every activity, every thought is directed toward that goal. The great spiritual uplifting one experiences when that freedom is finally granted is like being reborn—not as an innocent babe, not even as a footloose 17-year-old (I had turned 18 in jail), but as someone with a new awareness of the meaning of life, liberty, and happiness. It was an expensive lesson, but for me one that need never be repeated.

—Student Essay

EXERCISE 4: Your Own Transitions

Take an essay you've written recently, whether for this class or any other, and underline all existing transitions, both within paragraphs and between them. Supply additional transitions where you feel your paper needs them, and strengthen any that are weak.

CONCLUSIONS

It's not always easy to end an essay gracefully. Part of the problem is that many students are stuck on the idea that a paper's conclusion merely repeats, in abbreviated form, what the introduction and body have already said. Some writers even go so far as to conclude with an exact restatement of their thesis statement, perhaps introduced with a creaking "Thus I have shown that. . . ." The results are understandably redundant and dull.

How much you should repeat from the body of your paper depends on the length of the paper and the complexity of its ideas. A reader will probably appreciate a clear summary in a fifteen-page paper, but not in a 500-word essay. If you *do* decide to paraphrase your ideas at the end of a paper, make sure to reword them enough to avoid mechanically repeating what you've already said.

Though the main function of a conclusion is to give readers a sense of completion, leaving them with the ideas you wanted to emphasize, a conclusion may do other things as well. For instance, it may

- show why you have gone to the trouble of developing your argument, perhaps relating the topic to a larger context
- identify related topics beyond the scope of the essay and suggest areas for future study
- leave readers questioning their own attitudes toward the topic—perhaps challenging them to act upon what they have learned
- offer readers insight or information they would not have accepted or understood without having read the rest of the paper
- encourage readers to find out more about the topic

It's harder to illustrate a good conclusion than a good introduction, because a concluding paragraph depends on everything that has gone before. We don't have the space (nor you the time) to wade through several complete essays just to look at how they end. But we can at least show you a few of the most common ways to get out of an essay smoothly.

The Summing Up

In this concluding paragraph from a student essay, the writer brings together the ideas central to her thesis about the nature and value of our sense of the past.

> I cannot say that we are all perennial amnesia victims, forgetting our beginnings for the pleasure of the "moment," because there are too many signs of a yearning for the past. However, I do wonder whether our solutions to the problem of retrieving the past are not based on illusory nostalgia: an escape to the pastoral, a romantic view of a city or a revolution. We clamor after the past even while we are thinking of that new place we will be or that new, better paying job we will have tomorrow. When I think back on the secure feeling I had in that classroom with the rain beating down outside, I realize it was a result of the time and effort I put in that place and those people, of the pain I experienced and the happiness I enjoyed. A sense of the past doesn't appear out of mid-air; it comes from the caring for, commitment to, and experience of the place where we live, whether or not we voluntarily choose that place.

The Chronological Ending

When an essay is organized chronologically, it makes sense that it should end with the most recent development in a chain of events. An essay tracing the development of Thomas Jefferson's political philosophy might end with the view he came to late in life; an essay about a personal experience might conclude with the writer's present reflections on what happened to him earlier. The following is the conclusion of a paper describing a student's experiences during World War II, experiences that replaced his eager youthfulness with maturity, fear, and weariness.

> Things got awful bad around Tulagi and Guadalcanal, and the remnants of old Task Group 13 picked up their very tired butts and went there for a crack at it. Just off Steward Island the showdown came, and it was a black day. The Japanese air strike arrived at dawn and worked the old *Hornet* and *Enterprise* over with a passion, leaving the *Hornet* dead in the water. They returned every 36 minutes all day long and tore the ship up. The *Porter* was sunk and the *Enterprise* out of action but afloat. I got in the water at five in the evening and was picked up by the USS *Anderson* at dark. All night the Japanese closed while the *Anderson* and one other ship stayed back to try to sink the *Hornet* while the rest of Task Group 13 fled. During that day I was so afraid and shattered I thought my head would break. I stood on the deck of the *Anderson* and shook out of control. I had grown a million years old at the age of eighteen.
>
> I have raised four sons and watched them take years and years to mature, and I have not begrudged them any of the time they took because of the one day when I grew up. I was on two carriers later that saw a lot of action, but the fear and realization and the growing up was over. Them people were shooting at an old man.

And a student paper on Stephen Crane's short story "The Open Boat" concludes by examining the end of the story in light of a theme running through the work:

> The theme of man-helping-man is dramatically emphasized in the conclusion of Crane's tale. After several unsuccessful attempts to reach the shore, the men are making their final approach when the tiny boat overturns; they begin to swim toward the beach. In this desperate swim for life, the oiler—depicted as an individual suited to solitary action—races toward the shore, leaving the others behind. The injured captain, the cook, and the correspondent are not strong swimmers, but the cold water has not dissolved the bond they had established in the lifeboat; they remain in contact with each other, each man helping the others, in some small way, to reach the shore. With the aid of a rescuer, the three men safely reach dry land. There they find the lifeless body of the oiler: the man who left the group in an attempt to save himself has drowned. Against the violent and indifferent sea, a lone man did not survive; three men, working together for the benefit of the group, reached safety.

Putting Your Topic in Perspective

As we said earlier, many essays conclude by relating the topic to a larger context, somewhat the way a photographer fits the camera with a wider-angle lens to take in a wider view. The following conclusion is taken from a student paper arguing against the use of 2,4-D (an insecticide many believe to be dangerous) in the Oregon redwood forest. In his final paragraph, the writer places his topic in historical perspective, relating it to the way we have repeatedly waited too long to ban other chemical sprays and urging his reader to join in the battle against 2,4-D:

> This apparent blindness in the face of public outcry and conflicting scientific opinion has characterized our history of handling the chemical spray problem. DDT was not only legal but federally endorsed until flocks of birds and other wildlife disappeared. Substance 2,4,5-T (a close cousin of 2,4-D) was outlawed only in 1978, when contrary to industry claims the Environmental Protection Agency determined it was indeed a major factor in the high incidence of miscarriages among women living in areas where it was used. The deadly aftereffects of Agent Orange we are just now learning about. Must we wait to act until the Oregon woods are empty of all sound save the grinding of chain saws and the booming crash of fallen lumber? Let's stop the spray now.

And in the last paragraph of "The Arts of Selling," Aldous Huxley "widens the angle of his lens" by examining how the methods and spirit of commercial advertising (the topic he has been dealing with throughout) have encroached on American life to the point that they now determine how we elect our political leaders:

> In one way or another, as vigorous he-man or kindly father, the candidate must be glamorous. He must also be an entertainer who never bores his audience. Inured to television and radio, that audience is accustomed to being distracted and does not like to be asked to concentrate or make a prolonged intellectual effort. All speeches by the entertainer-candidate must therefore be short and snappy. The great issues of the day must be dealt with in five minutes at the most—and preferably (since the audience will be eager to pass on to something a little livelier than inflation or the H-bomb) in sixty seconds flat. The nature of oratory is such that there has always been a tendency among politicians and clergymen to over-simplify complex issues. From a pulpit or a platform even the most conscientious of speakers finds it very difficult to tell the whole truth. The methods now being used to merchandise the political candidate

as though he were a deodorant positively guarantee the electorate against ever hearing the truth about anything.
—*Brave New World Revisited,* Harper & Row, 1958

In My End Is My Beginning

Many conclusions return to something mentioned in the introduction. They have the effect of completing a circle, returning to where the essay began but suggesting the richness of everything that has come between. For instance, a student's essay about her grandmother began with the writer poised outside the grandmother's door, wondering whether to disturb her for a late-night heart-to-heart. The body of the paper "flashed back" to the writer's first meeting with her years before and their changing relationship over the years. The essay concluded with the writer's realization that her grandmother would still want and be able to help:

> It was late, but I knew Gram Marie would be awake. I knocked and went in.

The following excerpts from a student essay show how the details in a concluding paragraph can effectively contrast with those in the introduction. The paper begins:

> Ten years ago, when I graduated from high school, I decided to become an individual. I went out and bought a Volkswagen camper with a multicolored paint job, necessary dents, and mandatory missing hub-caps: the appropriate vehicle to have as a symbol of my newly found independence. I wore the clothes that showed my allegiance to the subculture to which I had decided to belong. I was never seen without my leather jacket with fringe hanging to the ankles and torn faded blue jeans with holes in the knees and patches on the crotch. Dirty worn-out hiking boots with long laces, tied behind the ankle instead of the conventional place, were the final touch to my outfit. I decided to live communally because that was the fashion of the lifestyle I had chosen. All day the five of us sat in the living room on huge pillows, listening to Dylan records, memorizing his profound lyrics, and reiterating his philosophy to each other as though his thoughts were our own. I had all the appropriate rhetoric memorized to be recalled when the conversation needed the "heavy" insight only Dylan could provide.

The body of the paper describes how the student gradually realized that far from succeeding in his quest to become an individual, he was only following the lead of other people. His conclusion shows how he has changed over the years:

> Today I drive an old beat-up car, not as a statement of my identity, but because it's what I enjoy and can afford. I dress in the way I feel comfortable, not because my clothes identify me with any group or philosophy. I live peacefully and simply, spending my free time nurturing my garden, not because it's the "organic" thing to do but because it gives me comfort. I try to develop my own ideas and express them in a way that shows something of myself and my experience. I think I have finally accomplished what I set out to do ten years ago.

The same "circular" pattern can work in an argumentative paper. In an essay maintaining that sports *don't* build character, *San Francisco Chronicle* sportswriter Lowell Cohn begins by describing an advertisement that reflects the cultural myths about sport: a boy is receiving his first gun as his father and grandfather look on with mingled love and pride. The essay concludes by returning for another look at the ad:

> I'd like you to imagine the ad for one last moment. What's missing in the picture? Think hard. The mother. For obvious reasons. He-men are not supposed to be mother-tied. Ever since we lived in caves, the important work of killing has been men's business. But there's something else the designers of the ad never thought of. If the mother were there, she might have put a crimp in the ritual scene by saying something deflating like, "Come off it, boys."

When Somebody Else Said It Better

A time-honored way to get out of an essay gracefully is to leave your reader with an apt quotation:

> But it is a mistake to regard any rules about writing as absolute. Near the end of his essay "Politics and the English Lanaguage," George Orwell gives six helpful guidelines for producing clear, effective prose. His sixth is "Break any of these rules sooner than say anything outright barbarous."

Another example, this one from a student essay arguing that adults all too often ruin sports for children:

> Instead of creating a love for sports, many coaches and parents teach children to play to win no matter what. As a result, many a discouraged child wishes to have nothing to do with an activity which brings only pressure and anxiety for him and glory for so few.

> If coaches defined sports the way *Webster's New Collegiate Dictionary* does, there would be more children *and* adults enjoying athletic pastimes today: "sport . . . (1a) a source of diversion: recreation; (1b) . . . a physical activity engaged in for pleasure. . . . *syn* see FUN."

Ending with a quotation by someone your reader is likely to respect can also lend support for the points you've been arguing in the body of the essay.

Leave Them with a Story

An essay may finish with a particularly appropriate anecdote that epitomizes the subject in some way. A student's affectionate (but humorous) look at his aunt concludes with this paragraph:

> Arriving home late one afternoon after a tiring day of screaming kids and parent-teacher conferences, Aunt Katharine sat down in front of her television to relax with a cup of tea and an old movie. After several minutes of viewing a singularly uninteresting dark screen, not daring to investigate further than the on-off switch, she telephoned for a repairman. When he arrived, he was left alone with the set and after only two or three minutes had completed the repairs. Aunt Katharine thanked him for his fast and efficient service, adding that she couldn't understand why the set, which was only about a year old, had malfunctioned. As he gave her the yellow billing slip, he replied, "Sometimes these newer models work better if you plug them in."

The Descriptive Closing

You can also conclude with an evocative description, one that relates literally or symbolically to your subject. One of our students recently handed in an excellent essay about a demolished seaside amusement park, itself a symbol for her family, once happily united but long since divided. The final sentence draws upon details mentioned earlier in the paper, including Laughing Sal, a motorized mannequin who presided over the entrance to the Fun House, rocking back and forth as she issued recorded laughter.

> As I search the trashy empty lot for something familiar, a feeling comes over me. I can feel my hands getting heavy with grief in my sweater pockets. I can see the dented Schlitz cans and cigarette butts on the ground blurring before me. I have learned and accepted that Playland, like my family, is gone and remains only in my memory.
>
> Finally I turn and walk off, but I find myself glancing behind my

shoulder as if still hoping to see Playland miraculously materialize with its winding roller coasters, peanut brittle, and mechanical lady laughing far off in the dense fog.

Some Last Thoughts on Conclusions

In our experience, many students worry too much about their conclusions. They feel as if every paper they write must end with a grand statement on life and humanity, as if they must always tie up their ideas with the verbal equivalent of a satin bow. Sometimes a note of simple sincerity is the most effective way to end a paper. The philosopher Bertrand Russell completed a section of his autobiography with two eloquently simple sentences: "This has been my life. I have found it worth living, and would gladly live it again if the chance were offered me."

One of us remembers returning an "A" paper to a student who was amazed at having done so well. "My paper didn't even have a conclusion," he explained. "After trying for an hour to think of a good ending, I just turned in the paper without one and hoped you wouldn't grade me down too much for it." Actually, the instructor hadn't even felt the absence of a concluding paragraph: the paper ended smoothly and appropriately. Perhaps this student had so much trouble thinking of a way to end the paper because he realized, unconsciously at least, that he'd said everything he had to say.

So if you're having trouble thinking of a way out of a paper, try looking at the last paragraph you've written to see if it already brings the paper to rest or if it can be revised to do so. As an alternative, you can look through the body of the paper to see whether there's a sentence or two you could move to the end without doing violence to the middle. Since writing a good conclusion is partially a matter of sound, you may even want to set aside a phrase or two that strikes you as particularly appropriate while you're writing the paper.

EXERCISE 5: Introductions and Conclusions

To help sharpen your sense of how different types of introductions and conclusions work, take a look at some professional essays that you find in anthologies, magazines, newspapers, etc. From among the ones you look at, find three that have the kinds of introductions we've discussed in this chapter, and three that have the kinds of conclusions we've just discussed. (You can pick an essay that does double duty—that has both a type of introduction and a type of conclusion we've covered.)

Be prepared to discuss how the introductions and conclusions work in relation to the rest of the essay and whether or not you think they're effective.

REVISING

> Do not be afraid to seize whatever you have written and cut it to ribbons; it can always be restored to its original condition in the morning, if that course seems best. Remember, it is no sign of weakness or defeat that your manuscript ends up in need of major surgery. This is a common occurrence in all writing, and among the best writers.
>
> William Strunk, Jr., and E.B. White, *The Elements of Style,*
> 3rd edition, Macmillan, 1979

The "best writers" mentioned in the quotation above don't always approach revising in the same way inexperienced writers do. While practiced writers may be afraid they will spoil the stew by tampering with it too much, unpracticed writers are often afraid to look at the brew at all, for fear that they might see odd bits floating around which don't belong, that they might notice that the taste is a little flat and requires additions, that they will discover they haven't followed the recipe very carefully and have instead wound up with some strange concoction.

In other cases it isn't fear at all that prevents student writers from revising. It's reluctance to write more, to work still harder. "After all," many reason, "I've worked hard enough just producing this one draft, so why should I go back and look at it critically? The teacher will do that." Unfortunately, that's just what will happen. The instructor will find, and mark, all the careless errors, all the weaknesses in organization and development, all the clumsy phrases and unclear sentences. And the paper's grade will suffer accordingly. What could have been an A or B paper, or at least a C, will slowly sink beneath that beautiful "pass" line into the murky regions below.

Try to get into the habit of revising what you've written. Note that we say "revising," not just recopying your work onto a fresh, unscribbled page. Revising involves re-examining your papers to discover their weak spots, so you can strengthen them. It means returning to check for mechanical and sentence structure errors. It means looking at your papers again with the critical eye of another person, in order to anticipate objections so you can counter or eliminate them. Revising means going back, and if necessary, redoing anything that needs work. If you can become your own most critical audience, you are on your way to producing better papers.

Like other stages of the writing process, revising takes different forms for different people. Here are some of the ways you can get perspective on your own work, so you can see it clearly and objectively enough to make the necessary changes or additions.

If you can put a rough draft aside for a while, you'll probably find that you can evaluate it more clearly when you look at it again. After some time has elapsed, you aren't so emotionally tied up in a paper, the pride of creation having passed and the memory of the difficulty involved having dimmed. It's often wise to leave a paper for a couple of days, but at the very least leave it for several hours.

When you return to your paper, try reading it out loud, to a friend if you can corral one for a while, to a mirror if you're alone. Chances are that you will stumble over some of the sentences: the ones that need revising. And perhaps certain sections will sound flimsy: the ones that need further support. Maybe you'll find yourself wanting to skip back and forth between sections: the ones that turn out to need reshuffling and reorganization. And certain passages may even make you uncomfortable: the ones that are shaky in reasoning or inappropriate in tone.

Many writers do exactly what Strunk and White suggest, and what we've suggested elsewhere in this book. They cut the paper up into sections, moving them around until the order seems appropriate, even adding sections and transitions to link the ideas more firmly together. Other writers go so far as to *outline* a completed essay, in order to check the relationship of the parts to the whole, and to see whether the paragraphs have enough specifics to be convincing.

Once you have the ability to temporarily disconnect yourself from your papers and view them critically, you can make the necessary revisions. One way to spot things that may need revising is to review old papers that your instructor has corrected. You might discover that you tend to generalize too broadly and to omit supporting evidence. Or you might see that four fragments did you in on your last essay. Or you might note that the remark "fuzzy thinking" occurs frequently in the margins of your papers. When you can identify the traps you have fallen into in the past, you can look for them when you revise. If necessary, you can look up "Fragments" in the Usage Manual of this text and learn what you are doing wrong. You can return to the section on development and remind yourself how to use specific details and examples to back up your thesis.

And in the case of marginal notes you don't understand, you can seek out your instructor and ask for help. Often, instructors will even go over a rough draft with you, if you have specific questions and have done what you can to revise.

You can also use the following checklist to help you in revising your papers. While it may look like a summary of steps you've already gone through, check your work carefully against this list to make sure you've really completed each step. Pay special attention to items 8 and 9, on proofreading for sentence and mechanical errors. You may be reluctant to read over the paper one more time, but if you do look at it critically, you'll probably spot a fragment, a spelling error, or some other minor, or major, problem.

Checklist for Revising Your Essays

1. Have I written an introductory paragraph that will interest my readers and give them enough, but not too much, background on the topic?
2. Do I have a thesis statement (or at least a very clear thesis idea) that controls my essay?
3. Do I "prove" my thesis, backing it up with sufficient examples and explanations?
4. Do I stick to my thesis, never wandering from the point and including irrelevant material?
5. Does each of my paragraphs have a main point, and does each of them connect to my thesis? (A convenient way to check this is to write out your thesis statement and list all the topic sentences underneath it.)
6. Do I link my paragraphs together with transitions, so that my readers move smoothly from one idea to the next?
7. Is my reasoning clear and logical? Have I avoided saying, in effect, "This is just how it is, and I know it's right because I believe it"?
8. Are my sentences correct? Have I avoided run-togethers, parallel structure errors, reference errors, and so on?
9. Have I proofread carefully for mechanical errors, checking areas like spelling, subject–verb agreement, and punctuation?
10. Have I varied my sentences enough so that they are interesting to read, not choppy and repetitious?
11. Have I concluded my essay effectively, leaving readers with a sense of completion?
12. Above all, have I made my meaning clear, so that anyone can follow my ideas?

7

The Sentence Base

Now that we've considered the larger units of the paragraph and the essay, we need to spend some time working with sentences, for paragraphs and essays are only as clear and effective as the sentences that form them. In this chapter and the next, we'll look at ways to add depth and variety to sentences, as well as to strengthen the core of every sentence: the subject and verb.

Students often ask us why we want them to be able to pick out the subject and verb in a sentence. After all, they've been using sentences regularly for years and aren't particularly heartsick that they can't point to one word and say, "That's the subject," then point to another and say, "That's the verb."

By way of analogy, Adrian Cohn, coauthor of *A Handbook of Grammar, Style, and Usage,* points out that a good carpenter doesn't necessarily need to know what a hammer is called, as long as he can use it—until, that is, someone says, "Hand me the hammer." We can apply the same logic to writing sentences. You don't have to know one grammatical term from another—until your instructor, or your own good sense, suggests that part of your sentence needs work. And you can follow your instructor's advice to "choose a more concrete sentence subject" or "change the verb to the active voice" only if you can confidently locate the subject and verb.

Sentences and Independent Clauses

We can define a sentence as a group of words that contains at least one **independent clause.** An independent clause is a group of words that:

- contains at least one subject and one verb
- can stand alone
- can be punctuated like any other sentence, beginning with a capital letter and ending with a period, question mark, or exclamation point

Take a look at the following sentences, in which we have labelled the independent clauses and underlined the subjects once and the verbs twice.

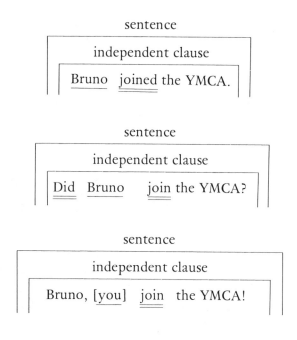

You'll notice that "after he rejected the neighborhood sandlot" contains a subject and a verb but is not marked as an independent clause. This is because it cannot stand by itself as a complete sentence.

Rather, it *depends* on the rest of the sentence for its meaning and is therefore a **dependent clause,** also known as a **subordinate clause.** (You'll have a chance to work extensively with subordinate clauses in Chapter 8.) You should not punctuate a subordinate clause as you do an independent clause; if you do, you will have produced a **fragment:**

> After he rejected the neighborhood sandlot.

Phrases

Groups of words that do not contain both subjects and verbs are called **phrases:**

- running across the crowded street
- under the window in the corner of the room
- in order to pass the course
- such as the Philippines, Guam, and other Pacific Islands
- the problem being my reluctance to get involved in that kind of situation

These, too, if punctuated as sentences, are fragments. (See also "Fragments," p. 334 of the Usage Manual.)

The Sentence Base

At the heart of every independent clause, and therefore also at the heart of every sentence, is the **sentence base:** the subject and verb. If you can recognize the subject and verb in an independent clause, you are ready to control them to your advantage, establishing a strong base which you can expand into an effective, efficient sentence.

- A **verb** can change tense (past/present/future).
- A **subject** answers who? or what? about the verb.

EXAMPLE:

Pavlov's dogs salivated in response to a bell.

Question:	What is the verb in the sentence above? In other words, which word can change tense?
Answer:	"Salivated" can change from past, to present ("salivates"), to future ("will salivate"). Therefore, the verb is "salivated."
Question:	What is the subject in the sentence above? In other words, who or what "salivated"?
Answer:	"Dogs" salivated. Therefore, the subject is "dogs."

EXAMPLE:

Not wanting to offend the policeman, Harry waited patiently at the red light.

> *Question:* What is the verb in the sentence above? Which word can change tense?
>
> *Answer:* "Waited" can change from past, to present ("waits"), to future ("will wait"). The verb is "waited." (Note that neither "wanting" nor "to offend" *has* a tense, as is evident if you try to decide whether they are past, present, or future. Therefore, neither "wanting" nor "to offend" can be the verb in this sentence.)
>
> *Question:* What is the subject in the sentence above? Who or what "waited"?
>
> *Answer:* "Harry" waited. Therefore, the subject is "Harry."

EXERCISE 1

Find the subjects and verbs in the sentences below. The following steps should help you:

 a. Eliminate phrases.
 b. Find the verb first, asking which word can change tense.
 c. Then find the subject, asking who? or what? about the verb.

Examples:

Often <u>scientists</u> <u>illustrate</u> time ~~in terms of space, comparing the history of the earth to the length of a football field, for example~~.

<u>One</u> ~~of the biggest problems facing students~~ <u>is</u> finding enough time ~~for study, work, and a social life~~.

~~In the shadows of the overgrown lot~~ <u>sat</u> a hideous, flea-infested <u>mutt</u>. (Note that in this last sentence, "mutt" is the subject even though it comes after the verb.)

1. My dog usually buries her bones in the backyard by the oak tree near the lawn.
2. The majority of students and teachers will attend the commencement ceremony.
3. In the morning please remind me of my dentist's appointment in Milpitas.
4. The President and the media are trying to work together for the good of the country.

5. My vacation begins next week.
6. On the highest branch of the tree sat a pair of squirrels.
7. Helping the children with their homework will be difficult for parents who haven't studied the new math and transformational grammar.
8. Not to be outdone, Carlos ate the entire apricot cobbler and drank two quarts of milk.
9. Willa Cather, among other women authors, is enjoying a return to popularity.

EXERCISE 2

Tell which of the following are sentences and which are fragments. Be prepared to explain your answers.

1. Going to sleep, he muttered incoherently the lyrics of some Broadway showtune.
2. Fearing the ramifications of his rash behavior.
3. Speak up!
4. Murmuring low.
5. Because he was a lover of music, attending every opera that came to his small town, sometimes taking standing-room tickets when his wallet was lean.
6. And there on the bench sat Flora, as cute as she was when she was a girl in San Antonio.
7. Due to the perseverance of scientists like Madame Curie.
8. It finally happened.
9. The staunchest reactionaries are threatened, too, when basic liberties are denied.

FOCUS

You've no doubt seen snapshots that are out of focus. You can usually get a general sense of the picture, but the fuzziness may irritate you and keep you from knowing exactly what, or whom, you're looking at. Readers are irritated in exactly the same way by unclear writing. And often sentences are fuzzy because their subjects are inappropriate. Notice the difference in the sentences paired below:

> The *incidence* of moonlighting in academia is high.
> Many *teachers* moonlight.

> The *use* of Valium is greater than that of any other prescription drug in the United States.
> *Valium* is the most widely used prescription drug in the United States.

The *composition* of an all-volunteer army serves our country better
than the composition of one drawn from draftees.
An *all-volunteer army* serves our country better than one composed
of draftees.

His *appearance* indicated tiredness.
He looked tired.

To most readers, the second sentence in each pair is clear and
forceful, while the first is unnecessarily wordy and abstract. These
pairs illustrate a rule of thumb about how to construct sentence
bases: When you can, *focus on human or concrete nouns and pronouns as grammatical subjects.*

A "human" subject is, obviously, one referring to a person. A
"concrete" subject refers to something you can see, hear, taste,
touch, or smell. Whatever your topic, when you start writing about it
you're apt to find that you are in fact writing about something
human or concrete. There can be no "art" without artists, no "politics" without voters and politicians, no "youth-oriented advertising
campaigns" without young people, advertisers, and radios, televisions,
magazines, and newspapers. The question you should ask yourself as
you form a sentence is "*Who* or *what* am I really writing about?"
The **focus** (or grammatical subject) of your sentence should reflect
your answer to that question.

EXERCISE 3

Even when trying to focus their writing more concretely, students often feel that their topic demands abstract sentence subjects.
If they're writing about economics, politics, education, business,
freedom, or intelligence, they will use these words, or equally abstract
synonyms, as their only sentence subjects. In fact, though, most
abstractions are really just shorthand ways of representing a set of
concrete or human components. "Medical science," for instance,
encompasses doctors, nurses, syringes, gas chromatographs, tongue
depressors, X-ray machines, and so on. As you found in Chapter 3
on paragraph development, even though you may begin with a fairly
abstract statement as your topic sentence, you need to reinforce and
clarify it with more specific, concrete examples. Similarly, though a
term like "medical science" may be the subject of a topic sentence,
the rest of the paragraph's sentence subjects should tend to be precise
and concrete.

This exercise lists several abstractions. For each one, list
ten human or concrete components, as we've begun doing with
"education":

1. Education: *students, teachers, textbooks, registration forms . . .*
2. Politics
3. Discrimination
4. Poverty
5. Business
6. Recreation
7. Fashion
8. Law

The Benefits of Concrete Focus

If, when possible, you choose concrete sentence subjects, your writing will often be more interesting, simply because people and concrete things are more interesting than abstractions. Think how many people would be eager to read an Ann Landers column about a guilty mother who, having been discovered sneaking a look at her teenage daughter's diary, regrets her inquisitiveness, as opposed to the limited number who would read even a short, exclusively philosophical article about intrafamilial trust and a child's right to privacy.

Second, well-focused sentences—those with human or concrete subjects—are less likely to lead to structural errors. If you have a solid subject, such as "she," "the President," "I," "the voters," "a 1969 Ford Mustang," "twelve students," or "my cat Alphonso," you will be inclined to follow it with a verb that does what a verb is designed to do, to express the action that the subject performs or experiences. *A politician* can mislead constituents, but *politics* can't. *Students* can demand a new bookstore, but *a student rebellion* can't. (We'll be talking more about the important relationship between subjects and verbs later in this section.)

Perhaps most important, knowing something about focus can help you avoid writing the kind of inflated, abstract, and often nearly meaningless prose many inexperienced writers think is the only kind appropriate in the lofty realms of a college course. Trying hard to give weight to his sentence, the writer of empty abstractions often produces something like "Society is responsible for the upsurge of crime in this country." We would find it nearly impossible to infer anything of substance from such a sentence, probably because the writer hasn't decided what he wants to say. A fuzzy subject like "society" can keep a writer from bothering to figure out what he thinks about a topic, but an alert reader won't be fooled.

Trying to use human beings or concrete entities as your grammatical subjects can help you as you write, and the concept of concrete focus is equally useful in editing. Whenever you have the feeling that a sentence you've written is weak or unclear, stop and see what you've made the grammatical subject. For instance, the sentence "The tendency for people not to cheat on their taxes comes from fear of getting caught" isn't essentially about anything as theoretical and nebulous as "tendency"; it's about people. So make "people" the subject: "Most people don't cheat on their taxes because they're afraid of getting caught." Often you won't have to look far for what should be your subject; you'll find it buried elsewhere in the sentence, as "people" got submerged in "the tendency for people not to cheat." And if you don't find your real subject in the sentence, remember to ask yourself what people or concrete things are involved in the subject or situation you're writing about.

EXERCISE 4

Some of the following sentences are poorly focused, but some are fine the way they are. For instance, the following sentence already has a human subject:

> Most students of history and philosophy agree that socialism will never flourish in the United States.

The writer of the next sentence wants to emphasize the abstraction he's discussing:

> Freedom is an elusive term, because each of us defines it differently.

However, this sentence is poorly focused:

> A reluctance to work steadily caused her to be unprepared for the presentation on Monday.

The subject of the sentence, "reluctance," is inappropriately abstract for a sentence that is really about a person. The sentence might be better written

> Because she was reluctant to work steadily, she was unprepared for the presentation on Monday.

Identify the grammatical subject in each of the following sentences, and then revise only those sentences that are poorly focused.

1. A great deal of learning took place in my physics class.
2. The intelligence necessary to understand this concept is possessed by few people.
3. Advocates of gun control laws often fail to consider the problems of implementation and enforcement.
4. The theory of relativity revolutionized modern science.

5. The view from my window enables me to see Central Park.
6. Weather forecasts are often so unreliable as to be useless.
7. His insistence on seeing the manager only caused the saleswoman to finally become angry.
8. My urge to laugh at his predicament had to be controlled.

THE ACTIVE VOICE

What do Tony Bennett, the author of the Book of Genesis, Jimmy Carter, Virginia Woolf, and Ronald Reagan have in common? They all used the *active voice* to make the clear, direct, and forceful statements below:

> I left my heart in San Francisco.
>
> In the beginning, God created the heaven and the earth.
>
> I will never lie to you.
>
> A woman must have money and a room of her own if she is to write fiction.
>
> If you've seen one redwood, you've seen them all.

Most of the sentences you write are in the active voice. *In the active voice, the subject of the sentence is the "agent" or "actor."* In the sentences just quoted, the subject "I" did the leaving, the subject "God" did the creating, and so on.

The active voice has a relative, the *passive voice*, which can often drain sentences of their clarity and force, as a look at the passive versions of the quotations reveals. (Note also that passive versions are appreciably longer.)

> My heart was left in San Francisco by me.
> In the beginning, the heaven and the earth were created by God.
> You will never be lied to by me.
> Money and a room of her own must be had by a woman if fiction is to be written by her.
> If one redwood has been seen by you, they have all been seen by you.

In these passive-voice sentences, the subject of the sentence is indeed passive: it passively *receives* the action. In other words the subject "heart" didn't do the leaving, it *got left.* The subjects "heaven" and "earth" didn't create; they *were created.* As you check the subjects in the three remaining sentences, you'll see that in each case, the subject receives rather than performs the action.

Disadvantages of the Passive Voice

Using the passive voice is not a crime for which writers are tossed into the grammatical clink. Indeed, the passive voice is an essential tool for good writing. But its uses are limited, and its potential drawbacks serious.

While the active voice directs attention forward through the sentence, helping the writer maintain readers' interest and momentum, the passive voice directs attention backward. Compare the following:

ACTIVE

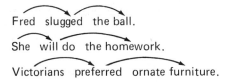

Fred slugged the ball.
She will do the homework.
Victorians preferred ornate furniture.

PASSIVE:

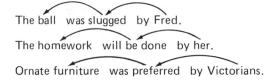

The ball was slugged by Fred.
The homework will be done by her.
Ornate furniture was preferred by Victorians.

The active voice follows the word pattern we're used to, first giving us the agent (actor), then the action, then the thing or person acted upon. It tells us, in other words, who did what to whom—in that order. The passive voice, though, gives us the receiver of the action, the action, and then—maybe—the agent.

We say "maybe" because it's possible to write a sentence in the passive voice and leave out the agent entirely:

> My heart was left in San Francisco.
> The heaven and the earth were created.
> You will never be lied to.
> Money and a room of one's own must be had if fiction is to be written.
> If one redwood has been seen, they all have been seen.

These sentences are not only clumsy, they're logically incomplete. It matters that Tony Bennett left his own heart in San Francisco. And it certainly matters that God is the creator in the second sentence. When you're in doubt about which construction to use, active or passive, ask yourself what your sentence is really about. Most often you'll find that you want the agent as your sentence subject and that you'll therefore be writing in the active voice. Virginia

Woolf's sentence, for instance, isn't really about "money" and "a room," but about "a woman" who would write fiction.

Passive sentences that omit the agent can be more than just awkward and incomplete. They can be carelessly or intentionally deceptive. Not coincidentally, official jargon is often peppered with passives.

> Before I can accept your application of employment, your personal character and professional background will be thoroughly investigated.

Here the passive voice makes it sound as though this investigation is an unquestionable fact of life, not the result of some person's or institution's actions. The sentence would sound very different if it read, "Before I can accept your application for employment, my assistant, Ed, will thoroughly investigate your personal character and professional background." Reading the active version of the same sentence, you might legitimately wonder who this Ed is, what business of his your personal character and professional background are, and just how he's going to conduct his investigation.

Sometimes a writer or speaker will use the passive voice in a related and equally deceptive way: to give the impression of wide acceptance and agreement when none exists.

> It is conceded that Smith will receive no more than a third of the total vote in the coming election.

The writer here implies that everyone, even Smith himself, admits that the election is in effect over. Yet in fact there is no agent in the sentence to *do* the conceding, no one whose credentials for making such a concession we can challenge. The active voice won't let a writer get away with such seemingly substantial but actually hollow statements. In the active version of this sentence, the writer would have to supply an agent:

> _____ concedes that Smith will receive no more than a third of the total vote in the coming election.

Who concedes? Smith? The opposing candidate? The political columnist for the local newspaper? The majority of citizens in a recent poll? Smith's mother? It makes a difference.

The active voice confers one final benefit on a writer or speaker. It discourages grammatical errors, particularly dangling modifiers, that the passive voice tends to foster. (See Chapter 9 for a more complete discussion of dangling modifiers.) The dangling modifier in the following passive sentence disappears when the sentence is rewritten in the active voice:

> *Passive:*   Shaking with hunger, large bowls of clam chowder were devoured by the campers.
> (The subject "bowls" makes no sense as the agent of the verbal phrase "shaking with hunger.")
>
> *Active:*   Shaking with hunger, the campers devoured large bowls of clam chowder.

In summary, the active voice has a number of strengths. The active voice:

- states clearly who or what is performing the action in a sentence
- is more concise
- is more direct and forceful

And the passive voice has a number of potential weaknesses. The passive voice:

- is often wordy
- is usually less forceful
- can lead to inappropriate focus (and dangling modifiers)
- allows a writer to avoid taking responsibility for the action in a sentence
- can imply wide agreement or acceptance when none exists

EXERCISE 5

Underline the passive constructions in the following sentences. (Some sentences may not contain any passive constructions.)

Example:

I was thinking of the time I had been caught shoplifting a model airplane from the toy store.

1. *Seize the Day* was written by Saul Bellow.
2. Everyone has been asked to contribute two dollars.
3. Shakespeare is generally considered the greatest English writer of all time.
4. The old lady was remembering how the wind used to sweep through the valley when she was a child.
5. If he is given the chance to prove himself, I know he will come through.

6. It has been requested that contributions in memory of the deceased be sent to the American Cancer Society.
7. Undoubtedly questions will be raised about the wisdom of the decision.
8. I found her job performance lacking in several respects.

EXERCISE 6

The following sentences are written in the passive voice. For each of them,

a. decide which of the drawbacks that we've discussed weaken them, and

b. revise to the active voice, clearing up the weakness.

1. Contempt is bred by familiarity. *familiarity breeds contempt*
2. It is recognized that the increase in our prices was necessary.
3. Unorthodox typography, capitalization, and punctuation are often used to underscore the meaning in e.e. cummings' poems.
4. Please try to find another place to park as this space is needed for my car. *I need*
5. It has been established that women executives can't handle pressure.
6. Your courage in the face of such widespread hostility is admired.
7. All your documents have been checked, and it has been decided that you are to be sent out of the country. *now that all*
8. After the 400 meter freestyle, an invigorating shower was taken by all the swimmers. *took*
9. These requirements will be completed by the time you graduate.
10. In his quiet moments, time was found by Bronstein to compose three light symphonies and a satirical opera. *in his quiet moments found time*

When the Passive Passes

You may be wondering why, if the active voice is indeed so much better, the passive voice is used at all. But there are times when the passive voice is desirable or necessary. Sometimes, for instance, a writer wishes to emphasize who or what is acted upon, rather than who or what is acting:

Yesterday, a three-billion-dollar tax cut was approved by the House of Representatives.

This sentence clearly emphasizes the tax cut and its unprecedented passage, not the House of Representatives.

Sometimes the actor is either unknown, unimportant, or too obvious to mention.

Mr. Job was cited for speeding on Highway 101.
The ornamental fastening at the top of a lamp is called a finial.
Because of heavy fog, the flight to London has been cancelled.

And at times, the passive construction is employed deliberately by the conscious writer, who uses it to heighten the reader's expectation by putting the actor last:

Much to our horror, we were surrounded by a pack of hungry, grasping Cub Scouts.

In California, a felon can be pardoned only by the governor.

EXERCISE 7

A. Change the following passive constructions to the active, supplying—even inventing—agents when necessary.

B. Decide whether one construction is better than the other, and if so, *why*.

Example:

Nathan Roberts was named gold medal winner in the cello competition.

A. The Music Department named Nathan Roberts gold medal winner in the cello competition.

B. You would probably want to emphasize the winner of the award, so the passive version is probably preferable.

1. The World Series is scheduled to begin on October 10.
2. It is felt that science fiction should have a place in university literature programs.
3. A stirring speech will be given by the Senator.
4. Music was played by Lawrence Welk until the crowd passed out.
5. My most rewarding experience was had in the summer of 1968 when my family took an extended vacation across the U.S.
6. The causes of crib death have not been conclusively determined.
7. Six passengers on the bus had been robbed by middle-aged hoodlums.
8. Light is directed toward a single point by the six main mirrors of the giant telescope.
9. My love of writing was first recognized when Miss Jenkins had me read my poetry in class.

10. People who make barrels are called "coopers."
11. When the presidential candidate returned to the convention floor, his running mate had already been selected.

(For more on the active and passive voices, see "Passive Voice" on page 357 of the Usage Manual.)

VERBS

Perhaps, like us, you were taught in elementary school that "verbs are action words." As was the case with a number of other things that seemed simple at the time, verbs turned out to be a bit more complicated than that basic definition suggests. But the definition does make an important point. Verbs can give your writing life. Because they do usually describe an action or a process, they tell the reader, quite literally, what's happening; the more precise and alive the verb, the clearer and stronger the reader's sense of your meaning. In the following sentences, the verbs range from those, like "was scraping," that describe an observable action to those, like "simplifies," that describe a more abstract process.

> As he was scraping the paint off the boat's hull, I was cutting patches of canvas and sewing them together into a new, if somewhat sloppy, sail.

> Koko, a female lowland gorilla under the care of psychologist Penny Patterson, can communicate with human beings through American Sign Language.

> The President demanded equal time on national television so that he could counter his opponent's accusations.

> A pass/fail grading system simplifies record-keeping for instructors and administrators.

A precise and appropriately vivid verb can make the difference between a fairly clear but pretty stodgy sentence and one with real zip. Compare

> The car came to a stop in front of our house.

with

> The car skidded to a stop in front of our house.

or

> The car sputtered and wheezed to a stop in front of our house.

or

    The car <u>coasted</u> to a stop in front of our house.

or

    The car <u>jerked</u> to a stop in front of our house.

In a general sense, "came to a stop" tells the reader what happened. But as we found in our earlier discussion of levels of generalization in the paragraph, a general statement alone usually can't let the reader know exactly what you have in mind. "The car came to a stop in front of our house" is not only less vivid but less specific than the alternative sentences, which tell the reader exactly *how* the car might have stopped.

EXERCISE 8

    Inexperienced writers often plug into a sentence the first verb that comes to mind, rather than finding the most exact and vigorous one. In the following sentences, the underlined verbs are less precise and vivid than they might be, given the context of the rest of the sentence. For each underlined verb, suggest a more appropriate substitute.

Example: When confronted with the charge, the suspect lowered his head and, in words we could barely make out, *said* something about having been out of town that week.

Possible revisions: muttered, whispered, stammered

1. Wisely fearing for its safety, the cat <u>got</u> up into the tree, just out of reach of its canine pursuer.
2. My boss's relentless, sarcastic criticism of my report <u>bothered</u> me.
3. Obviously furious, John <u>walked</u> across the room and <u>closed</u> the bedroom door.
4. Americans <u>use</u> energy thoughtlessly, leaving lights turned on in the daytime and thermostats up at night.
5. Many people <u>criticize</u> the American Nazi Party of the 1980s because they still <u>dislike</u> the German Nazi Party of the '30s and '40s.
6. Few students can <u>have</u> a high grade point average if they are also working full time.
7. When attorneys, defendants, witnesses, or spectators disrupt court proceedings, judges must <u>request</u> order.

8. Losing only in Massachusetts and the District of Columbia, Richard Nixon <u>defeated</u> George McGovern in the 1972 election.

We're not suggesting though, that you always plug in the most energetic verb you can find. Occasionally, a writer will pick a verb that is *too* vivid, that delivers more punch than the situation demands. (Theodore Bernstein calls these overwrought word choices "atomic flyswatters.") The writer may decide that "believe" is too bland for his tastes, so after consulting a thesaurus, a dangerous weapon in the hands of the inexperienced, he ends up writing, "I theorize that everyone should have the chance to attend college." Or, opting for something less pedestrian than "begin," he may write, "A new football season will dawn on September 15."

EXERCISE 9

The writers of the following sentences have overdone it a bit. For each underlined verb, find a more suitable, less dramatic substitute.

Example: The field mice had <u>gouged</u> into the side of the hill, creating scarcely visible hiding places.

Possible revisions: dug, burrowed

1. As the wind picked up, the few remaining leaves <u>plummeted</u> from the trees and drifted to the ground.
2. Asked when his next record would be released, the singer <u>retorted</u> that it would be out next summer.
3. The minister <u>exhorted</u> the crowd to be seated.
4. Holding no strong opinion one way or the other, the congressman <u>resolved</u> to vote against the measure.
5. Though other countries may not like us, they will still <u>revere</u> us if we remain strong militarily.

(See also "Wrong Word" on page 425 of the Usage Manual.)

"To Be"? Probably Not

Verbs are "action words" not only because they most often *describe* an action or process, but because they also impart a sort of grammatical action to your writing. A dynamic verb propels readers through your sentence; a dull, static verb forces them to trudge through your prose like someone slogging through snow against a headwind. Compare these two sentences:

Franklin Delano Roosevelt <u>restored</u> Americans' belief in their own future and <u>infused</u> the White House with warmth and dignity.

> During the administration of Franklin Delano Roosevelt there <u>was</u> a restoration of Americans' belief in their own future, and warmth and dignity <u>were</u> in the White House.

From our earlier discussion of focus, you know that the first sentence is more effective because it has a human subject that reflects what the sentence is really about. But it's also better because its verbs, "restored" and "infused," help move readers through the sentence, keeping them from getting mired in the relative lifelessness of the second version.

Both of the verbs in the second version, "was" and "were," are forms of the verb "*to be*," along with *am, are, is, have been, will be,* and so on. We use this verb more often than any other, and it does indeed come in handy. We can use it in its most basic sense to say that something exists: "There is a mailbox on the corner of Market and Third," "There were too many flaws in his proposal," "There will be a parade on Arbor Day." We can also use it to make what we can loosely term a grammatical equation, in which we match a person or thing with some attribute or identifying information: "My boss is a jerk," "Warren G. Harding was the 29th President of the United States," "Her most recent novel is tedious."

We use the verb *to be* so often, though, that we may reach for it automatically even when we could choose a more dynamic and exact alternative. Overuse of *to be* can rob writing of descriptive and grammatical momentum because this verb, like its overworked cousins *to have, to seem, to appear,* and a few others, doesn't fit the rudimentary definition of a verb; that is, it does not express action. Compare the following sentences:

> Throughout the night, there *was* the sound of cats squalling and hissing outside my window.
> Throughout the night, cats *squalled* and *hissed* outside my window.
>
> Since the new management took over, there *has been* a deterioration of service in this restaurant.
> Since the new management took over, service in this restaurant *has deteriorated.*

These sentences aren't really about the existence of "sound" or "deterioration," nor do they involve any kind of grammatical equation. Therefore the real action in these sentences—"squalled and hissed" and "has deteriorated"—should be conveyed through appropriate verbs, not undercut by the static "to be."

If the verb *to be* were only listless and overused, that would be enough to discourage us from grabbing it at every opportunity. But misuse of *to be* can lead to other problems just as serious, if not just as obvious.

Because *to be* is a static verb, it creates a certain sense of finality and completeness that tends to cut off further discussion and development; neither the reader nor the writer is moved to consider the full implications of a statement. The following have a nice, self-contained ring:

> There *is* no time like the present.
> The only good Indian *is* a dead Indian.
> Whatever *will be, will be.*
> Everything *is* relative.

Aphorisms like these are not supposed to invite discussion or disagreement; one doesn't feel driven to ask some basic questions about these statements, which range from the racist to the inane to the indecipherable. In your own writing, you're less likely to recognize the bald generality of an assertion and less likely to summon the support it demands if you couch statements in the flat and final tones of the verb *to be.* Even a generally good writer might let the following sentences slip past, not recognizing how broad they are and how extensively he would have to develop them to make them work.

> There *are* no serious objections to a ban on smoking in all public places.

(Had the writer phrased this differently—"No one objects seriously to a ban on smoking in all public places"—he would have been much more apt to note the indefensibly unqualified character of his statement.)

> Politicians *will* always *be* untrustworthy, so it doesn't matter whom we vote for.

(Here the writer has based a drastic conclusion on an unsupported premise. What does the writer mean by "will always be untrustworthy"? What exactly will politicians always *do* that will make them undeserving of our trust, and what evidence does the writer have for his prediction of politicians' behavior? The answers to these questions demand a great deal of thought and explanation, but the form of the writer's statement makes it unlikely that he'll realize how much work he's cut out for himself.)

Finally, the verb *to be* can lead not only to problems in logic and effectiveness but also to outright errors in grammar, errors that indicate a lapse in logic as well as in syntax. We noted earlier that *to be* can be used to form grammatical equations—"Most of the students in my history class <u>are</u> sophomores." Occasionally this kind of equation goes awry, but its form sometimes prevents inexperienced writers from catching their own mistake. For instance, consider this sentence:

The complaint the university band makes most often *is* its uniforms.

This statement makes no grammatical or logical sense because the equation is faulty; uniforms are not a complaint. "The university band complains most about its uniforms" corrects this deficiency and, because it also employs a human sentence subject, makes it easier for the writer to continue his development of the idea concretely.

We're not suggesting that you should purge the verb *to be* from your writing, any more than we'd suggest that you should write every sentence in the active voice or that you should never use an abstract sentence subject. But unless you're using *to be* for a good and specific purpose—indeed, unless you're using *any* word for a good and specific purpose—you're better off taking the time to find a clearer, and often less troublesome, substitute.

EXERCISE 10

The verb *to be* appears in each of the following sentences. After you've located the *to be* form(s) in a sentence, determine how the verb is being used. If the writer seems to be merely asserting the existence of something or someone, decide whether the sentence really centers only on the idea of existence, or whether some action is more important.

Take, for instance, the following sentence:

There <u>is</u> strong disagreement between the governors of the two states on the proposed flood control project.

The writer has stated that an abstraction, "disagreement," exists even though the sentence more directly concerns the governors and how they *feel* about this issue:

The governors of the two states <u>disagree</u> strongly about the proposed flood control projects.

If "to be" isn't being used to denote existence, check to see whether it's being used to make a grammatical equation. If so, is the equation logical? For instance, "A student in this class who would deliberately cheat <u>is</u> an idea I refuse to believe" doesn't work because the writer has illogically equated "student" with "idea." Better:

> I refuse to believe that a student in this class would deliberately cheat.

Also check to see whether the sentence demands further proof or explanation, despite how complete it might sound:

> Since tourists are the best tippers, cab drivers shouldn't take advantage of their ignorance of city geography.

It's nice to see somebody sticking up for the tourists, but the writer would still need to *demonstrate* his assertion about their relative generosity.

Below, identify the sentences in which *to be* was used carelessly or incorrectly, and revise them if possible.

1. The elephants are my favorite moment in the circus.
2. There were many students idly strolling across the lawn during registration week.
3. Our college is a haven for middle-class reactionaries.
4. I refuse to discuss this issue any further because there is a fallacy in your argument.
5. A college education prepares one for the business world and is a time, in an interview, when many prospective employers become particularly interested.
6. There is something distasteful about having to study inside today when there is so much happening right outside my window.
7. Most of my thinking is in the center of the room because that's where my bed is.
8. Part of this assignment is difficult because it is hard to follow.
9. But the subtle moral of the story was the priceless ability to take an objective look at oneself.
10. Your cooperation will be the key figure in our panel discussion.

A Final Word on Verbs

Although *to be* seems to cause particular problems, any verb can be used illogically. **Predication errors** result from the mismatching of the subject and predicate. (The predicate consists of the verb and its direct object or complement—in other words, the verb plus whatever words complete the basic meaning of the sentence.) For instance, the following sentence doesn't work:

> The activities in the alley included an old stray cat and a group of teenagers setting fire to a trash can.

Neither a cat nor a group of teenagers can be included among activities. Similarly, this sentence is a nearly unqualified disaster:

> His insistence on doing everything himself degraded his own respect among the group.

The basic prediction—"(his) insistence/degraded/(his own) respect"—is meaningless. Maybe the writer meant something like, "The other members of the group didn't respect him because he insisted on doing everything himself." (See also "Predication" on page 360 of the Usage Manual.)

EXERCISE 11

Each of the following sentences contains a predication error. Briefly explain the problems, and then revise the sentence.

Example: The pressure of finals created many sleepless students.
(The basic predication here is *pressure/created/ students,* obviously nonsensical.)

Possible revision: A number of students hadn't slept because of the pressure of finals.

1. Her failure to show up on time was stared at in disbelief.
2. He is unlike most of us: his enthusiasm for acting eliminates other people's hobbies and outside interests.
3. The 4.3 per cent growth rate is considered optimistic by many economists.
4. Only scientists can understand the difficulty of the highly theoretical report.
5. The glass in the street will require careful drivers in this area.

EXERCISE 12

Exercises 12 and 13 give you additional practice with several of the concepts covered in this chapter.

Rewrite the following paragraph, revising any sentences that are poorly focused or in which the passive voice or the verb *to be* is used inappropriately.

> There is a resentment among children of arbitrary rules, but parents must often impose them anyway. For instance, staying up until midnight to watch *Invasion of the Giant Gila Monsters* on TV

might be insisted upon by a six-year-old boy; despite his parents' patient, logical arguments about the child's need for rest and his obligation to attend school the next day, he would probably remain unmoved—and immobile. In that case, there must be an assertion of parental authority and the child must be ordered to bed. A nine-year old girl might decide that her bicycle is to be ridden by her through busy city streets to visit a friend. To her, this feeling might be an obligation to her peer group. She would probably resent any observations about the dangers of city traffic, so the time-honored "because I say so" doctrine might need to be invoked by her parents. Any detailed explanations for the seemingly callous refusals by the parents in both of these examples would probably have to be postponed—perhaps for quite some time.

EXERCISE 13

Write a 125-word paragraph on a subject of your own choice. Make sure that your sentences are well-focused. If you use the verb *to be* or the passive voice, be sure you have a logical reason for doing so. When you check your work, underline subjects once and verbs twice.

8

Coordination and Subordination

Most of us get justifiably annoyed when the directions for a product— an unassembled bookcase, a sewing pattern, an electronics kit—are incomplete and disjointed. But because these products are tangible, we may still be able to see how the parts fit together despite the manufacturer's muddled directions. Essays and paragraphs don't come with visual aids, though, so it's particularly important that the reader be able to see how the ideas fit together; the only clues to the writer's thoughts are the words on the paper. This section offers some ways to make sure those clues point in the right direction.

The techniques in the next two chapters can be loosely grouped together as methods of joining. These methods can be used to connect words, phrases, and whole clauses that you've already written as well as to create new ones. The writer of the following paragraph has used these techniques effectively, creating a passage that communicates clearly and smoothly.

> During the past few years, racquetball has surged in popularity because it demands relatively little from the casual player. The novice at tennis must spend hours practicing forehands and backhands against a backboard, serving buckets of balls either into the net or

out of the court, and rallying ineptly with other newcomers before he can expect to play an even adequate game. The beginning racquetball player, on the other hand, can be reasonably sure that his racquet will strike the ball and that the ball, in turn, will manage to hit the wall. The handball player must suffer the ceaseless sting of the ball against his palm and must propel the hard little sphere with just his own strength; the racquetballer uses the larger, resilient surface of the racquet not only to spare his tender skin but also to aid the ball in its flight. It would be insulting and simplistic to suggest that all tennis players are patient and hard-working, while racquetballers are lazy, or that handball players are strong, skillful, and stoic while racquetball players are weak and inept. Nevertheless, racquetball continues to attract people with neither the time nor the diligence required by more disciplined sports.

This paragraph has a number of strengths common to most good writing. Its most important asset is its clarity, which the writer ensures by showing the connections between ideas and supplying enough details and examples to support his observations. He explains, for instance, that racquetball is popular *because* it demands relatively little; he describes the *specific* kinds of tedious practice tennis players must engage in. In addition, he has eased his readers' path by writing sentences long enough to create some momentum and provide variety.

In the following version of the same passage, the techniques of joining to be covered in this section have been left out. We now have to guess at the connections between most ideas, important details have been dropped, and the paragraph as a whole is choppier.

During the past few years, racquetball has surged in popularity. It demands relatively little from the casual player. The novice at tennis must spend hours practicing. Only then can he expect to play an adequate game. The beginning racquetball player can be reasonably sure that his racquet will strike the ball. The ball will probably hit the wall. The handball player must suffer the ceaseless sting of the ball against his palm. He must also propel the hard little sphere with just his own strength. The racquetballer uses the larger, resilient surface of the racquet to spare his tender skin. He also uses it to aid the ball in its flight. It would be inaccurate to suggest that all tennis players are patient and hard-working. It would be just as wrong to suggest that handball players are better than racquetball players. Racquetball does continue to attract people without the time and diligence required by more disciplined sports.

In comparing the two versions of this paragraph, you should notice the following shortcomings of the second:

Loss of clarity: we are no longer told *why* racquetball is popular, for example.

Lack of detail: the writer leaves out the examples of tennis practice and the specific ways in which handball players might wrongly be presumed to be better than racquetballers.

Choppiness: the second version consists mostly of short, simple, "Dick and Jane" sentences. The disconcerting jerkiness that results makes us feel as though we're riding in a pickup truck driven by somebody who has never operated a stick shift before.

Monotony: most of the sentences follow the same pattern, many unnecessarily repeating the subject and even the verb of previous sentences.

COORDINATION

You already use the most basic tools of joining, known in grammatical circles as **coordinating conjunctions:**

> and
> but
> for
> or
> nor
> yet
> so

Coordinating conjunctions can be used to join independent clauses (clauses that can stand alone as complete sentences):

Christmas, Thanksgiving, and Easter are supposed to be joyous occasions, (yet) more suicides occur around holidays than at any other time of year.

Jane Austen received only £15 for writing Pride and Prejudice, (and) her income from all six of her novels didn't exceed £600 during her lifetime.

Coordinating conjunctions can also be used to join *elements* within sentences:

The Washington Post (and) *The New York Times* have often led the newspaper industry in revealing government scandals.

During his long convalescence, the patient couldn't <u>eat</u>, <u>sleep</u>, <u>watch</u> <u>TV</u>, (or) <u>talk</u> without great pain.

In his quest for the great whale, Captain Ahab pursued Moby Dick down the coast of South America, around the Cape of Good Hope, (and) into the Pacific Ocean.

Tired (but) cheerful, the students returned from a weekend of skiing in time to attend their morning classes.

What Can Coordinating Conjunctions Connect?

You can see from the preceding examples that whether they are connecting whole sentences or parts of sentences, coordinating conjunctions always link like units. The units that coordinating conjunctions join are alike in two ways. First, the elements joined by coordination should be grammatically parallel: in our examples, nouns are paired with nouns, verbs with verbs, prepositional phrases with prepositional phrases, adjectives with adjectives, independent clauses with independent clauses.

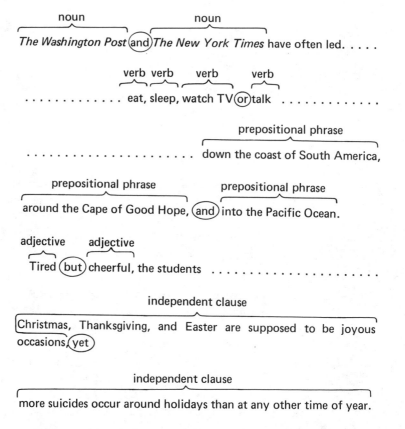

The elements joined by coordinating conjunctions are alike in another way as well. When you join two or more constructions with a coordinating conjunction, you are giving them roughly *equal emphasis.* (This is an especially important consideration when you're deciding how to join clauses. Clauses can also be linked in ways that give one clause more emphasis than another, as we'll see later in this chapter and in the next.)

Using Coordination to Extend

Coordination can do more than join existing elements. It can also add new information, amplifying and extending your ideas. You might find, for instance, that "Exhausted, I finished the marathon" doesn't fully recapture your feelings at the end of the race. Using coordination, you could extend the sentence to "exhausted but exhilarated, I finished the marathon." Similarly, you might at first write

Our country normalized relations with China in the 1970s.

Again, you'd no doubt realize that this statement alone is incomplete, because it doesn't explain what caused this dramatic change in U.S. policy. So you could try the sentence:

Our country normalized relations with China in the 1970s, for we feared the political and military course an isolated China might pursue.

Better, but still not quite complete. You might round out the picture by using coordination to add a second important reason:

Our country normalized relations with China in the 1970s, for we feared the political and military course an isolated China might pursue and sought the substantial economic benefits of improved American-Chinese relations.

In short, you want to remain conscious not only of joining ideas you already have but of selecting useful information to add, and coordination is one tool to that end.

Which Coordinating Conjunction to Use?

As you'll see from the following chart, each coordinating conjunction expresses a particular logical relationship. When using coordination, be sure to pick the appropriate conjunction.

Logical Relationship	**Conjunction**
addition	**and**

Examples: A stack of unwashed dishes sat in the sink, and the week's laundry lay in piles on the living room floor.

You need a tourist card and proof of insurance if you're driving into Mexico.

---

contrast	**but, yet**

Examples: Tom is a Republican but his brother is a Democrat.

Tom is intellectually gifted but emotionally immature.

Zorba the Greek was uneducated, yet he had wisdom most educated men would envy.

Zorba the Greek was uneducated yet wise.

---

cause and effect	**for**

Example: Attempts to change our environment often backfire, for every time we disturb a life cycle, we set in motion a series of repercussions we may not be able to cope with.

---

alternative	**or**

Examples: The price reduction may be postponed for a couple of weeks, or it may even be cancelled entirely.

To be or not to be, that is the question.

---

indicates the general sense of "and not" (generally follows neither, not, never, no)	**nor**

Examples: The news media have neither the obligation nor the inclination to save government figures from personal or political embarrassment.

I did not take the exam, nor do I intend to.

---

result	**so**

Examples: Only three students signed up for the course, so it was cancelled.

Many folk remedies have a basis in sound medicine, so doctors are reluctant to dismiss home cures automatically.

EXERCISE 1: Coordination

A. To sharpen your ability to recognize parallel grammatical units, draw a line connecting the matching elements in the following columns.

Example:

into the room ————————— that he had only ten dollars
an alligator ————————— under the stone
that the engine needed repairing   a dog

of the people	rapidly
hoping somehow to win the game	to manipulate
that their notes were incomplete	ominous
a group of new immigrants	some self-help groups such as Synanon have been investigated
various religious cults have been discredited	pretended it was Saturady instead of Tuesday
dark	for the people
to direct	knowing he would be lucky to come out of it in one piece
who had never been to a disco before	that the instructor would give a difficult test
quietly	their cardboard suitcases
snuggled down under the covers	who believed in trying anything

B. Circle the coordinating conjunction(s) and underline the set or sets of parallel elements in the following sentences.

Example:

I base what I am saying not on one semester's experience (but) on four full years as a college student.
Sodium nitrite, red dye #5, (and) cyclamates are only a few of the dangerous additives found in processed foods.

1. The majority of classes I took were monotonous, useless, and simplistic.
2. I have no time to wait, so I'll leave a message.
3. After the first quarter of school, he knew he had to study harder or suffer the consequences.
4. Automobile insurance is an expensive but necessary part of owning a car.
5. Many pioneers discovered that their belongings were too burdensome, that they lacked basic skills necessary for survival in the wilderness, and that they had underestimated the dangers of the trail west.

6. It is sad that so many young Americans have become disenchanted with politics as a career, for the nation needs future leaders with the idealism of youth.
7. Attempting to untangle themselves from the problems of inflation yet losing buying power every year, many Americans have lost faith in the future of the economy.
8. "Out of the closets and into the streets" was the rallying cry of the gay liberation leaders in the early 1970s, and men and women who had always hidden their sexual preferences responded by joining marches, demanding equal rights, and talking openly with their friends and families.

C. Pick five of the pairs of matched elements from Part A. For each pair, write a sentence, joining the elements with a coordinating conjunction.

Example:

Knowing that the engine needed repairing but that he had only ten dollars, Tom decided to hope for the best.

D. Add interest and detail to the following sentences by adding parallel elements.

Example:

During the argument, Laverne chased Shirley _____ , _____ , and _____ .

Possible addition: During the argument, Laverne chased Shirley around the kitchen table, out the side door, and into the sprinkler running on a neighbor's front lawn.

1. When I think of the country, I think of _____ , of _____ , of _____ , and of _____ .

2. _____ yet _____ , many adolescents are torn by conflict.

3. I thought back over some of the most depressing moments in my life: the time _____ , the time _____ , and the time _____ .

4. During the past fifteen years, our lives have been made easier; _____ , for _____ .

5. Flipping the channels restlessly, I was subjected to a barrage of commercials for a dozen things I didn't want to buy, including

_____ , _____ , _____ ,

_____ , and even _____ .

6. The first woman President will probably _____ ,

_____ , and _____ .

7. _____ but _____ ,
   I staggered into the room.

8. By _____ , _____ , and _____ ,
   the atomic bomb exploded at Hiroshima drastically changed the way many people saw their world.

9. Working with a medium that can be as _____ and

_____ as life itself, serious film-makers try to

_____ , to _____ ,

or to _____ .

10. Scuba diving requires both training and stamina, so _____

_____ .

The "Uh/You Know" Syndrome

Listen carefully to a friend talking and notice the number of times he says "uh" or "you know." If he's like most of us, he'll probably use one or both of these phrases to fill verbal dead space and get from one thought to another. Writers can't "uh" on paper, but they often use *and* in a similar manner, connecting ideas in the handiest way rather than the most logical one. Even though *and* is the quickest and simplest method of joining phrases and sentences, it's often not the best.

And expresses no logical relationship beyond mere addition. Its overuse can also mark a passage as unsophisticated and even tedious. Because they lack a mature vocabulary (and are usually breathlessly eager to relate their adventures), children frequently connect spoken narratives with a seemingly ceaseless stream of *ands:* "First we went to the show and when we got there it was full and we decided to wait for the next show and that wasn't until an hour later and then we went in and it was really scary and we wanted to stay and see it again and it was time to leave and we left and . . . ." A mature writer, though, will take the time to search for the right connection between ideas, using *and* only when it's the most precise choice.

Note the over-reliance on *and* in the following passage. In which cases might the writer have used a different coordinating conjunction (or other appropriate construction) rather than the *and* that sprang so effortlessly to mind?

> Personal counseling is available free at most colleges, and many students are reluctant to seek counseling for their personal problems, and they continue to try, often unsuccessfully, to cope with them alone. They feel that a counselor would be shocked at their troubles and, on the other hand, might dismiss them as trivial or unrelated to school. In fact, a counselor does not judge and merely tries to help. Faced with a student's revelations about difficulties with drugs, sex, teachers, family, and friends, the trained counselor will not lecture and reproach the student and will try to help find solutions. A good counselor also recognizes that there's no such thing as a trivial emotional problem, and if a student is bothered enough to seek counseling, the problem deserves to be taken seriously. Finally, a student's life outside school affects his work in school, so a counselor won't discount a problem as irrelevant to the student's education.

EXERCISE 2: Picking the Right Conjunction

In each of the following, *and* is used to join sentence elements, even though in some cases another coordinating conjunction might be more appropriate. Correct all the sentences in which *and* should be replaced by a more precise conjunction. (You might want to refer to the chart on page 194.)

Example: I never thought I'd see England ~~and~~ ^{but} I was wrong.

OK as is: Howard Jarvis felt property taxes in California were far too high, and the majority of California voters agreed with him.

1. We decided to ask for a different table, and the waiter wouldn't move us.
2. The Office of Energy realized it had to force people to drive their cars less, and it proposed a plan to ration gasoline.
3. I was not enthusiastic and not even vaguely pleased about the President's decision.
4. Many universities spare no time, money, and effort in recruiting athletes, and later they completely ignore these players when they have academic problems.
5. In the last decade, marriage has increasingly been replaced by "meaningful relationships" and divorce has been justified by "a need for one's own space."

6. She didn't know how to tell him that she wanted to end the relationship, and she knew how badly he would react.

7. Contrary to popular belief, most people who learn speedreading do not suffer a loss of comprehension when their reading rates go up, and they do not have more difficulty remembering the material later.

8. Prominent critics panned the movie as phony and trite, and it turned out to be a box office smash.

Eliminating Needless Repetition

By using coordination carefully, you can eliminate useless repetition. In the following sentences, for example, it's not necessary to write both "James Joyce" and "he."

> James Joyce was born in Ireland. Later he moved to Italy.
> *Revision:* James Joyce was born in Ireland but later moved to Italy.

When more than the subject is repeated, more can be removed. Notice in the following sentences that the beginning of the second sentence repeats almost word for word the beginning of the first.

> *Joyce spent several years* teaching in Milan. *He also spent several years* travelling around Europe trying to get *Ulysses* published.

The example reads more smoothly when coordination is used to eliminate repetition.

> Joyce spent several years teaching in Milan and travelling around Europe trying to get *Ulysses* published.

Such editing may unnerve writers who pad their sentences, but the edited, streamlined prose is much less likely to bore the reader. The writer has stopped giving out signals that he has little to say and a lot of room to say it in.

EXERCISE 3: Eliminating Repetition

Use coordination to combine the following sentences, eliminating any needless repetition.

Example: Playing blackjack for high stakes is exciting. Playing it for high stakes is usually not very lucrative.

Revision: Playing blackjack for high stakes is exciting but usually not very lucrative.

1. Historians surmise that Stonehenge was, at one time, a religious temple. They also believe that it was a sophisticated astronomical device capable of predicting such events as lunar eclipses.
2. Sir Bernard Lovell, the British astronomer, said that UFO sightings in New Zealand were no more than meteorites. He said this even though he knew that a pilot and crew had observed the objects. He held to his position despite the fact that four or five of the objects had been tracked on radar.
3. Faulkner's portrayal of Benjy in *The Sound and the Fury* is a masterful piece of writing that completely captures the perceptions of a childlike mind. The writing is also masterful because it manages to tell a story from that mind at the same time.
4. Perhaps because of a perennial interest in sex and sophomoric humor, male college students used to read *Playboy.* For more or less the same reasons, this group now reads *National Lampoon.*
5. Despite progress in civil rights, it is unlikely that we will have a black president within the next couple of decades. It is equally unlikely that there will be a female president within the next twenty years.

Punctuation

Because sentences with coordinating conjunctions are punctuated differently from sentences that use other connecting words and techniques, you'll need to be able to remember the seven coordinating conjunctions without continually referring to a text. There's an easy, if somewhat bizarre, solution: just remember the clue FAN-BOYS.

F̲or
A̲nd
N̲or
B̲ut
O̲r
Y̲et
S̲o

Usage does permit some variation in punctuating sentences that contain coordinating conjunctions, but you should generally follow some standard rules:

1. When a coordinating conjunction joins two independent clauses, you need a comma just *before* the conjunction.

    Doctors used to believe that eating rich foods before bedtime caused people to have bizarre dreams, <u>but</u> today we know that the indigestion resulting from such eating simply causes people to be more aware of their dreams.

2. If the two independent clauses being joined by a coordinating conjunction are very brief, you can omit the comma (though it is never wrong to include it).

The students supported the new schedule <u>but</u> the faculty didn't.

3. When joining just two elements that are *not* independent clauses with a coordinating conjunction, do not use a comma before the conjunction.

Hemingway worked on newspapers early in his career <u>but</u> later turned to writing novels.

The young Senator from Boston <u>and</u> the old Senate hand from Texas had little in common.

4. When joining three or more items (words, phrases, or clauses) in a parallel series, separate them with commas.

Sally sells sea shells, barnacles, beer, <u>and</u> dehydrated squid down by the sea shore.

After the tragic fire, people speculated endlessly on its causes, blamed various government agencies for negligence, <u>and</u> then allowed a ballot initiative on fire ordinances to fail.

(Although some authorities consider the final comma optional in most cases, you're better off including it to avoid ambiguity.)

A Cure for the Comma Splice

Coordinating conjunctions provide one simple means of correcting a major and very common punctuation error—the **comma splice** (also discussed in the Usage Manual). You create a comma splice if you try to join two independent clauses with only a comma:

My parents were convinced that I was perfect, no amount of mischief on my part could make them change their minds.

The Bakke decision did little to clarify the Supreme Court's position on affirmative action, so test cases will continue to be brought be- the court.

It is somewhat misleading to distinguish Shakespeare's poetry from his plays, the plays themselves are poetry.

More than merely a punctuation error, the comma splice weakens the joined sentences by depriving them of a logical connection between parts. To fix a comma splice, you need only add the appropriate co-ordinating conjunction after the comma. (We'll introduce several other ways to correct comma splices later in the book.)

> My parents were convinced that I was perfect, and no amount of mischief on my part could make them change their minds.

> The Bakke decision did little to clarify the Supreme Court's position on affirmative action, so test cases will continue to be brought before the court.

> It is somewhat misleading to distinguish Shakespeare's poetry from his plays, for the plays themselves are poetry.

Occasionally a writer will jam together two independent clauses without any punctuation at all, creating what is called a **run-together** or **fused sentence**. (See "run-together sentence" in the Usage Manual.)

> In Nathaniel Hawthorne's "Young Goodman Brown," the main character discovers the universality of sin this new awareness embitters him.

> There are thousands of English composition texts on the market not all of them are suited to the beginning writer's needs.

If the writer chooses to fix a fused sentence with a coordinating conjunction, he must also remember to supply the necessary comma before it.

> In Nathaniel Hawthorne's "Young Goodman Brown," the main character discovers the universality of sin, and this new awareness embitters him.

> There are thousands of English composition texts on the market, but not all of them are suited to the beginning writer's needs.

EXERCISE 4: Punctuation

A. Correct the punctuation in the following sentences when necessary. You may have to add, delete, or move commas. A sentence may be correct as it is.

Example: Most of us complain loudly about rising food costs but, how many of us are willing to change our eating habits, or shop more carefully?

COORDINATION AND SUBORDINATION

Correction: Most of us complain loudly about rising food costs, but how many of us are willing to change our eating habits or shop more carefully?

1. The heat was intense but exhilarating.
2. Architects should design the interiors of buildings as carefully as they do the exteriors for, the pattern of our indoor environment probably affects our sense of well-being much more dramatically than does the facade of a building.
3. My mother always predicts a narrow, and bleak future.
4. The tax initiative was passed by a two-to-one margin yet many people are still very much opposed to it.
5. It was 7:30 but he still had not started dinner.
6. The Nobel Prize Committee wanted to influence world politics so, they awarded their prize to Begin of Israel and Sadat of Egypt.
7. Apparently a simple sport, ping-pong requires a subtle touch aggressive strategy and good defensive techniques.
8. Fred realized that we were late so we turned off the television grabbed our coats, sprinted to the car and roared off down the road.

B. Some of the following contain comma splices. Correct them as necessary, inserting the appropriate coordinating conjunction.

Example: I've never been to Europe, I plan to go for nine weeks next summer.

Correction: I've never been to Europe, *but* I plan to go for nine weeks next summer.

1. Many people dogmatically support the death penalty, they simply refuse to recognize evidence that it does not deter crime.
2. The United States has weathered several bleak economic periods in the past several years, none has been as severe as the depression of the 1930s.
3. Before applying for a job, you should find out as much as possible about your prospective employer.
4. The President admitted he couldn't exert much influence over his family, they would just rebel if he tried.
5. The decline in basic writing skills is distressing, the situation seems to be getting steadily worse.

C. In the following paragraph, supply any commas necessary according to the rules presented in this chapter.

Colleges sometimes accommodate the needs of younger students in the form of scholarships grants and other financial assistance but they often neglect the more practical concerns of the older students with parental responsibilities. For instance, this college provides no day-care facilities for students with small children so the parents struggle on their own to find someone to care for their children during classes. They waste time money and emotional energy hiring babysitters they may not know or trust or they leave the children with relatives, forcing unwanted responsibilities on them and guilt on themselves. Parents need a safe and convenient place to leave their kids so this college should provide a day-care center. Students with children could then attend classes use the library or study on campus with greater convenience and less distraction.

The Pleasures of Parallel Structure

Earlier in this chapter we mentioned that when you use coordination, you set up *parallel units,* units that are grammatically alike. Coordination is not only an effective joining tool but also a means of balancing a sentence and setting up readers' expectations about the rhythm of the language to come. In his Inaugural Address, John F. Kennedy made eloquent use of this technique.

Let the word go forth from this time and place, to friend and foe alike, that the torch has been passed to a new generation of Americans: born in this century, tempered by war, disciplined by a hard and bitter peace, proud of our ancient heritage—and unwilling to witness or permit the slow undoing of those human rights to which this nation has always been committed and to which we are committed today at home and around the world.

Aside from simple connections of "time and place" and "friend and foe," the passage makes effective use of parallel units in series to describe the new Americans: "*born* in this century, *tempered* by war, *disciplined* by a hard and bitter peace, *proud* of our ancient heritage—and *unwilling* to witness. . . ." By the time we've read as far as "tempered by war," we've begun to sense the rhythm of the sentence and to expect another phrase like the first two that will describe these Americans. Though we can't anticipate the content of the message, we expect the speaker to maintain the rhythm he's established. The fulfillment of our expectations has a great deal to do with how readable and even enjoyable a passage is.

Kennedy employs coordinated parallel elements again towards the end of the sentence; here he wants to make one more point, to complete the thought, perhaps even to balance out the long "which" clause.

> . . . unwilling to witness or permit the slow undoing of those human
> rights *to which* this nation has always been committed [form and
> rhythm would have allowed him to stop here, but accuracy wouldn't] ,
>
> *and*
>
> *to which* we are committed today at home and around the world.

Though not the only uses of parallel structure in the paragraph, these
are probably the most dramatic.

Imagine how awkward the passage might have sounded had
Kennedy not been aware of how to use parallel elements correctly.
The description of the new generation of Americans might have read
something like this:

> . . . the torch has been passed to a new generation of Americans:
> born in this century, tempered by war, people who have been disci-
> plined by a hard and bitter peace, proud of an ancient heritage
> and we won't witness or permit the slow undoing of those human
> rights . . .

When a writer violates our expectations of language, we're forced to
pay attention to the form of the writing rather than to the content.
Like an audience listening to a pianist with no sense of rhythm,
readers become more conscious of the faulty technique than of the
content of the passage. Employed properly, then, this technique of
parallelism is much like the tempo in good music: the audience
appreciates it but is not forced to pay attention to it. Employed
improperly, it becomes your strongest message, one you hadn't
intended to deliver, about your competence with the written
language.

In order to avoid using coordination incorrectly, making what
are termed **parallel structure** errors, you need to tune up your
ear, becoming conscious of sentence balance and listening for this
balance when you proofread.

How to Spot Parallel Structure Errors

If your ear tells you something is wrong with a sentence, as it probably does in our rewrite of Kennedy's sentence, here's how you can
identify the problem. This sentence should also sound funny to you:

> Cynthia is a person with a good mind <u>and</u> who has high standards.

The two items joined by and—"with a good mind" and "who has
high standards"—are not like elements. The last is a clause (with a
subject, "who," and a verb, "has"), while the first is a phrase (with-

out a subject and verb). You need to make these units parallel—grammatically alike. To do so, you can take one of two approaches: either change the clause to match the phrase or change the phrase to match the clause.

PHRASE APPROACH

Cynthia is a person <u>with</u> a good mind <u>and</u> high standards	("And" now connects two nouns that are part of the "with" phrase.)

CLAUSE APPROACH

Cynthia is a person <u>who has</u> a good mind <u>and</u> high standards	("And" now connects two nouns that are part of the "who" clause.)

If you have trouble spotting which units are parallel, the following test will make the process much easier: look at the kind of language that comes after the conjunction. Then simply look for similar language just *before* the conjunction. If you find the same type of elements on both sides, the construction is parallel. If you don't, something is wrong. In the original "Cynthia" example, there is nothing before the conjunction that works like "who has high standards," so the sentence has to be revised.

As you use parallelism to link not just two but three or more items, the problems you may run into become a bit more subtle and not quite so jarring to the ear. See if you can spot the parallelism problem in the following sentence:

"Doonesbury" is a comic strip filled with sarcasm, dry wit and peopled with some of the most frighteningly realistic characters ever to hit the funny papers.

The writer here is calling attention to three attributes of the "Doonesbury" comic strip, but if we list them, it's immediately clear that the last one is not parallel with the other two:

"Doonesbury" is a comic strip filled with
  sarcasm,
  dry wit, *and*
  peopled with some of the most frighteningly realistic characters . . .

The first two items lead us to expect a like item after the "and," but we get something that matches "filled with" instead. There are a couple of ways to make the elements parallel. If you want to keep the structure much as it is now, simply plug in an "and" between "sarcasm" and "dry wit."

> "Doonesbury" is a comic strip
> *filled* with sarcasm (and) dry wit, (and)
> *peopled* with some of the most frighteningly realistic characters . . .

Now we have two sets of parallel elements (sarcasm/dry wit, and filled/peopled). But sometimes this doubling up of "ands," though grammatically correct, sounds awkward. If you think it does, you can restructure the series so that all the elements match:

> "Doonesbury" is a comic strip filled with
> *sarcasm,* (noun)
> dry *wit,* (and) (noun)
> *some* of the most frighteningly realistic characters . . . (noun phrase)

These aren't the only solutions to the problem, but they're probably the best for retaining the emphasis and basic structure of the original.

EXERCISE 5: Parallelism

Underline the elements which should be parallel in each of the following sentences. Then restructure each sentence so that the elements are parallel.

Example: A good student must be <u>patient</u>, <u>diligent</u>, and <u>have the ability</u> to ask questions.

Possible revision: A good student must be patient, diligent, and inquisitive.

1. At my grandmother's house, one has a choice of greasy chicken soup, overcooked boiled beef, or one can have an egg salad sandwich.
2. He helped to wash the car and with cleaning out the garage.
3. Many influences shape a child's development: family, church, peer groups, economic, social, and school.
4. Have you ever had an application for a loan or credit card rejected because at some time a collection agency came out to collect a bill or a bad payment record?
5. Some people are not able to take charge or cannot handle tough situations that crop up and to make quick decisions.
6. I remember how my uncle used to be able to get first row baseball tickets which he was supposed to use for business clients, but instead he took me.

7. The students' evaluation indicated a respect for their professor but that he needed to lighten the workload of the course.
8. In the event of an emergency and you cannot reach the operator by dialing "0," call the County Office at 555–9388.
9. The conclusion simply restates the author's thesis that the refrigerator offers too many conveniences, makes us lazy, and unconcerned with planning ahead for our food needs.

CORRELATIVES

Though it may seem to you at this point that nothing else could, or should, be said about coordination, there is one last variation on the theme you should know about: **correlative conjunctions.** Correlative conjunctions offer an important stylistic addition to the seven basic coordinating conjunctions. They're the caviar of coordination: more sophisticated and less familiar than the basic seven. Unlike the seven, they're always used in pairs:

> [Man] is immortal, <u>not</u> because he alone among creatures has an inexhaustable voice, <u>but</u> because he has a soul, a spirit capable of compassion, and sacrifice and endurance.
> —from William Faulkner's Nobel Prize speech

The correlatives (not . . . but) give special emphasis to what follows each of them, heightening the reader's attention. Both reasons receive more emphasis than "Man is immortal," even though the second receives more than the first.

Below is a list of the most common correlative pairs, with explanations and sample sentences.

Logical Relationship	Correlative Pairs
choice or option	**either . . . or . . .**

Examples: Either the movie <u>or</u> the play would be entertaining.

The U.S. will <u>either</u> find new energy sources <u>or</u> become increasingly dependent on Arab oil.

equal negation of two elements	**neither . . . nor . . .**

Examples: I <u>neither</u> want <u>nor</u> need another drink.

As the politician spoke, the hostess insisted the party was <u>neither</u> a fund raiser for him <u>nor</u> a convenient political platform.

addition—emphasis on the   **not only . . . but (also)* . . .**
second element

Examples: Underground fires are <u>not only</u> hard to combat <u>but also</u> extremely difficult to escape from.

James A. Michener is <u>not only</u> successful <u>but</u> highly pro-lific (also).

---

contrast—emphasis on the   **not . . . but . . .**
second element

Examples: <u>Not</u> talent <u>but</u> continuous effort is the source of most success.

Our efforts at times seem focused <u>not</u> on solving the literacy crisis <u>but</u> on perpetuating it.

---

addition—emphasis on both   **both . . . and . . .**
elements

Examples: <u>Both</u> New Orleans <u>and</u> San Francisco suffer from an overdependence on tourism.

Surprisingly, the new government is <u>both</u> less popular than expected <u>and</u> weaker than a provisional government can afford to be.

We've written two versions of the following sentences, one *with* correlatives and one *without.* Notice the difference in emphasis and rhythm.

1. The stock market dropped 50 points last month, <u>and</u> the cost of living index rose 1.6 per cent as well. (*without*)
2. <u>Not only</u> did the stock market drop 50 points last month, <u>but</u> the cost of living index rose 1.6 per cent as well. (*with*)

1. I haven't the time <u>or</u> the desire to dust the woodwork. (*without*)
2. I have <u>neither</u> the time <u>nor</u> the desire to dust the woodwork. (*with*)

Like coordinating conjunctions, correlatives must join like grammatical units. Because the correlatives set the units off, it's easy to find the units and make sure they're parallel.

---

*Sometimes "also" may not appear directly after "but," or may be omitted entirely.

1. Not only   did the stock market drop . . .
                          (*conjunction followed by an independent clause*)
   but   the cost of living rose . . .
                          (*conjunction followed by an independent clause*)

2. I have neither   the time
                          (*conjunction followed by a noun*)
   nor   the desire
                          (*conjunction followed by a noun*)

Problems in parallel structure occur when like units no longer follow each conjunction; this sometimes happens when one of the correlatives is misplaced.

He not only is an authority on butterflies but also antique airplanes.

In the above example what follows the first conjunction (a verb phrase) is not the same as what follows the second (a noun and its modifier). There are two solutions to the problem. You can change the language after "but also" to read like that after "not only":

He not only is an authority on butterflies but also is an authority on antique airplanes.

Better still, you can change the first unit so that it matches the second to eliminate needless repetition.

He is an authority not only on butterflies but also on antique airplanes.

Correlatives are a bit like the additional engines put in the middle of a long freight train. They give certain parts of the sentence an extra boost and can sometimes make the difference between an emphatic sentence that has good rhythm and balance and a sentence that is just adequate.

EXERCISE 6

A. In some of the following sentences one or both of the correlatives have been misplaced. In these sentences, put the correlatives in the proper place. In some cases you may have to delete repetitious information when you move the conjunction.

Example: My father not only subscribes to *Plain Truth* but also *The Daily Worker.*

Revision: My father subscribes to not only *Plain Truth* but also *The Daily Worker.*

1. My roommate both is messy and lazy.
2. Some people think detective novels are not true literature but are trash.
3. Neither rain, sleet, personal sorrow, nor will a right to privacy keep the television cameras and reporters away.
4. The Pittsburgh Steelers beat not only the Dallas Cowboys but they beat the bookies' predictions as well.
5. A good crossword puzzle is both an exercise in expanding your vocabulary and understanding vague clues.
6. Einstein's equations prove both that time is relative to an object's speed and that no object can travel faster than the speed of light.
7. In either our lifetime or in the lifetime of our children, America will no longer dominate international economics.
8. Not only is Bill an ace driver, but also an excellent mechanic.

B. Write five sentences; in each, use a different correlative pair.

(For more on parallel structure, see the corresponding entry in the Usage Manual, page 348.)

Coordination is not the only way to combine equal elements, though it is certainly the most common joining technique, especially for linking clauses. Semicolons and colons also allow you to combine and expand independent clauses, thereby expanding your ideas and the variety of your sentences.

Semicolons

Somebody once said that the semicolon [;] was invented by a writer frustrated by a lack of alternatives in English punctuation. The writer wanted a strong break between two closely related ideas, the story goes, but not a full stop. A comma indicated too weak a break. The period, on the other hand, was too final, too complete: it allowed no continuation of the thought into the next sentence. The writer reasoned that what was really needed was a mark that fell in between the two, something that created a stronger break than a comma but that wasn't as strong as a period. Adhering to the maxim that the simplest solution is usually the best, the writer combined the period and the comma piggyback fashion, creating the perfect compromise— the semicolon.

Whether this story is true or not, it can help you remember how to use this problem child of English punctuation: use the semicolon to show your reader that two sentences are closely related and might have been separated by a period if you hadn't been convinced of their connection. For example:

Jim likes Stravinsky; his sister prefers Sinatra.

The writer *could* have put a period after Stravinsky, but the resulting two choppy sentences would then have been completely separate even though it was really the writer's intention to present them as two parts of a whole.

He could also have joined the two sentences with a comma and the coordinating conjunction *but* (Jim likes Stravinsky, but his sister prefers Sinatra). Although the ideas would have been ably coordinated and the contrast between Jim and his sister made explicit, the balance, and the reader's sense of making the connection, would have been diminished.

Remember, when a writer uses only a semicolon between two independent clauses, he's actually coordinating the two ideas without a coordinating conjunction, confident that the relationship between the ideas is unmistakable. So when you use a semicolon, make sure the reader can understand the connection you have in mind between the clauses you are presenting together. And note these points:

1. Never break two sentences with a comma alone. "Jim likes Stravinsky, his sister prefers Sinatra" contains a comma splice, so named because the writer is using a comma to "splice" together two complete sentences.
2. Never use a semicolon between an independent clause and a fragment, as in "Jim likes Stravinsky; not Sinatra," or "Jim likes Stravinsky; although his sister prefers Sinatra."

Colons

Sometimes an independent clause serves to *amplify* or *explain* the independent clause before it. In this case, a writer can choose to indicate the relationship by using a colon [:] between the two clauses.

1. I was sure something was wrong: I could smell the smoke before I got up the first flight of stairs.
2. Madame Curie stared into the microscope with growing excitement: she was convinced that she had made an important discovery.
3. Farley Mowat completed some impressive research before writing *Never Cry Wolf:* he lived in the Canadian wilds and carefully observed a family of wolves for over two years.
4. Winston Churchill could be both eloquent and humorous: "The inherent vice of capitalism is the unequal sharing of blessings; the inherent virtue of socialism is the equal sharing of miseries."

In 1, the sentence after the colon tells us what was "wrong." In 2, the second sentence lets us know what was behind Madame Curie's stare and excitement. In 3, the second sentence clarifies "impressive research." And in 4, the sentence after the colon specifically illustrates Churchill's eloquence and humor.

TRANSITIONAL EXPRESSIONS

Transitional expressions are known by a number of aliases which all more or less describe their function (we've heard them called conjunctive adverbs, adverbial conjunctions, introductory adverbs). There are numerous transitional expressions, which

- indicate a logical relationship between independent clauses (as conjunctions do)
- provide continuity from one sentence to another (as other transitional devices do)

The following chart is by no means complete, but it can give you a sense of the kind of expressions we're referring to:

Logical Relationship	Transitional Expression
cause and effect	**consequently**
	hence
	then
	therefore
	thus
	as a result

Examples: Willie Mays played baseball with boldness of wit and muscle; <u>as a result</u>, he was elected to the Hall of Fame.

The chemistry final will cover everything we learned from the beginning of the semester. It is essential, <u>then,</u> that I study not only the whole text, but also every note I ever jotted down in class.

contrast	**however**
	nevertheless
	still
	on the other hand
	even so
	in contrast
	nonetheless
	instead

Examples: Most people finish the day lamenting that they haven't accomplished more; <u>however</u>, few will take the time to organize the day effectively.

I'd seen *Gone With the Wind* six times by the time I was 20. <u>Even so,</u> I cried at each showing as if it were the first.

---

comparison   **likewise**
                                              similarly

Examples: Newspaper headlines seem to capitalize on our need for the gory truth. <u>Likewise,</u> TV newscasts are apt to begin with startling statements that capture our blood-thirsty but fact-seeking appetites.

Everyone from the music devotee to the social butterfly comes to the opera. The symphony audience, <u>similarly,</u> is made up of an incongruous array.

---

time   **meanwhile**
                                              subsequently

Examples: The chili bubbled over onto the back burner; the tortillas, <u>meanwhile</u>, were heating up in the oven, taking their time.

Children learn to differentiate between their parents before they reach their first birthday; <u>subsequently</u>, their perceptions about everyone they encounter become increasingly precise.

---

addition   **also**
                                              besides
                                              furthermore
                                              moreover
                                              additionally

Examples: The processes of thinking and writing are in many ways inseparable. <u>Moreover,</u> when we write extensively about a given subject, our thoughts about it are likely to become more complex.

It's enough for me just to dream of being devilishly handsome; <u>besides,</u> I'd never have time to ward off the admirers.

---

amplification	**indeed**
	in fact
	for example
	for instance
	in effect

Examples: The ballet didn't contain any more action than the music could keep up with; <u>indeed</u>, the choreography was practically toe to toe with the musical score.

Roger seems to be losing his "mad dog" personality. <u>In fact,</u> I saw him the other day and he actually smiled when he said hello.

Although transitional expressions are like conjunctions in some important ways, there are a couple of important differences. Unlike conjunctions, transitional expressions can be moved around. Thus in our example in the chart, the independent clause beginning with "however" could also read:

Most people finish the day lamenting that they haven't accomplished more; few, <u>however,</u> will take the time to organize the day effectively.

Most people finish the day lamenting that they haven't accomplished more; few will take the time, <u>however,</u> to organize the day effectively.

Most people finish the day lamenting that they haven't accomplished more; few will take the time to organize the day effectively, <u>however.</u>

(Try to do the same thing with *but,* a conjunction that also expresses contrast, and you'll end up with nonsense: "Few, but, will take the time. . . .")

Because transitional expressions are *not* conjunctions, they cannot *join* independent clauses. You must separate the two independent clauses with a semicolon or a period.

Wrong: Igor pounced greedily on the flaming lizards, indeed I've never seen Igor so eager.

Right: Igor pounced greedily on the flaming lizards; indeed, I've never seen Igor so eager.

or

Igor pounced greedily on the flaming lizards. Indeed, I've never seen Igor so eager.

Punctuating Transitional Expressions

When transitional expressions come at the beginning of independent clauses, they're usually followed by a comma:

> College professors often go to some lengths to create a relaxed atmosphere. <u>For example</u>, some ask their students to sit cross-legged on the floor or on big pillows.

When transitional expressions come in the middle of an independent clause, they're usually surrounded by commas:

> . . . Some, <u>for example</u>, ask their students to sit . . .

When transitional expressions come at the end of a sentence, they're usually preceded by a comma:

> . . . Some ask their students to sit cross-legged on the floor or on big pillows, <u>for example</u>.

EXERCISE 7: Semicolons and Transitional Expressions

A. Some of the following sentences are punctuated incorrectly. Correct them as necessary.

1. She drank coffee he was addicted to Dr. Pepper; however.
2. The judge found the young girl innocent, consequently, she was immediately released from custody.
3. Many early writers signed their works "Anon," Virginia Woolf speculates that many of them were women.
4. The term "comics" is something of a misnomer; since most of the strips in the "funny pages" don't even purport to be amusing.
5. Melville wrote "Bartleby the Scrivener" in 1853; nevertheless, the story remains a timely portrait of the kinds of problems people face today.
6. I enjoyed my Italian class this summer. It may; in fact, be the most pleasant course I've taken.
7. Every American knows the dangers of smoking, nevertheless, many continue their self-destructive habit.
8. Franklin Roosevelt's "New Deal," John Kennedy's "New Frontier," and Jimmy Carter's "New Foundation" suggested vague but attractive programs of action, who, for example, could resist the modern ring of "new" linked with the adventurous tradition of the "frontier"?

B. Write three sentences of your own using *only* semicolons between independent clauses.

C. Write sentences of your own conforming to the following models:

1. _____ . Transitional expression, _____

_____ .

2. _____ ; _____ , transitional expression,

_____ .

3. _____ ; _____ , transitional

expression.

EXERCISE 8: Colons

A. Below we've provided one independent clause (followed by a colon) that you are to amplify or explain in a second independent clause.

Example: Dwayne made the right choice:

Possible answers: Dwayne made the right choice: he jumped out the window before the smoke asphyxiated him.

Dwayne made the right choice: he decided to go to med school.

Dwayne made the right choice: he married Mary Elizabeth.

1. My uncle was shy and kept to himself:
2. The house had been neglected for years:
3. A teacher must do more than just stand before a class and lecture:
4. A good bibliography is a useful research tool:
5. This movie was unusually boring:

B. Write three sentences of your own using colons.

(For a more complete discussion of the colon, see page 368 of the Usage Manual.)

SUBORDINATION

As we've seen, coordinating conjunctions and transitional expressions are useful tools for joining related ideas. But these devices— particularly the seven coordinating conjunctions—can't express the full range of logical relationships (there is no coordinating conjunction or transitional expression that lets you show that one event is conditional on another, for instance).

And since they express a connection between two *independent clauses,* giving both clauses equal emphasis, coordinating conjunctions and transitional expressions don't let you emphasize one idea over another.

Consider, for instance, these two sentences:

Good writing requires hard work yet can be very rewarding.

The inflation rate continues to rise; moreover, families have a hard time making ends meet.

In the first sentence, the coordinating conjunction *yet* is used correctly to contrast two ideas. But suppose we feel that these two ideas aren't equally important, that the rewards of good writing outweigh the work it requires. We could recast the sentence like this:

<u>Although</u> good writing requires hard work, it can be very rewarding.

The second sentence presents other possibilities. As it stands, the transitional expression *moreover* expresses only the general relationship of addition. And, as in the first sentence, the two clauses are given equal weight. The following revisions express more precise connections between the clauses and give more emphasis to the idea that families are having financial trouble:

Because the inflation rate continues to rise, families have a hard time making ends meet.
(*expresses a cause/effect relationship*)

As long as the inflation rate continues to rise, families will have a hard time making ends meet.
(*expresses a time relationship*)

Words like *although, because,* and *as long as* are **subordinating conjunctions,** and the clauses they introduce are **subordinate clauses.*** The word *subordinate* comes from Latin and means "below in rank." A subordinate clause, then, expresses an idea that you choose to make less important than the idea you express in an independent clause.

Compare the following sentences, both of which contain exactly the same words:

---

*You may have heard subordinate clauses referred to as *dependent* clauses. The terms are interchangeable.

Although he is frequently late for work, he does an excellent job with everything he is assigned.

Although he does an excellent job with everything he is assigned, he is frequently late for work.

If the supervisor wants to play down the employee's tardiness, she can acknowledge it in the subordinate clause, using the independent clause to stress the high quality of the employee's work. This is what the first sentence does. If, on the other hand, she wants to emphasize the employee's tardiness and only mention his good work, she can write the sentence as it appears the second time. The two sentences create a very different impression, simply because of where the writer chooses to place the "although."

Whenever you begin a clause with a subordinating conjunction, you turn that clause into a subordinate clause, thereby making it less important than the independent clause it's attached to.

Here is a list of the most common subordinating conjunctions, grouped according to the relationships they express:

Logical Relationship	Subordinating Conjunction
cause and effect	**because**
	since
	now that
	inasmuch as

Examples: Because I have a headache, I'm going to stay home.

Since young children are often unable to distinguish between television commercials and regular programming, many consumer advocates believe commercials aimed at small children should not be allowed on the air.

contrast	**although**
	though
	even though
	while
	whereas
	even if
	no matter how

Examples: I asked for a raise, even though I was pretty sure the answer would be no.

Whereas ferns thrive on a moist environment, African violets are inclined to sulk if their leaves get wet.

condition	if
	unless
	provided (that)
	in case

Examples: If a person is feeling overworked and under pressure, he may come down with a psychosomatic illness to give him an excuse to stay in bed and rest.

Many economists believe we are bound for another depression unless we can curb inflation.

comparison	as
	as if
	as though

Examples: You are acting as though I didn't care for you.

He drove us to our house as a seasoned taxi-driver would have, with sureness of direction and a sense of urgency.

purpose	in order that
	so (that)

Example: Many writers procrastinate on assignments so that they will have a built-in excuse for accomplishing less than their best work.

time	after
	before
	as
	as soon as
	now that
	since
	until
	when
	while
	as long as
	whenever
	once

Examples: After the proposition was passed, schools had to curtail their athletic programs.

In late autumn, as the days are getting shorter, the number of accidents occurring during the afternoon rush hour rises dramatically.

---

other   **whatever**
                                        wherever

Examples: Whatever you do, don't forget to proofread a paper.

They saw police barricades wherever they looked.

(If you have trouble expressing logical relationships through subordination, see the entry "Faulty Subordination" on p. 413 in the Usage Manual.)

Other Advantages of Subordination

We've already mentioned the most important advantages of subordinate clauses: they allow you to emphasize certain ideas in a sentence while playing down others, and they help you to express relationships between your ideas that might not otherwise be apparent.

But that's not all subordinate clauses are good for. They also allow you to qualify generalizations you may want to make. For instance, if a writer wanted to complain about the poor public transportation in her city, but felt she should mention the reason for this problem, she could, and should, take advantage of subordination. Instead of writing,

Public transportation in San Francisco is slow, unreliable, and above all dangerous,

she could write

Because the city can't afford to maintain it, public transportation in San Francisco is slow, unreliable, and above all dangerous.

Or if a writer wanted to argue that ski areas in Colorado are superior to all others in the United States, he could give necessary recognition in a subordinate clause to the advantages of another locale:

Even though New England has some terrific slopes, I think Colorado's ski areas are the best in the country.

Subordinate clauses are also good for smoothing out choppiness. Very often you'll find that you can use subordinate clauses to combine ideas that might sound choppy if they each appeared as a separate sentence. For instance, "Agatha Christie's detective stories make light reading. Her plots are often extremely complex, however." Too many such sentences, monotonously succeeding each other like telephone poles set at regular intervals along a highway, will make your ideas seem simplistic and lackluster. Notice how much more smoothly the sentence reads if you combine your ideas and subordinate the less important of the two: "Though Agatha Christie's detective stories make light reading, her plots are often extremely complex."

Subordinate Clauses Can't Make It Alone

You should know that subordinating conjunctions are grammatical karate experts. When you put one in front of an independent clause, a subordinating conjunction instantly transforms a perfectly self-sufficient complete sentence into a dependent, inconclusive fragment. For example:

> *Sentence:*   I took out the trash.
>
> *Fragments:*   After I took out the trash
> Unless I took out the trash

The last two leave you hanging in mid-air; you feel the need for an independent clause for these subordinate clauses to latch onto:

> *Sentence:*   After I took out the trash, I was irritated to discover an overflowing wastebasket I had forgotten to empty.
>
> *Sentence:*   Unless I took out the trash each evening, the cockroaches and ants descended on the kitchen in the night.

Actually, most of the students we've encountered who make the mistake of punctuating subordinate clauses as complete sentences tend to do so when the subordinate clause comes *after* an independent one. Here's an example:

> It is almost as important to know the connotations of a word as it is to know its literal definition. So that you will know what contexts to use it in and will recognize its full implications when you see it in print.

These two sentences should, of course, be joined:

> It is almost as important to know the connotations of a word as it is to know its literal definition so that you will know what contexts

to use it in and will recognize its full implications when you see it in print.

Note that it would *not* be correct to use a semicolon before the subordinate clause, since semicolons are generally used to separate two independent clauses.

Punctuation

Fortunately, the guidelines for punctuating subordinate clauses are simple. We can illustrate them as we give them to you:

1. *When a subordinate clause begins a sentence,* it is usually followed by a comma.
2. A subordinate clause, *when it comes in the middle of a sentence,* is almost always surrounded by commas; that is, one goes before it and one comes after it.
3. A subordinate clause is not usually set off from the sentence base *when it comes at the end of a sentence.* In this kind of sentence, there is usually no need to set off the clause since the subordinating conjunction ("when" in the sentence you just read) signals the beginning of a less important idea. *If* you still feel you need to set off the subordinate clause, you may use a comma:

I didn't go to the meeting, though I certainly would have if I had known she would be speaking.

EXERCISE 9

Circle the subordinating conjunctions in each of the following sentences, and underline the clauses they introduce. Then supply any necessary punctuation.

Example: If I study hard for the chemistry final I may get an "A" in the course.

Answer: (If) I study hard for the chemistry final, I may get an "A" in the course.

1. Whenever I went on stage I thought about the consequences I would suffer if I forgot my lines.
2. After she escaped to the North Harriet Tubman helped to free other slaves.
3. I am amazed now that I look back on my years in high school at

the number of classes that were offered as well as their diversity and scope.

4. It doesn't pay to read a textbook as if it were recreational reading because you will be held responsible for the information the text contains.

5. We will be subject to gas rationing unless we drastically reduce our fuel consumption.

6. After the orthodontist had propped my mouth open squirted all sorts of vile-tasting solutions into it and filled it with wires which dangled from the sides of my mouth he decided to begin a friendly chat.

EXERCISE 10: Subordinate Clauses and Real Life

1. You're annoyed at the discourteous treatment you received the last time you were in the stereo store and decide to write the manager a letter about it. Using a subordinate clause, write a sentence in which you acknowledge the good service you have generally received there, but emphasize your displeasure over the recent incident.

2. You're watching an old movie on TV and are suddenly amazed to recognize a former teacher in the role of a dangerous killer. If you were writing a sentence about this discovery, which fact would you put in the subordinate clause—that you were watching television or that you recognized your former teacher? Write the sentence.

3. You're writing a paper for your film class about the silent comedies of Buster Keaton. You want to say that it's necessary to see some of the typical, mediocre slapstick comedies of that time in order to appreciate Keaton's artistry fully. Write a sentence conveying this idea, using a subordinate clause.

4. You have just fallen in love, and you're writing a note to the object of your desire. Write a sentence containing a subordinate clause and emphasizing how dreary your life had been up until the time the two of you met.

5. You are asked by the company you work for to contribute to a worthwhile charity.

   a. Write a sentence containing a subordinate clause and explaining that you would like to contribute at another time but can't afford to right now.

   b. Then write a sentence in which you reverse the emphasis of the two clauses (making the subordinate clause in your first sentence the main clause in the second, and vice versa).
   Which is the more positive reply?

EXERCISE 11: Joining with Subordinate Clauses

Join the following pairs of sentences, using subordinate clauses. Whenever possible, write more than one version of the new sentence,

   a. using different conjunctions to convey different relationships between the two ideas and

   b. emphasizing first one clause, then the other. Be prepared to discuss the differences in meaning these changes create.

Example: The chartered 727 taxied down the runway. I wondered whether I would live to see home again.

Possible revisions: As the chartered 727 taxied down the runway, I wondered whether I would live to see home again.

Until the chartered 727 taxied down the runway, I wondered whether I would live to see home again.

The chartered 727 taxied down the runway as I wondered whether I would live to see home again.

1. You walk up the steps to my grandmother's house. Ceramic owls and bare-bottomed Cupids peek out of the shrubbery at you.
2. The professor sputtered through his lectures at 250 words per minute in an effort to save time. He only ended up having to repeat himself at least twice.
3. "Oh, no!" were my only words. I stared blankly at the test I had forgotten to study for.
4. I had an hour to kill. I went to the library to study.
5. We get home in the evening, tired from our day and ready to relax. We discover our mailboxes bursting with junk mail.
6. In ancient China, a tiny foot was considered a very attractive attribute in a woman. The tale of Cinderella is believed to have originated there.
7. You dream of strangling your best friend with the greatest of vindictive pleasure. It is probably a sign that you have some unresolved anger against this person.
8. Sometimes a substitute took over the class. We had a wonderful time then, sitting in the wrong seats, pretending not to understand any of her questions, and belching loudly when she assigned homework.
9. *Huckleberry Finn* is ostensibly a children's book. It can be enjoyed and interpreted on a number of levels.
10. Air traffic regulations need to be tightened to insure greater safety. If this does not happen, air traffic controllers have threatened to go on strike.

EXERCISE 12

To each of the following sentence bases, add a subordinate clause which provides more information about the base. Use as many of the subordinating conjunctions as you can, and try to vary the placement of the subordinate clauses, putting some at the beginning, some in the middle, and some at the end of the sentence.

Example: Making good coffee is an art.

Possible additions: As Mrs. Olson once remarked, making good coffee is an art.

Making good coffee, though few people realize it, is an art.

Making good coffee is an art whereas anybody can pour boiling water over a teabag.

1. The clock struck eight.
2. Children need kindness tempered with discipline.
3. Reading fiction can be just as educational as reading textbooks.
4. Hubert strolled confidently across the dance floor.
5. Fortunately, a person makes few mistakes which cannot be corrected.
6. For many people who enjoy it as a hobby, gardening provides an opportunity to be outdoors, to cultivate the earth, and to watch things grow.
7. Holiday seasons seem more and more to belong to commercial interests.
8. The banning of many pesticides created problems for the consumer as well as for the farmer.
9. To be an individual is increasingly difficult in a society which rewards people for "following the crowd."
10. Too much television, newspaper, and magazine advertising is aimed at making people over thirty wish they could have stayed eternally twenty-one years old.

9

Expanding the Sentence Base

Looking around at all the things that delight his eye, a young child attempts to communicate his joy. His thoughts come out as discrete units, drop by drop:

Look at the flower.
It is pretty.
It is red.
It smells like cherry Jell-O.

It takes the child four repetitious sentences to express what an older child might consolidate into a single sentence:

This pretty red flower smells like cherry Jell-O.

As adults, though our observations and sentences are of course more complex, we apply the same principle of consolidation to connect our ideas and elaborate on them when we think, speak, and write. Good writers command a variety of constructions to fuse related information into sentences that don't waste words and to sharpen their observations by adding interesting, pertinent detail.

227

While the methods of coordination and subordination in the last chapter are the most common ways to link ideas and show their relationships, other techniques often distinguish amateur prose from professional writing. Accomplished writers use the constructions we're about to show you not only to develop their sentences but to add interest, variety, and momentum to their writing.

The constructions we discuss in this chapter can work for you in several ways. Sometimes you'll use them to combine separate, disconnected sentences into smooth, coherent statements, as the older child joined the four choppy sentences. At other times, when you realize you haven't said enough, they'll provide ways to expand on an idea in order to give your readers a clearer picture of what you're thinking or feeling. And since these constructions appear often in published writing, but much less often in student essays, you'll be working toward a more mature, polished style. For all of these reasons, the constructions you'll practice in this chapter can make the difference between inert, lackluster prose and writing that is lively and engaging.

VERBAL PHRASES

I had been a little fearful of attending a concert with 14,000 people. I had beard the reports of the chaos and mass hysteria which always accompanied Elvis and Beatles concerts; the terror of the Stones concert at Altamont was still fresh in my memory. But sitting, waiting for the show to begin, watching the red, blue, and yellow Frisbees swoop and soar from one end of the stadium to the other, hearing the laughter and talk between strangers ("How did you get your ticket?", "How much did you have to pay?", "Where are you from?", "Did you see him eight years ago in Monterey?"), I began to realize that an audience is a direct reflection of the performer. We had all come to hear Dylan the poet, the spokesman of our generation, not a Rock Super-Star whose ego depended on the hysterical ravings of teenage groupies. My fears abated.

The student who wrote the above passage follows several of the principles we've discussed in this book. She logically organizes the paragraph according to time, focuses consistently on first-person pronouns, and gives us explicit concrete details, down to the colors of the Frisbees. But the paragraph works for another reason, too.

Take a closer look at the third sentence in the paragraph, the one that begins "But sitting, waiting for the show . . ." You'll see that the main clause, "I began to realize that an audience is a direct reflection of the performer," doesn't come until the very end, after the writer has built up momentum in the sentence by recreating for herself and the reader the activity before the concert, putting herself in the middle of the anticipation, exuberance, and conversation that helped her start to see the connection between audience and performer.

If you'll look carefully at the series of phrases describing this activity, you'll notice that each begins with a word ending in "-ing." *Sitting, waiting, watching,* and *hearing* are called **verbals** since they come from verbs but don't function as main verbs within the sentence. A group of related words with a verbal at the beginning (*waiting for the show to begin,* for example) is called a **verbal phrase**.

The writer has used these verbal phrases to combine actions and observations that might otherwise have staggered across the page in a series of choppy sentences: "I sat and waited for the concert to begin. I watched the red, blue, and yellow Frisbees." Like subordinate clauses, verbal phrases have the added advantage of helping us show relationships between ideas: here the writer emphasizes her realization about audiences by expressing it in the main clause of her sentence, preparing readers to accept this idea by her careful arrangement of the subsidiary details that lead up to it. The verbal phrases help her to thrust us into the center of her experience, through interesting descriptive details that substantiate the main clause. While "I began to realize that an audience is a direct reflection of the performer" is not a bad sentence, the writer has created a stronger one by adding verbal phrases.

Verbals come in three basic models. The most popular is the *-ing* form:

> By skillfully <u>reshuffling</u> the cards, he was able to turn the game around.

> He was shot after <u>laying</u> five aces on the table.

> <u>Reflecting</u> on this later, he decided that he may have been too greedy for his own good.

There is also the *to* form:

> <u>To convince</u> her of my sincerity, I brought her a note from my analyst.

> <u>To win</u> her approval, I translated all of Shakespeare's works from English into Russian and back again.

> You need a gimmick <u>to get</u> an "A" in a composition class.

And there's also the *had* form, so named because it is derived from the past participle, or *had* form, of the verb: *pleased, written,* and *seen,* for example:

> Pleased by all the attention, the mayor choked on his gum.
>
> The epic poem "Scuba Diving in Nevada on Ten Dollars a Day," written in 1904, continues to dazzle literary critics even today.
>
> Seen in the gold of an autumn sunset, my laundry looks beautiful, hanging proudly on the sleek clothesline and flapping majestically in the breeze.

Although verbals can be used anywhere in a sentence, they usually appear at either the beginning or end, as in the sentence about the laundry, where they do both. Remember that when a verbal is preceded or followed by other words, it becomes part of a verbal phrase, like "by skillfully reshuffling the cards," "pleased by all the attention," or "to get an 'A' in a composition class." Armed with this information (there's one now), go through the following student paragraph and find the verbal phrases.

> As a child, I spent one summer visiting Aunt Estelle, who had a profound preoccupation with food. Equipped with three shelves of cookbooks, pots and pans of every size and shape, and a set of kitchen appliances that would have put a Sears Roebuck catalogue to shame, she cooked as industriously as a research scientist working on a cancer cure. She started the day by serving an early breakfast of tea and charred toast, bits of which I stealthily dropped behind the heater in order to save room for the culinary horrors to follow. Our midmorning snack was relatively unalarming: a few cookies and a Coke. Much to my alimentary apprehension, though, lunch was a dieter's dream, often consisting of steak, greens, an enormous disc of cornbread, salad smothered in thick, creamy Thousand Island dressing, the dauntless "dirty potatoes" that looked it, and a triumphant slab of boysenberry pie to reward me for finishing everything on my plate. Then in the humid heat of afternoon, Aunt Estelle would suddenly appear on the front porch, bearing a tray of Popsicles or ice cream. Later came her stringent request "Eat your supper!"—a threatening portion of eggs and plump sandwiches which I either threw, undetected, behind the cabinet or threw up, fully observed. At bedtime it was peppermint sticks and a kiss. Disappointed in love, Aunt Estelle had long ago made a nuptial commitment to the kitchen, and by the end of the summer the size of my stomach bore witness to the sanctity of her vows.

ANSWERS:

> visiting Aunt Estelle; Equipped with three shelves . . . to shame;
> working on a cancer cure; by serving an early breakfast of tea and
> charred toast; in order to save room for the culinary horrors to fol-
> low; consisting of steak . . . on my plate; smothered in thick, creamy
> Thousand Island dressing; to reward me for finishing everything on
> my plate; bearing a tray of Popsicles or ice cream; undetected; fully
> observed; Disappointed in love.

EXERCISE 1: Verbal Phrases

A. Combine these sentences, using verbal phrases.

Example: She clutched her head and moaned. She reached for the Anacin bottle.

Answer: Clutching her head and moaning, she reached for the Anacin bottle.

Or: Reaching for the Anacin bottle, she clutched her head and moaned.

1. Auto makers often seem to correct potentially dangerous defects only when forced to by government action. They apparently hope their negligence will go unnoticed.
2. The politician had been defeated and dishonored. He could no longer face the public.
3. You should write according to a plan, leave yourself plenty of time for revising, and proofread your work carefully. You should do these things in order to compose a successful essay.
4. Marx's theories have never been tried in their pure form. They might prove practical if human greed and tyranny did not interfere.
5. People made their way to the beach. They were burdened by striped umbrellas, canvas rafts, and coolers full of lemonade.
6. This paper surveys the development of film in the early years of the twentieth century. It emphasizes the improvement of editing techniques.
7. I was confused by the test question. I sat still. I stared into space. I hoped inspiration would strike.

B. From each of the main clauses that follow, write three expanded sentences. Leaving the main clause as it stands, write one
sentence with an "ing" verbal, another with a "had" verbal, and a
third with a "to" verbal.

Example: The librarian ordered the students to leave.

Revisions: *Shaking his fist angrily,* the librarian ordered the students to leave.

Driven beyond endurance by their continual talking, the librarian ordered the students to leave.

In order to restore quiet to his domain, the librarian ordered the students to leave.

1. Katherine dismantled the engine piece by piece.
2. The butler skidded on the freshly waxed floor.
3. The United States entered World War II.
4. Americans tend to live for the moment.

C. Expand the main clauses of the following sentences by using several verbal phrases.

Example: The thin November sun warms the hard soil.

Expanded sentence: Shining wanly, the thin November sun warms the hard soil, glinting off the pebbles on the path, bathing the withered stalks and bronze blossoms.

1. I finally left the chaotic party.
2. She was an outstanding teacher.
3. Advertisers attempt to manipulate the public into buying products they don't want or need.

Dangling Modifiers

Because a verbal doesn't come with its own subject, it needs to latch onto one. A verbal must have an agent, a word telling who or what is its implied subject:

> To become a member of our organization, an <u>applicant</u> has to give each officer fifty dollars in small bills and a turkey.

> At last week's meeting, I walked into a room full of <u>turkeys</u> clucking apprehensively and <u>initiates</u> clutching bags full of small bills.

> Inspired by our example, the <u>President</u> has decided to require a similar membership donation from each member of the cabinet.

In each of the sentences above, the underlined word tells who or what is the implied subject of the adjacent verbal. Most of the time the verbal's agent will be the subject of the clause the verbal is attached to; the verbal phrase is then set off by a comma, as in the first and third sentences above. When the verbal's agent is the noun just before it (as in the second sentence), the verbal phrase is usually not set off by a comma.

One problem arises as you use verbal phrases, but once you understand how it comes about, it's easy to correct. Occasionally you may write a verbal phrase that "dangles" at either end of the sentence, that doesn't make sense with the word that is grammatically its agent.

> Gasping for breath and dripping with sweat, the bus pulled out as I ran to the stop.

> Bored and distracted, the report was read with no enthusiasm.

> A college education is necessary to get a good job.

> The test was passed by taking enough time to think about each question before answering it.

Sentences like the first one are good for a laugh, but most of us wouldn't let a verbal dangle quite that blatantly. If we weren't paying attention, though, we might let sentences like the other three slip by. Although not so obvious as the dangling modifiers in the first sentence—a bus can't gasp or drip with sweat—the verbals in the other sentences dangle too: the report wasn't bored and distracted, a college education can't get a job, and the test didn't take time to think about questions.

How to Correct Dangling Modifiers

You can correct a dangling modifier by performing surgery on either of the two parts of the sentence. The first, and in most cases the better way to undangle a troublesome verbal is to change the subject of the sentence so it *can* be the implied subject of the verbal. For example, "Bored and distracted, the chairman read the report with no enthusiasm."

Another way to correct the problem is to turn the verbal phrase into a clause, which by definition has a subject and therefore can't dangle: "If you want a good job, a college education is necessary."

This brings us to a closely related point. If you write a sentence in the passive voice or one whose focus is abstract, you may well compound these problems by also writing a dangling modifier. If you correct any one of these problems, the others will probably clear up. For example, the sentence "Family planning should be taken into consideration before getting pregnant and having to cope with the consequences" contains dangling modifiers, has abstract focus, and is in the passive voice. Simply making *you* the subject of the sentence eliminates all three problems: "*You* should consider family planning before getting pregnant and having to cope with the consequences." Similarly, in the previous example about the test, getting rid of the passive also disposes of the dangling modifier: "Mortimer passed the test by taking enough time to think about each question before answering it."

EXERCISE 2: Dangling Modifiers

Some of the following sentences contain dangling modifiers; some do not. Identify and correct those that do, being careful to focus the sentence by choosing the most appropriate subject. Whenever possible, correct the sentence in two ways.

1. Coming into the room, an ancient, mouldy fish tank and a hat-rack covered with cobwebs are seen by the curious visitor.
2. Mt. Shasta loomed formidably in the moonless night, illuminated only by thousands of stars.
3. Entering the party, the sound of hard rock music almost blew out our eardrums.
4. By avoiding complex language, the readability of insurance policies can be increased.
5. Being from a large family with six sisters and one brother, quarrels, battles, and screams of "I hate you!" were not uncommon.
6. My father's finger firmly hit the disconnect button upon hearing it was a member of the opposite sex I was dialing.
7. To help create equality of opportunity, objections to civil rights legislation had to be overcome.
8. Not wishing to hurt his feelings, she told him his striped green slacks and purple polka dot tie complemented each other.
9. Coming back to school after several years in the outside world, the educational experience can be difficult.
10. A door was forced open to escape from the burning theater.
11. Startled by the force of the accusation, yet remembering that every reporter in the crowded press room had a microphone and camera aimed at her, the senator drew a deep breath, paused, and began her answer, speaking with an assurance born of years in public life.

(For more practice, see "Dangling Modifiers" pp. 328–329 of the Usage Manual.)

VERBAL ABSOLUTES

Though philosophical absolutes like "All roads lead to Rome" or "I never met a man I didn't like" are perhaps best avoided, verbal absolutes provide you with yet another way to expand and vary your sentences. Moreover, they offer an advantage that, having just learned about verbal phrases, you'll appreciate: they can't dangle. And the reason they can't is one of the keys to understanding how they work:

Verbal absolutes are simply verbal phrases *with nouns or noun equivalents in front of them.* And they have the benefit of allowing you to take a sentence like the following, which contains a dangler—

> Frayed and torn, Cinderella limped home in her old clothes while a large pumpkin rolled along clumsily beside her.

—and turn it into a logical descriptive sentence by making the simple and succinct correction of placing the noun that can indeed be "frayed and torn" in front of the verbals:

> verbal absolute phrase
>
> (noun) (verbal) (verbal)
> Her old clothes frayed and torn, Cinderella limped home while a large pumpkin rolled along clumsily beside her.

Verbal absolutes are perhaps most effective when describing action:

> The runner jogged smoothly down the beach, his breathing paced, his arms barely cocked.

Here the verbal absolutes add living detail to a general action (the jogging), detail without which that action might appear simplistic or boring. Taking the process a couple of steps further, we can see how effective the absolute can be in a long, fluid statement in which nothing dangles or runs together:

> The early morning light throwing the runner's shadow long on the sand, he jogged smoothly down the beach, his breathing paced, his arms barely cocked, not pumping, but swaying slightly forward and back, his hips rotating to extend his stride, the balls of his feet pushing off, throwing puffs of sand out behind him, and the whole figure moving rhythmically, motion without waste, growing smaller, flowing away into the distance.

The exciting thing about this sentence is that the writer has been able to show so many parts of the jogger in motion—his arms, his hips, the balls of his feet, and, finally, his whole figure—the absolutes magnifying the detailed parts of the whole just as a zoom lens of a camera might focus on and magnify specific actions in a large scene.

Now that you know how to use verbal absolutes, the next obvious question is how to construct them. Think of them as transformations of complete sentences whose subjects remain, but whose verbs change into verbals:

    (subject) (verb)   (subject)   (verb)

1. His fiddle was broken and his musical inspiration was dashed.

    (noun) (verbal)   (noun)   (verbal)

His fiddle broken and his musical inspiration dashed, Nero suddenly realized that Rome was, indeed, burning.

                (subject) (verb)

2. Each tuna fish sandwich sat in its own cozy parsley bed.

The table was covered with an abundance of food, each tuna fish
(subject) (verbal)
sandwich sitting in its own cozy parsley bed.

    (subject)   (verb)

3. The need for rationing had passed.

    (noun)   (verbal)

The need for rationing having passed, restrictions on once-scarce commodities could be lifted.

Adjectives, like verbals, can be incorporated into absolute phrases. You simply place the noun or noun equivalent you're describing in front of the descriptive words. Thus:

    (subject) (adjective)
       | (verb) | (adjective)

Choppy: Her hair was curly and black. The actress glowed with a dark beauty.

       (absolute phrase)

Flowing: Her hair curly and black, the actress glowed with a dark beauty.

    (subject) (verb) (adjective)

Choppy: His face was mottled. Burton was burning with anger for the fifth time that day.

      (absolute phrase)

Flowing: His face mottled, Burton was burning with anger for the fifth time that day.

EXERCISE 3: Absolutes

In the following exercises, join each series of sentences together by making absolute phrases out of all but one of the sentences, using the remaining one as your main clause. In some cases you'll need to change only one sentence to an absolute phrase, while in others you'll need to change two or three.

Example: His kite was struck by lightning. Ben Franklin returned to his house electrified by his discovery.

Rewrite: His kite struck by lightning, Ben Franklin returned to his house electrified by his discovery.

1. His temper was rising uncontrollably. The cop pulled the car over to the side of the road.
2. The motorist waited patiently. Her heart beat wildly. Her anxiety level was quietly yet clearly reaching psychotic heights.
3. The importance of "pure" research has become suspect. The public's enthusiasm for nonindustrial science has started to wane.
4. His knees were broken. The linebacker crawled off the field. His body convulsed with pain. His head drooped. His eyes were swollen almost shut.
5. His imagination was dulled to a prosaic bluntness. His inspiration was irretrievably lost. The student stared at the blank sheet of paper that was to have been his composition.
6. Its leaves resembled oversized spinach. Its stalks climbed clear through the hothouse roof. Its blossoms reeked like the most concentrated French cologne. The African violet had definitely overreacted to the fertilizer.
7. The timing is erratic. The use of dynamics is apparently arbitrary. The musicianship is atrocious. This recording of *Also Sprach Zarathustra* is almost unbearable.
8. Holmes left the scene of the crime. His hat was tilted precariously on his head. His pipe was securely clamped between his teeth. His magnifying glass was tucked safely in the lower right-hand pocket of his trench coat.

Now that you've gotten a feel for putting the above language into absolutes, you might want to try creating your own. To each of the following sentence bases, add two or three absolute phrases.

Example: The Ferrari rounded the corner in a four-wheel drift.

Expanded sentence: A police car close behind, the Ferrari rounded the corner in a four-wheel drift, its driver clutching the steering wheel, his knuckles white and his forehead dripping.

1. She pored over her physics text.
2. The ballerina crossed the stage in a series of pirouettes.

3. Older students are usually quite dedicated.
4. The cook madly dashed around trying to fix all the short orders at one time.

Now make up five of your own sentences with absolute phrases.

ADJECTIVE CLAUSES, ADJECTIVE CLUSTERS, AND APPOSITIVES

Have you ever tried to tell a friend about your troubles with your roommate, who is hassling you about money, your erratic house-keeping, and your disposition, only to realize that your listener isn't really appreciating the extent of your misery? You try, "My room-mate is driving me crazy." As you watch your friend's eyes, you realize that although he wants to be sympathetic, he just doesn't understand, maybe because you haven't found the right assortment of words to convey your despair. Desperate to communicate some of your pain, you search for a way to make your predicament clearer, to supply the details that will answer the questioning look in your friend's eyes.

As a writer, you face the same problem of getting through to your audience. Just as the good conversationalist tries to provide details that clarify and add interest, the clever writer anticipates a reader's questions and supplies specific answers. In addition to verbals and verbal absolutes, there are other constructions that help you make your sentences more complete and precise, redefining and explaining your main idea.

Let's return to the original problem and suppose that you are writing, rather than speaking, about your roommate.

Being a methodical person, and having read our suggestions on pre-writing, you try to list all the things about your roommate that drive you crazy.

1. My roommate is rigid in his habits.
2. He is always griping about my leaving socks on the floor.
3. He is always complaining that I run out of money before payday.
4. He constantly groans that I'm too emotional—sometimes cheerful, sometimes depressed.
5. My roommate is always worried.
6. He is irritable and very stingy.

Keeping in mind that your object is to sum up your problems with your roommate as concisely and concretely as possible, you try to compose a single sentence that sets forth your problem:

Rigid in his habits, my roommate, a nervous, fretful tightwad who never seems to stop complaining, is giving me an ulcer with his constant attacks on my housekeeping, my moods, and my extravagance.

Notice that by writing the sentence this way, you have compressed bits of information into a brief but explicit description of his character, a compression made possible by three constructions: the adjective clause, the adjective cluster, and the appositive. Each of these constructions provides an efficient way for you to add information to a sentence, particularly information about a person or thing.

Adjective Clauses

As the name suggests, an **adjective clause** is a group of words that describes a noun (the definition of an adjective) and that has a subject and a verb (the definition of a clause). Adjective clauses can generally make a more complete statement than an adjective, which is usually just a single word.

(adjective)

The salesclerk ignored the impatient customer.

(adjective clause)

The salesclerk ignored the customer, who drummed his fingers on the counter, conspicuously stared at his watch, and finally sighed heavily and muttered something to himself while striding out the door.

Signal Words for Adjective Clauses

Most adjective clauses are introduced by one of seven words, each of which is used differently.

Who refers to people ("Golda Meir, who led Israel for many years, cared little for the pomp and ceremony of public office.") Note that who acts as the subject of an adjective clause.

Whom also refers to people. ("The type of person for whom this magazine is written does not exist any longer.") Note that whom acts as the object of a verb or a preposition.

Which refers to things (including ideas). ("The new budget, which must still be approved by the legislature, calls for cutbacks in police services.")

That refers to things or people, though most authorities prefer who or whom for references to people. ("A university ship that had

been scheduled to arrive last week has still not been heard from.''
''He is the kind of son that every parent hopes for.'')

Whose shows possession. (''**Dr.** Adams, whose specialty is walruses,
enjoys teaching at the University of Alaska.'' ''We moved into an
old house whose exterior badly needed painting.'')

Where refers to places. (''Costa Rica, where many Europeans now
live, is a small, beautiful country in Central America.'')

When refers to time. (''Surprisingly, many adults don't remember
the day when President Kennedy was murdered.'')

EXERCISE 4: Adjective Clauses

In each of the following sentences, underline the adjective
clause and circle the noun it modifies.

Example:

Human memory is a (process) that psychologists and biologists still
scarcely understand.

1. The foreman fired the auto worker who kept attaching windshield
   wipers to the inside of the car windows.
2. On my first visit to the university library, I got lost in the stacks,
   where the librarian finally discovered me at closing time.
3. Travelling gives you the chance to meet people whom you might
   otherwise never have encountered.
4. For dinner last night, I had antipasto, lasagna, veal piccata, roasted
   peppers, and zabaglione, an orgy of eating that caused me to gain
   five pounds and lose a night's sleep.
5. She was an author whose work I had never read.
6. If a consumer is dissatisfied with a product, he or she should let
   the manufacturer know, for complaining is a strategy that often
   gets results.

How to Punctuate Adjective Clauses

Read the following two sentences aloud:

Any actor who plays Hamlet is compared with all others who have
played the role.

Richard Burton, who played Hamlet on Broadway, was compared
with all others who had played the role.

Your ear probably tells you that the adjective clause ''who played
Hamlet on Broadway'' in the second sentence is parenthetical, or not

essential. Because it doesn't provide information needed to identify the noun it modifies—Richard Burton—the clause is set off with commas. Such clauses are called **nonrestrictive**.

As you read the first of those sentences, though, you probably don't pause before and after the adjective clause "who plays Hamlet." This clause *is* necessary, because without it you don't know what type of actor the sentence is about. ("Any actor is compared with all others who have played the role" doesn't make much sense.) This kind of adjective clause is called **restrictive**.

Put commas around an adjective clause if you don't need it to identify the noun it modifies. You'd probably pause before and after such a clause if you read it aloud. (These not-absolutely-essential clauses are the nonrestrictive clauses.)

But don't put commas around an adjective clause if you *do* need it to identify the noun it modifies—(these are the restrictive clauses.)

Here are some examples of nonrestrictive clauses:

> Margaret Mitchell, who wrote *Gone with the Wind,* tried a variety of inappropriate names—Robin, Angel, and Pansy among them—before settling on Scarlett as a name worthy of her headstrong protagonist.

Since "Margaret Mitchell" can stand alone without further identification, the adjective clause is set off by commas.

> My father, who has a quick temper, once hurled a beer stein at a stray dog that failed to treat his prized petunia bed with proper regard.

"My father" tells you who the writer is talking about, so the adjective clause is set off with commas.

> The television film *Holocaust,* which was first aired in West Germany in 1979, stunned many young Germans who had never been told about the horrors of Nazi concentration camps.

"Holocaust" specifies which film is being discussed, so the adjective clause is set off by commas.

And here are some examples of restrictive clauses:

> People who live in glass houses should be exhibitionists.

(Without "who live in glass houses" we don't know which kind of people the sentence is about, so the adjective clause is not set off by commas.)

> The newspaper route which I had as a boy netted me all of ten dollars a month, but that seemed like big money at the time.

(Try the sentence without the adjective clause: "The newspaper route netted me all of ten dollars. . . ." Which newspaper route? You need the adjective clause, so it's not set off by commas.

> Many people think ex-convicts who commit the same crime again should receive stiffer sentences the second time.

(Again, without the adjective clause "who commit the same crime again," it's not clear which particular ex-convicts the writer is discussing. So no commas around the adjective clause.)

EXERCISE 5: Punctuating Adjective Clauses

Add commas where necessary:

1. Major controversies have erupted recently over condominiums and apartment buildings which exclude people who have children.
2. Ruth Gordon who starred in *Where's Poppa?* and *Harold and Maude* has proven that an actress' career need not be over when she reaches the traditional retirement age.
3. Any student who intends to take courses that require many papers should learn how to type.
4. One of my greatest heroines is Jane Addams who gave up a comfortable upper-middle-class existence to found Chicago's first settlement house in a tenement district.
5. My next-door neighbor who is inclined to get hysterical immediately telephoned the police when he opened a closet door to find a snake inside.
6. I used to suffer untold torment on Valentine's Day when we would all take Valentines to school (I was afraid I wouldn't get any).
7. Queen Elizabeth II whose sister Margaret became the first member of the Royal Family to secure a divorce is known for her exemplary home life.
8. Last summer I got the chance to visit Minneapolis where my grandfather grew up and to see the house where he was born.

EXERCISE 6: Joining with Adjective Clauses

Using adjective clauses, combine each set of sentences into one smooth sentence.

Example: The Office Manager had proven himself to be efficient and industrious. He would soon rise to the position of Assistant Vice-President.

Revision: The Office Manager, who had proven himself to be efficient and industrious, would soon rise to the position of Assistant Vice-President.

1. If I were to inherit a fortune, I would give it away to my adventuresome sister. She would know better than I how to enjoy it.
2. When I was a child, I took piano lessons from a lovable woman named Mrs. Oglethorpe. I always liked to tease her because she believed everything I told her.
3. An adjective clause is a sentence expander. Its function is to make the reader's understanding of a noun more precise and complete.
4. The senator promised to lower taxes, fight crime, and enact a new law. This law would force dog owners to clean up their canines' unsolicited additions to neighborhood lawns.
5. One of the best places to go at five o'clock in the morning is the flower market. Thousands of blooms spill out onto the sidewalks there, awakening the drowsy visitor with their colors and scents.
6. This autumn something happened. It completely changed my way of looking at the world. It made me understand better than I ever had before what it meant to be alone and afraid.

EXERCISE 7: Adding Adjective Clauses

A. For each of the following sentences, construct an adjective clause which provides more information about the underlined noun.

1. Before I could begin to tackle all my assignments, I had to have a plan.
2. I began to dream of my trip to Tahiti.
3. Campus child-care centers would be a great convenience to many university students with children.
4. I have a collection of 324 hats, but my favorite is the blue felt fedora with the peacock feathers.
5. The man put down his makeshift sign, mounted his soap box, and proclaimed that the end of the world was at hand.
6. The successful city planner devises projects.
7. Many respected educators believe that the standard college grading system should be abolished.
8. Startling as it may seem, behavioral scientists are now teaching apes to use human sign language.

B. Write seven sentences of your own with adjective clauses. Each adjective clause should start with a different signal word (*who, whom, whose, that, which, where, when*).

Adjective Clauses with Prepositions

You're reading over a rough draft of your latest essay, hoping you can revise what you've got into something approximating an "A" paper, when you come across the following sentence:

> He asked me a peculiar question in which several different responses were possible.

You stop and read it again. Your ear has caught the fact that something is wrong, but you're not sure exactly what. You have the feeling, though, that it has something to do with that peculiar-sounding "in which."

The problem is that you've used the wrong preposition before "which." "Which" refers to "question" in this sentence, and usage dictates that we say responses are possible *to* questions, not *in* questions.

You can see the mistake more clearly if you turn the adjective clause into a sentence:

> Several different responses were possible to it [the question].

The rule is that you use the same preposition (*in, from, to, about, on, for,* etc.) that you would use if the adjective clause were a separate sentence.

EXERCISE 8: Adjective Clauses with Prepositions

The adjective clauses in the following sentences contain prepositions. Some are correct, and some aren't. Fix those that aren't.

Example: The economy is something to which we have no control.

Correction: The economy is something over which we have no control. (When the adjective clause is turned into a sentence, it's clear that "We have no control to it" is incorrect.)

1. Mr. Walker was an extraordinary teacher of whom I would be willing to tackle any assignment.
2. *The Exorcist* was a shocking, vulgar, and violent film which there was a great deal of controversy about.*
3. Loyalty is a virtue for which most people pay too little attention.

---

*Note that, contrary to prevalent superstition, it is not necessarily incorrect to end a sentence with a preposition. In fact, prepositions sometimes sound more graceful and less conspicuous at the end.

4. The price of books is set according to a system in whose intricacies the general public knows little.
5. He ushered me into his office, which I had not been prepared of; it was cluttered and dark, yet strangely pleasant.
6. The attorney whom you addressed your letter to has been disbarred.

Adjective Clusters

An **adjective cluster** consists of a lead adjective followed by other closely connected words. Unlike adjective *clauses*, adjective clusters do not contain subjects and verbs. Yet they serve much the same function: they provide information about a person or thing.

You can sometimes create an adjective cluster by joining information from two separate sentences:

My roommate is <u>rigid in his habits</u>.
He is giving me an ulcer.

Joined: <u>Rigid in his habits</u>, my roommate is giving me an ulcer.

The underlined portion, the essence of the first sentence, becomes the adjective cluster in the fused sentence. We call this group of words a cluster because the words "in his habits" must stay with the lead adjective "rigid." While we can't treat these clusters like simple adjectives (we wouldn't write "My rigid in his habits roommate"), we can move the entire cluster around within a sentence. We can, for example, write, "Rigid in his habits, my roommate is giving me an ulcer," or, "My roommate, rigid in his habits, is giving me an ulcer." Take a look at some choppy sentences followed by their fusions:

There were hundreds of flies. They were <u>black and glintingly metallic</u>. They sparkled blue and green when the sunlight hit them.
There were hundreds of flies. <u>Black and glintingly metallic</u>, they sparkled blue and green when the sunlight hit them.

We just muddle along in the same wasteful, inefficient manner. We are <u>content to play the game and occasionally sneak in an improvement</u>.
We just muddle along in the same wasteful, inefficient manner, <u>content to play the game and occasionally sneak in an improvement</u>.

I dropped onto the sofa. I felt <u>limp and dejected</u>.
<u>Limp and dejected</u>, I dropped onto the sofa.

EXERCISE 9: Adjective Clusters

A. For each of the following, use adjective clusters to produce one smooth sentence.

1. Tom was enthusiastic but uncoordinated. He lost every game of tennis.
2. Melissa suddenly got up, left the class, and ran twelve blocks home to get her assignment. She was furious with herself for being so forgetful.
3. She was aware of his weakness for small chocolate candies. She led him on with kisses.
4. The workings of the Electoral College are obscure to most voters. These workings are rarely mentioned even during an election year.
5. Professor Stevens was a bit irresponsible, but he was also extremely attractive. He began another math class with an amusing excuse for being twenty minutes late.

B. Write five sentences of your own with adjective clusters.

Appositives

So much of grammar seems arbitrary that it's nice to encounter a construction whose name actually describes its function. Derived from the Latin word for "to put or place," an **appositive** is a noun or noun equivalent placed beside another noun to explain it more fully. But while *opposition* indicates that elements work against each other, *apposition* means that elements work together, side by side. Take a look at the following sentence, for example:

> (noun)   (noun)
> Mr. Crumpet, the baker down the street, makes the best doughnuts in town.

Notice that the appositive the baker down the street, a noun followed by a series of associated words, simply renames and thus further identifies Mr. Crumpet.

Just as adjective clusters can be used to fuse more than one thought, appositives too can transform two or more sentences into one.

> Mr. Crumpet is the baker down the street.
> Mr. Crumpet makes the best doughnuts in town.

Notice how much smoother the appositive sounds. By using appositives, you avoid needless repetition of the subject and verb (and especially the weak *was*, a *to be* verb that, as you learned in Chapter 5, doesn't really move the sentence or thought forward). However, appositives are more than just efficient. As we pointed out in the introduction to this section, appositives give you another chance to get your point across, probe a little more deeply into your idea. Consider, for example, the following sentence:

> Vegetarianism introduced me to a new range of foods—fernshoots, alfalfa sprouts, pickled burdock root, and nasturtium leaves.

A "new range of foods," no matter how much it conveys to the writer, is essentially an abstraction, and thus difficult for anyone else to understand. Notice, though, that when the writer takes the trouble to further define this abstraction, she can make her concept concrete.

(As we noted in the definition above, a "noun equivalent" can also be an appositive. For example: "His goal, to earn a black belt in karate, often seemed unreachable." Note that the appositive here is what is called an infinitive phrase, a "noun equivalent" because it could itself serve as the sentence subject: To earn a black belt in karate was his goal.)

Since the function of the appositive is to rename a noun, it is only logical that appositives need to remain fairly close to the words they identify. But as long as they do stay close to their nouns, appositives, like adjective clusters, may be moved about within the sentence.

> My little brother, a perfectionist in everything he does, reassembled the clock after discovering exactly what made it tick.

> A perfectionist in everything he does, my little brother reassembled the clock after discovering exactly what made it tick.

For purposes of punctuation, you might regard appositives this way: since they are renaming a noun, they are most often not strictly necessary to the sense of the sentence and so could be eliminated. When we wish to indicate that an element in a sentence could be left out, we set it off by commas, as we do with nonrestrictive adjective clauses. Depending on where the appositive comes in the sentence, then, it will usually be followed by a comma, surrounded by commas, or preceded by a comma.

Appositives can *introduce* sentences, *interrupt* the standard subject-verb-object pattern, or *conclude* sentences.

> *Introducer:*   A woman in love with her Porsche if I ever saw one, Samantha ignored the men in her English class.

> *Interrupter:* Samantha, <u>a woman in love with her Porsche if I ever</u> <u>saw one</u>, ignored the men in her English class.
>
> *Concluder:* The men complained bitterly about Samantha, <u>a</u> <u>woman more in love with her Porsche than with any</u> <u>mere male.</u>

EXERCISE 10: Appositives

A. Transform each of these pairs or groups of sentences into one smooth sentence by using appositives.

1. My mother is a woman of great energy and determination. She amazed me during a recent phone conversation.
2. I carried two images of myself in my head. One image was of a knock-kneed urchin in blue jeans. The other was of a princess of the realm, regal, ethereal, forever pursued and loved.
3. Most patients regard their doctor with a mixture of fear and awe. These are feelings not especially conducive to clear doctor-patient communication.
4. Any type of prejudice is the tool of the ignorant. It is the weapon of the unthinking.
5. Since I was always on a diet, I hated to walk through that neighborhood. It was a place redolent with glorious aromas. There were many scents which tempted me with promises of homemade pasta, freshly ground coffee, and still-warm cinnamon rolls.
6. The silver coffee urn was an heirloom handed down through generations. It gleamed softly on the sideboard.
7. She decided to drop out of school. It was a place she hated and would never be sorry to leave.
8. My father is a frustrated man. He is a pilot who was born in the wrong century. He is a wild-eyed visionary who should have been young when the Wright brothers were first experimenting with the possibilities of flight.
9. Travellers are often relieved to find that other languages contain a helpful smattering of cognates. Cognates are words that sound like their English equivalents, such as *haus* (house) in German or *aeropuerto* (airport) in Spanish.
10. Louise was a woman who was convinced that Freud had all the answers. She discovered, to her dismay, that the computer dating service had matched her up with Louie. Louie was a devoted follower of Werner Erhardt's est theories.

B. Write five sentences of your own with appositives.

Appositives and Adjective Clusters as Sentence Tighteners

In the interests of economy and directness, you'll often find that adjective clauses can be trimmed down to appositives or adjective clusters. This is especially true of adjective clauses with linking verbs like *to be* or *to seem*.

For example, the adjective clauses in the following sentences are unnecessarily wordy, given the more concise alternatives available:

> Willie Mays, who is a ballplayer who was more popular with New Yorkers than with San Franciscans, always seemed to consider New York his home.
> Willie Mays, a ballplayer more popular with New Yorkers than with San Franciscans, always seemed to consider New York his home.

> Unilateral disarmament, which seems like an appealing idea to many liberals, is dangerous and impractical.
> Unilateral disarmament, an appealing idea to many liberals, is dangerous and impractical.

> John often returned to his old high school, which was a place that had memories that were both pleasant and painful.
> John often returned to his old high school, a place with memories both pleasant and painful.

Anything Can Work in Apposition

You've seen how the principle of apposition works with nouns; you can also use apposition with other grammatical units. Just remember that you must place like grammatical units next to (in apposition to) each other. Just as you put a noun by a noun, so you must follow a verbal phrase with a verbal phrase, an adjective clause with another one, a prepositional phrase with a like construction, and so on. Below, we provide some examples of various constructions working in apposition to one another.

1. *Nouns and Verbals:* <u>A part-time toy store clerk,</u> I try to dodge through the customers who are determined <u>to stop me, to find out</u> exactly where each toy on their Christmas list is stacked.
2. *Prepositional Phrases:* I stared <u>at the class, at the faces, at the legions of eyes.</u>
3. *Subordinate Clauses:* We most often act as we do because our actions give us pleasure or save us trouble; we rarely perform an act <u>because it is right, because it squares simply with our sense of what is fair and moral.</u>

4. *Adjective Clauses:* When I was living in San Francisco, I owned a dog that was completely bald and extremely ugly, a scrawny, naked runt of a dog <u>who</u>, in spite of being hopelessly cross-eyed, <u>loved to watch</u> daytime soap operas on TV, <u>who would howl</u> pitifully if prevented from watching "As the World Turns," <u>who ignored</u> all my pleas to do something more constructive than sit transfixed by the boob tube all day long.

EXERCISE 11: Putting It All Together

In the last two chapters, we've demonstrated how well-developed sentences can help writers by eliminating terminal choppiness, linking ideas, and curing the blahs. You know that one of the most useful things you can do is to expand each sentence by adding details, and you also have at least a nodding acquaintance with some constructions that are natural expanders: subordinate clauses, adjective clauses, appositives, adjective clusters, verbal phrases, and absolutes. You've practiced each construction in isolation; here's a chance to come closer to what you do in actual writing by using several different constructions to expand upon a main clause:

A. Take the sentence base "I had a best friend."

1. Put a clause beginning with *when* before it.
2. Put a clause beginning with *who* right after "friend."
3. Follow that *who*-clause with an appositive, a word or phrase that renames "friend."
4. After the appositive, write another *who*-clause.
5. Stop and reread what you have so far to be sure it makes sense. (You might want to have someone else look at it too.)
6. Continue the sentence where you left off by writing two verbal phrases joined by *and.*

Continue your description by expanding the sentence base "We went everywhere together," using a variety of constructions. Don't forget absolutes and adjective clusters.

B. We began with sentences that are basically descriptive, but here are a couple of sentences which call for more analytical thinking. Once again, expand them by using as many constructions as you can, without overdoing it.

1. I talked to an employment counselor yesterday.
2. I am now beginning to question the value of a college education.

10

Words, Words, Words

The best writing is concrete and direct. Good writers aren't afraid to take and defend a stand, and they work hard to put their ideas across clearly and to support them solidly. They also strive to actively engage their audience, choosing words, examples, and details that keep readers interested. This standard of good writing is hard to achieve, but good writers put forth the necessary effort.

Yet even if we are good writers, we may sometimes fail to reach or even try for that difficult standard. We may be tempted to look for shortcuts, to give the illusion of meeting our obligations to our readers without actually going to the trouble of doing so. These shortcuts, whether we use them consciously or unconsciously, dilute our prose, confusing, intimidating, or pacifying our readers rather than informing and interesting them.

WORD PRECISION

The Overburdened Word

In preparing ad copy, one novice ad man wrote, "The fanny pack is gravity-centered in the small of the back." Asked what he meant to convey by "gravity-centered," he responded, "The pack fits so that its center of gravity is practically the same as the individual's. The closer the centers of gravity are to each other, the better the balance." He thought his two-sentence explanation was conveyed by one word, "gravity-centered." He *overburdened* this one word, trying to make it convey a concept that demands more than a one-word explanation.

When a writer "overburdens" a word, it's usually because he or she doesn't understand that the single word chosen cannot encapsulate the whole idea the writer intends. "Overburdened words" need to be replaced by sentences or paragraphs that can more fully and precisely explain what the writer has in mind. A single word might be perfectly clear in one context but not in another. Take this sentence, for example:

> The chairman of the committee illustrated how *irresponsible* he was
> by failing to draw up an agenda for the meeting or even to show up.

In this case, it is immediately clear why the chairman is irresponsible. The two examples define his irresponsibility, so the word needs no further explanation. Put the word in a different context, however, and the term requires further explanation.

> Their handling of the 1979 oil crisis and their subsequent reaping of
> windfall profits proved once again how *irresponsible* the oil com-
> panies are.

The writer of this sentence does not make clear what he means by "irresponsible." He assumes that mentioning the 1979 crisis and large oil company profits proves his point, but two questions remain: (1) what was "irresponsible" about the oil companies' handling of the crisis? (2) why are big profits necessarily "irresponsible"? In this context the term "irresponsible" is overburdened and requires further explanation. This writer doesn't realize that there is no one word that captures his meaning. To his credit, his thought is more involved than a one-word explanation permits, and it requires an extra sentence, perhaps even a paragraph, of explanation.

The Wrong Word

A simpler but related problem crops up when a writer is unfamiliar with the meaning of a word. While the writer of the sentence about oil companies extended the meaning of the word beyond its limits, the writers of the following sentences picked words that miss their intended meanings completely.

> Dwight watched the changing *facade* of his father's features as he
> explained the details of the accident.

The protesters believed they would be *futile* in their attempt to change the government's position on draft registration.

The three kindergarteners formed a cheerful *triumvirate* as they skipped their way to school.

In the first sentence, the writer doesn't have a clear enough understanding of "facade" to know that it usually applies to the front of buildings rather than to people's features. In the second sentence, the writer probably means "unsuccessful" or "frustrated," since only protests and not protesters can be "futile." And in the last sentence, the writer mistakenly assumes that a "triumvirate" means something like any "team" or "group" of three when in fact it refers to a ruling or governing body of three.

The wrong word error is usually the result of a misguided sense of how to choose words. The writer either has seen the word before and, having a hazy recollection of what it means, proceeds to use it wherever it seems appropriate, or has decided to extend his or her vocabulary, throwing in a few gems from the thesaurus.

No matter why these errors occur, the result is the same: the reader begins to doubt the writer. Basic communication is not usually in question; most readers can make sense out of the three sentences we've discussed. But in permitting errors like these, the writer indicates he or she can't use language critically, a shortcoming that makes the writer's entire thinking process suspect. As a general rule, then, stick with words you thoroughly understand. The dictionary and thesaurus are basic, even essential, references, but they should be used carefully and thoughtfully, not casually.

In addition to these obvious barriers between what a writer intends to say and what he or she actually says, there are a number of obstacles that block meaning in various ways. Some are difficult to detect and eliminate because we're so used to them in speech, as well as in poorly written academic and political prose, that we come to think of them as appropriate in our own writing. (See "Wrong Word" in the Usage Manual, pp. 425–426.)

TECHNICAL LANGUAGE AND A LAY AUDIENCE

Technical language can be effective and precise, as when one doctor tells another, "My patient has an aneurism of the aortic arch." Between two specialists who understand the terms of their profession, such language acts as a valuable shorthand for communicating a complex problem. Addressed to the layman, however, such language would be practically meaningless. A doctor speaking to a patient would probably go on to rephrase this technical description in terms the patient would clearly understand: "You have a weak spot, a ballooning out of the blood vessel wall, on the artery that carries blood to your lower body." How extensively a speaker or writer draws on accurate technical terms should depend on the audience's familiarity with the subject. Even when used appropriately, these terms are almost always more effective if followed by concrete examples, analogies, and definitions. If you're in doubt about your audience, address yourself to the patient, not the doctor.

Below are two different explanations of the same phenomenon, one written to the "doctor" (in this case, a group of scientists) and the other written to the "patient" (in this case, a general audience). Though both are written by the same writer, Carl Sagan, the first obviously addresses itself to a highly professional scientific group who would expect scientific data, the second to a general audience who probably wouldn't understand, let alone appreciate, that technical data.

The modern theory of stellar evolution implies that the Sun has increased in brightness by several tens of per cent over geological time. Were all other global parameters held constant, this would imply that the mean temperature of the Earth was below the freezing point of seawater about 2×10^9 yr ago. There is, however, excellent geological and palaeontological evidence that there were extensive bodies of liquid water on the Earth between 3 and 4×10^9 yr ago. A possible solution to this puzzle, first postulated by Sagan and Mullen, is that the Earth's primitive atmosphere contained small quantities of NH_3 and other reducing gases which significantly enhanced the global greenhouse effect. NH_3 is especially effective in the 8-13 nm window in a CO_2-H_2O atmosphere. It was argued that plausible changes in other global parameters, such as the infrared emissivity or the Russell Bond albedo, would have been ineffective. The increase in solar brightness over geological time seems model-invariant even under extreme model perturbation for the solar interior, as has recently been reconsidered in a straightforward stellar structure scaling argument. Cosmochemical considerations point strongly to a higher abundance of reduced constituents in the primitive than in the contemporary terrestrial atmosphere; and reduced atmospheric components such as NH_3 and CH_4 are required to understand the accumulation of prebiological organic compounds necessary for the origin of life in this same period, between 3 and 4×10^9 yr ago.

—Carl Sagan, "Reducing Greenhouses and
Temperature History of Earth and Mars,"
Nature, 15 September, 1977

If we assume that the earth four billion years ago had the same distribution of land and water, clouds and polar ice, so that it absorbed the same relative amount of sunlight that it does today, and if we also assume that it had the same atmosphere it has today, we can calculate what its temperature would have been. The calculation reveals a temperature for the entire earth significantly below the freezing point of seawater. In fact, even two billion years ago, under these assumptions, the sun would not have been bright enough to keep the earth above the freezing point.

But we have a wide variety of evidence that this was not the case. There are in old mud deposits ripple marks caused by liquid water. There are pillow lavas produced by undersea volcanoes. There are enormous sedimentary deposits that can only be produced by ocean margins. There are biological products, called algal stromatilites, that can only be produced in water.

So what is wrong? Either our theory of the evolution of the sun is wrong or our assumption that the early earth was like the present is wrong. The theory of solar evolution seems to be in good shape. What uncertainties exist do not appear to affect the question of the sun's early luminosity.

The most likely resolution of the apparent paradox is that something was different on the early earth. After studying a wide range of possibilities, I conclude that what was different, two billion years ago and earlier, was the presence of small quantities of ammonia in the earth's atmosphere. Ammonia is present on Jupiter today; it is the form of nitrogen expected under primitive conditions. It absorbs very strongly at the infrared wave-lengths that the earth emits to space. Ammonia on the primitive earth would have held heat in, increasing the surface temperature through the greenhouse effect and keeping the global temperature of earth at congenial levels. Ammonia would have made possible the origin and early history of life and the abundance of liquid water early in the history of the planet. Ammonia is one of the atmospheric constituents needed for making the building blocks of life. The study of the sun's evolution leads us to information about the early history, chemical composition, and temperature of the earth, and therefore, to the circumstances of its habitability. Stellar and biological evolution are connected.

—Carl Sagan, "A Younger Sun, a Colder Earth,"
The Cosmic Connection: an Extraterrestrial Perspective,
Doubleday and Sons, 1973

Notice that the first sample is slanted towards a critical audience expecting to be convinced by empirical evidence, while the second is geared toward a receptive, less critical audience that wants information. Sagan judiciously assumes that his lay audience will probably have no idea what the "Russell Bond albedo" was and that they will not care that a change in it has no bearing on the "greenhouse effect." He rightly understands that they will be interested in an easily comprehensible explanation of this effect. Hence, in the second version he devotes half his discussion to this explanation. At no point does he refer to numbers and scientific terms, though in the first version he relies on them heavily.

In order to successfully make this switch from the technical explanation to the general explanation, you may want to refer to some helpful guidelines, for while Sagan makes the switch appear easy, you may find it a bit tricky in your own writing.

KNOWING YOUR AUDIENCE

Before you address your subject, know both your audience and your terms. If you're writing a report on learning disabilities for an education class, you can use terminology you'd probably want to avoid if you were writing an article for the student newspaper on the same subject. Regardless of your audience, be sure your terms are accurate. A newspaper audience that read "dispepsia" where the proper word would be "dyslexia" would no doubt be as unnerved as your education teacher would.

BUILDING DEFINITIONS

If you take the time to build a series of definitions of your technical terms, you help your audience follow your thinking. In the doctor/patient example at the beginning of this section, for instance, notice that "aneurism" is defined in easily understood terms as "a ballooning out of the blood vessel wall." Similarly, you can see that if an accounting major were writing a paper for a general audience and wanted to discuss P & L sheets and negative and positive cash flow, he'd need to define those terms, elaborating on just what a profit and loss statement is and what negative and positive cash flow refers to.

In combination with definitions, analogies can help bridge the gap between your specialty area and the realm of knowledge familiar to all of us. In explaining how the heart works, for example, a doctor might describe it as "a biological pump," comparing its function to that of a machine we're all familiar with. In explaining cash flow problems, our accounting student might compare cash flow in a business to water flow in a reservoir: just as water flows in and out of a reservoir, money flows in and out of a business. If there is more coming into the reservoir than is being let out, cash flow is positive. But if there is less flowing in than is being let out, cash flow is negative. By comparing the unfamiliar to the familiar, writers draw on shared knowledge to help us understand new information.

JARGON

Jargon is defined as terminology common to a particular profession or discipline. But the term usually implies the inappropriate use of such terminology. Though, as we've seen, such language can be mistakenly directed to the wrong audience, it is much more often simply misused. In casual conversation, we often carelessly use terms whose technical definitions are quite different from what our application would suggest. While we shouldn't have to edit our every word when talking with friends, we do the language and ourselves an injustice if we don't distinguish between casual oral language and more formal writing.

When we accuse a friend of being "paranoid," for example, we rarely mean that he has delusions of greatness, though the definition of the term includes that meaning. We usually mean he has fears of some sort, which comes close to another part of the definition of paranoia, delusions of persecution. While the listener would probably understand our use of the word *paranoid*, in writing we want to avoid misinterpretation, for the result could be as strange as that in a recent news article in which a politician says of a former Ronald Reagan aide that he is "paranoid, has been for a long time. He can't stand to have anybody disagree with him . . . ." From this statement we might assume that "paranoid" meant "irritated by criticism."

A supermarket recently displayed a sign that informed its patrons that it was "back on-line" after a union strike. Presumably the management of the market meant that the strike was over and that union employees were back on the job, but anyone familiar with the term *on-line,* drawn from computer jargon, might reasonably have been confused. Did management mean to say the strike was over? Or that they had experienced temporary problems with their computer terminals? The misapplication of the term created confusion instead of communicating the intended message.

Parameters, originally a term referring to variables in a math problem, has come (perhaps through confusion with *perimeters*) to mean little more than "borders" in daily usage. Now if that change were uniformly accepted, it would not create confusion; it would simply exemplify the continuing evolution of language. In this case, however, both definitions exist simultaneously. Notice, for example, that Carl Sagan uses the technical meaning of the word: "Were all other global parameters [variables] held constant. . . ." The layman, assuming Sagan meant "borders," would be hard pressed to understand the sentence.

Jargon Used to Obscure

One particular brand of shampoo claims that it is a "polymeric shampoo" that "lathers into the hair's structure a cross-linking, strengthening lattice-work of body building, cuticle intensifying attributes that greatly enhance the integrity of the hair." This claim sounds impressive—precisely, of course, how it is supposed to sound. Advertisers know that a product's success depends on its packaging. So to draw attention to a product pretty much like all the others of its type, they resort to the worst form of jargon: obscure technical-sounding language—"polymeric," "lattice-work," "cuticle intensifying attributes"—combined with overly complex sentence structures.

Jargon can be used to impress, sometimes to intimidate, and often to obscure. Used in this manner, it is practically devoid of content. When writers push this kind of language on a perceptive reader, they not only fail to intimidate or impress, they put their intellectual bankruptcy on paper as well. Rather than saying something they believe, they say nothing, or pump up a simple message, perhaps afraid they have nothing to say at all. In the following paragraph, for instance, the writer confuses a very short, straightforward message for just this reason.

> The term *efficient,* when used to refer to financial management, is usually used when discussing aspects of management performance. Efficient performance is that which maximizes results obtained from the resource that the management has control of regardless of whether the result achieved, met, or was congruent with the goals of the firm or segment. An example of this term used correctly is: "The building contractor was efficient because he stretched his available funds to accomplish the most building construction he possibly could; however he did not complete the building site on the agreed-upon date." Thus the term *efficient* is always used to describe a project or job that has been done with the least possible cost expenditure.

Using jargon like "maximize," "congruent with," "cost expenditure" and "segment," terms he's probably borrowed from a business text, the writer thinks his discussion sounds educated and probably even articulate. He may also realize that technical words and overly complicated sentence structures lengthen his paragraph. Perhaps he's simply trying to sound like a textbook and doesn't yet have a clear idea of what he wants to say beyond something like, "In business the term *efficiency* refers to how well resources are used, not to whether a specific firm's goals are met." One succinct, simple sentence and an example would probably have conveyed the writer's meaning better than any amount of jargon.

We don't mean to imply that when you have a thought requiring technical language, you should reduce it to a banality. But always try to use the language that conveys your meaning most directly. Don't over-simplify the complex, but don't complicate the simple either.

EXERCISE 1: Jargon

Each of the following sentences contains jargon—technical language from some specialized field. For each sentence, decide whether
a. the use of jargon is legitimate and clear, or
b. the jargon is apt to confuse a general reader unfamiliar with the field the jargon is drawn from, or
c. the jargon seems to have been used to intimidate and impress the reader.

Example:

The interface between the communications parameters of an effective T-group facilitator and the constituent members depends to some extent on the facilitator's ability to sublimate his own passive-aggressive tendencies. (While it's possible that the author of this sentence felt he was using technical language clearly, it's more likely that this mound of technical-sounding verbiage is supposed to awe the reader.)

1. Transistors, silicon chips, and microcircuits have made life more convenient for most of us, though we probably have very little idea what these tiny, almost magical components are, let alone how they work.
2. Few students seem to realize that a participle used as a substantive can be considered—syntactically if not always grammatically—a noun.
3. The signal-to-noise ratio that the ANRS in my new receiver/ pre-amp/tuner package delivers beats the specs of any other unit with Dolby, and this doesn't even take into account the RMS power rating.
4. One of the things that always amuses me about customers at the printing plant where I work is that they'll frequently ask for a set of dup film on a print job but not specify whether they want it right-reading emulsion down or right-reading emulsion up.
5. The ASA rating of film (for example, ASA 100 or ASA 400) tells you how sensitive the film is to light; the higher the ASA rating, the more sensitive the film.
6. Failure to merge-purge management objectives against a bottom-line-oriented fiscal cycle can lead inexperienced middle-level managers into a negative cash flow situation.

7. The archetypal totems of this culture recur in industrial, nonindustrial, and neoindustrial societies, proving that the anima of which Jung spoke is culture-invariable.

ABSTRACT LANGUAGE

Abstract words and phrases as varied as *freedom, democracy, political upheaval, artistic success, decision-making process, essential liberties, quality merchandise,* and *equal rights,* are difficult to interpret, their meaning varying from context and from person to person. Each is an abstraction—something with no concrete physical reality—that manages to encompass neatly a broad range of ideas. For example, the notion *political upheaval* can encompass specifics ranging anywhere from military takeover of a civil government to rioting in the streets, imposition of curfews, or nationwide campus rebellions. Abstract concepts are complex, so abstract language shouldn't be used lightly.

Yet, since abstract words and phrases often sound "high level," writers may be tempted to use them, thinking they can make their readers believe that a subject is more difficult or complex than it really is. Writing filled with abstractions is often simply confusing. Look at this sentence, for example:

The course of action represents interface on the forefront of scholarship.

While at first glance these words might seem pretty impressive, we are hard put to interpret them when we read them closely. Look at the questions this one sentence raises: In what ways does the action "represent" anything? What is "interface" and what kind is the writer referring to? What is a "forefront of scholarship"? And what exactly does "scholarship" mean here? If we need explanations to interpret just one sentence like this, imagine how confusing it would be to read a number of such sentences strung together. Yet sometimes we do get whole paragraphs that *sound* as if they mean something, but we can't figure out what. For example:

A theory of cultural change is impossible without knowledge of the changing sense ratios effected by various externalizations of our senses. It is very much worth dwelling on this matter, since we shall see that from the invention of the alphabet there has been a continuous drive in the Western world toward the separation of the senses, of functions, of operations, of states emotional and political, as well as of tasks—a fragmentation which terminated, thought Durkheim, in the *anomie* of the nineteenth century. The paradox presented by Professor von Bekesy is that the two-dimensional mosaic is, in fact, a multidimensional world of interstructural resonance. It is the three-dimensional world of pictorial space that is, indeed, an abstract illusion built on the intense separation of the visual from the other senses.

Notice some of the abstractions:

theory of cultural change
changing sense ratios
various externalizations of our senses
drive toward the separations of the senses
fragmentation
anomie
multidimensional world
interstructural resonance
three-dimensional world
pictorial space

One page of this sort of confusing and obscure abstract writing is enough to stop even the most tenacious reader. But when a writer presents abstract ideas clearly, then abstract language is appropriate and even essential. Look, for example, at the following paragraph:

I know that some people say the idea of Law of nature or decent behaviour known to all men is unsound, because different civilizations and different ages have had quite different moralities. But they haven't. Just think what a *quite* different morality would mean. Think of a country where people were *admired* for running away in battle, or where a man felt *proud* for double-crossing all the people who had been kindest to him. You might just as well try to imagine a country where two and two made five. Men have differed as regards what people you ought to be unselfish to—whether it was only your own family, or your fellow countrymen, or every one. But they have always agreed that you oughtn't to put yourself first. Selfishness has never been admired. Men have differed as to whether you should have one wife or four. But they have always agreed that you mustn't simply have any woman you liked.

—C.S. Lewis, from "The Law of Right and Wrong"

Lewis' meaning is not hidden behind the abstract language he uses. While the paragraph revolves around a central abstraction, human morality, we understand this abstract notion because Lewis grounds it in specific examples, just as our earlier discussion of paragraph development stressed that the main idea in a paragraph should be clarified and supported with specifics.

Unfortunately we often see and hear abstract language when it hides meaning, not when it clarifies it as Lewis' language does. We hear politicians promising "strength against oppression," "economic independence," and "the eternal dignity of humankind." We even hear a manufacturer advertising a "new era in which pride and quality are a way of life." When we come across such statements, we must ask ourselves whether they are direct and to the point, helping us to think clearly, or whether they are deceptive.

For example, it is difficult for anyone's thoughts and feelings to remain unaffected by a term like *economic independence*—the unemployment check recipient can see in that phrase the promise of a job; the middle-income professional can see in it the promise of lower taxes. There are simply not enough specifics to alienate anyone, and the legislator who uses the phrase can attract a wide variety of voters without making any hard commitments. However, discriminating voters won't have been manipulated. They will try to cut through the abstract promises, realizing that they haven't gotten specific answers to the problems that affect their lives.

As you can see, models of abstract language are there for the taking. Yet, as a responsible writer, you don't want to be put in the position of either manipulating or confusing readers by using such language. If you find yourself using phrases like those in the preceding examples, ask yourself whether you justify them in the rest of your essay.

For no matter how strongly you might feel about subjects like civil liberties, young love, or quality in engineering, if you give your readers nothing more than such abstract phrases, you will not have made the point you had in mind. Ask yourself what you mean by *civil liberties* (or whatever abstract concept you want to deal with), and then check to see whether you have clarified and limited the term through examples, illustration, or explanation. If you're not certain whether you have rescued your message from obscurity, then go over what you know about developing paragraphs in order to check yourself. If you can develop your writing clearly and concretely, abstract subjects and the abstract words you use to talk about them will probably be of the kind in the Lewis paragraph—that is, the kind you want. After all this, if you still find that you're using too many abstract words, ask yourself a difficult question: am I depending on abstract language to appear impressive?

This leads to our next concern, the writer who attempts to impress a reader by choosing yet another sort of language.

POMPOUS OR INFLATED LANGUAGE

How would you react if you were to walk into your science lab and find the person next to you in a silk lab coat trimmed with lace and fastened with diamond buttons? Or if you were to go to the neighborhood fast food restaurant for a burger and some fries, and were greeted by a maitre d' who insisted that you couldn't sit down at a table unless you'd first made a telephone reservation? You'd probably think your lab partner and the management of the fast food chain were pretentious, even ludicrous. They'd make an impression all right: you'd think they were fools.

While such incidents would never occur in real life, pomposities involving *language* occur all the time, and they can make speakers or writers appear just as foolish as the lab technician in diamonds. Pompous language is simply language too fancy for the occasion. Why, then, do we often fall into the trap of using it? We use pompous language because we want to make ourselves or our subject sound important. We use it because we want to impress people. We use it because we think that if we write "the ball game is due to commence at one o'clock" or "my friend Lily is going through a period of remunerative unproductivity," people will take more notice than if we write that the ball game is *supposed to start* at one o'clock or that Lily is *earning little money.* When we have a dictionary or thesaurus in front of us to provide synonyms for everyday words, or when we have a vague recollection of the fancy words we've seen other writers use, we often succumb to the temptation to gild our prose. Take, for example, the following paragraph in which a student describes her nephew as he sat immovable in front of the television set:

> Dinner was ready but Terry didn't notice. He sat staring at the TV screen, his face showing no ebullience whatsoever. In fact, a stranger might have thought he was an icon, were it not for the fact that, halfway into *Lassie,* a tear streamed down his visage and he wiped it away with the back of his hand. Nothing we could say would convince him to come to the table, and when Aunt Alice finally walked over to the set and turned it off, Terry broke into one of his dolorous tirades.

What this writer failed to take into account when she chose words like *ebullience* and *visage* was that she was presenting an account of an everyday event. She might legitimately write about King Lear's visage or his dolorous tirades, for the scope, language, and literary stature of Shakespeare's tragedy justify a serious, even formal response to it. But she sounds ridiculous using such language to relate a homey, minor anecdote about little Terry. A writer can't make an idea or a writing task any more important or impressive than it is by covering it in "high-toned" diction, nor should he or she want to.

You can avoid writing inflated language by thinking about whether the words you've used are appropriate to your subject, audience, and purpose. You'd be more correct, for example, to use *the mountain* instead of *the mount* in a description of local scenery or in an exposition of present-day ecosystems. Similarly, you wouldn't talk about *utilizing* the vacuum cleaner when *use* is more suited to the occasion of vacuuming, and you'd probably want to choose *worthy* instead of *meritorious* when wondering whether you deserved a recent compliment on your new hat. The point is not that certain "fancy" words are to be avoided, but that every word has its place. And there are many places where "fancy" words just don't belong. Worthwhile ideas needn't hide behind pompous language, and weak ideas ultimately can't.

EXERCISE 2:

For almost every situation, there is appropriate language. As you read the following paragraphs, decide whether the words the authors have chosen reflect the occasions they have written about. If a paragraph contains inappropriate words or phrases, underline those words and be prepared to discuss just why they are inappropriate. Then consider how the weak passages could be fixed. Finally, rewrite those inappropriate paragraphs so that they are more suitable to the occasions or subjects they describe.

1. I was only a child when I witnessed my first and only coronation of a Queen. It was an intensely cold day, too cold for a child to be standing for hours, pressed against the barricades, waiting for even a glimpse of the procession that would find its way to the Abbey and forge my link with history. The intense cold was aggravated by a fine icy mist that began at dawn when I arrived. By mid-morning, it was raining cats and dogs, and I had grown more and more uncomfortable. But finally it began, and as my hands grew numb and my chin trembled, I caught my first vision of the Queen's carriage regally bearing her through the throng and knew with the certainty of my youth, that the ceremony was at last getting off the ground. I shall never forget my feelings of awe as I watched that swell lady raise her hand to wave, her head proudly lifted under the weight of the dazzling crown.

2. Miss Totten's figure, as she sat tall at her desk or strode angularly in front of us rolling down the long maps over the blackboard, had that instantaneous clarity, one metallic step removed from

the real, of the daguerreotype. Her clothes partook of this period too—long, saturnine waists and skirts of a stuff identical with that in a good family umbrella. There was one like it in the umbrella stand at home—a high black one with a seamed ivory head. The waists enclosed a vestee of dim but steadfast lace; the skirts grazed narrow boots of that etiolated black leather, venerable with creases, which I knew to be a sign of both respectability and foot trouble. But except for the vestee, all of Miss Totten, too, folded neatly to the dark point of her shoes, and separated from these by her truly extraordinary length, her face presided above, a lined, ocher ellipse. Sometimes, on drowsy afternoons, her face floated away altogether and came to rest on the stand at home.

3. There are several steps to pursue if you want to bring your first vegetable garden to consummation. First, locate a plot that gets good strong solar illumination for several hours each day. Check this area at different times of the day to make sure about the light patterns. Then, ascertain which members of the vegetable kingdom you want to cultivate and in what quantities. You might keep in the forefront of your consciousness the fact that experienced horticulturalists suggest that a diminutive plot of comestibles is best for the neophyte. It will let you become familiar with gardening *modus operandi* but will not be so formidable a task that all the bliss is drained from your inaugural experience. Be sure to draw up a planting schema that signifies where each crop will be implanted in the earth. A graphic design of your intention will allow you to make the optimum utilization of your region. Moreover, your actual labor in the garden will be accelerated because you will be cognizant of exactly where to put which crop and in what order of precedence to disseminate each one. Finally, you are ready for the journey to your neighborhood nursery to purchase seeds for later dispersal. When you procure seeds at a local garden supply center, you can start sowing them immediately, since you can select among varieties that are appropriate for your territory. By selecting these varieties, you take a large step toward ensuring a bountiful harvest. Even if you are entirely inexperienced, you will find growing your own viands at home a rewarding and delectable experience.

EUPHEMISM: THE ART OF EVASION

Sometimes we wish to speak or write indirectly rather than directly. We avoid saying,

Sorry that your mother got fired.
I hear your uncle died.

My brother rammed a police car, then threw a beer bottle at the officer.

Instead we regret that someone has been "laid off," offer sympathy that someone has "passed away," and may refer to our brother's "being in trouble." In these and other situations that may be embarrassing or painful to talk about, we turn to euphemisms. Taken from a Greek word meaning "to use words of good omen," **euphemisms** are pleasant words substituted for harsh or painfully direct ones.

Euphemisms are socially useful, allowing us to spare our own and others' feelings when we must refer to potentially embarrassing subjects—such as death, bodily functions, and sex. To spare people's feelings—to avoid rubbing their noses in the more earthy aspects of life—is certainly a legitimate function of euphemisms.

Unfortunately, euphemisms aren't always employed for such humane reasons. If our boss asks us how a certain report is coming along and we reply that we're "having a little trouble polishing off the rough edges" when we really mean that we haven't even started the job, we're guilty of using euphemism in a self-serving way. When used to deceive either others or ourselves, euphemisms can be dangerous, encouraging us to hide reality and perhaps even blocking clear thought.

Most of us are familiar with deceptive euphemisms. Thanks to countless advertisements, we know that a "pre-owned Cadillac" is a *used* one and that medicine "designed to relieve the discomfort caused by facial blemishes" will help our *acne,* or at least cover up the *pimples.* Recent political and social events have taught us to look again when *bombing* is referred to as "air support" or when *ghettos* are called "substandard housing." No doubt the most frightening example of euphemisms used to distort the truth occurred in Nazi Germany when Hitler's Ministry of Propaganda came up with the phrase *endgültige Lösung* ("final solution") to describe the murder of 6,000,000 human beings in gas ovens.

These grossly deceptive uses of euphemisms are most often perpetrated *against* us, not *by* us. So we need to be alert when we read. But we may also need to acknowledge that we're sometimes guilty of using euphemisms ourselves, either to hide something or to spare others. Suppose, for example, that you've worked closely with X and found him to be very unreliable, irritable, and slow. A friend later asks for your opinion of X because he is seriously considering doing a semester-long project with him. You reply, "Like all of us, X has his little quirks." You may think you're sparing your friend's feelings, but actually you're hiding the truth and not doing him any favors. This euphemistic response is especially bad if you've been asked in confidence what you really think. In this situation, the euphemism causes actual misunderstanding that can hurt your friend.

It's not as if you've said you're "going to the restroom," a tactful phrase we all understand and can hardly misinterpret.

When You Write: Legitimate and Illegitimate Uses of Euphemisms

How can you determine whether you are using euphemisms legitimately or not? Simply ask yourself why you want to use euphemisms in a particular situation, and then decide whether or not your reason is valid.

There are legitimate reasons for using euphemisms in your papers, just as there are times when good manners call for euphemisms in conversation. For example, imagine that you're writing about your experiences in Europe, concentrating on some surprising differences you encountered. In such a paper, you wouldn't have to describe in detail (and we won't here) the peculiar but challenging layout of the toilets in Greece. You could write instead about the "rudimentary facilities," explaining that often there are no porcelain fixtures at all. How many or how few euphemisms to use would depend to an extent on the point of the paper. If the entire essay revolved around a comparison of toilets here and there, you could hardly get by with a vague and fleeting description. But, in general, a desire to politely spare yourself and your reader by using euphemisms is defensible.

On the other hand, wanting mainly to protect yourself from a reality painful or difficult to write about is not a valid excuse for employing euphemisms. Say, for instance, that you're writing an essay defending the nuclear family of the U.S. as opposed to the extended family system of other nations. You argue that the other cultures are forced to keep the extended family system because of economic necessity. Here in the U.S., you argue in contrast, we have choices about how to structure the family unit. For instance, the family isn't forced to keep the grandparents at home. The older members can either live on their own if they can care for themselves, or they can choose to live in a convalescent home.

Here is the euphemism: *convalescent home.* By using this word, the writer of our hypothetical essay has allowed himself to ignore the biggest objection to his defense of the nuclear family, the argument that rather than being built on real choices, the nuclear family reflects an inhumane and selfish refusal to care for the elderly. The term *convalescent home* conjures up pleasant images of a comfortable place where people get well, an image exploded by a single visit to one of these places in which old people do not recover from their age, and for which *home*—a place where families live together—is scarcely an appropriate term.

The point is that as writers we have an obligation to deal honestly and directly with the difficult parts of our topics, not skirt them or look away from them by resorting to euphemisms.

Having discussed the clearly legitimate and illegitimate uses of euphemisms, we come to the gray area in between, the often misguided attempt to spare a reader's feelings. We all want to avoid stepping unnecessarily on others' sensibilities. But if you find yourself talking about "problems many *athletes* on scholarship face at X University," when what you really mean is *black athletes* in particular, you're not being clear. In fact, you're causing misunderstanding, because few people will be able to guess which athletes you really mean.

Similarly, you're bound to be misunderstood if you write on a course evaluation that "teachers in the physics department tend to have unusually high expectations of students," when you mean actually that "teacher X never gives any grade higher than a C and makes disparaging remarks about students in class." Couched in such misguided euphemisms, your criticism of a teacher winds up sounding like a comment on the department's high standards, something the chairman is likely to pride himself on. Your legitimate objection will probably be completely lost.

If you're genuinely convinced that a subject or your opinion will shock or offend a reader, don't bring it up. But once you do bring an idea up, don't backtrack into an obscuring haze of euphemism.

EXERCISE 3: Euphemisms

Read the following sentences and decide (1) whether or not they use euphemisms legitimately, and (2) how to revise the unacceptable euphemisms.

Example: When Caesar passed away, all Rome mourned.

Revision: When Caesar died, all Rome mourned.

1. I had so much to drink at the party that on the way home my car went out of control and hit a telephone pole.
2. Many city dwellers find it annoying that pet owners allow their animals to go to the bathroom on the sidewalks.
3. Because of increased administrative costs, we have found it necessary to revise the minimum payment due on your account each month.
4. Berk's Department Store is pleased to announce that it now carries a new line of fashions for the large man and woman.
5. In several instances, his handling of the corporation's finances was inconsistent with federal laws.

6. Mick Jagger's performance on stage relies heavily on romantic overtones.

7. The president announced that in the interests of national security, it might become necessary to detain aliens in administrative centers until the current international crisis has passed.

FIGURATIVE LANGUAGE

The goal of good writing is always to communicate clearly; to do that, you'll sometimes want to go beyond the literal meaning of your words. You may wish to elicit an emotional response from your readers, for instance, or to engage their imaginations.

> "I see a mouse," she said, pointing to the furry, long-tailed creature scurrying through the hole in the wall.

> "I see a mouse," she said, pointing to the timid soul huddled in the corner, trying to hide from the rowdy bustle of the partying crowd.

There's an obvious difference between the two sentences above. In the first, the writer is referring to an actual animal, using the word *mouse* in its literal sense. In the second, though, the writer has used the word *mouse* figuratively, to suggest an idea, to convey an impression of the person being described. The first use of the word is surely precise, but it permits readers only to visualize an actual mouse; the second sentence goes further, allowing the readers to use what they know about mice, gathered from our shared experience, to better understand a person.

Figurative language says one thing and means another; it can't be taken literally. Often, as in the case of the mouse above, it is built on comparisons between one idea and another. It can be a powerful tool because it offers you and your readers the chance to make connections, to compare something concrete, a mouse, with something more abstract, an idea such as shyness.

Suppose you are describing a scene that includes a pond and a large tree. You begin:

> On the edge of the pond there was a big tree that extended over the water.

Sensing that you haven't described the scene fully enough, you come up with this:

> On the edge of the pond grew an enormous willow tree, spread open like an umbrella whose ribs extended halfway across the still water.

By comparing the branches of the tree to the ribs of an umbrella, you've given your readers an image, something they can picture. But you've done more than that, for your image suggests not just a picture, but ideas of safety, shelter, and tranquility. Consider the difference between:

New York is ruined by commuters.

and E.B. White's

Then there is the New York of the commuter: the city that is devoured by locusts each day and spat out each night.

The first sentence is merely a statement. Readers can do little more than read it and absorb the information, if they're even interested enough to do that. But when they read the second sentence, readers can understand the ideas the writer associates with New York and commuters: that commuters are like voracious insects, ravenous and uncaring, consuming the city to feed their hunger by day, fleeing it at night when they have digested all it offers.

In an essay discussing why he would choose to banish the past from his life, a student wrote:

Lost loves, and jobs that I might have done better, hang around my mind's attic clanking their chains, and the racket distracts my concentration on the present.

The writer has suggested more than his distaste for the past; through the images of attics and chains he has allowed us to understand why he feels as he does. And the heavy burden of past regrets, inescapable and disturbing, becomes more than the writer's private experience; the connection he has drawn invites his readers to think about their own pasts in a new way.

Each of these writers knew the power of figurative language to play on associations between one idea and another; they understood that such connections can often convey ideas more clearly than literal statements might.

Clichés

Figurative language often works so well in its original form that it gets adopted into common use, losing its originality in the process. If someone were to start off a sentence about her familiarity with Boston, for instance, with the phrase, "I know Boston like . . ." and asked you to complete it, chances are your immediate response would be something close to ". . . the palm of my hand." You'd be able to finish the phrase so easily because you've heard it before, many times. Similarly, when someone describes his nervousness at making his first speech in debate class by telling you that his hands were "as cold as ice," you understand that his hands were very cold because he was tense, but you may feel as though you've heard his story before.

The first person to use phrases like the following was creating original, inventive images:

happy as a lark	in the limelight
slept like a log	knight in shining armor
nip in the bud	pass with flying colors
a mind like a steel trap	worth his weight in gold

Because such images seemed apt, they caught on, eventually becoming clichés—stale expressions that are often simply the first thing to come into one's mind.

Because clichés are so handy, they can too easily substitute for careful thought or detailed description. A careful reader will demand more than tired phrases and will perhaps be inclined to gloss over what you say, because it seems too familiar. Instead of settling for a cliché when one occurs to you, try to invent a fresh image, draw a new connection, or create a precise and thoughtful description of your own. If, as you write, you choose your words to suit *your* purpose, reflect *your* ideas, you won't have to settle for borrowed phrases.

Automatic Phrases

The primary danger of clichés, then, is that they can bore an audience and encourage careless thought and expression. More dangerous, because more insidious, are automatic phrases. These are the trite expressions we hear everywhere, every day, and so are lulled into employing ourselves, usually when we can't or won't think through an idea.

If someone in the office complains about the high cost of funding the hot meal program at the local elementary school, someone else is sure to chime in, "That's right, there's no such thing as a free lunch," even though the phrase actually means something quite different and has nothing to do with whether or not we should publicly finance hot lunches for young children. Similarly, if a woman who has worked long and hard to acquire the skills necessary for an important promotion on her job is passed over in favor of someone else, an unthinking "friend" is all too likely to offer the dubious comfort of a platitude—"Well, win some, lose some."

In both instances, the people responding with the automatic

phrase aren't thinking, perhaps because it's difficult, perhaps because it's uncomfortable, perhaps because it might force them to act or to acknowledge feelings they'd rather ignore. Take the "Win some, lose some" response, for example. Here a serious and perhaps complex situation is dismissed as if it were as simple as flipping a coin in a bet, sometimes winning with heads, sometimes losing with tails. The reply allows the speaker to ignore almost completely the friend's efforts, her feelings of frustration and failure, even perhaps the possible issue of fairness or unfairness. The lost promotion is thereby reduced to an accident of fate, beyond anyone's control. As writers, though, we *do* have control over what we say. The surest way to gain that control is to think an idea through, wrestle with it, and examine all its implications, instead of settling for an automatic and often thoughtless interpretation.

CONNOTATIONS

A familiar joke describes a person analyzing a personality trait by saying to a friend:

I am resolute; you are stubborn; he is pig-headed.

We smile at this because we recognize that it's based on our knowledge that we can select words to reflect our purposes and that words not only have literal, or *denotative* meanings, but *connotative* meanings as well, associations and implications beyond their literal definitions. When we hear the joke, we understand that while each term describes a person not easily persuaded, each also has emotional colorations as well. *Resolute* suggests strength in the face of obstacles that might force a lesser person to yield his convictions to someone even stronger; *stubborn* implies someone who probably should bend a little but usually doesn't; and *pig-headed* is clearly negative, suggesting someone who simply will not change his mind regardless of the good reasons for doing so. Note that *pig-headed,* because of the associations it carries with a "dumb animal," is really quite different in its effect from the other two words.

The point is that few words in English are neutral. Even words whose literal meanings are very similar can differ in the effect they have or the meanings they convey. What's the difference, for instance, between *bachelor* and *spinster*? Both words describe unmarried people, but *spinster* carries with it cultural connotations that are negative, even insulting, although stating that a woman "isn't married" doesn't have the same effect. Consider the words *dine* and *eat*. What was on the menu when you "dined?" How was the table set?

Who served the food? What was the atmosphere? While we all eat every day, most of us "dine" only occasionally.

A careful writer can exploit the associations words carry with them to suit his or her purpose. Automobile manufacturers did not choose the names of their various models carelessly. "Cougar," "Jaguar," and "Mustang" are not just kinds of animals; they are *wild* animals, and the names given to these automobiles impart just the right hint of daring and speed which, the manufacturers try to convince us, will transfer to the people who drive them. Similarly, "Seville" and "Monte Carlo" connote the sophistication and luxury associated with pleasure spots foreign to Americans and therefore exotic and desirable.

You can make your words work for you by first deciding what idea you want to convey to your readers and then seeing what associations certain words have. The word *portly* suggests a rather large person, yet one who is dignified, distinguished, a gentleman, perhaps. *Fat,* on the other hand, does more than merely define a person's body shape; the word implies a negative judgment of the person being described. So, if you want to describe a considerably overweight person and put him in a favorable light, you might choose *portly, imposing,* or *heavy-set* to make your point. In an essay describing the plight of old people living on limited incomes in which you call for a change in your reader's attitude, you might choose to refer to your subjects as "the elderly" rather than as the more condescending "old folks," particularly if you want your reader to be convinced of the dignity due those who have reached old age.

In addition to your purpose, you need also to consider your audience. When writing to your traditional-minded parents to ask for help with your rent, you'd be more likely to refer to the man or woman you live with as your *roommate* than as your *lover*—even though he or she is literally the "one who loves you"—simply because the word "lover" may spark the very association you know your parents would rather not make.

If you're unsure of the connotations a particular word carries, check it out carefully. You can ask other people what the word conveys to them, but remember that their knowledge of connotations may be no broader than yours. In fact, they may have highly personal, idiosyncratic associations with a certain word. You can look the word up in a dictionary, but this won't be enough if you choose a small, paperbound one. For this kind of search, your best resource is a large, reputable desk dictionary, such as the *American Heritage Dictionary* or *Webster's Seventh Collegiate Dictionary,* which often includes not only the definition—the meaning of a word—but synonyms, words with related meanings but different connotations. A word with the wrong connotations can seriously change, even pervert, your meaning. In writing about the vivid imagery in Wordsworth's nature poetry one of our students called the language "sensual." A quick check in the dictionary would have prevented this misleading statement:

> **Sensual:** pertaining to or consisting in the gratification of the senses, or the indulgence of appetite; fleshly. Devoted to the pleasures of sense of appetite; voluptuous; sometimes, lewd. Indicating sensuality, or voluptuousness; as in, a *sensual* mouth. SYN. See **Carnal: Sensuous.**

The cross-reference to "sensuous" would have taken the student to the appropriate word, and in addition, given him more information about the difference in connotation between the two words:

> **Sensuous:** Of or pertaining to the senses or sensible objects; addressing the senses. Characterized by sense impressions or imagery addressing the senses; as, *sensuous* description. SYN: **Sensuous, sensual, luxurious, voluptuous, epicurean** mean giving pleasure by gratifying the senses. **Sensuous** implies delight in the beauty of color, sound, form, etc.; **sensual,** gratification of appetites impelled by gluttony or lust; **luxurious,** inducing a pleasant languor, delightful ease, etc.; **voluptuous,** abandonment to sensuous, or especially sensual enjoyments; **epicurean,** sensuous, or less often, sensual delight in eating, etc.

EXERCISE 4: Connotation/Denotation

The writer of the following sentences had at his disposal a thesaurus but not a dictionary. Consequently, the underlined words, while in the right family of meanings, are inappropriate in context. Explain why the underlined words are incorrect and come up with acceptable replacements.

1. She illuminated the proper method of tying shoes.
2. We need to utilize the milk before it sours.
3. The child had difficulty ascertaining his way to school.
4. Determined to fight inflation, every Sunday he would sever the money-saving coupons from the newspaper.
5. The walls were covered with signs reading, "Please abstain from smoking in the theater."
6. The young woman was bombarded with flowers and gifts after she was hospitalized for appendicitis.
7. The city council voted to build a new aqueduct to bear water from the mountains to the local reservoir.

8. After the earthquake, measuring 7.9 on the Richter scale, rocked San Francisco, most people were unable to cope with the resulting <u>inconvenience</u>.
9. His <u>ability</u> to do the work of four people was really <u>noticeable</u>.
10. Every time her boyfriend came over, her younger brother would <u>persecute</u> them by peeping at them from behind the door.

EXERCISE 5: Words, Words, Words

Below are several phrases that are either clichéd, inflated, obscure, euphemistic, or unnecessarily abstract. Decipher the meaning of these phrases and put them into intelligible words. If you decide that a phrase is actually meaningless, strike it out.

1. Canine control officer.
2. After the grief specialists had prepared the deceased for his repose, he was laid to rest in the memorial park.
3. Since overpopulation is a serious world problem, she decided that her third obstetrical experience would be her last.
4. I hear you, and I can get behind what you're saying, but you've got to get your head together and get clear about your priorities before we can really relate to each other in a meaningful way.
5. One area of confusion concerns the degree of generality of specificity in personality.
6. Whenever I curl up in my sleeping bag, I feel as snug as a bug in a rug.
7. The deprivation of those less economically favored in our society inflicts upon them diminished expectations and inculcates resentment manifested in violence.
8. The president had difficulty in initiating a decision-making process in reference to the escalation of costs and prices in all sectors of the economy.
9. The Pentagon argued that during a guerrilla war, such as that fought in Vietnam, it is necessary to "pacify the enemy infrastructures," often by using defoliants.
10. Adolescents whose subcutaneous foramen produce an excess of oily secretions are advised to consult with a physician specializing in dermetics.

EXERCISE 6:

Read the following passage from *Final Payments* by Mary Gordon, in which two characters, Isabel and John, address a group of young people who are about to undertake a series of interviews with some elderly shut-ins who have been placed in private residences in order to be taken care of. Isabel is the first speaker.

> "Well," I said, "I don't know what to say. This is a very complex issue. I suppose the most important thing is not to make people feel as though they're being invaded. After all, it's their lives we're going into. We mustn't make them feel as if we were stealing something from them, or that we thought our lives were more important than theirs."
>
> "Point number one," said John. "Sensitivity. Awareness. The old third eye. Is that what you're driving at?"
>
> "Yes, I suppose so."
>
> "Only let me add a little piece of advice," said John. "Sure, you don't want to come over as Mrs. Bureaucrat—or *Miz* Bureaucrat as the case may be . . . but you're there to get information, not to make friends. You've gotta break some eggs if you wanna make an omelet. Go on Belle."
>
> . . . "I think what we ought to do among ourselves," I said, ideas coming to me like little windfalls as I talked, "is to try to figure out what seems to make these people happy and what doesn't. Perhaps if we can understand the good things that people do we can tell other people about them. It's easier for people if they don't feel so alone in these things."
>
> "Point number two. Efficiency Analysis. Information Dissemination. *Communication,* that's the name of the game, right baby?"
>
> "Yes," I said, not really listening, anxious to go on. "I think what we should all do is to listen to the way people talk; find out if they have private jokes with the people they're taking care of. Jokes are very important."
>
> "Back to the magic word *communication.* I swear to God, it's everything."

1. Whose ideas seem more original and thoughtful, John's or Isabel's?
2. Pick out as many words and phrases as you can that you feel exemplify weak uses of abstraction, jargon, cliché, or euphemism. You may find categories overlapping.
3. Who uses more abstractions, jargon, clichés, and euphemisms, John or Isabel?
4. Do these phrases detract from the dialogue? What might the dialogue be like if these phrases weren't there? What effect do all these phrases have on the rest of the conversation? What effect do you think they might have on the young people listening to Isabel and John?
5. Can you find acceptable uses of either abstraction, cliché, jargon, euphemism, or figurative language? Why do you find them acceptable?

Usage Manual

You can use this section in at least three ways.

First, it's a quick reference for most of the technical questions you'll run into in writing your papers (Do I want a comma here or a semicolon? Should I use *a* or *an* before the word *X-ray*? Do I mean *affect* or *effect*?).

Second, you should use this Usage Manual to look up errors your instructor marks on your papers. (There is a list of the most common marking symbols on the inside back cover.) For example, if you find "dangling modifier," "fragment," "predication," or "spelling" marked—especially more than once—you should turn to the corresponding entry in the Manual, which is arranged alphabetically. There you will find an explanation of the error, some suggestions for avoiding it, and exercises to make sure you understand the concept. Some entries in the Usage Manual also include references to portions of the main text, where there are more detailed discussions of particular items.

Third, you can use the diagnostic test that begins on the next page to help you spot errors that might give you trouble. When you miss a question in any entry (or get it right but aren't sure how you did it), look up the corresponding entry in the Usage Manual. If you miss questions on many entries, your instructor can suggest which ones you should work on first.

DIAGNOSTIC TEST

Since answers appear directly after each set of questions, you should place a piece of paper over the page and lower it as you go through the test. Write down your answer to each question, and make a note of any that you miss.

A/An

Choose the correct form:
1. He has to wear (a, an) uniform on his job.
2. (A, An) honorable defeat means more than a hollow victory.

ANSWERS

1. **a**
2. **An**

Adjective/Adverb Confusion

Choose the correct adjective or adverb in the following sentences:
1. I felt (strange, strangely) entering the deserted house alone.
2. In order to win a division championship, a team must play (good, well) throughout the entire season.
3. During the last part of our vacation, time passed (real, really) (quick, quickly).

ANSWERS

1. **strange**
2. **well**
3. **really, quickly**

Agreement of Pronoun and Antecedent

Select the proper pronoun in each of the sentences below.
1. The class was optimistic, for (it, they) knew the professor's exams were usually not unreasonably difficult.
2. If anyone can't get to the sorority meeting on time, (she, they) should let the organizers know.
3. Neither of the boys left (his, their) books on the school bus.

ANSWERS

1. **it**
2. **she**
3. **his**

Agreement of Subject and Verb

Select the proper verb form in each of the sentences below.
1. Which of these two cakes do you think (taste, tastes) better?
2. The professor's list of readings (were, was) too long.
3. Each of the club members (has, have) paid dues.

ANSWERS

1. **tastes**
2. **was**
3. **has**

As/Like

Choose the correct version:
1. It looked (like, as if) it might snow, so I drove home (like, as) a maniac.
2. I sent in the forms (like, as) you requested.

ANSWERS

1. **as if, like**
2. **as**

Broad Reference

Decide whether or not the references "this" and "which" are used correctly in the following sentences. If they are not, correct the sentences.
1. The presidential candidate studied under the foremost foreign policy expert at Harvard. Then, after graduation, he worked for several years as a successful executive at General Motors. This gave him the experience required of a national leader.
2. Every year he makes a great show of giving money to the United Crusade, which I find hypocritical.

ANSWERS

1. Too broad. Replace last sentence with something like the following:
   Both types of training gave him the experience required of a national leader.
2. Ambiguous. *Two* readings and corrections are possible.
   . . . **Crusade, a display I find hypocritical.**
   . . . **Crusade, an organization I find hypocritical.**

Capitalization

Which of the following words should be capitalized?

geology   english   aunt jane   my father   psychology 1-A
the old man and the sea   united states senate   the senator
senator hayakawa   a psychology course   middle ages   empire
state building   *death of a salesman*

ANSWERS

**English, Aunt Jane, Psychology 1-A, *The Old Man and the Sea*,
United States Senate, Senator Hayakawa, Middle Ages, Empire State
Building, *Death of a Salesman***

Case of Pronouns

Select the proper pronoun in each of the following sentences:
1. Jerry and (I, me) are planning to bicycle across Italy this summer.
2. My father surprised my mother and (I, me) not only by cooking
   dinner but by cleaning up afterwards, too.
3. Among (us, we) four runners, Sue ran the fastest mile.
4. (Us, We) procrastinators always have to face the moment when
   time finally runs out.

ANSWERS

1. **I**
2. **me**
3. **us**
4. **We**

Colloquialisms/Slang

Replace any slang in the following sentences:
1. Catalytic converters are a bummer because they screw up a car's
   performance.
2. For a dude who was supposed to be a career soldier, MacArthur
   was a jerk because he got on his commander-in-chief's case.

SUGGESTED REVISIONS

1. **Catalytic converters are irritating/troublesome because they interfere with/impede a car's performance.**
2. **For a man who was supposed to be a career soldier, MacArthur
   was unprofessional/a hypocrite because he argued with/disobeyed
   his commander-in-chief.**

Comma Splice

Correct any comma splices in the following sentences:

1. When I got home on Saturday night, I was horrified to discover a piece of lettuce stuck to my upper right front tooth, I had wondered why my date had looked at me oddly several times during the evening.
2. The hospital was both overcrowded and understaffed, the nurses, however, did a heroic job under the difficult circumstances.
3. In this country it is extremely easy to obtain false identification cards, a problem which costs banks, retailers, credit card companies, and ultimately the honest citizen hundreds of thousands of dollars a year.

ANSWERS

1. **When I got home on Saturday night, I was horrified to discover a piece of lettuce stuck to my upper right front tooth; I had wondered why my date had looked at me oddly several times during the evening.** (You could also put a period or dash after *tooth.*)
2. **The hospital was both overcrowded and understaffed; the nurses, however, did a heroic job under the difficult circumstances.** (A period or dash after *understaffed* would also be correct.)
3. **Correct**

Comparative/Superlative

Choose the correct form:

1. The decathlon is the (gruelinger, gruelingest, more grueling, most grueling) test of an Olympic athlete's skill and endurance.
2. Many people prefer Disneyland to Walt Disney World, even though the Florida complex is (newer and bigger, newest and biggest, more new and big, most new and big).

ANSWERS

1. **most grueling**
2. **newer and bigger**

Comparison, Faulty

Correct the following sentences:

1. I keep my room much cleaner than my brother.
2. The miniskirt always looked like women trying to be girls.
3. This month's heating bill was higher than last month.

ANSWERS

1. This one has three possible revisions, depending on what meaning the writer intends:
   I keep my room much cleaner than I keep my brother.
   I keep my room much cleaner than my brother keeps it.
   I keep my room much cleaner than my brother keeps his.
2. Women who wore miniskirts always looked as if they were trying to be girls.
3. This month's heating bill was higher than last month's.

Coordination, Faulty

Rewrite the following sentences, using appropriate coordinating conjunctions, subordination, or both:
1. The supervisor was late to work every day and was never around when needed, and the company promoted her.
2. I was under a great deal of pressure to do well in school, and I almost thought of paying someone to write my term papers, and I knew I would feel guilty if I did.

POSSIBLE REVISIONS

1. **The supervisor was late to work every day and was never around when needed, but the company promoted her.**
2. **Because I was under a great deal of pressure to do well in school, I almost thought of paying someone to write my term papers, even though I knew I would feel guilty if I did.**

Dangling Modifier

Do the modifiers in these sentences "dangle"? If so, correct them.
1. After determining the cost of the fabric and the labor involved, the suit was unreasonably expensive.
2. Attached to the apparatus by bolts, the scientist was especially interested in the manometer.
3. To graduate from college, many general courses must be taken.

ANSWERS

1. Yes.
   After determining the cost of the fabric and the labor involved, she decided the suit was unreasonably expensive.
2. Yes.
   The scientist was especially interested in the manometer, which was attached to the apparatus by bolts.

3. Yes.

To graduate from college, a student must take many general courses.

Division

If you had to divide the following words at the end of a line, where would you put the hyphen?
better   return   disruptive   certificate   punctuation   technical
prosperity   radio   permanent   differences   representative
unconstitutional   stretched   wretched

ANSWERS

You may divide the words in *any* of the places indicated:
bet-ter, re-turn, dis-rup-tive, cer-ti-fi-cate, punc-tu-a-tion, tech-ni-cal, pros-per-i-ty, ra-dio, per-ma-nent, dif-fer-en-ces, rep-re-sen-ta-tive, un-con-sti-tu-tion-al, stretched (cannot be divided), **wretch-ed**

Fragment

Which of the following are fragments? Make them into complete sentences.
1. In case you ever need to know something like the number of table-spoons in a gallon.
2. We had to move several times while I was growing up. The reason being that my father was in the military.
3. You might think it would be fun to live in seven different states. It wasn't.
4. One of my most embarrassing experiences was falling into my grandmother's pond. While drinking champagne at a family re-union. An incident no one has ever let me forget.

ANSWERS

Corrections other than these are possible, of course. If you're in doubt about yours, read the section.
1. A fragment.
   In case you ever need to know something like the number of table-spoons in a gallon, a table of equivalents is useful.
2. Second sentence is a fragment.
   We had to move several times while I was growing up because my father was in the military.
3. Both sentences are complete.
4. Second and third sentences are fragments.
   One of my most embarrassing experiences was falling into my grandmother's pond while drinking champagne at a family reunion, an incident no one has ever let me forget.

Logic

Briefly explain any problems in the logic of the following sentences:

1. People who travel abroad should either learn the languages of the countries they visit or stop complaining about being treated rudely on their travels.
2. Cowboys exemplify the great American virtue of independence: have you ever seen one standing in a welfare line?
3. People who rave about the craftmanship behind foreign cars must be stupid or crazy. My German subcompact has been in the shop four times in the past six months.

ANSWERS

1. Either/or reasoning: the sentence implies, incorrectly, that the only two alternatives open to travelers are to learn new languages or to uncomplainingly endure what they perceive to be rude treatment.
   Buried premise: the sentence implies that travelers are treated rudely only if they don't speak the language of the host country.
2. Glittering generality: "the great American virtue of independence" is an attractive but empty phrase.
   Hasty generalization: the writer is asking readers to assume that there must not be any cowboys on welfare if readers haven't seen them in welfare lines (if indeed readers have seen a welfare line at all and could recognize a cowboy standing in one).
3. Name calling: "crazy" and "stupid" insult rather than explain.
   Hasty generalization: the writer makes an inference about the reliability of foreign cars in general on the basis of only his experience with one car.

If you were able to explain the logical problems in these sentences, you needn't be concerned if you were unfamiliar with the specific terms used to describe the problems—"hasty generalization" and "glittering generality," for example.

Misplaced Modifier

Correct any misplaced modifiers in the following sentences:

1. The sniper's bullets only killed one person in the large crowd.
2. In the chic new restaurant, vintage wine is served to elegant guests in plastic cups.
3. He lived in a small, box-shaped room with one window and barely any light for reading in the poorest section of town.

ANSWERS

1. **The sniper's bullets killed only one person in the large crowd.**
2. **In the chic new restaurant, vintage wine is served in plastic cups to elegant guests.**

3. He lived in the poorest section of town in a small, box-shaped room with one window and barely any light for reading.

Modification Errors

Revise the modification in the following sentences to eliminate any errors:

1. I tried to tell him that it wasn't fair to grade by his personal view of a student.
2. Many new products do not perform to the extent of their advertising.
3. Psychiatrists may be able to give sound advice even with personal problems themselves.

POSSIBLE REVISIONS

1. I tried to tell him that it wasn't fair to base his grades on his personal view of a student.
   or:
   I tried to tell him that it was unfair to let prejudice influence his grading.
2. Many new products do not perform as well as their advertising claims they will.
3. Psychiatrists may be able to give sound advice even though they may have personal problems themselves.

Note: Quite often sentences with severe modification errors are improved only by complete revision, not a change of one troublesome phrase.

Parallelism

Correct any problems in parallelism in the following sentences:

1. I had come to detest his arrogance when he beat me at backgammon, Scrabble, or caught me in a grammatical slip.
2. Some feminists argue that restricting the draft to men discriminates against women, perpetuates archaic sexual stereotypes, and that excluding women from the draft is unconstitutional.
3. She not only tried to upstage the other actors, but she forgot her lines at a crucial moment in the second act.

ANSWERS

1. I had come to detest his arrogance when he beat me at backgammon or Scrabble—or caught me in a grammatical slip.
   or perhaps less awkwardly:
   I had come to detest his arrogance when he caught me in a grammatical slip or beat me at backgammon or Scrabble.
2. Some feminists argue that restricting the draft to men discrimi-

nates against women, perpetuates archaic sexual stereotypes, and is unconstitutional.
3. She not only tried to upstage the other actors but forgot her lines at a crucial moment in the second act.

Passive Voice

Is the passive voice used appropriately in the following sentences? If not, change the passive constructions to the active.
1. The book was published in 1968.
2. It is agreed that private schools are better than public schools.
3. Their objection to the ruling was voiced by the committee.

ANSWERS

1. Appropriate
2. **Many parents agree that private schools are better than public schools.** (Other subjects besides "Many parents" are possible, of course.)
3. **The committee voiced their objection to the ruling.**

Point of View Shift

Correct any inappropriate shifts in point of view in the following:
1. If one is to get a well-rounded education, he or she should take a number of general education courses, for these provide you with an overall framework in which to place more specialized information.
2. As a Japanese Sumo wrestler, you don't try to keep your weight down; on the contrary, one stays what could only be termed obese by Western standards, his mass adding to both the aesthetic and the practical sides of the sport.

SUGGESTED REVISIONS

1. **If you are to get a well-rounded education, you should take a number of general education courses, for these provide you with an overall framework in which to place more specialized information.**
2. **A Japanese Sumo wrestler doesn't try to keep his weight down; on the contrary, he stays what could only be termed obese by Western standards, his mass adding to both the aesthetic and the practical sides of the sport.**

Predication

There is a problem with the basic structure of each of the following sentences. Briefly explain the problem and revise the sentence accordingly.

1. A democracy is when everyone has a say in the government.
2. Louis' reckless driving faced him with the fact that he would never be able to get a driver's license in the State of New York.
3. Steep and rocky mountains can be a frustrating athletic experience.
4. The structure of the cell is in a circle.

ANSWERS

1. Since a democracy is not a time, the use of *when* is incorrect.
   A democracy is a system in which everyone has a say in the government.
2. People can be faced with a fact, but an action (like driving) cannot do the facing. **Because of his reckless driving, Louis was faced with the fact that he would never be able to get a driver's license in the State of New York.**
3. Mountains can't constitute an experience.
   Trying to climb steep and rocky mountains can be a frustrating athletic experience.
4. According to this sentence, the "structure of the cell" is located "in a circle." But the writer is trying to describe the cell's *shape,* not its location:
   The structure of the cell is circular.

PUNCTUATION:

Apostrophe

1. The most popular spot in the neighborhood was the (Smiths, Smith's, Smiths') swimming pool.
2. (Mens, Men's, Mens') fashions tend to change more gradually than (womens, women's, womens').
3. The attorney for the defense tried to convince the jury that the crime was actually (societys, societies, society's, societys') fault.
4. Thinking the pen was (hers, her's, hers'), Barbara dropped it into her purse.

ANSWERS

1. **Smiths'**
2. **Men's, women's**
3. **society's**
4. **hers**

Colon

Correct any punctuation errors in the following sentences:
1. The applicant must be: neat, courteous, efficient, and willing to take responsibility.

2. Even the TV commercials seemed to be against me, they conspired to remind me of the perfect body and fulfilling lifestyle I lacked.

ANSWERS

1. **The applicant must be neat, courteous, efficient, and willing to take responsibility.**
2. **Even the TV commercials seemed to be against me: they conspired to remind me of the perfect body and fulfilling lifestyle I lacked.** (You could also correct the comma splice here by using a semi-colon, dash, or period. But the colon is particularly appropriate since the second clause explains the first.)

Comma

Add any necessary commas to the following:

Although the earthquake that hit San Francisco on April 18 1906 caused extensive damage the effect of a similar disaster would probably be far worse today. Given the relatively greater concentration of people and buildings the destruction from the earthquake itself would be greater and the disruption of power communications fire and police services and emergency medical facilities would be harrowing often fatal.

ANSWER

Although the earthquake that hit San Francisco on April 18, 1906, caused extensive damage, the effect of a similar disaster would probably be far worse today. Given the relatively greater concentration of people and buildings, the destruction from the earthquake itself would be far greater, and the disruption of power, communications, fire and police services, and emergency medical facilities would be harrowing, often fatal.

Dashes

Correct any punctuation problems in the following sentences:
1. He was a determined old man—always driving his '49 Packard at racing-car speeds—always getting to the bank teller's window at 10:00 sharp Monday morning—and always betting big money on the least favored horse in the race.
2. Native speakers will master their language—no matter how complex that language is, by the age of five.

ANSWERS

1. Any of the following:
   a) **He was a determined old man, always driving his '49 Packard**

at racing-car speeds, always getting to the bank teller's window at 10:00 sharp Monday morning, and always betting big money on the least favored horse in the race.

b) He was a determined old man—always driving his '49 Packard at racing-car speeds, always always getting to the bank teller's window at 10:00 sharp Monday morning, and always betting big money on the least favored horse in the race.

c) He was a determined old man, always driving his '49 Packard at racing-car speeds, always getting to the bank teller's window at 10:00 sharp Monday morning—and always betting big money on the least favored horse in the race.

2. Either change the comma after *is* to a dash, or change the dash before *no matter* to a comma.

Hyphen

Hyphenate the following words and phrases where necessary:
twentieth century music   my twelve year old brother   thirty five years old   widely accepted beliefs   a self centered person   well informed   in the seventh grade   seventh grade history teacher   his ex wife   anti Communist

ANSWERS

twentieth-century music, my twelve-year-old brother, thirty-five years old, a self-centered person, well-informed, seventh-grade history teacher, his ex-wife, anti-Communist

Parentheses

Correct any punctuation errors in the following sentence:
Jane Austen's premature death at the age of 42 ended her career, (which lasted only from 1811 to 1816.)

ANSWER

Jane Austen's premature death at the age of 42 ended her career (which lasted only from 1811 to 1816).

Quotation Marks

Put quotation marks where needed in the following sentences:
Did David get a chance to re-read Whitman's poem Grass? Jesse asked. If he did, he continued, I'd like to ask him what he thinks uniform hieroglyphic means.

ANSWER

"Did David get a chance to re-read Whitman's poem 'Grass'?" Jesse asked. "If he did," he continued, "I'd like to ask him what he thinks 'uniform hieroglyphic' means."

Semicolon

In the following sentences, correct any errors involving semicolons. You may have to add, remove, or replace them.

1. It wasn't enough to be fatigued from playing an instrument all day. Each of us had to hurt otherwise we weren't giving one hundred percent.
2. For Monday, read the following sections; Chapter 2, pp. 27–54, Chapter 3, pp. 55–62, Chapter 6, pp. 98–127, and Chapter 7, pp. 128–141.
3. Many people thoughtlessly gobble aspirin for every minor pain; despite the drug's potentially serious side effects.
4. Few people associate California with cotton, however, it produces more cotton than any other state.

ANSWERS

1. It wasn't enough to be fatigued from playing an instrument all day. Each of us had to hurt; otherwise we weren't giving one hundred percent.
2. For Monday, read the following sections: Chapter 2, pp. 27–54; Chapter 3, pp. 55–62; Chapter 6, pp. 98–127; and Chapter 7, pp. 128–141.
3. Many people thoughtlessly gobble aspirin for every minor pain, despite the drug's potentially serious side effects.
4. Few people associate California with cotton; however, it produces more cotton than any other state.

Redundancy

Correct any redundancies in the following passage:

In the minds of many public employees, they believe that the unstated, but nevertheless significant and important, positive benefits of their vocational type of work include such factors and elements as job security, a noncompetitive working environment in which to practice their chosen professions, and routine, normal, and expectable promotions into better positions.

POSSIBLE REVISION

Many public employees believe that the unstated, but significant, benefits of their type of work include job security, a noncompetitive working environment, and routine promotions.

Repetition

Revise the following to eliminate any inappropriate repetition of words, sounds, or sentence structure:

Motion pictures' fictional depiction of blacks often lacks depth and credibility. In early films, grown blacks were usually shown as simple-minded, like some childlike creatures that could register only fear or happiness. In later films, blacks were usually shown as the embodiment of one stereotype or another. In these films, blacks were shown as either ruthless criminals or cops or commendable individuals with the intellect of Einstein and the patience of Mother Teresa.

POSSIBLE REVISION

The depiction of blacks in films is often shallow and unrealistic. In early films, adult blacks were usually shown as simpleminded, as though they were childlike creatures that could register only fear or happiness. Blacks in later films usually embodied one stereotype or another: either ruthless criminals or cops at one extreme or, at the other, exemplary individuals with the intellect of Einstein and the patience of Mother Teresa.

Note: You should be concerned not with how closely your revision matches ours but with how thoroughly you managed to identify and eliminate the various repetitions. Among the offenders:

the repetition of *ict* sound in *pictures, fictional, depiction*
the *blacks/lacks* rhyme
repetition of *like* and *childlike*
the two *or*'s in a row in the last sentence
the *criminals/cops/commendable* alliteration in the last sentence
the repetition of the words *blacks were shown* toward the beginning of the last three sentences

Run-Together Sentences

If any of the following are run-together sentences, correct them.

1. I had no inkling that they would give me a party it came as a complete surprise, especially since they weren't friends of mine.
2. The ever-growing presence of word-processing machines in large offices has made life easier for many secretaries, who no longer have to spend time on tedious tasks such as typing individual copies of form letters and retyping pages on which minor errors or revisions have been made.
3. My weekend was ruined I couldn't seem to get rid of a headache that plagued me for the better part of two days.

ANSWERS

1. I had no inkling they would give me a party. It came as a complete surprise, especially since they weren't friends of mine.
2. Correct
3. My weekend was ruined. I couldn't seem to get rid of a headache that plagued me for the better part of two days. (A semicolon, dash, or colon after *ruined* would also be correct.)

Spelling

Which of the following words are misspelled? Correct them.

recieve   truly   insureance   unmanageable   commited
occurred   offerring   fryed   retrieve   quizzes   wierd
advertisement   potatos

ANSWERS

receive, truly, insurance, committed, offering, fried, weird, potatoes

Subjunctive

Where necessary, put the verbs in the following sentences in the sub-junctive mood:

1. I wish that my final wasn't on Friday because I'd rather go to the concert. But if I was to miss the exam and go to the concert instead, I'd probably feel guilty.
2. My parents demand that my boisterous friend Pete either sits quietly at the dinner table or goes straight home without eating as if he was two years old.

ANSWERS

1. **I wish that my final weren't on Friday. . . . But if I were to miss the exam. . . .**
2. **My parents demand that my boisterous friend Pete either sit quietly at the dinner table or go straight home . . . as if he were two years old.**

Subordination, Faulty

Correct the subordination problems in the following sentences:

1. The television executive talked about the value of watching television because many programs are informative or genuinely entertaining.
2. Unless two people live together before they marry, they can avoid some of the difficulties of learning to share and get along with another individual.

3. Although I enjoy cooking in the French manner, I like to prepare Italian recipes.

SUGGESTED REVISIONS

1. The television executive talked about the value of watching television, pointing out that many programs are informative or genuinely entertaining.
2. If two people live together before they marry, they can avoid some of the difficulties of learning to share and get along with another individual.
3. Although I enjoy cooking in the French manner, I really like to prepare Italian recipes best.

Tense Sequence

Correct any problems in sequence of tenses in the following sentences:
1. If I would have realized how hard it was going to be, I would have prepared more thoroughly for my driving test.
2. Although I traveled there many times before, Greece never looked as inviting as it did on my last trip.

ANSWERS

1. If I had realized how hard it was going to be, I would have prepared more thoroughly for my driving test.
2. Although I had traveled there many times before, Greece had never looked as inviting as it did on my last trip.

Tense Shift

Fix the verb tenses in the following paragraph:

London may be rated the most expensive city in the world, but I found a way to beat the high cost of living during the week I spent there. After the motorcoach from the airport drops me at Victoria Station, I find a nearby bed-and-breakfast that isn't too expensive. The next day I moved to an even cheaper "bed-sitter" in Chelsea. So what if the bath and WC were down the hall? My refrigerator and stove, along with a nearby supermarket, solve my food problems, so I was able to spring loose some extra pounds for the theater. Maybe there is still such a thing as a bargain—even in London.

ANSWER

London may be rated the most expensive city in the world, but I found a way to beat the high cost of living during the week I spent there. After the motorcoach from the airport *dropped* me at Victoria Station, I *found* a nearby bed-and-breakfast that *wasn't* too expensive. The next day I moved to an even cheaper "bed-sitter" in Chelsea. So what if the bath and WC were down the hall? My refrigerator and stove, along with a nearby supermarket, *solved* my food problems, so I was able to spring loose some extra pounds for the theater. Maybe there is still such a thing as a bargain—even in London.

Titles

Make sure the titles in the following sentences are punctuated correctly—either placed in quotation marks or underlined (italicized). Add the appropriate punctuation where none exists.

1. *I Am the Very Model of a Modern Major General,* a song with a typical Gilbert and Sullivan title, is from their operetta "The Pirates of Penzance."
2. David Perlman's article The Wilderness, which originally appeared in the San Francisco Chronicle, is included in the anthology Popular Writing in America.

ANSWERS

1. "I Am the Very Model of a Modern Major General," a song with a typical Gilbert and Sullivan title, is from their operetta *The Pirates of Penzance.*
2. David Perlman's article "The Wilderness," which originally appeared in the *San Francisco Chronicle,* is included in the anthology *Popular Writing in America.*

Who/Whom

Choose the correct form in the following sentences:

1. The first space shuttle pilots, (who, whom) remained unflappable throughout their mission, are out of the same mold as Chuck Yaeger, (who, whom) first flew a plane fast enough to break the sound barrier.
2. Caligula was a man (who, whom) many feared and few admired.

ANSWERS

1. who, who
2. whom

Wordiness

Rewrite the following sentences to make them more concise:

1. Prior to the undertaking of a purchase of a major nature, you should in most instances make a comparison of prices, features, and overall quality.

2. In terms of the boredom of the audience, the tendency of the film toward the creation of confusion was to blame.

SUGGESTED REVISIONS

1. **Before making a major purchase, you should usually compare prices, features, and overall quality.**
2. **The audience was bored because the film was confusing.**

Commonly Confused and Misused Words

Choose the correct word in each of the following pairs of words:

The family was (already, all ready) to (accept, except) the (complement, compliment) when the chairman stopped mid-sentence and scratched his brow. "I don't want to adversely (affect, effect) this fine ceremony," he said, "or (imply, infer) that because there are twenty-five children in your family you can't share the award (among, between) you. But I (don't hardly, hardly) know how such a large (amount, number) of people are going to manage to split one Big Mac."

ANSWERS

all ready	imply
accept	among
compliment	hardly
affect	number

Below is a list of the entries in the Usage Manual. (For convenience, all punctuation entries are arranged alphabetically under "punctuation.")

parts of speech
  noun
  pronoun
  verb
  adjective
  adverb
  preposition
  conjunction
  interjection
passive voice
point of view shift
predication
punctuation
  apostrophe
  colon
  comma
  dash
  ellipses
  exclamation point
  hyphen
  parentheses and brackets
  period
  question mark
  quotation marks (see also "dialogue")
  semicolon
  underlining (italics)
redundancy
reference—see "agreement of pronoun and antecedent" and "broad reference"
repetition
run-together sentences
sequence of tenses—see "tense sequence"
slang—see "colloquialisms/slang"
spelling
subjunctive mood
subordination, faulty
tense sequence
tense shift
titles
who/whom (see also "agreement of pronoun and antecedent")
wordiness
wrong word
commonly confused and misused words

A/AN

Use *a* before a word that begins with a consonant sound; use *an* before a word that begins with a vowel sound. Thus:

a tree	an elephant
a book	an orange
a tired old man	an angry dog
a unit	an honest mistake

Notice that you can't always tell whether you should use *a* or *an* simply by looking at the first letter of the word that follows; you must *hear* the word in your mind. Thus you should use *a* before "union," since the word begins with a consonant *sound* ("yoon-yon"), but *an* before "umbrella," which begins with a vowel sound. Similarly, "honest," which sounds as if it were written "on-est," requires *an*, while "house," in which the "h" sound *is* pronounced, should be preceded by *a*.

EXERCISE:

Put *a* or *an* before each of the following:

1. _____ typewriter
2. _____ old typewriter
3. _____ devastating fire
4. _____ immense fire
5. _____ hour's conversation
6. _____ hostess
7. _____ euphemism
8. _____ unreasonable request
9. _____ universal desire
10. _____ honorable mention

Answers:

1. a
2. an
3. a
4. an
5. an
6. a
7. a

8. an
9. a
10. an

ADJECTIVE/ADVERB CONFUSION (See also "Wrong Word," page 425.)

Writers sometimes make the wrong choice between the adjective and adverb form of a word. Remember that *adjectives modify nouns* and that *adverbs modify verbs*, as well as adjectives and other adverbs. We therefore write

He gave an <u>enthusiastic</u> performance.
(The adjective "enthusiastic" modifies the noun "performance.")

He performed <u>enthusiastically</u>.
(The adverb "enthusiastically" modifies the verb "performed.")

We would never write "He performed enthusiastic" or "He gave an enthusiastically performance." But some incorrect choices aren't as grating, and we may fail to notice that we've chosen an adjective when we should have used an adverb, or vice versa. Compare the following sentences with their revisions:

Incorrect: Even a conscientious scientist may not always spot his or her own mistakes as quick as is necessary.

Revision: Even a conscientious scientist may not always spot his or her own mistakes as <u>quickly</u> as is necessary.
(Since "spot" is a verb here, it must be modified by an adverb, "quickly.")

Incorrect: Most parents soon learn to be <u>real</u> patient with their children's seemingly endless questions.

Revision: Most parents soon learn to be <u>really</u> patient with their children's seemingly endless questions.
(The adjective "patient" must be modified by an adverb, "really.")

Occasionally, writers are tripped up by **linking verbs,** which include *to be, to seem, to appear, to act,* and verbs having to do with the senses, like *to taste, to smell, to sound,* and *to feel.* When these verbs link the subject of a clause with a word describing that subject, the descriptive word is an adjective. For example:

linking
subject   verb   adjective
John's attitudes on race relations are surprisingly short-sighted.

```
                    linking
            subject verb adjective
So far, Vonnegut's new novel seems boring.
```

```
                                    linking
    subject                         verb adjective
The bread one buys at supermarkets often tastes stale by the next
day.
```

```
                            linking
    subject                 verb   adjective
The itinerary the speaker outlined sounded exciting.
```

In most cases, we instinctively reached for the adjective rather than the adverb in this situation. We would never write "John's attitudes are *short-sightedly*," "The novel seems *boringly*," "The bread tastes *stalely*," or "The itinerary sounded *excitingly*."

As we noted earlier, some wrong sentences don't sound as wrong as others. Even though the original sentences in the pairs below may sound all right, they're incorrect:

Incorrect: In view of my short time on the job, I felt rather <u>awkwardly</u> about having to confront my boss.

```
                                        subject
                                        │ linking
                                        ▼ verb
```
Revision: In view of my short time on the job, I felt rather
adjective
<u>awkward</u> about having to confront my boss.

Incorrect: Most visitors to Hawaii find that poi, a pasty staple of the Island diet, tastes rather <u>oddly</u>.

```
                                    subject
```
Revision: Most visitors to Hawaii find that poi, a pasty staple of

```
            linking
            verb      adjective
```
the Island diet, tastes rather <u>odd</u>.

EXERCISE

Choose the correct form (adverb or adjective) in the following sentences:

1. Sometimes people fail their driving test because they drive too <u>cautious/cautiously</u> and thereby impede the flow of traffic.
2. Even though the team played <u>good/well</u>, their opponents played better.

3. John's been acting irritable/irritably for the past few weeks.

4. Public personalities who seem arrogant may in fact be real/really shy.

5. My stereo doesn't sound as good/well as yours.

Answers:

1. cautiously   4. really
2. well   5. good
3. irritable

AGREEMENT OF PRONOUN AND ANTECEDENT

A pronoun usually refers to an antecedent, a noun or another pronoun that comes before it.

> (antecedent)   (pronoun)
> The bank robbers found their getaway car right where they had left it.

Because the pronoun refers to the antecedent, it must agree with the antecedent in gender and number. Also, the pronoun must be clear and unambiguous.

Number Agreement

1. Plural antecedents require plural pronouns; singular antecedents require singular pronouns.

> (singular) (singular)
> *Correct:* The student put his copy of *The Divine Comedy* in the locker.
>
> (plural)   (plural)
> *Correct:* The physicists put on their lab suits before entering the sterile environment.
>
> (singular)
> *Incorrect:* It has not been unusual for a President to use cabinet
> (plural)
> and even judicial appointments to reward their political allies.

2. Use a singular pronoun to refer to a collective noun (platoon, committee, group, etc.) when the collective noun is thought of as

one unit. Use a plural pronoun if the members of the group are considered individually.

> The third platoon showed <u>its</u> wisdom by retreating gracefully in the face of superior forces.
> The third platoon all cleaned <u>their</u> rifles.

3. In most cases, use a singular pronoun when referring to an antecedent that is an indefinite pronoun (*anybody, everybody, each, someone, everyone*, etc.). You can remember that these are singular by keeping in mind that most of them end in "body" (a singular) or "one" (also a singular).

> Everybody who voted stuffed <u>his</u> or <u>her</u> ballot in the ballot box.

Person Agreement

Pronouns must agree in *person* as well as in number with the pronoun antecedent that they refer to.

> *Incorrect:* If <u>someone</u> wants knowledge badly enough, <u>you'll</u> find a way to get it.
> (A third person antecedent, "someone" is used with a second person pronoun, "you.")
> *Correct:* If <u>someone</u> wants knowledge badly enough, <u>he'll</u> find a way to get it.
> *Correct:* If <u>you</u> want knowledge badly enough, <u>you'll</u> find a way to get it.

Unambiguous Reference

Be sure pronouns refer clearly to *one* antecedent only.

> *Ambiguous:* Michelangelo met Lorenzo di Medici when <u>he</u> was a young boy.
> *Clear:* When Michelangelo was a young boy, <u>he</u> met Lorenzo di Medici.

Clear Antecedent

Avoid using a vague pronoun that in fact has no antecedent.

> *Incorrect:* I like to go to that store because <u>they</u> treat customers well. (Who are "they"? Insert a noun naming "them.")
> *Correct:* I like to go to that store because <u>the salespeople</u> treat customers well.

Gender Agreement

Besides agreeing in number, singular antecedents and their pronouns must agree in gender (a classification of nouns and pronouns according to their sex). In English there are four genders: (1) the masculine gender, (2) the feminine gender, (3) the common gender denoting either sex, and (4) the neuter gender denoting the absence of sex.

Masculine	Feminine	Common	Neuter
man	woman	adult	mirror
boy	girl	child	sofa
king	queen	ruler	radio
father	mother	parent	phonograph
he	she	they	car
him	her	them	it

Indefinite pronouns create a special problem in gender, for they often refer to both sexes. In the past, the standard has been to use a masculine pronoun for both sexes. However, some people now believe that this standard indicates a bias in the language and argue that we need a more equitable rule. There is little general agreement at present about how this problem should be handled, but here are three approaches that have become generally accepted:

1. If the sentence clearly shows that the antecedent refers to only one sex, use the pronoun of that gender.

> Anyone who joins the sorority can pick her own big sister.
> Someone in the fraternity left his shorts hanging on the shower knob.

2. If the gender of the antecedent is unknown or is clearly a combination of both sexes, try naming both genders.

> Everyone in the audience got to his or her (or his/her) feet.
> The writer should realize that s/he must treat the subject honestly.

(We find the slash awkward, though it's a common solution to this problem.)

3. Often the best solution to problems of gender agreement is to write the sentence either in the plural or in the second person.

> The audience got to their feet.
> As a writer, you should realize that you must treat your subject honestly.

EXERCISE

Correct any errors in pronoun/antecedent agreement in the following. In sentences 8 and 9 pick the appropriate pronoun to fill in the blank.

1. The citizen was outraged at the cost of their water bill.
2. Both art and engineering contribute its unique characteristics to achitecture.
3. The contractor will use either paint or shingles for its decorative effect.
4. The delegates were prepared to cast his or her ballots by the end of the debate.
5. Joan told her girlfriend that she had been chosen as a delegate to the Democratic National Convention.
6. Any time anyone wants to borrow my car, you can just give me a ring.
7. The organization polled their members in a straw vote.
8. No one at the picnic brought _____ baseball glove.
9. Three pieces of cake miraculously found _____ way into my stomach.

Possible Answers:

1. The citizen was outraged at the cost of *his* water bill.
2. Both art and engineering contribute *their* unique characteristics to architecture.
3. The contractor will use either paint or shingles for *their* decorative effect.
4. The delegates were prepared to cast *their* ballots by the end of the debate.
5. When the Democratic National Convention elected Joan as a delegate, *she* told her girlfriend.
6. Any time anyone wants to borrow my car, *he or she* can just give me a ring. *or* Any time *you* want to borrow my car, *you* can just give me a ring.
7. The organization polled *its* members in a straw vote.
8. No one at the picnic brought *his or her* baseball glove.
9. Three pieces of cake miraculously found *their* way into my stomach.

AGREEMENT OF SUBJECT AND VERB

Verbs must agree with their subjects in both person and number: a first-person singular subject (*I*) must be followed by a first-person singular verb (*am, was, have, need,* etc.); a third-person plural subject (*they, books, days, Americans,* etc.) must be followed by a third-person plural verb (*are, were, have, need,* etc.).

> *Incorrect:*   He <u>don't</u> stand a chance of winning the election.
> ("Don't" would be correct with "I," "you," or a plural subject but doesn't agree with the subject "He.")
>
> *Correct:*   He <u>doesn't</u> stand a chance of winning the election.
> (The subject and verb agree.)

Usually we make our verbs agree intuitively, without having to stop and think about how the parts of our sentences fit together. This section will deal with the situations in which it's easy to get confused.

The Subject of the Sentence

1. The subject is not always the noun directly preceding the verb. Because you write more slowly than you think, you may get fooled into making your verb agree with a noun that comes before the verb instead of with the real subject. For example:

> *Wrong:*   The bag of honey date <u>cookies are</u> in the cupboard.
> *Right:*   The <u>bag</u> of honey date cookies <u>is</u> in the cupboard.
>
> *Wrong:*   The tedium of changing diapers, getting up in the middle of the night with a crying baby, and constantly having to subordinate one's own wishes to the needs of a child <u>have driven</u> many new parents into severe depressions.
> (The amount of detail in this sentence can obscure the real subject—<u>tedium</u>.)
>
> *Right:*   The <u>tedium</u> of changing diapers, getting up in the middle of the night with a crying baby, and constantly having to subordinate one's own wishes to the needs of a child <u>has driven</u> many new parents into severe depressions.

2. When you're unsure about what the subject in your sentence is, ask yourself who or what goes with the verb. What is or are in the cupboard? A *bag* is. What has or have driven parents into depressions? *Tedium* has. (See Chapter 7, The Sentence Base, p. 167.)

Bracketing off prepositional phrases mentally can also help you isolate the subject and verb since neither can be part of a prepositional phrase.

> The package [of books] was delivered yesterday.

Compound Subjects

1. When you have two or more subjects joined by *and,* the verb is almost always plural.

Wrong: My father sadly told me that his faith and trust in me <u>was</u> gone.

Right: My father sadly told me that his <u>faith and trust</u> in me <u>were</u> gone.

(Again, you can get distracted into using a singular verb if the noun just preceding the verb is singular. Try to notice when your verb has more than one subject.)

Once in a while two subjects joined by *and* are considered one unit, in which case the verb is singular:

<u>Bread and water</u> <u>was</u> once the staple of prison fare.

2. Subjects joined by *or, either . . . or,* and *neither . . . nor* require special treatment.

A. If both subjects are singular, use a singular verb. Either <u>John</u> or <u>his brother</u> <u>is</u> going to phone us. (one <u>or</u> the other . . . not both)

B. If both subjects are plural, use a plural verb. Neither <u>tarantulas</u> nor <u>scorpions</u> are my favorite pets.

C. If one subject is singular and the other plural, make the verb agree with the subject closer to it. Usually the sentence will sound better if you put the plural subject second and use a plural verb.

Correct and preferred: Neither the secretary of state nor the president's closest <u>advisors</u> <u>know</u> what the state of the union is.
(closer subject is plural) (plural verb)

Also correct: Neither the President's advisors nor the <u>Secretary of State</u> <u>knows</u> what the state of the union is.
(closer subject is singular) (singular verb)

3. If you're joining subjects that differ in *person* ("he and I"), the verb should agree with the subject nearer to it. But because these sentences usually sound terrible, they should be rewritten if possible.

Correct but awkward: Neither she nor I am to blame for the problem.

Better: She isn't to blame for the problem, and neither am I.

Collective Nouns

A collective noun names a group usually considered as a unit: *couple, committee, class, team, audience, group,* etc. Depending on how they are being used, collective noun subjects can take either a singular or a plural verb.

1. If the collective noun in a sentence is acting as a *unit,* use a singular verb:

> The committee is not in favor of the proposal.
> The class was dismissed ten minutes early.

2. If, on the other hand, you want to show that the members of the collective noun acted as individuals, use a plural verb:

> The couple are hoping to spend their honeymoon in Honolulu.

Note: Usually when the people in a group are acting individually, it is smoother to use expressions like "committee members":

> *Correct:* The committee were asked for their ideas.
> *Better:* The committee members were asked for their ideas.

3. The subject *number* deserves your special attention. As subject, *a number* is plural, but *the number* is singular:

> A number of students were clustered around the drinking fountain.
> The number of unwanted pregnancies among high school girls is increasing.

Indefinite Pronouns

1. Some indefinite pronouns—*one, no one, anyone, everyone, someone, nobody, anybody, everybody, somebody, each, either,* and *neither*—are always singular.

> No one was there.
> Each of the suggestions has possibilities.
> Neither of them is going.

2. Some indefinite pronouns—*several, few, both,* and *many*—are always plural.

> Both of them are going. (*But:* Each of them is going.)
> Many are called; few are chosen.

3. A few indefinite pronouns—*some, none, any,* and *all*—can be either singular or plural, depending on the context.

(singular)

None of the cake was left. (*Compare:* It <u>was</u> left.)

(plural)

None of us were there. (*Compare:* We <u>were</u> there.)

4. Note that when *each, every,* and *many a* act as adjectives modifying a subject, the verb must be singular:

Each window <u>was</u> broken.

Every book, magazine, and pamphlet <u>has been</u> catalogued.

Many a student <u>has</u> lived to regret signing up for too heavy a course-load.

Special Cases

1. A few nouns look like plurals because they end in -s, but are actually singular. They include *news, physics, mathematics, economics, politics.*

2. A plural noun showing extent or quantity takes a singular verb:

Eight miles <u>is</u> about my limit on a hike.

Five dollars <u>seems</u> a lot to spend for a movie.

3. When a clause begins with "there" or "here," you must match your verb with the actual subject, which comes after the verb.

There <u>is</u> no <u>excuse</u> for his rudeness.

There <u>were</u> several <u>possibilities</u>.

Here <u>is</u> some <u>coffee</u>.

Here <u>come</u> <u>Helen and Jean</u>.

4. In adjective clauses beginning with *who, which,* and *that,* the verb must agree with the antecedent—the word the *who, which,* or *that* refers to.

<u>Dreams</u> that <u>recur</u> are usually psychologically important.

A <u>dream</u> that <u>recurs</u> is usually psychologically important.

EXERCISE

Correct any subject/verb agreement errors in the following sentences.

1. Every one of his colleagues swear he's the best qualified for the job.
2. Economics pose problems no one have solved yet.
3. The album containing the old man's will and childhood photographs were found hidden beneath a trapdoor in the closet.
4. When young children lose a parent, their grief and loneliness often leads them to become withdrawn.
5. Neither Mr. Forbes nor Miss Johnson were in the classroom when the fire broke out.
6. The team was given a standing ovation after it won the game.
7. The number of problems that turned up was disheartening.
8. There was a number of complaints; here's two of them.
9. Both Bob and Carol feel that Ted and Alice are too old to trick-or-treat.
10. The sociologist believes that commercials usually exaggerate the happiness that comes with buying products and leads us to develop unrealistic expectations.

Answers:

1. Every one of his colleagues *swears* he's the best qualified for the job. (*Every* is always singular.)
2. Economics *poses* problems no one *has* solved yet.
3. The album containing the old man's will and childhood photographs *was* found hidden beneath a trapdoor in the closet.
4. When young children lose a parent, their grief and loneliness often *lead* them to become withdrawn.
5. Neither Mr. Forbes nor Miss Johnson *was* in the classroom when the fire broke out.
6. *Correct*
7. *Correct*
8. There *were* a number of complaints; here *are* two of them. ("A number" is plural.)
9. *Correct*
10. The sociologist believes that commercials usually exaggerate the happiness that comes with buying products and *lead* us to develop unrealistic expectations. ("Commercials usually exaggerate . . . and lead")

AS/LIKE

The troublesome distinction between *as* and *like* appears to be eroding, but not so fast that you don't need to know the difference.

Both *as* and *like* can be used to mean something along the lines of "to the same degree," "similar to," or "equally." The choice between *as* and *like* depends not so much on meaning as grammar: *as* introduces clauses and *like* introduces nouns or phrases.
For instance:

```
                        clause
He runs as gracefully as a cheetah does.
                            noun
My father doesn't look like my grandfather.
```

Sometimes this can be confusing, because we often write "He runs as gracefully as a cheetah," omitting the implied "does." Still, we would never say or write "He runs as gracefully like a cheetah." We run into trouble when both *as* and *like* sound right.

You tend to react to adversity just like I do.
You tend to react to adversity just as I do.

From the rule given in the first paragraph of this section, we know that, since "I do" is a clause, the second sentence is correct. Given the fact that we tend to use *like* in place of *as* in casual conversation, the first sentence may sound better than the second. To resolve that dilemma between what our ear likes and what grammar prescribes, we could concoct the following revision, which would satisfy both our ear and our English teacher:

"You tend to react to adversity just like me."
Or, "You and I react to adversity in the same way."

The simplest rule is this: "If *as, as if,* or *as though* make sense in the sentence, *like* is incorrect. If they do not make sense, *like* is the right word."*

For instance, we wouldn't write or say, "He looks just *as/as though/as if* his brother," but we would say, "He looks just *like* his brother."

On the other hand, since "My boss sometimes treats me *as*

*Frank O. Colby, quoted in *A Dictionary of Usage and Style.*

though I were an imbecile" sounds correct, we shouldn't write, "My boss sometimes treats me *like* I were an imbecile."

So when in doubt, try *as, as if,* or *as though* first. If none of them fit, then go with *like.*

EXERCISE

Fill in the blanks below with either *like* or *as, as if,* or *as though.*

1. In many ways, the United States today is _____ Great Britain a hundred years ago.
2. You'll probably get yourself into trouble if you try to study in college _____ you did in high school.
3. Although meteorologists may sometimes sound _____ they think they're infallible, they're the first to admit that weather prediction is far from an exact science.
4. The reporter felt intensely about the issues that had sparked the demonstration, but his professionalism compelled him to act _____ an indifferent observer.
5. Throughout much of the play, Hamlet behaves _____ he's insane.

Answers:

1. like
2. as
3. as if *or* as though

4. like
5. as if *or* as though

BROAD REFERENCE

Don't overwork the indefinite pronouns *this* and *which.* Follow the accepted practices regarding their usage:

1. *This* can be used to refer generally to an idea expressed in a preceding sentence as long as no confusion results. However, *this* can be ambiguous if it encompasses too many ideas.

Acceptable: In the mid-seventies, an increasing number of families were separated by divorce. This has led many family therapists to speculate on the future of the nuclear family in America.

Incorrect: In past decades, a college education practically guaranteed one a good job, a comfortable salary, and a secure future. Anxious parents urged their children to attend college. But the increasing numbers of college graduates made competition for the limited number of jobs increasingly tough, and the fluctuating state of the economy only intensified the problem. <u>This</u> confused the incoming college students and made them unsure about which path would actually help them reach their goals.

In the above paragraph, the word *this* refers to several ideas, not just one. To correct the broad reference error, insert a noun or a phrase that accurately explains what *this* refers to. In the example above, the phrase "This changing situation" would do the trick.

2. The relative pronoun *which* is often used ambiguously. Do not use *which* to refer to the entire preceding sentence if it could also modify only the last word and thus cause confusion:

Incorrect: I often arrive late at my office, which isn't surprising since I don't own an alarm clock.

This sentence may at first seem confusing, because we are likely to read it as saying that the office is surprising, clearly a ridiculous idea. We misread it because we are accustomed to expect *which*-clauses to modify a single noun, as in

I often arrive late at my office, which is in the financial district.

Common usage dictates that we can use *which*-clauses to refer broadly to the entire idea in the preceding clause *if the last word in the clause isn't a noun.*

Acceptable: I often arrive at my office late, which isn't surprising since I don't own an alarm clock.

CAPITALIZATION

The conventions of written English call for capital letters in the following instances.

1. Capitalize the first word in a sentence, or in an expression punctuated as a sentence (ending in a period, question mark, or exclamation mark).

Can we actually blame him? Probably not. His motives are very understandable.

2. Capitalize the first word of a direct quotation that is itself a complete sentence.

> Patrick Henry is famous for his statement, "Give me liberty, or give me death!"

> She said, "He wants to study French this quarter."

But do not use a capital letter when quoting less than a complete sentence.

> Freud believed that when man became civilized he "exchanged a portion of his possibilities of happiness for a portion of security."

3. Capitalize the first, last, and all important words in titles of books, magazines, pictures, songs, articles, movies, and so on. Articles (*a, an, the*), coordinating conjunctions, and prepositions of fewer than five letters are generally considered unimportant. (See also "Titles" in this Usage section.)

The Heart of Midlothian	*The War Between the States*
"The Rime of the Ancient Mariner"	"How to Raise and Train Dogs"
	Meet the Press
The New York Times	*All Quiet on the Western Front*

4. Capitalize proper nouns, those that name specific people, places, and things. Also capitalize proper adjectives, those that derive from proper nouns.

Harry S Truman	the Truman Doctrine
England	English tweeds
America	an American ear
Chicano	Latino music

Jane Austen	Joe Homes	Germany	Texas	Finn	Jew
Cadillac	Levi's	Blacks			

Note: If a word has acquired a special meaning, it is no longer capitalized.

> french fries   china cabinet   navy blue

5. Because they are proper nouns, capitalize the following:

A. Geographic names and names of definite regions:

Africa	Drake's Bay
Angel Falls	Straits of Gibraltar

the Midwest   the South Pole
the Far East   the Sun Belt

B. Names of streets, monuments, buildings, bridges, and so on:

Fleet Street   Frontier Boulevard
the Washington Monument   the Doe Building
Southern Pacific Railroad   Clarendon Hotel
the *Queen Mary* (ship)   Boulder Dam
Golden Gate Bridge

C. Names of historical events, periods, and documents:

World War II   Declaration of Independence   the Middle Ages
Fourteenth Amendment

D. Names of government bodies and departments:

Supreme Court of the United States   the Senate
the House of Representatives   Department of Education
General Accounting Office

E. Names of political parties, business, fraternal organizations, institutions:

Pacific Telephone   Boy Scouts of America   New York Library
University of California at Los Angeles   Oxford University
Democratic Party

6. Capitalize titles of rank *only* when joined to a person's name. (Exceptions: titles of very high rank, well-known to all, such as Queen of England and President of the United States.)

President Johnson   Professor Galbraith
Congresswoman Chisholm   Dame Edith Evans   Dr. Julia Easton

He decided to write a letter to his congresswoman protesting the income tax increase.
In her answer to her constituent, Congresswoman Chisholm acknowledged that middle-income families are being taxed heavily.

7. Capitalize the days of the week, months of the year, and holidays.

Tuesday   December   Easter Sunday   Memorial Day
Mother's Day

Note: Do not capitalize names of the seasons, unless you are personifying them, as in poetry.

> I won't go to school this summer.
> Penetrating through all three layers of my heavy woolens, Winter's
> icy breath chilled me unmercifully.

8. Capitalize *north, south, east,* and *west* only when they refer to sections of the country, not when they refer to directions.

> He comes from the Far West.
> Lately the East has endured severe winters.
> We drove west for seven miles, then turned south.

9. Capitalize all words referring to the Deity, the Bible, and other sacred books.

> God   Koran   New Testament   Holy Spirit   Talmud
> Bible

10. Capitalize names of school subjects only when they refer to specific courses. Language courses and languages are always capitalized.

> history   History IB
> science   Physics II
> psychology   Psychology 243
> English   Spanish

11. Capitalize words showing family relationship only when used with a person's name or when used alone as the equivalent of nicknames.

> Uncle Charles   my uncle   Cousin Mary   his favorite sister
> She wrote to her mother asking for suggestions.
> I'm going to ask Dad for some help with this project.

12. Do *not* capitalize common nouns, those naming any one of a class of persons, places, or things.
Capitalize common nouns only when they are part of a proper name.

> steamboat   catfish   (*but* Steamboat Springs, Catfish Hunter)
>
> John studied for years to become a doctor.
> Should we call Dr. Keroes or Dr. Hastings?

She wanted to swim in the ocean.

The Pacific Ocean is larger than the Atlantic Ocean.

EXERCISE:

Correct any errors in capitalization in the following sentences.

1. In the fall, I plan to go east to college, perhaps to pennsylvania state university, where I will study architecture and economics in hopes of someday joining the department of urban planning in washington, d.c.
2. Shelley was right when he said that poets are "The unacknowledged legislators of the world."
3. "I don't think I can go," she replied, "because I have about three hours of homework left."
4. Of all the Periods in History, the english renaissance seems the most exciting.
5. Well-known as a melting pot of Races, the United States has large settlements of scandinavians in the north, irish in the east, chicanos in the west, and blacks in the south.
6. Late in the Summer, our family always goes up to the Lake, where we laze around, fish, swim, read, and eat. My favorite way to spend the day is to read a mystery such as Bill Boyce's *Going through the Eye of The Needle,* to catch a few Rainbow trout, and then to drive into town for some mexican food.

Answers:

1. In the fall, I plan to go east to college, perhaps to Pennsylvania State University, where I will study architecture and economics in hopes of someday joining the Department of Urban Planning in Washington, D.C.
2. Shelley was right when he said that poets are "the unacknowledged legislators of the world."
3. *Correct*
4. Of all the periods in history, the English Renaissance seems the most exciting.
5. Well-known as a melting pot of races, the United States has large settlements of Scandinavians in the North, Irish in the East, Chicanos in the West, and Blacks in the South.
6. Late in the summer, our family always goes up to the lake, where we laze around, fish, swim, read, and eat. My favorite way to spend the day is to read a mystery, such as Bill Boyce's *Going Through the Eye of the Needle,* to catch a few rainbow trout, and then to drive into town for Mexican food.

CASE OF PRONOUNS

I hit the ball.
The ball hit me.

"I" and "me" refer to the same person in the above pair of sentences; the form the pronoun takes depends on its grammatical role in the sentence. If the pronoun is acting as a subject, it appears as *I;* if it is acting as an object, it becomes *me.* The same holds true for *he* and *him, she* and *her, we* and *us,* and *they* and *them.*

Subjective Case	I	he	she	we	they
Objective Case	me	him	her	us	them

We've never had a student who wrote "Me hit the ball" or "The ball hit I." But you can get into trouble when you have a *pair* of subjects or objects. In those cases, there's a quick test to tell you which form of the pronoun to use. Try simplifying the sentence so that you come to the pronoun in question more quickly. For instance, should you write, "Was the package for John or I?" or "Was the package for John or me?" If you try temporarily leaving out "John or," you'll know in a second. You would say "Was the package for me?" so "Was the package for John or me?" is correct.

Wrong	*Right*
The same principle applies to you and I.	The same principle applies to you and me.
The personnel manager complimented her and I on our work.	The personnel manager complimented her and me on our work. (*Or perhaps smoother:* The personnel manager complimented us on our work.)
Her and her brother make me sick.	She and her brother make me sick.

You may also get confused by a sentence like this one:

Us secretaries resented the cavalier way he would give us orders.

That's probably what most of us would say in speech, but formal English requires

We secretaries resented the cavalier way he would give us orders.

Why? Because *we* resented the way he gave orders; you would never say, "Us resented." On the other hand, "He infuriated all of us secretaries" is correct because "He infuriated all of us."

EXERCISES:

Choose the correct form:

1. George hoped both (he, him) and his brother would be accepted at the college they had applied to.
2. Helen Keller acknowledged that both her teacher, Anne Sullivan, and (her, she) would at times become frustrated and angry.
3. (We, Us) Puritans all know that hard work is good for our characters.
4. Please return the completed forms to my secretary or (I, me).
5. To (we, us) kids, Vietnam was just a name on the 6:00 news.

Answers:

1. he
2. she
3. We
4. me
5. us

COLLOQUIALISMS/SLANG

Although these two categories of words are sometimes lumped together, they are in fact quite different.

Colloquial Language

Colloquial language is appropriate in conversation and, by extension, in writing that we want to sound conversational or informal. It has been described as "the language used in the speech of educated people."

Below are some illustrations of some formal terms and their colloquial equivalents:

Formal	**Colloquial**
to become familiar with the proper method of doing something	to get the hang of something

to agree to participate in or give one's active support to	to play along with
prohibiting or opposed to the sale of liquor	dry
something of inferior or shoddy quality	junk

You'll notice that the formal terms are longer than their colloquial counterparts. They would also sound stilted in an informal essay, in which it would be perfectly appropriate to write

> It sometimes takes people a few days to get the hang of using a sophisticated electric typewriter.

> I would often play along with my brother's schemes, only to regret my involvement later.

> Despite the repeal of prohibition nearly fifty years ago, many counties in Southern and Midwestern states are dry.

> The junk that passes for appliances these days is often so poorly designed and manufactured as to be useless and, at times, dangerous.

Naturally, if you were preparing a formal report for a class discussing consumer protection, you might use a less colloquial and more neutral, precise term than "junk" to describe inferior appliances. But since you generally want your reader to get a feeling for your individual voice, it makes sense to draw on the language that you use in speech.

Slang

This is not to suggest, though, that your entire speaking vocabulary is appropriate for even an informal essay. Aside from the occasional vulgarity we may let slip in conversation with peers, most of us use *slang* in our casual conversations as well. Slang is different from colloquial language in a couple of key ways: slang terms tend to be understood by only one segment of the general population, and they tend to appear in the language and then disappear relatively quickly. For these reasons, slang is usually not effective in an essay. You can't be sure that your readers will understand a slang term, for they may not belong to a group that uses it. For instance, to a pop or jazz musician an *ax* is a musical instrument; to the rest of us, it's something used to chop wood. You may also be either ahead of or behind your readers in your choice of slang, using a term that they may not have heard yet or that they may have heard so long ago that it's outdated. Describing something as "the bee's knees" or "the cat's pajamas," for example, wouldn't earn you many points for trendiness.

Because slang is informal and even rebellious, it can jar a reader's sensibilities as well. If you were reading an essay on *Pride and Prejudice,* you'd probably be a bit put off by a writer who referred to the social milieu of the novel as "a drag" or to Mrs. Bennett, one of the characters in the novel, as "a pain in the butt."

If you're in doubt about the status of a particular word or expression, check a current dictionary—the New College edition of *The American Heritage Dictionary* is especially good for this. If a word is designated as "standard," you can use it fearlessly. If it's designated as "colloquial" or "informal," you're probably still safe, at least in an informal essay. If it's designated as "slang," you'd probably do better to find a more standard substitute.

For instance, if you check your dictionary, you'll find that the word "junk" is *standard* when used to mean "trash" or "discarded goods that have outlived their usefulness." "Junk" is *colloquial* when used to describe shoddy merchandise. And "junk" is *slang* when used as a synonym for narcotics in general or heroin in particular.

COMMA SPLICE

A comma splice occurs when a writer, using only a comma, puts together two independent clauses (independent clauses can stand alone as sentences).

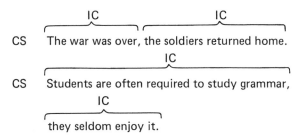

These mergers are unacceptable. There are four main ways to correct comma splices:

1. Use a period to separate the independent clauses:

The war was over. The soldiers returned home.
Students are often required to study grammar. They seldom enjoy it.

2. Use a semicolon to separate the independent clauses:

The war was over; the soldiers returned home.
Students are often required to study grammar; they seldom enjoy it.

3. Use a coordinating conjunction (*and, but, for, or nor, yet, so*) after the comma.

The war was over, so the soldiers returned home.

or

The war was over, and the soldiers returned home.
Students are often required to study grammar, but they seldom enjoy it.

4. Turn one of the independent clauses into a dependent clause, one no longer capable of standing alone.

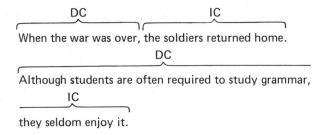

DC   IC

When the war was over, the soldiers returned home.

DC

Although students are often required to study grammar,

IC

they seldom enjoy it.

Of the four methods, numbers 3 and 4 are often preferable because they help eliminate choppiness and show the reader the logical relationship between the clauses.

Many writers have trouble with comma splices because they confuse *transitional expressions* with *coordinating conjunctions.* Thus they think that words such as *then, however, for example, therefore,* etc. can legally join independent clauses. They can't. Only the seven coordinating conjunctions (*and, but, for, or, nor, yet, so*) can join independent clauses with just a comma. (For more on transitional expressions, see Chapter 8, Coordination and Subordination, page 213.)

       CS   Someone running for President as an Independent could win the election, however it's not very likely.

Revision: Someone running for President as an independent could win the election; however, it's not very likely.

       CS   The students promptly finished their work, therefore the teacher dismissed them early.

Revision: The students promptly finished their work; therefore, the teacher dismissed them early.

Comma splices are treated at greater length in Chapter 8, "Coordination and Subordination."

EXERCISE:

Correct any comma splices in the following sentences.

1. I wanted to finish my work and go outside, the beautiful weather beckoned me.
2. The rate of inflation is still climbing, people are feeling the pinch more and more.
3. Stuffing the last sleeping bag into the car, they completed the arrangements for the camping trip, then they collapsed into bed.
4. Science offers hope for the cure of many diseases, it can't always promise miracles.
5. City governments are now acknowledging the need for more public housing, although funding is difficult to obtain given the larger problems of recession and inflation.

Answers:

Use any of the four methods presented above. Try to determine which method is most effective in any given sentence.

1. Because the beautiful weather beckoned me, I wanted to finish my work and go outside.
   I wanted to finish my work and go outside, for the beautiful weather beckoned me.
   I wanted to finish my work and go outside ; the beautiful weather beckoned me.
2. The rate of inflation is still climbing, and people are feeling the pinch more and more.
   The rate of inflation is still climbing; people are feeling the pinch more and more.
3. Stuffing the last sleeping bag into the car, they completed the arrangements for the camping trip; then they collapsed into bed.
   Stuffing the last sleeping bag into the car and completing the arrangements for the camping trip, they collapsed into bed. (*Note:* This sentence uses still another method of eliminating the comma splice. It involves turning the first independent clause into a *phrase* that is parallel with the opening phrase. Try for variety when you can.)
   Stuffing the last sleeping bag into the car, they collapsed into bed after they had completed the arrangements for the camping trip.
4. Science offers hope for the cure of many diseases, but it can't promise miracles.
   Science offers hope for the cure of many diseases; however, it can't promise miracles.
   Although science offers hope for the cure of many diseases, it can't promise miracles.
5. *Correct*

COMPARATIVE/SUPERLATIVE

Although the convention regarding the use of the comparative and superlative is eroding, if not disappearing, you should still use these two adjective forms correctly. The comparative or *-er* form of the adjective signifies "more"; the superlative or *-est* form signifies "most." Basically, the rule is this: if you're comparing only *two* things or people, you use the *comparative,* or *-er* form of the adjective:

> the <u>better</u> of the two dancers
> the <u>more</u> even-tempered twin
> the <u>sillier</u> of the two movies
> the <u>more</u> intelligent of the pair

If you're comparing more than two things or people, you use the *superlative,* or *-est,* form of the adjective:

> the <u>best</u> dancer of the troupe
> the <u>most</u> even-tempered member of the family
> the <u>silliest</u> movie ever made
> the <u>most</u> intelligent of the threesome

All one-syllable adjectives have a comparative or superlative form, usually formed by the addition of *-er* and *-est;* nice, nicer, nicest. A few adjectives have irregular comparative and superlative forms: *good, better, best; bad, worse, worst; many, more, most.*

If you're not sure what the comparative or superlative form of a particular adjective is, check your dictionary. With a few exceptions, adjectives of more than one syllable are made comparative or superlative merely by the addition of *more* or *most:* "beautiful, more beautiful, most beautiful."

Exercise:

Choose the correct form in the sentences below.

1. Paul Simon was the <u>more/most</u> talented member of the team of Simon and Garfunkel.
2. This is one of the <u>hardest/most hard</u> problems I've ever faced.
3. Many of the voters who watched the 1960 Kennedy-Nixon debates decided who the <u>best/better</u> candidate was on the basis of his appearance and mannerisms alone.
4. Perhaps Iceland is the <u>less/least</u> known member of NATO.
5. Van Gogh, like many artists, became <u>more famous/famouser</u> in death than in life.

Answers:

1. more
2. hardest
3. better
4. least
5. more famous

COMPARISON, FAULTY

Sometimes writers carelessly compare things that can't logically be compared. This happens usually because what they've written isn't what they actually mean. For instance, the writer of the first sentence below didn't really mean to compare books and schools:

Faulty comparison: The books for this class are easier than high school.

Revision: The books for this class are easier than the ones I had to read in high school.

Similarly, the writer of the following sentence didn't intend to equate weather and cities:

Faulty comparison: The fog in our town is sometimes as dense as London.

Revision: The fog in our town is sometimes as dense as London's.

A comparison is like an equation, so the two sides of the comparison must match. Make sure that the comparison you've written is the comparison you intend.

EXERCISE:

Correct any faulty comparisons in the following sentences. If a sentence is correct, leave it as it is.

1. His neck looks like a giraffe.
2. After World War II, many Black American soldiers remained in France, feeling that the French attitude toward race was more enlightened than America.
3. The stereo was as loud as a jackhammer.
4. Plutonium is more expensive than the cost of gold.
5. The current President's rapport with the press is even less stable than his predecessor.

Answers:

1. His neck looks like a giraffe's.
2. After World War II, many Black American soldiers remained in France, feeling that the French attitude toward race was more enlightened than America's.
3. *Correct*
4. Plutonium is more expensive than gold.
5. The current President's rapport with the press is even less stable than that of his predecessor (*or* "than his predecessors").

COORDINATION, FAULTY

Faulty coordination is the stringing together of two or more independent clauses with one of the coordinating conjunctions (*and, but, for, or, nor, yet, so*) when logic or style requires either a different coordinating conjunction or another type of construction.

Sentences that use excessive coordination are usually wordy and monotonous:

> *Wordy:* Fort Wayne, Indiana, is a small, uninspiring Midwest town, <u>and</u> my brother lives and works there, <u>but</u> he's used to living in a cosmopolitan setting.
>
> *Better:* My brother, accustomed to living in a cosmopolitan setting, lives and works in Fort Wayne, Indiana, a small, uninspiring Midwest town.

As the example shows, such sentences can be rewritten to replace the coordinating conjunctions with subordination (see Chapter 8) or other more sophisticated constructions.

Because *and* is the most frequently used coordinating conjunction, it is also the most abused. Often it is thrown carelessly into a sentence where another conjunction would be more appropriate.

> *Imprecise:* Shel Silverstein writes perceptive children's stories <u>and</u> children are usually not as impressed by them as their parents are.
>
> *Clearer:* Shel Silverstein writes perceptive children's stories, <u>but</u> children are usually not as impressed by them as their parents are.

The sentence can also be rewritten so that one clause is subordinated to another:

Although Shel Silverstein writes perceptive children's stories, children are usually not as impressed by them as their parents are.

EXERCISE:

Where necessary, rewrite the following sentences, using appropriate coordinating conjunctions, subordination, or both.

1. A person smokes a menthol cigarette and thinks it's not irritating his throat and the smoke feels so cool.
2. Politics is often a messy business and we must feel it's a necessary part of government and we tolerate it.
3. People thought gas prices were high in the early '70's, and they would have thought them low by today's standards.
4. Government officials are quick to decry genetic studies and they fear a "brave new world," and they fail to realize that these same studies benefit cancer research.
5. "Room temperature" as it applies to wine is a great deal chillier than most people suspect, and the term originated during a period when rooms were largely made of stone, for stone rooms are exceptionally cold.

Possible Answers:

1. a. When a person smokes a menthol cigarette, he thinks it's not irritating his throat because the smoke feels so cool.
   b. A person smokes a menthol cigarette, thinking it's not irritating his throat because the smoke feels so cool.
2. a. Politics is often a messy business, but we must feel it's a necessary part of government, for we tolerate it.
   b. Though politics is often a messy business, we must feel it's a necessary part of government, for we tolerate it.
3. a. People thought gas prices were high in the early '70's, but they would have thought them low by today's standards.
   b. Although people thought gas prices were high in the early '70's, they would have thought them low by today's standards.
4. a. Government officials are quick to decry genetic studies for they fear a "brave new world," yet they fail to realize that these same studies benefit cancer research.
   b. Government officials are quick to decry genetic studies, fearing a "brave new world," but they fail to realize that these same studies benefit cancer research.
5. "Room temperature" as it applies to wine is a great deal chillier than most people suspect, for the term originated during a

period when rooms were largely made of stone, and stone rooms are exceptionally cold.

DANGLING MODIFIER (INCLUDING DANGLING PARTICIPLE)

Barking and yelping, the postman was chased by a pack of dogs.

This is (literally) a textbook example of a *dangling modifier*, a verbal phrase that doesn't make logical or grammatical sense with the rest of the sentence. Its agent (implied subject) is not the same as the subject of the sentence in which the verbal phrase appears—the postman didn't bark and yelp.

The verbal phrases in the following sentences dangle:

In preparing dinner, one disaster after another ensued.
("disaster," the subject of the sentence, doesn't make sense as the agent of "preparing" a disaster can't prepare dinner)

To analyze the budget usefully, last year's expenditures must be considered.
("last year's expenditures" cannot be the agent of "to analyze," since expenditures can't analyze anything)

You can correct a dangling modifier in two ways.

1. Change the subject of the clause so it makes sense as the agent of the verbal:

In preparing dinner, Fritz faced one disaster after another.
To analyze the budget usefully, you must consider last year's expenditures.

2. Change the verbal phrase into a clause, which by definition always has its own subject and therefore cannot dangle:

While Fritz was preparing dinner, one disaster after another ensued.
If you want to analyze the budget usefully, last year's expenditures must be considered.

For a more complete discussion of verbal phrases, see Chapter 9, including the section on dangling modifiers, page 232.

EXERCISE

Correct any dangling modifiers in the following sentences.

1. Climbing up onto the chair, the birdcage was within the cat's reach.
2. A difficult written examination must be completed in order to pass the course.
3. After walking to work in the rain, my hair was a sodden mess.
4. Uninformed about growing resentment against him, Paraguay seemed like a perfect retreat for ousted Nicaraguan strongman General Anastasio Somoza.
5. Seen from the perspective of history, one might feel that President Nixon's accomplishments in foreign policy overshadow the political misfortunes of Watergate.

Possible Answers:

1. Climbing up onto the chair, the cat was within reach of the birdcage.
2. You must complete a difficult written examination in order to pass the course.
3. After I walked to work in the rain, my hair was a sodden mess.
4. Uninformed about growing resentment against him, ousted Nicaraguan strongman General Anastasio Somoza thought Paraguay was a perfect retreat.
5. One might feel that, seen from the perspective of history, President Nixon's accomplishments in foreign policy overshadow the political misfortunes of Watergate.

DIALOGUE

1. In general, separate dialogue from the rest of a sentence with a comma and quotation marks:

"Good morning," she said coldly.
He looked at her and said, "Something seems to be bothering you."

Notice that both commas and periods go *inside* quotation marks.

2. Even after a full sentence of dialogue, use a comma rather than a period unless you've come to the end of *your* sentence:

"Your powers of observation are amazing," she told him.
Even though she knew it was childish, she couldn't help answering sarcastically, "Your powers of observation are amazing."

3. Sometimes you'll want to interrupt a line of dialogue:

"And that," he said, "was that."

"In this world there are only two tragedies," remarks a character in one of Oscar Wilde's plays. "One is not getting what one wants, and the other is getting it."

Note that, logically enough, the punctuation differs according to whether the interrupted dialogue is one sentence or two. If you have a new sentence when you resume the dialogue (as in the example from Oscar Wilde above), put a period before it and begin the quotation with a capital letter. Otherwise, just set the dialogue off from the rest of the sentence with commas.

4. Use question marks and exclamation points as they are required within your dialogue. If you have a question mark or exclamation point, you do *not* use a comma as well.

Wrong	*Right*
"What did you say?," I asked.	"What did you say?" I asked.
"Get out of here!," he shouted.	"Get out of here!" he shouted.

5. Begin a new paragraph every time *the speaker* changes. This convention allows you to show who's talking without tiresomely repeating people's names.

"My dear," Charles said. "Have you heard the news?"

"No!" replied Laura, her eyes widening with interest. "What?"

"Billy Peabody has been arrested. It happened last night. They say he's confessed everything."

"But I don't understand. I thought he was devoted to his wife."

"That's what we all thought. But I guess we were wrong."

6. A special problem comes up when you have one speaker exactly repeating the words of another. In this case, you use *single* quotation marks (the apostrophe on your typewriter) for the "quotation inside the quotation."

"Imagine my horror when I came into the room to hear him say 'I love you' to another woman!" she exclaimed.

7. Another special case involves a long speech, one that goes on for more than a paragraph. In this situation, convention requires that you remind your readers you're quoting someone by using quotation marks at the beginning of each paragraph, though you do not use *ending* quotation marks until the whole speech is over. The following

passage, from a short story by Agatha Christie called "The Blue Geranium," illustrates the complexities of punctuating dialogue when one person is quoting others. Throughout the passage, Dolly Bantry is telling a story about something that happened to some friends of hers: note the double quotation marks at the start of every paragraph to remind us that Dolly is speaking. The people whom she quotes talk in single quotation marks.

> "Very unwisely George laughed.
>
> " 'Well, you have had your money's worth this afternoon.'
>
> "His wife closed her eyes and took a long sniff from her smelling bottle.
>
> " 'How you hate me! You would jeer and laugh if I were dying.'
>
> "George protested, and after a minute or two she went on.
>
> " 'You may laugh, but I shall tell you the whole thing. This house is definitely dangerous to me—the woman said so.'
>
> "George's formerly kind feeling toward Zarida underwent a change. He knew his wife was perfectly capable of insisting on moving to a new house if the caprice got hold of her.
>
> " 'What else did she say?' he asked.
>
> " 'She couldn't tell me very much. She was so upset. One thing she did say. I had some violets in a glass. She pointed to them and cried out:
>
> " ' "Take those away. No blue flowers—never have blue flowers. Blue flowers are fatal to you—remember that." . . .' "

In the last paragraph, Dolly Bantry is quoting George's wife quoting Zarida the fortuneteller—hence the double quotation marks within the single ones. Fortunately, it's unlikely that you'll ever find yourself in such a complicated situation—but if you do, you'll know how to handle it.

EXERCISE

Supply quotation marks, commas, question marks, and paragraph breaks wherever necessary:

We were all sitting around the table talking about what to do on our summer vacation. Why don't we drive across the country I asked. I've never been out of state before. If you think I'm going to spend my vacation in a car full of screaming kids said Mother you've got another think coming. Well, what about going on the train asked my father. That's an idea! I said. But my sister didn't like it. I thought we were going to go camping she said. I distinctly remember Dad saying When you kids are older, we'll go on a long camping trip.

Answer:

We were all sitting around the table taking about what to do on our summer vacation.

"Why don't we drive across the country?" I asked. "I've never been out of state before."

"If you think I'm going to spend my vacation in a car full of screaming kids," said Mother, "you've got another think coming."

"Well, what about going on the train?" asked my father.

"That's an idea!" I said.

But my sister didn't like it. "I thought we were going to go camping," she said. "I distinctly remember Dad saying, 'When you kids are older, we'll go on a long camping trip.'"

DIVISION OF WORDS INTO SYLLABLES

When you come to the end of a line and have to divide a word, be sure to divide it *between syllables.* That means that a one-syllable word (even a long one, like *through* or *stretched*) cannot be divided. Try to divide as few words on a page as possible (it's better to have a slightly ragged right-hand margin than to disrupt your readers' concentration by continually splitting up words). Do not divide words on consecutive lines, and never divide the last word on a page. Also, you save nothing by splitting a word so that only the last letter appears on the next line (*radi-o,* for instance), since that last letter could just as well have appeared where you put the hyphen. Nor should you divide a word with only one letter on the first line (*a-tone*).

But if you do have to divide a word, how do you know where the syllable breaks come? When you're really in doubt, consult a dictionary (dictionaries don't always agree, by the way). You can usually figure out how to divide a word yourself. First, try pronouncing the word slowly and clearly. The syllable breaks will probably come where you pause (free-dom, dis-com-fort, re-pro-duc-tion).

There is also a rule that covers most instances:

Divide a word between two consonants or before one consonant.

For example:

Between two consonants:	let-ter
	im-pair
	pur-suit
	col-lec-tion
	pas-sen-ger

Before one consonant:	re-view
	la-ment
	spe-cies
	beau-ti-ful
	pla-ce-bo
Words that apply both principles:	cin-na-mon
	sen-ti-men-tal
	ac-com-mo-da-tion
	dis-con-so-late-ly

There are also a few corollaries to this rule:

1. Treat two consonants pronounced together as one: drink-a-ble
moth-er
hand-i-cap

2. When you have three consonants in a row, divide between the two that *aren't* sounded together: Christ-mas-time
tum-bling
dis-tinc-tion
sur-prise

3. An *r* usually goes with the vowel preceding it if the *r* and the vowel are pronounced as one sound: Or-e-gon
su-per-in-ten-dent
gre-gar-i-ous

But: e-ra-sure
o-ra-tion

4. In general, divide a word *after* a prefix or *before* a suffix:
pre-oc-cu-py   driv-ing (not dri-ving, as the word sounds)
re-en-ter   forc-i-ble

EXERCISE

Without consulting a dictionary, try dividing the following words into syllables.

1. champagne
2. prevent
3. middle
4. division
5. daffodil
6. contribution
7. accompaniment
8. derivation
9. fisherman
10. eruption
11. origin
12. nonappearance
13. noodle
14. unattached
15. uniformitarianism

Answers:

1. cham-pagne	9. fish-er-man
2. pre-vent	10. e-rup-tion
3. mid-dle	11. or-i-gin
4. di-vi-sion	12. non-ap-pear-ance
5. daf-fo-dil	13. noo-dle
6. con-tri-bu-tion	14. un-at-tached
7. ac-com-pa-ni-ment	15. u-ni-form-i-tar-i-an-ism
8. der-i-va-tion	

FRAGMENT

You probably remember the standard definition of a sentence: "a group of related words, containing both a subject and a verb, which together make a complete statement." A fragment, as its name implies, is a *piece* of a sentence:

When you get home tonight.
A plan with no drawbacks.

Obviously these "sentences" don't make sense by themselves; they leave you wanting to hear more.

Usually, however, students don't write fragments in isolation—they put them next to another sentence that makes sense of the fragment:

Then came the main dish. A platter filled with Alaskan King Crab sautéed in butter, fresh snipped parsley, lemon juice, and Worcestershire sauce.

This kind of fragment is easy enough to correct; just join it to the sentence it belongs with.

Then came the main dish—a platter filled with Alaskan King Crab sautéed in butter, fresh snipped parsley, lemon juice, and Worcestershire sauce.

There are two ways to distinguish fragments: a grammatical approach and a more intuitive one.

For most students, the best test is simply to read a questionable sentence carefully to see if it makes a complete statement. For instance, "The funds that would ordinarily be spent on athletic programs" is a fragment because it doesn't complete an idea about the funds. The fragment can be turned into a sentence in a number of ways:

> The funds that would ordinarily be spent on athletic programs are now being used to support the academic curriculum at some schools. Many schools are finding it difficult to raise the funds that would ordinarily be spent on athletic programs.
> (*or even*) The funds would ordinarily be spent on athletic programs.

You can also spot a fragment grammatically by checking to see that each sentence you write has a main subject and verb. "The ever-increasing spiral of inflation" has a potential subject but no verb; "Asked me what I meant" has a verb but no subject (*who asked me?*). Note, however, that a subject and a verb alone won't guarantee a complete sentence. A subordinate clause ("If you want to get the most from life," for instance) has both a subject and a verb but stops short of making a complete statement because it is introduced by a subordinating conjunction (discussed in Chapter 8).

The word "being" is one to watch out for if you have a tendency to write fragments:

> I flunked the test. The reason being that I had not studied at all.

The problem is that "being" is not a verb; it is a *verbal* and must be attached to a clause. Again, you can make a correct sentence by joining the fragment to the sentence before:

> I flunked the test, the reason being that I had not studied at all.
> *Even better:*   I flunked the test because I had not studied at all.

Or if for some reason you want to write two sentences, change *being* to *was:*

> I flunked the test. The reason was that I had not studied at all.

EXERCISE

Some of the following sentences are complete; others are fragments. Make the fragments into complete sentences, either by joining them to independent clauses or by adding words.

1. Days at Boy Scout camp bashing canoes, telling dirty stories around the campfire, and filling the seniors' sleeping bags with snakes and "meadow muffins."

2. Poetry can be extremely difficult to understand. The reason being that it is the most concise form of literature.

3. Freud postulated the existence of an unconscious full of thoughts and desires too shocking to be admitted into the conscious mind. An idea which many of his contemporaries indignantly repudiated.

4. It finally happened. I got a job.

5. As the warm weather set in, I came down with spring fever. The major symptom being a desire to go to the beach instead of to school.

6. His theories mocked, his methodology attacked, his colleagues' support withdrawn.

7. Bill thought the 1959 Pontiac he had picked up for $65 would be easy to get running. It wasn't.

8. When you're writing a paper, it's a good idea to begin early. Unless you happen to like typing at four o'clock in the morning with one eye open.

9. I found several delightful curiosities in the attic. Love letters postmarked 1905 and 1906 and addressed to Ruth Wilkins and Charles Allen. A souvenir newspaper chronicling Charles Lindbergh's 1927 transatlantic flight. Even a photograph album containing faded snapshots of a smiling young couple that I recognized as my grandparents.

Possible Answers:

Note: Fragments can be corrected in a variety of ways. These answers are meant only as illustrations; if you're in doubt as to whether your version is correct, ask someone you trust to check it for you.

1. *A fragment.* I spent my days at Boy Scout camp bashing canoes, telling dirty stories around the campfire, and filling the seniors' sleeping bags with snakes and "meadow muffins."

2. *Second sentence is a fragment.* Poetry can be extremely difficult to understand since it is the most concise form of literature.

3. *Second sentence is a fragment.* Freud postulated the existence of an unconscious full of thoughts and desires too shocking to be admitted into the conscious mind—an idea which many of his contemporaries indignantly repudiated.

4. *Neither sentence is a fragment.* You may have marked the first sentence as one since you didn't know what "It" referred to. However, the sentence "It finally happened" contains a subject ("it") and a predicate ("finally happened") and is an independent clause. Thus these sentences are correct as they stand, though there would be nothing wrong with joining them with a colon, semicolon, or dash.

5. *Second sentence is a fragment.* As the warm weather set in, I came

down with spring fever, the major symptom being a desire to go to the beach instead of to school.

6. *A fragment.* His theories were mocked, his methodology was attacked, and his colleagues' support was withdrawn.

7. *Neither sentence is a fragment. See explanation for Sentence 4.*

8. *Second sentence is a fragment.* When you're writing a paper, it's a good idea to begin early, unless you happen to like typing at four o'clock in the morning with one eye open.

9. *All but the first sentence are fragments.* I found several delightful curiosities in the attic: love letters postmarked 1905 and 1906 and addressed to Ruth Wilkins and Charles Allen, a souvenir newspaper chronicling Charles Lindbergh's 1927 transatlantic flight, and even a photograph album containing faded snapshots of a smiling young couple that I recognized as my grandparents.

LOGIC ERRORS

When you write an essay, you should present your ideas logically. The following list of fallacies should alert you to the most common logical traps:

1. The Hasty Generalization

In everyday life generalizations made from our own experience can be useful. Every time you've visited San Francisco in the summer, the weather has been cold and foggy at least some of the time, so you pack a coat. Your two history midterms both emphasized dates, so you make it a point to memorize the most important ones for the final.

But some generalizing can be dangerous. In particular, some writers tend to generalize too freely from their own experience. "I spent two weeks visiting my sister in Memphis last summer," a student writes, "so I know what Southerners are like." The student fails to take into account that his knowledge of Southerners is based on only one person's experience for only two weeks in only one Southern city. The generalization is further weakened by the unstated but clear assumption that all Southerners are alike.

You leave yourself wide open when you use *absolutes* in your writing, words like *all* and *no, always,* and *never.* You'll gain more respect from your readers if you substitute the more reasonable *many* and *few, usually* and *seldom,* and if you admit the limitations of your own experience: "Although my observations are based on only two weeks' experience in one Southern city, I felt that I learned something important about the South."

2. The Unsupported Generalization

Even worse than the generalization based on only a couple of experiences is the generalization that isn't supported at all. "Police are more messed up than the people they arrest," writes a student, convinced that she's said the last word on the subject but actually having proved nothing at all. Remember that nothing is true simply because you say it is.

3. The Buried Premise

In formal logic, a particular fact is held up against a basic premise to arrive at a conclusion. Here's the old stand-by:

Premise: All men are mortal.
Fact: Socrates is a man.
Conclusion: Socrates is mortal.

Very seldom in an essay do you go through these exact steps (and it would probably make pretty boring writing if you did). But many statements do in fact turn out to be derived from premises. Take this one, for example: "Kay is a Lesbian, so she must hate men." Without realizing it, this writer is actually drawing a conclusion from an unstated premise:

Premise: All Lesbians hate men.
Fact: Kay is a Lesbian.
Conclusion: Kay hates men.

The basic premise here is suspect: Just because a woman is a Lesbian, we cannot legitimately conclude that she hates men.

Note the "buried premises" in the following statements:

Since Joe advocates socialized medicine, he must be a Socialist.
(All people who advocate socialized medicine are Socialists.)

Barnes will make a good governor. He's a fine husband and father.
(Anyone who is a fine husband and father will make a good governor.)

4. Either/Or Reasoning

A few things in life *do* boil down to only two possibilities: we can either go out or stay home, the team will either win or lose, I will get the job or I won't. But most issues are more complex, encompassing a whole range of possibilities. The writer who is guilty of the either/

or fallacy mistakenly implies that there are only two choices when in fact there are more.

> *Example:* America—love it or leave it.
> (These are your only options.)
>
> A man is either honest or he isn't.
> (He can't be honest some of the time, or honest about some things and not others.)
>
> You'll have to decide whether you're going to end the relationship or accept Maria as she is.
> (No compromise solution is possible.)

5. Argument to the Man (*ad hominem*)

Sometimes a writer will distract readers from the issues by attacking something on the grounds that the wrong person favors it. For example: "If Nixon was for that policy, it *must* be a mistake." Note that the writer has given us no reasons to oppose the policy; he has rejected it solely on the grounds that Nixon was for it. (The "buried premise" of such a statement would be that "Everything Nixon ever favored is a bad idea.")

6. Transfer (*ad vericundiam*)

The opposite of argument *ad hominem,* "transfer" involves borrowing *prestige* from someone or something to gain support for an idea. You see the technique used all the time in advertising: a TV commercial shows a movie star drinking a certain beverage, and you are supposed to "transfer" your associations with the star to the drink itself. An example from writing:

> If our forefathers were alive today, they would be vehemently opposed to the draft.

Instead of discussing the *issue* of draft resistance, the writer has distracted us by bringing in our forefathers, hoping we'll transfer our feelings of respect for them to the writer's opposition to the draft.

7. Appeal to Emotion—Loaded Language

This fallacy involves playing on the feelings your readers are likely to have, rather than convincing them by reason. By using words with strong connotations, words that carry an emotional weight beyond their literal definitions, the writer attempts to make readers feel favorably or unfavorably about a person or idea without giving any *reasons* to do so. The two most common forms of loaded language are *name-calling* and *glittering generalities.*

A. NAME CALLING

Instead of logically persuading readers that they should be against someone or something, the writer just slings a little mud in the direction of whatever it is he or she wants to condemn. Politicians resort to this device particularly often: Democrats are called "bleeding-heart liberals," while Republicans are accused of having "Stone Age mentalities." Sometimes the person who is guilty of name-calling is a little more subtle. A candidate running against an elected official manipulates the voters by asking them if they are sick of the lies the government has been feeding them, implying that his opponent is a liar without supplying any evidence.

B. GLITTERING GENERALITIES

Here a writer tries to win support by using positive but nebulous catch-phrases like "the American way," "honor and decency," "true, honest government," or "a meaningful relationship." These expressions appear to say a great deal without supplying any concrete images to show what the writer actually means. This approach may appeal to unalert readers because they can fill in exactly what they want to hear, but glory words won't fool experienced readers. Once again, the solution is to come right out and say what you mean, supplying examples and details that will show readers *your* definition of any general terms you need to use.

Please note that we are *not* telling you to strike emotional appeals from your writing. Part of the art of persuasion involves choosing examples you hope will appeal to your readers' feelings as well as to their intellects. But responsible writers do not try to distract readers from the real issues by stirring up their emotions. For further discussion of the legitimate uses of emotional appeals, see Chapter 5, pages 116–117.

8. After This, Therefore Because of This (*post hoc, ergo propter hoc*)

Writers who fall prey to this common fallacy assume that because B followed A, B was *caused* by A. For instance, some Republicans have taken pleasure in pointing out that all four wars we have been involved in during this century (World Wars I and II, the Korean War, and the war in Vietnam) began during the administrations of Democrats, but it does not follow that these wars began *because* Democratic Presidents were in office. Nor is it fair to say, without further evidence, that because Jack's grades started to go downhill after his parents split up, their divorce caused his problems in school.

9. It Does Not Follow (non sequitur)

One way to convince readers of something is to present a series of statements leading them to the conclusion you want them to agree with. But if at any point in this chain of reasoning there is a missing or weak link, the whole argument breaks down. A statement that doesn't grow logically out of what has previously been presented is called a *non sequitur*. For instance, a car dealer may tell his TV audience, "This year, I'm especially proud of the new lineup of cars from Ford. So you'll want to come on down and test drive one of these fine automobiles." This is a fairly obvious *non sequitur*, since the car dealer's pride in *his* product does not motivate *us* to test drive a car.

Here is another example, this one from an essay: "Being a college student involves living with pressure and competition. Therefore we should eliminate grades and evaluate students entirely on a pass-fail basis." The conclusion that students should not receive grades is a *non sequitur* because the preceding sentence has not adequately led up to it. We are left with a couple of questions:

1. Are pressure and competition necessarily things to be eliminated?
2. Would pass–fail grading end pressure and competition?

10. False Analogy

Analogies (likening one thing to something else) can be very helpful in getting your readers to visualize your meaning. If you say that arriving for the first time at an unfamiliar campus is like playing blind man's buff, you help your readers imagine your feelings as you wander around, looking for buildings, information, classes, new friends. The only problem with analogies is that they don't, in themselves, prove anything. For instance, one of us was once criticized by a more experienced professor for getting to class early and chatting with her students before the class began. "Teaching a class is like giving a performance," he said. "You should walk in exactly at 8:10—as the curtain goes up." While teaching is in many ways like giving a performance, the analogy failed to take into account the many differences: students come to class to learn rather than be entertained; in a composition class "performer" and "audience" interact; the students, unlike members of an audience, were coming to class three times a week for a whole semester. The professor's analogy failed to explain why he thought it a mistake for an instructor to come into class early and chat with students.

11. Begging the Question

Writers guilty of this fallacy use language that simply assumes the truth of whatever they're trying to prove. For example, referring to "Ronald Reagan's incompetence during his years as governor of California" doesn't establish that Reagan was incompetent but may give a writer the illusion of having proved it.

Sometimes begging the question involves redundancy: "It is wrong to commit adultery because it is immoral." This sentence merely lets us know—twice—that the writer considers adultery morally wrong. The "because" is totally misleading, for the second clause does not explain the first.

12. Card Stacking

A writer naturally wants to make the strongest possible case to support a thesis. But sometimes the writer will "stack the cards" in his or her favor, either deliberately or accidentally. Card stacking involves arranging information so that it is all favorable to one's point. Usually this involves omitting unfavorable information altogether.

A classic example of card stacking occurs in an address General George Patton made to his troops in World War II. Knowing of his recruits' fears, Patton said:

> You are not all going to die. Only 25 per cent of you right here today will be killed in a major battle.

The card stacking occurs in the final phrase, "in a major battle." Even if Patton's statistic is correct (and one wonders where he got it), the final phrase makes it nearly meaningless to anyone who looks behind the arranged information and asks, "What did Patton leave out? What didn't he tell me?" The questions to ask in this example are the following: How many men will die in minor battles or skirmishes? How many will not die immediately but later, in a hospital or elsewhere? How many will not die but be maimed for life? Above all, how many will die of disease, exposure, and so on?

For obvious reasons, card stacking is often called "lying by omission." Inexperienced writers, perhaps thinking they are just putting forth the best interpretations of their information, will resort to this tactic. But careful readers will immediately start asking questions and may begin to doubt not only a writer's point, but his or her integrity.

EXERCISE

After reading the following entries, identify the logical fallacy in each and explain why the entry is illogical.

1. Although some people believed that the Vietnam war weakened the U.S. economy, the gross national product rose during every year in which U.S. involvement was most extensive. Thus, the war must have strengthened rather than weakened the U.S. economy.

2. Every young person who accepts the challenge of athletic competition emerges a victor. For by participating in the competitive spirit central to all sports and by testing his own tenacity, prowess, and courage, he is preparing himself for the biggest game of all: life.

3. Because of the increasing amount of air traffic in major metropolitan airports and the danger that increased traffic represents, we will have to either build more airports to accommodate the overflow or close down existing airports in the interests of safety.

4. Howard Cosell's "friendship" with Muhammed Ali was obviously nothing more than a self-seeking publicity ploy on Cosell's part. Cosell regularly insults his audience's intelligence by mangling the English language and expecting the audience to believe that the patently phony toupee he wears is his own hair.

5. Senator Davis arrived at the campaign rally 45 minutes late, thereby showing that he didn't mind keeping 1,500 people waiting.

Answers

1. *Post Hoc Fallacy:* The fact that the GNP went up doesn't prove that the Vietnam war caused it to rise. In fact, one wonders how much higher the GNP might have been, had the U.S. not been involved in a war. Also, a high GNP doesn't by itself mean that the economy is strong.

2. There are several errors in this one, including glittering generalities, unsupported generalizations, and faulty analogy.

   GG: "Challenge of athletic competition," "competitive spirit central to all sports," as well as "glory" words such as "tenacity," "prowess," and "courage," and "victor."

   UG: Not all sports test the above-named virtues. Not every one who plays or tries to play has these virtues tested. What is a "victor" anyway? In common usage, victor means one who wins the contest, whatever it is, and not every player wins every time. Some never do win.

   FA: Life isn't a game.

3. *Either/or Reasoning:* There *are* other alternatives. If the problem is too many airplanes, one could find out how many too many there are and eliminate some flights. It might also be possible to

re-route airplanes to adjacent airports, to encourage people to use other modes of transportation, and to improve safety procedures to compensate for the increased air traffic.

4. *Non Sequitur:* The assertions here, having to do with Cosell's friendship with Ali, his control of English, and his toupee, have nothing to do with each other.

Argument ad hominem: The sentences are unsupported, unqualified generalizations that also smack of name-calling. Terms like "patently phony" and "self-seeking" are more accusatory than explanatory.

5. *Buried Faulty Premise:* If set out, the premise would look like this:

1. People are late for meetings only when they don't care about people waiting for them.
2. Senator Davis was late for the rally.

Conclusion: Senator Davis was indifferent to his audience.

The premise is clearly illogical. There could be a number of causes, all quite legitimate, for his late arrival at the rally.

MISPLACED MODIFIER

Generally, a modifier (adjective, adverb, prepositional phrase, etc.) should be close to what it modifies. A modifier is said to be *misplaced* when it is awkwardly or confusingly separated from what it modifies.

Misplaced Modifier:	The cat padded into the silent, dimly lit bedroom at the end of the hall <u>noiselessly</u>.
Revision:	The cat padded <u>noiselessly</u> into the silent, dimly lit bedroom at the end of the hall.
Misplaced Modifier:	Al Jolson was a popular vaudeville entertainer in the 1920s, <u>whose maudlin style would make most people cringe today</u>.
Revision:	Al Jolson, <u>whose maudlin style would make most people cringe today</u>, was a popular vaudeville entertainer in the 1920s.

(In the first example, the adverb "noiselessly" should be close to "padded," the verb it modifies. In the second example, the underlined adjective clause should follow "Al Jolson," the noun it modifies.)

Perhaps the best illustration of the importance of correct and logical placement of modifiers is the following type of sentence, whose meaning changes as the word "only" is moved about:

Only I borrowed his shirt yesterday. (I and no one else)

I only borrowed his shirt yesterday. (I didn't steal it, only borrowed it.)

I borrowed only his shirt yesterday. (Just his shirt, nothing else)

I borrowed his only shirt yesterday. (He had only one shirt)

I borrowed his shirt only yesterday. (Not any earlier)

I borrowed his shirt yesterday only. (And on no other day)

EXERCISE

Correct any misplaced modifiers in the following sentences. If a sentence is all right, leave it as it is.

1. The 1936 Olympics served as a showcase for Nazi propaganda, which were held in Hitler's Germany.
2. I just intended to read the first chapter but wound up reading the whole book.
3. Refusing to be pinned down, the attorney only hinted that he had a surprise witness.
4. Individual freedom without direction and discipline from others almost is worse than direction and discipline without individual freedom.
5. As though he knew his opponent was expecting a lob, McEnroe disguised his drop shot, which barely cleared the net, cleverly.

Answers:

1. The 1936 Olympics, which were held in Hitler's Germany, served as a showcase for Nazi propaganda.
2. I intended to read just the first chapter but wound up reading the whole book.
3. *Correct*
4. Individual freedom without direction and discipline from others is almost worse than direction and discipline without individual freedom.
5. As though he knew his opponent was expecting a lob, McEnroe cleverly disguised his drop shot, which barely cleared the net.

MODIFICATION ERRORS

A *modifier* is a word or a group of words which limits or qualifies the meaning of some other word. Modifiers include adjectives, adverbs, prepositional phrases, verbal phrases, adjective clauses, and appositives. Basically, modification errors involve any part of the sentence beside the *core* (the subject-verb-complement/object part). This leaves a writer with a lot of room in which to make errors in a sentence.

Two types of modification errors, misplaced modifiers and dangling modifiers, are fairly easy to spot and correct. (Refer to the appropriate entries in this Usage Manual for explanation and exercises.) The more general modification error is harder to spot and correct. Often, a writer knows a sentence "sounds funny" but doesn't know how to correct the problem. Following are three common types of modification errors.

1. In using a prepositional phrase, be careful that you are modifying the part of the sentence you wish to modify.

Incorrect: One of the main attractions of Disneyland is Space Mountain, a place which reveals the positive attitude of our travels. (This sentence literally says that our travels have attitudes, clearly an impossibility.)

Revision: One of the main attractions of Disneyland is Space Mountain, a place which reveals our positive attitude toward travel.

Incorrect: The Empire State Building represented advanced technology and the necessity of gigantic buildings for more working space. (Again, the sentence doesn't mean what it actually says—that big buildings needed working space.)

Revision: The Empire State Building represented advanced technology and the necessity for gigantic buildings that would provide more work space.

2. When beginning a sentence with a prepositional phrase, be careful not to repeat the sentence subject.

Faulty: For a student talented in the arts, he should be given every encouragement.

Correct: For a student talented in the arts, a great deal of encouragement is necessary.

Better: A student talented in the arts should be given every encouragement.

3. The overuse and misuse of the preposition *with* often leads to modification errors. Try to eliminate the *with* altogether and modify more tightly, or be sure you really mean "with."

Incorrect: The speed and convenience of McDonald's restaurants are greatly appreciated by mothers always on the go with their children's activities.

(The mothers aren't going anywhere with activities.)

Revision: The speed and convenience of McDonald's restaurants are greatly appreciated by mothers always on the go with their children.

or Better: The speed and convenience of McDonald's restaurants are greatly appreciated by mothers always on the go, hauling their children from one activity to another.

Incorrect: Every individual in our society has conflicting values with his fellow human beings.

(We don't have values with others. Our values conflict with the values of others.)

Revision: Every individual in our society has values that conflict with those of his fellow human beings.

4. Sometimes faulty modification occurs when a writer uses a *phrase* instead of a *clause* (See Chapter 7, pp. 166–167).

Incorrect: McDonald's restaurants are so well-known that they are almost as famous as the American flag. However, it is unlikely of the American people to accept McDonald's as the number one American symbol.

Revision: McDonald's restaurants are so well-known that they are almost as famous as the American flag. However, it is unlikely that the American people will accept McDonald's as the number one American symbol.

EXERCISE:

Correct any faulty modification in the following sentences.

1. The death rate in a car has recently soared because of unbelted drivers.
2. The space program itself illustrates the optimistic views of the American people's confidence in the future.
3. At Disneyland, every type of environment from land, sea, and sky is represented.
4. Because the country is so large and spread out, Americans lose a lot of time getting places more than anything else.
5. It's surprising that private ownership of handguns is still permitted with the high number of accidental deaths caused by them.

Suggested Answers:

1. The death rate in traffic accidents has recently *soared* because drivers aren't wearing their seat belts. *Or, better:*
The number of traffic fatalities has recently soared because drivers aren't wearing their seat belts.
2. The space program itself illustrates the American people's optimistic, confident view of the future.
3. At Disneyland, every type of environment from land and sea to sky is represented.
4. Because the country is so large and spread out, Americans lose more time getting places than doing anything else.
5. It's surprising that private ownership of handguns in still permitted, given the high number of accidental deaths involving handguns (*or,* the high number of accidental deaths they cause).

NUMBERS (Words vs. Numerals)

Generally, low numbers should be spelled out and high numbers should be written as numerals. Where you draw the line between low and high depends mainly on your own sense of style, but most writers spell out numbers under ten, and many spell out numbers under one hundred.

There are some additional conventions in this area, most of which you probably follow already. For instance, dates are not spelled out; you shouldn't begin a sentence with numerals (in other words, you'd write, "Fifty people were crammed into the closet-sized classroom"); related figures should be treated alike ("five or ten minutes," not "five or 10 minutes").

As with much else in matters of usage and judgment, the main thing is to be unobtrusive and consistent.

PARALLELISM

When elements in a sentence are parallel in meaning, they must also be grammatically parallel.

> Writing a good paper is a task that demands hard <u>work</u>, <u>patience</u>, <u>perseverance</u>, and a <u>willingness</u> to be self-critical.
> (The four nouns are parallel.)

> I <u>rushed</u> home, <u>threw</u> my assorted debris into a closet, and <u>ran</u> the vacuum cleaner over the worst of the crumbs on the living room rug.
> (The three verbs are parallel.)

If you lose track of how you began your sentence, though, you may wind up with a series that is not parallel:

> My favorite composers are Mozart, Beethoven, Rachmaninoff, and Wagner's operas.

The last element, "Wagner's operas," is not parallel with "Mozart," "Beethoven," and "Rachmaninoff." The error becomes even more glaring if you simplify the sentence by seeing how the last element matches up with the beginning of the sentence:

> My favorite <u>composers</u> are Mozart . . . and Wagner's <u>operas</u>.

The sentence could be corrected in at least two ways. You could simply change *Wagner's operas* into *Wagner* (which would be parallel with Mozart, Beethoven, and Rachmaninoff). Or, if you wanted to differentiate Wagner's operas from his other works, you could put this information in a separate clause:

> My favorite composers are Mozart, Beethoven, and Rachmaninoff; I also love Wagner's operas.

Some other examples of faulty parallelism:

Wrong

On weekends, Roberto likes <u>playing</u> golf or <u>to build</u> furniture in his workshop. (<u>playing</u> is not parallel with <u>to build</u>)

Right

On weekends, Roberto likes <u>playing</u> golf or <u>building</u> furniture in his workshop.

or

On weekends, Roberto likes to <u>play</u> golf or <u>build</u> furniture in his workshop.

There are several procedures which you must learn in order to operate a camera effectively: <u>loading</u> and <u>unloading</u> the film, <u>setting</u> the camera controls, <u>gauging</u> the correct exposure, and composition of your picture. (The last element, <u>composition</u> is not parallel with <u>loading</u>, <u>setting</u>, and <u>gauging</u>.)

There are several procedures which you must learn in order to operate a camera effectively: <u>loading</u> and <u>unloading</u> the film, <u>setting</u> the camera controls, <u>gauging</u> the correct exposure, and <u>composing</u> your picture.

The dog rolled off the couch onto the coffee table, knocking over a plant, two cups of coffee, and crushing the birthday cake. (The second element, two cups of coffee, is not parallel with the verbals knocking and crushing.)	The dog rolled off the couch onto the coffee table, knocking over a plant, spilling two cups of coffee, and crushing the birthday cake.
	or
	The dog rolled off the couch onto the coffee table, knocking over a plant and two cups of coffee and crushing the birthday cake. (The noun "plant" is parallel with the noun "cups," and the verbal "knocking" is parallel with "crushing.")

If your instructor marks one of your sentences for parallelism and you can't immediately spot the problem, it usually helps to write the sentence down in outline form. For instance, take the last sentence in the "wrong" column above:

The dog rolled off the couch onto the coffee table,
    A. knocking over a plant,
    B. two cups of coffee, and
    C. crushing the birthday cake.

Obviously (B) is not parallel with (A) and (C).

When you're using correlatives (*both . . . and, either . . . or, neither . . . nor, not . . . but,* and *not only . . . but* [*also*]), you must be especially careful with parallelism.

Similar grammatical units should follow each half of the correlative. For instance:

Wrong:	*Right*
The new series of textbooks is favored both by teachers and students. (There is a by after both but not after and.)	The new series of textbooks is favored by both teachers and students.

EXERCISE:

Straighten out the parallelism errors in the following sentences:

1. He loved to give large parties, drink huge quantities of champagne, and swimming with his guests in the nude.
2. Despite their many differences, both my parents are from the Mid-

west, are strongly religious in their views, and both of them know how to love children and make them feel wanted.

3. I have clerical skills such as filing, bookkeeping, shorthand, and I can accurately type 65 words per minute.

4. Fewer and fewer Americans are buying houses these days, not because they don't want to own homes, but the interest rates are so high.

5. That concept applies neither to you nor me.

Answers:

1. He loved to give large parties, drink huge quantities of champagne, and swim with his guests in the nude. *Or:* He loved giving large parties, drinking huge quantities of champagne, and swimming with his guests in the nude.

2. Despite their many differences, both my parents are from the Midwest, are strongly religious in their views, and know how to love children and make them feel wanted. *Or:* Despite their many differences, both my parents are from the Midwest, both are strongly religious in their views, and both of them know how to love children and make them feel wanted.

3. I have clerical skills such as filing, bookkeeping, shorthand, and the ability to type 65 words per minute. *Or:* I have clerical skills such as filing, bookkeeping, and shorthand; I can also accurately type 65 words per minute. (Other variations on this sentence are possible too.) Note that although shorthand and ability don't end in -ing, they are parallel with filing and bookkeeping since they are nouns.)

4. Fewer and fewer Americans are buying houses these days, not because they don't want to own homes, but because the interest rates are so high.

5. That concept applies neither to you nor to me. *Or:* That concept applies to neither you nor me.

PARTS OF SPEECH

It's perfectly possible to become a good writer without ever learning anything about grammar. But if you ever want to talk about how the words in a sentence function, or explain an error to someone, or understand a mistake you've made yourself, it helps to know the terminology and understand the concepts.

Every word in every sentence ever spoken or written fits into one of the following eight parts of speech. (Most of our definitions—the ones in quotation marks—are taken from the 1969 edition of *The American Heritage Dictionary of the English Language.*)

The Noun

A noun is "a word used to denote or name a person, place, thing, quality, or act."

> *Examples:* Marilyn Monroe   Chicago   table   honesty
> thinking

Nouns are fairly easy to recognize because they are usually words you can put *the, a,* or *an* in front of:

> the furniture
> a mess
> an angel

Anything you can *count* will also be a noun:

> five cars
> two situations
> a dozen reasons

The Pronoun

A pronoun is "one of a class of words that function as substitutes for nouns or noun phrases and denote persons or things . . . previously specified, or understood from the context."

> Thomas Jefferson invented the dumbwaiter.
> He invented the dumbwaiter.
>
> Children are often oversensitive.
> They are often oversensitive.

Pronouns also save you from having to repeat words:

> Where is your coat? I left it at the restaurant.
> Queen Elizabeth II was only 26 when her father died.
> Unmarried men who are under 25 pay the highest car insurance premiums.

The Verb

A verb is "that part of speech that expresses existence, action, or occurrence."

> *Examples:* is   were   run   gasped   will happen
> was thinking   had been stunned

The verb usually tells you what is *going on* in a sentence:

> Many men experience a sudden identity crisis when they reach their forties.
> We bought a bookcase and carried it home on the bus.

Verbs are the only words that change when the *time* of a sentence changes. For instance:

Present:	I am furious.	She plays soccer.
Past:	I was furious.	She played soccer.
Future:	I will be furious.	She will play soccer.
Present Perfect:	I have been furious.	She has played soccer.
Past Perfect:	I had been furious.	She had played soccer.

The Adjective

An adjective is "any of a class of words used to modify a noun [or pronoun] by limiting, qualifying, or specifying."

> *Examples:* old   green   romantic   infuriating   unfortunate
> an old lady   the green house   a romantic comedy
> the infuriating delay   an unfortunate remark

A good way to recognize adjectives is to compare them:

> old, older, oldest
> romantic, more romantic, most romantic

A special form of adjective is the *article,* which comes in three forms: *the, a,* and *an.*

The Adverb

Adverbs are ". . . a class of words that modify a verb, adjective, or other adverb."

> *Examples:* well, very, sadly, enjoyably, tomorrow
> She plays the piano well.
> (well tells us how she plays; it modifies the verb)
> She plays the piano very well.
> (very tells us how well she plays; it modifies the adverb well)
> Jerry looked at me sadly.
> (sadly tells how Jerry looked; it modifies the verb)

> We spent an <u>enjoyably</u> lazy Sunday morning in bed.
> (<u>enjoyably</u> tells us what kind of a lazy Sunday we spent;
> it modifies the adjective <u>lazy</u>)
> He should be here <u>tomorrow</u>.
> (<u>tomorrow</u> tells us when he should be here; it modifies
> the verb)

Adverbs very often end in *-ly* (*quickly, drastically, enormously*). Some, however, do not (*very, so, quite, not,* etc.).

The Preposition

Prepositions are "function words" used to show location or relationships. The following are the most common:

across	*for*	*on*
after	*from*	*over*
at	*in*	*through*
because of	*into*	*to*
before	*like*	*under*
between	*near*	*until*
by	*of*	*with*

Prepositions usually appear before nouns in prepositional phrases:

in the room	under the table
to her credit	after World War I
from the very first	through the years
on target	

The Conjunction

Conjunctions are "words . . . that connect other words, phrases, clauses, or sentences."

There are two classes: *coordinating* and *subordinating* conjunctions.

The coordinating conjunctions are *for, and, nor, but, or, yet,* and *so* (you can remember them by the acronym FANBOYS).

Subordinating conjunctions are the words used to connect subordinate clauses with main clauses. Among the most common are *when, if, because, although, before, after, since,* and *while*.

> I called the bank <u>when</u> I discovered the error.
> Let me know <u>if</u> you need any help.
> Children often have trouble with arithmetic <u>because</u> they cannot relate it to their own lives.

Notice that we can reverse the word order so that the sentence begins with the conjunction:

When I discovered the error, I called the bank.

The Interjection

An interjection is "a word of exclamation, capable of standing alone."

Examples: oh damn wow whew! help!

Note that sometimes a word can be more than one part of speech; you have to see how it is used in a sentence. For instance:

I love sports of all kinds. ("love" is a verb.)
Love is a powerful emotion. ("Love" is a noun.)
After the movie, we went to a restaurant. ("After" is a preposition.)
After you left, the trouble really started. ("After" is a conjunction.)

EXERCISE 1:

Identify the part of speech of each of the following groups:

1. dark, intelligent, angry, one-sided
2. to, on, of, through, beyond
3. woman, telephone, energy, success
4. gosh, ah, darn, goodness
5. them, her, it, this, which
6. a, an, the
7. go, was asking, recovered, will hope
8. and, though, but, while, unless
9. happily, not, very, sadly

EXERCISE 2:

Identify the part of speech of each word in the following sentences:

1. Ernestine drank two quarts of beer and ate a pizza after the game.
2. Many women today are delaying pregnancies until they are over the age of 35.
3. "Well!" said the duchess angrily as she swept from the room.

4. Banging his baton on the music stand, the conductor hurled insult-ing remarks at everyone in the orchestra.

5. Americans firmly rejected the Susan B. Anthony dollar when it was introduced in 1979.

Answers:

EXERCISE 1:

1. adjective	6. article
2. preposition	7. verb
3. noun	8. conjunction
4. interjection	9. adverb
5. pronoun	

EXERCISE 2:

1. Ernestine   drank   two   quarts   of   beer   and   ate
    noun   verb   adj.   noun   prep.   noun   conj.   verb

  a   pizza   after   the   game.
art.   noun   prep.   art.   noun

2. Many   women   today   are delaying   pregnancies   until
   adj.   noun   adv.   verb   noun   conj.

  they   are   over   the   age   of   35.
  pron.   verb   prep.   art.   noun   prep.   noun

3. "Well!"   said   the   duchess   angrily   as   she   swept
   interj.   verb   art.   noun   adv.   conj. pron.   verb

  from   the   room.
  prep.   art.   noun

4. Banging   his   baton   on   the   music   stand,   the
   adj.[1]   pron./adj.[2]   noun   prep.   art.   noun[3]   noun   art.

---

[1] Technically, "banging" is a special kind of adjective called a verbal. Although it looks like a verb, it is only *derived* from one. (Note that it would not change form if the time in the sentence shifted: Banging his baton on the music stand, the conductor *hurls* insulting re-marks at everyone in the orchestra.)
Verbals are treated more fully in Chapter 9, pp. 228–232.
[2] Some grammarians call "his" a pronoun, some a possessive adjective.
[3] "Music" is technically a noun although it functions as an adjective in this sentence. If you marked it an adjective (what kind of stand), that's fine.

conductor   hurled   insulting   remarks   at   everyone

   noun   verb   adj.   noun   prep.   pron.

in   the   orchestra.

prep. art.   noun

5. Americans   firmly   rejected   the   Susan B. Anthony   dollar

    noun   adv.   verb   art.   noun[4]   noun

when   it   was introduced   in   1979.

conj. pron.   verb   prep. noun

PASSIVE VOICE

There are two ways of stating many sentences in English:

Active voice: The boy hit the ball.
                  (Focus is on boy, the one who acts)
Passive voice: The ball was hit by the boy.
                  (Focus is on ball, the thing that receives the action)

Generally speaking, the active voice is more direct, forceful, and economical than the passive. Note that it takes the passive sentence above seven words to say what the active version can say in five. Other examples:

Active voice: I bought a new jacket.
Passive voice: A new jacket was bought by me.

Active voice: Ever-increasing numbers of young women are attending law schools.
Passive voice: Law schools are being attended by ever-increasing numbers of young women.

Even worse than being awkward and wordy, some passive sentences are vague. Note that by writing a sentence in the passive, you can leave out altogether the person or thing performing the action:

A mistake was made. (by whom?)
I was shown that I was wrong. (by whom or what?)

Sometimes the passive voice allows you to make statements that

[4]The same holds true for "Susan B. Anthony" in this sentence: the name is technically a noun, but functions here as an adjective.

have the ring of authority until someone notices that you've actually said nothing. For instance:

> It is widely believed that the two-party system is dead. (*who* believes it?)

If your instructor marks a sentence "passive," you should look at it carefully to see (1) how you could have written it in the active voice; and (2) why the sentence is objectionable as it stands. (Is it simply awkward and wordy? Or does it fail to show *who or what* you're really talking about?)

For a more complete discussion of the passive (including an explanation of when the passive voice *is* acceptable), see Chapter 7, pp. 173–178.

EXERCISE:

Rewrite the following passive sentences in the active voice. (Note that in the last two sentences, you must guess at the writer's meaning, supplying your own subjects for the verbs when you turn the sentences around.)

Example: The project was completed last week.

Possible Revisions: We completed the project last week.
                        The class completed the project last week.
                        The committee completed the project last week.

1. The meeting was attended by everyone.
2. A good idea was thought of by John.
3. Until recently, owning a car and driving it as much as they like have been regarded as inalienable rights by most Americans.
4. Her performance was found lacking in several important respects.
5. It was asked whether any problems were seen by the group.

Suggested Answers:

1. Everyone attended the meeting.
2. John thought of a good idea.
3. Until recently, most Americans regarded owning a car and driving it as much as they like as inalienable rights.
4. We/The audience/The dancer/etc. found her performance lacking in several respects.
5. The group asked itself whether it saw any problems. The counsellor asked the group whether it saw any problems, etc.

POINT OF VIEW SHIFT

"Point of view" refers to the person or persons a particular passage is about. Don't shift point of view except for a good reason. (Obviously, if you're writing about a heated argument between two athletes, for example, you'd need to focus on both of them in your paragraph.)

In the following passage, the writer shifts needlessly and probably unconsciously from one point of view to another.

> If a politician is continually exposed to petty, and not so petty, temptations, they may find it difficult to resist every offer of money, merchandise, or special favors. You might turn down the $500 "donation for miscellaneous expenses" and send back the new television sent as "an expression of gratitude for public service," but see nothing wrong with accepting a powerful constituent's offer of a relaxing weekend at his cabin in the mountains. If one accepts any such potentially compromising offer, a politician is open, understandably, to charges of corruption. But if politicians were required to report all transactions of potential monetary value, no matter how trivial, you would be less likely to do anything you wouldn't want voters to know about—and more likely to remain the honest person you started out as.

The problem, of course, is that the writer skips from "a politician," to "they (politicians)", to "you," to "one," to "a politician," to "politicians," and back to "you." In each case, though, the writer is really talking about the same type of person, and should therefore be consistent in this point of view. One solution might be to focus on "politicians" throughout. Another might be to involve the reader by making him or her the hypothetical subject:

> If, as a politician, you are continually exposed to petty, and not so petty, temptations, you may find it difficult to resist every offer of money, merchandise, or special favors. You might turn down the $500 "donation for miscellaneous expenses" and send back the new television sent as "an expression of gratitude for public service," but see nothing wrong with accepting a powerful constituent's offer of a relaxing weekend at his cabin in the mountains. If you accept any such potentially compromising offer, you are open, understandably, to charges of corruption. But if you were required to report all transactions of potential monetary value, you would be less likely to do anything you wouldn't want voters to know about—and more likely to remain the honest person you started out as.

EXERCISE:

Unify the point of view in the following paragraph, leaving the first sentence as it is.

Many of us have serious misconceptions about therapy and the way that therapists work. People may believe that therapy is only for those with such severe emotional problems that they cannot cope with their daily lives. Thus you may not seek professional help because you do not want to think of yourself as "sick" or unable to manage your life. We should realize that many people begin therapy for more positive reasons, because they feel it can help them get more enjoyment and fulfillment out of life. At the other end of the spectrum, some people have gotten the idea from Hollywood that a therapist is a demigod who can magically solve all their problems. One must understand that therapists are human beings with their own limitations and capacity to make mistakes, and that if a person is going to get anything out of therapy, he must be prepared to take an active part in the proceedings.

Suggested Revision:

Many of us have serious misconceptions about therapy and the way that therapists work. We may believe that therapy is only for those with such severe emotional problems that they cannot cope with their daily lives. Thus we may not seek professional help because we do not want to think of ourselves as "sick" or unable to manage our lives. We should realize that many people begin therapy for more positive reasons, because they feel it can help them get more enjoyment and fulfillment out of life. At the other end of the spectrum, some of us have gotten the idea from Hollywood that a therapist is a demigod who can magically solve all our problems. We must understand that therapists are human beings with their own limitations and capacity to make mistakes, and that if we are going to get anything out of therapy, we must be prepared to take an active part in the proceedings.

Note: Although it isn't necessary to make all the pronouns in this paragraph the same, the shifts in the original version are more capricious than is advisable, and thus a reader starts to notice the number of shifts rather than the point of the paragraph.)

PREDICATION

The core of a sentence—its subject, verb, and completer (complement or direct object)—must fit together logically. When these three core parts aren't logically linked, we say that the predication is faulty.

```
                   s                    v                                    c
Faulty:   The term "janitor" is considered to be a very difficult job.
          (A term is a job?)
                         s    v                        c
Correct:  Janitorial work is considered very difficult.
                                     s     v                       c
Or:       Many people think a janitor has a very difficult job.

                       s                        v           c
Faulty:   My first impression of the senator was proud and antag-
          onistic.
          (An impression is proud?)
                         s       v                   c
Correct:  My first impression was that the senator was proud and
          antagonistic.
                   s          v      c
Better:   The senator impressed me as being proud and antagonistic.
```

PREDICATION ERRORS WITH *TO BE.*

Most predication errors involve some form of the verb *to be.* This verb says that one thing *is* another. If the two things can be logically equated, all is well, as in the following examples:

```
        s    v          c
My uncle is a state senator.
        s    v        c
My uncle is often cross.
                  s      v      c
My uncle's office is on 52nd Street.
```

But if the two parts (subject and completer) can't be logically connected by the verb *to be,* you should look at the core of the sentence and pinpoint the problem. Often you wind up asking simple questions, such as "Is a term a janitor?" "Is an impression proud, or is the senator proud?" and so on.

PREDICATION ERRORS WITH OTHER VERBS.

Predication errors can occur with other verbs besides *to be.*

```
                 s                                        v
Faulty:   The tennis court, which was flooded, meant that the
                 c
          referees had to cancel the match.
          (How could tennis courts "mean" anything?)
```

$$\overset{s}{\qquad}\qquad\overset{v}{\qquad}\qquad\overset{s}{\qquad}\overset{v}{\qquad}$$

Correct: Because the <u>tennis court</u> <u>was flooded</u>, the <u>referees</u> <u>had to</u>

$$\overset{c}{\qquad}$$

<u>cancel</u> the <u>match</u>.

PREDICATION ERRORS WITH CONJUNCTIONS.

Predication errors often occur because writers follow some form of *to be* with a clause beginning with *because, before, when,* etc.

$$\overset{s}{\qquad}\qquad\overset{v}{\qquad}\overset{c}{\qquad}$$

Faulty: The <u>reason</u> I went <u>is</u> <u>because</u> I was tired of studying.
(The reason is because?)

$$\overset{s}{\qquad}\qquad\overset{v}{\qquad}\qquad\overset{c}{\qquad}$$

Correct: The <u>reason</u> I went <u>is</u> <u>that I was tired of studying</u>.

$$\overset{s}{\quad}\overset{v}{\quad}\qquad\overset{s}{\quad}\overset{v}{\quad}\overset{c}{\quad}$$

Better: <u>I</u> <u>went</u> because <u>I</u> <u>was</u> <u>tired of studying</u>.

$$\overset{s}{\qquad}\qquad\overset{v}{\qquad}\overset{c}{\qquad}$$

Faulty: <u>Happiness</u> <u>is</u> <u>when you pass</u> your final exams.

$$\overset{s}{\qquad}\qquad\overset{v}{\quad}\overset{c}{\quad}$$

Correct: When you pass your finals, <u>you</u> <u>are</u> <u>happy</u>.

Faulty: A simile is where you compare two unlike things using the words "like" or "as."

Correct: A simile is a figure of speech that compares two unlike things using the words "like" and "as."

PREDICATION ERRORS WITH PREPOSITIONAL PHRASES.

Predication errors also occur when a writer uses a prepositional phrase as the sentence subject or complement.

$$\overset{s}{\qquad}\qquad\qquad\overset{v}{\qquad}\overset{c}{\qquad}$$

Faulty: Another <u>way</u> to study efficiently <u>is</u> <u>during your lunch</u>
<u>break</u>.
(A way is during a break?)

$$\overset{s}{\qquad}\qquad\overset{v}{\qquad}\overset{c}{\qquad}$$

Correct: <u>Studying</u> during lunch <u>is</u> an efficient <u>way</u> to use time.

$$\overset{s}{\quad}\qquad\overset{v}{\qquad}\overset{c}{\qquad}$$

Or: <u>You</u> may efficiently <u>use</u> your lunch <u>break</u> to study.

$$\overset{s}{\qquad}\qquad\qquad\overset{v}{\qquad}\overset{c}{\qquad}$$

Faulty: <u>By watching</u> one's diet carefully <u>means</u> <u>losing</u> weight.
(<u>By watching</u> <u>means</u>?)

$$\overset{\text{S}}{} \quad \overset{\text{V}}{} \qquad \overset{\text{C}}{} \qquad \overset{\text{S}}{} \quad \overset{\text{V}}{} \quad \overset{\text{C}}{}$$

Correct: If <u>one</u> <u>watches</u> one's <u>diet</u> carefully, <u>one</u> <u>can lose</u> <u>weight</u>.

$$\qquad\qquad\qquad\qquad\qquad\qquad\overset{\text{S}}{} \quad \overset{\text{V}}{} \quad \overset{\text{C}}{}$$

Or: By watching one's diet carefully, <u>one</u> <u>can lose</u> <u>weight</u>.

(For a fuller treatment of predication, see Chapter 7, pp. 183–186.)

EXERCISE

Check the core of the following sentences to see if the predication is faulty. If it is, try to revise the sentence. Often, you can correct a predication error by making sure the sentence subject is a concrete word, one that stands for a human being or a concrete thing, not an abstraction.

1. Communal living is no place to raise a child.
2. Just because we disagree with Iran's foreign policy does not justify our harassment of Iranian students.
3. The viciousness of English teachers and other shady characters is well-known.
4. Another example of wasted tax money is in little-used parks and recreation centers.
5. The reason people dislike reading is because it requires concentration.
6. Misery is when you have three final exams scheduled for the same day.

Possible Answers:

1. A commune is no place to raise a child.
2. Just because we disagree with Iran's foreign policy, we have no reason to harass Iranian students. *Or:*
   Our disagreement with Iran's foreign policy does not justify our harassment of Iranian students.
3. *Correct.*
4. Little-used parks and recreation centers are also a waste of tax money.
5. The reason people dislike reading is that it requires concentration.
   [*or*] People dislike reading because it requires concentration.
6. When you have three final exams scheduled for the same day, you feel miserable.

PUNCTUATION

The Apostrophe

USE OF THE APOSTROPHE.

Apostrophes are used to show possession or ownership: *Mary's car, Bob's house, Edison's invention.* These are shortened ways of saying "the car of Mary," "the house of Bob," "the invention of Edison."

1. The need for an apostrophe is fairly easy to see in the case of particular people possessing definite things, as in the above examples, but a little harder to recognize in a phrase like "the car's defects." However, you're still writing in shorthand form "the defects of the car." Other examples:

the world's problems	the problems of the world
today's special	the special of (for) today
the fabric's design	the design of the fabric
women's liberation	the liberation of women

2. Use an apostrophe for expressions of *time* and *value:*

a week's vacation (the vacation of a week)
two weeks' severance pay (the severance pay of two weeks)
a moment's notice (the notice of a moment)
a month's work (the work of a month)
a dollar's worth (the worth of a dollar)

3. Occasionally, you need an apostrophe when the thing possessed is understood but not stated. For instance:

Her hair is much shorter than her brother's.

You'll see the need for the apostrophe if you realize that this is a shorthand way of writing:

Her hair is much shorter than her brother's hair is.

Similarly:

His eyes were as innocent as a child's [eyes are].

PLACEMENT

Once you've decided you need an apostrophe to show possession, how do you know where to put it? Turn the phrase around and insert *of,* as in the examples above. The noun following *of* takes an apostrophe.

1. If the noun following *of* ends in *-s,* simply add the apostrophe to it:

the basketball team of <u>girls</u>	the girls' basketball team
the visit of Prince <u>Charles</u>	Prince <u>Charles</u>' visit

2. If the noun following *of* does not end in *-s,* form the possessive by adding *'s.*

the basketball team <u>of the women</u>	the <u>women</u>'s basketball team
the visit <u>of Queen Elizabeth</u>	Queen <u>Elizabeth</u>'s visit

Note that in some cases, the position of the apostrophe is the only way to show whether a word is singular or plural:

Singular	*Plural*
my daughter's toys	my daughters' toys
his aunt's house	his aunts' house
my friend's parties	my friends' parties

3. Be sure to add the apostrophe to the base word; do not insert it in the middle:

Wrong	*Right*
Mr. Jone's lawn	Mr. Jones' lawn
Dicken's first story	Dickens' first story

4. What is the proper way to show possession involving two or more people? Should you write *George and Bill's* golf clubs or *George's and Bill's* golf clubs? If George and Bill own the golf clubs together, the first choice is correct; if each has his own set of clubs, the second choice is the right one. That is, you show *joint ownership* by making just the last word in a series possessive:

Jack and Jill's accident (it happened to both of them)

You show *individual ownership* by making both words possessive:

Jack's and Jill's clothes (both had their own)

WHEN NOT TO USE AN APOSTROPHE

5. Never use an apostrophe just to show a plural. (Students have a tendency to do this with names of families especially.)

Wrong	*Right*
The Henderson's are on vacation.	The Hendersons are on vacation.
Several hundred bird's suddenly descended on the island.	Several hundred birds suddenly descended on the island.

6. The possessive pronouns *his, hers, its, ours, yours, theirs,* and *whose* are never written with apostrophes.

Wrong	*Right*
We picked up your address book by mistake—do you have our's?	We picked up your address book by mistake—do you have ours?
The dog hurt its' paw. The dog hurt it's paw.	The dog hurt its paw.

OTHER USES OF THE APOSTROPHE

1. Use an apostrophe to indicate the missing letter(s) in a contraction:

don't (do not)
shouldn't (should not)
it's (it is *or* it has)
they're (they are)
who's (who is *or* who has)

2. Form the plural of letters and numbers by adding *'s.*

Instead of trying for A's, she is content with B's.
Although he was born in Omaha, he insisted on writing his 1's and 7's the European way.
There are two m's in accommodate.

3. Use an apostrophe before abbreviated dates:

I was born in '58.
For years she drove a beat-up '71 Volkswagen.

EXERCISES

A. Rewrite using apostrophes:

Example: the scent of the rose
　　　　　　the rose's scent

1. the wife of my brother
2. apparel for boys
3. the apartment of Kay and Nancy
4. the complexities of the issue
5. the flavor of the mushrooms

B. Rewrite *without* apostrophes, using prepositional phrases (*of,
belonging to,* or *for*)

Example: the rose's scent
　　　　　　the scent of the rose

1. Bill's telephone
2. a men's room
3. the witches' brew
4. an hour's delay
5. the buildings' exteriors

C. Choose the correct form:

1. Several thousand (people's, peoples, peoples') lives were lost in unnecessary traffic deaths last year.
2. (Womens, Women's, Womens') rights became a major issue early in
   the twentieth century.
3. Bob and Shirley occasionally borrow each (others, other's, others')
   cars.
4. The movie premiere was thronged by hundreds of (celebrity's,
   celebrities, celebrities').
5. When we heard you had cancelled your travel plans, we decided to
   cancel (ours, our's, ours') too.
6. The speaker contended that the proposed bill would limit (citizens,
   citizen's, citizens') constitutional rights.
7. Many Americans who had never before paid much attention to international politics were outraged when the (Soviets, Soviet's,
   Soviets') invaded Afghanistan in 1979.

D. Add apostrophes where necessary:

1. Two of Uncle Henrys cars, a 45 Buick and a 39 Pontiac, are quite
   valuable.
2. A years study went into the planning for the new municipal park.
3. In todays crowded schools, teachers assistants play an important

role in helping with clerical tasks and tutoring students who need help.

4. Many Americans, determined to keep up with the Joneses standard of living, run seriously into debt because they feel they must have cars, clothes, furniture, and even swimming pools as fine as their neighbors.

5. Many people fear that the worlds energy reserves will not be enough to keep up with our demands by 1990.

Answers:

A. 1. my brother's wife
   2. boys' apparel
   3. Kay and Nancy's apartment
   4. the issue's complexities
   5. the mushrooms' flavor
B. 1. the telephone of Bill
   2. a room for men
   3. the brew of the witches
   4. a delay of an hour
   5. the exteriors of the buildings
C. 1. people's
   2. Women's
   3. other's
   4. celebrities
   5. ours
   6. citizens'
   7. Soviets
D. 1. Henry's, '45, '39
   2. year's
   3. today's, teachers'
   4. Joneses', neighbors'
   5. world's

The Colon

Basically, we use a colon [:] to say to the reader, "What I am talking about is *this.*" The "*this*" is what follows the colon. Specifically, the colon should be used in the following ways:

1. Use a colon after an independent clause to introduce a list:

I have several things I need to do tomorrow: check out some books for my term paper, buy a birthday present for my brother, write up a chemistry lab report, and get the apartment in some semblance of order.

2. Use a colon to separate independent clauses when the second clause explains or expands on the first:

Only later did I understand: she was trying to tell me that she loved me.
Writing a good essay is a little like having a baby: getting the words out can be agony, but afterwards you feel awed at having created something that now exists outside yourself.
Perhaps there is no such thing as true mental health: the healthy personality is simply very well-adjusted to its neuroses.

3. Use a colon to introduce a quotation if it explains the beginning of your sentence or if the quotation is more than one sentence long:

Oscar Wilde loved to take a cliché and turn it into a *bon mot:* "In married life three is company and two none."

The last act of *Macbeth* contains one of Shakespeare's most famous speeches:
    Tomorrow, and tomorrow, and tomorrow,
    Creeps in this petty pace from day to day,
    To the last syllable of recorded time;
    And all our yesterdays have lighted fools
    The way to dusty death. Out, out, brief candle!
    Life's but a walking shadow, a poor player,
    That struts and frets his hour upon the stage,
    And then is heard no more; it is a tale
    Told by an idiot, full of sound and fury,
    Signifying nothing.

4. Use a colon after the greeting in a business letter:

Dear Ms. Fenton: Dear Mr. Adams: Dear Alan:

5. Use a colon between the chapter and verse in Biblical references:

Proverbs 4:7

6. Use a colon between hours and minutes in giving a specific time:

10:15 a.m.   9:43 p.m.

There are a few other things you should know about colons.

1. Do not use a colon in the middle of a clause:

Wrong	*Right*
Next semester I plan to enroll in: French 1, English 2, Biology 10, and History 4A.	Next semester I plan to enroll in French 1, English 2, Biology 10, and History 4A.

or

Next semester I plan to enroll in the following courses: French 1, English 2, Biology 10, and History 4A.

2. Colons go *outside* quotation marks:

One of Faulkner's most effective short stories is "That Evening Sun": its power comes partly from the fact that its terrible events are viewed through the eyes of children who only partially comprehend what is happening. (This rule is logical enough when you realize that the purpose of the colon is to separate and relate clauses in *your* sentence; it has nothing to do with what you are quoting.)

3. When a complete sentence follows a colon, you may capitalize the first word or have it begin with a small letter. Just be consistent.

4. To avoid confusion, use only one colon in a sentence.

5. When you're typing, it is customary to space *twice* after a colon (as opposed to once after a semicolon).

The Comma

Read the following sentence aloud, noticing where the pauses naturally fall:

Crossing Alma Avenue I managed to drop my briefcase which disgorged its contents all over the street.

The chances are you paused after "Avenue" and after "briefcase." That's where the commas go:

Crossing Alma Avenue, I managed to drop my briefcase, which disgorged its contents all over the street.

But knowing where to use commas shouldn't be entirely a matter of ear. Here are some rules to help you out:

1. When a sentence begins with something other than the main clause, the introductory element is usually set off with a comma (this helps the reader see where the main idea begins):

> If you get home first, turn on the oven.
> Having been through the throes of writing essays ourselves, we know how frustrating it can be.
> In fact, I would never have come to enjoy opera if someone hadn't dragged me to a production of *The Marriage of Figaro.*
> To become a librarian, you must earn a master's degree in library science.
> Well, I disagree.

Note: If the introductory element is very short and you don't want a pause, you should omit the comma:

> Of course I understand.

2. Use a comma to separate items in a series of three or more:

> His favorite foods are peanut butter, hamburger, watermelon, and lemon meringue pie.
> Bacon wrote that some books are to be tasted, others are to be swallowed, and a few are to be chewed and digested; by that he meant that some books should be read only in parts, others should be read casually, and a few should be read completely and attentively.

Note: Authorities differ about whether to omit the comma before the conjunction in such a series, as in "roses, carnations and sweet peas." Some instructors will allow you to omit the comma (providing you do so consistently); others, including the authors of this text, prefer that you include it. Without the comma, "carnations and sweet peas" is apt to appear as a unit instead of two separate entities. And leaving out a comma before the last element in a series can occasionally create ambiguity, as in this sentence:

> The other guests—an elderly transvestite, a harpist from the London symphony, an opera singer with a passion for strawberry daiquiris and various young men—all appeared quite at home.

How many other people were in the room—three or several more? Whether the "various young men" referred to were fellow guests or merely absent recipients of the opera singer's passion isn't clear the way the sentence is punctuated.

3. Put a comma before the coordinating conjunction in a compound sentence. (A compound sentence contains two independent clauses connected by a coordinating conjunction—*for, and, nor, but, or, yet, so.*)

> I dropped by his house about eight o'clock last night, but he wasn't at home.
> An old Wedgewood stove stood in the corner, and the walls were covered with prints and post cards from the turn of the century.
> Many inexperienced writers never plan what they're going to say, nor do they allow enough time to polish and revise their rough drafts.

Note: If the first clause is short, you may omit the comma (though it is not wrong to include it):

> Carol plays tennis and her husband plays golf.

You usually do not use a comma before a coordinating conjunction if it is connecting anything besides independent clauses.

Wrong	*Right*
I rushed home, and frantically looked through the mail.	I rushed home and frantically looked through the mail.

4. Use commas to separate parenthetical elements—that is, any part of the sentence that *could* be put in parentheses. For instance:

> Mr. Franklin, my eleventh-grade math teacher, used to give tests that were the terror of the school.

The words "my eleventh-grade math teacher" could go in parentheses:

> Mr. Franklin (my eleventh-grade math teacher) used to give tests that were the terror of the school.

Some other examples:

> Nijinski, who is generally considered the greatest male dancer of all time, could give the illusion of pausing in mid-air as he leapt across the stage.

> The clerk turned his attention to another customer, apparently annoyed by my inability to decide what to buy.

> Jesse Owens won four gold medals in the 1936 Olympics, a feat still unmatched in Olympic track and field.

> *But:* I still didn't understand the problem after the professor fin-
> ished his explanation.
>
> (The subordinate clause "after the professor finished his ex-
> planation" could not go in parentheses.)

5. Remember to put the comma *after* the parenthetical element even when it comes in the middle of a sentence:

Wrong	Right
The result of advertising, say psychologists is the continual cycle of arousal and disappoint-ment.	The result of advertising, say psychologists, is the continual cycle of arousal and disappoint-ment.

Note: Restrictive elements—parts of a sentence that are necessary to identify the words they modify—are not set off with commas. Another way of looking at this rule is to say that restrictive elements could not be put in parentheses.

> Shakespeare's tragedy *Hamlet*
> (he wrote more than one: *Hamlet* identifies which tragedy we're dealing with.)
>
> my friend Kevin
> (I have more than one friend; Kevin identifies which one)
>
> People who live in glass houses shouldn't throw stones.
> (We're not talking about people in general, only those who live in glass houses.)

(See also the discussion of adjective clauses and appositives in Chapter 9, pages 240–242 and 247.)

6. In general, use commas to separate transitional expressions from the rest of the sentence:

> However, Roosevelt had a different plan in mind.
> Roosevelt, however, had a different plan in mind.
> Roosevelt had a different plan in mind, however.

Note that *however,* a word that can float around in the sentence, is different from a conjunction like *but,* which can come only at the beginning of the clause and should not be followed by a comma:

Wrong	Right
But, Roosevelt had a different plan in mind.	But Roosevelt had a different plan in mind.

Other common transitional expressions usually set off by commas are *for instance, for example, of course, furthermore, as a result, that is, consequently, nevertheless, moreover, in addition,* and *on the other hand.*

Note: As in many other situations, you must let your ear be your guide in deciding whether to set off transitional expressions with commas. For instance, depending on whether or not you want a pause, you may punctuate the following sentence in two different ways:

> In fact, the economic picture continues to look dim.
> In fact the economic picture continues to look dim.

(Transitional expressions are covered more thoroughly in Chapter 8, pp. 213–216.)

7. Use a comma to separate dialogue or brief quotation from the rest of the sentence:

> John said, "_____."
> "_____," he added, "_____."
> "_____," he concluded.

8. Use a comma to set off words used in direct address:

> May I help you, ma'am?
> Clark, I have had enough of your foolishness.
> Frankly, my dear, I don't give a damn.

9. Use a comma to separate coordinate adjectives. (Adjectives are coordinate if you could insert *and* between them.)

> A cold, raw wind swept along the pier.
> (*Cold* and *raw* are coordinate, since you can say "a cold and raw wind.")
>
> He is a charming, generous man.
> (You can say "a charming and generous man.")
>
> My grandfather suffered three debilitating heart attacks.
> (No comma, since you cannot say "three and debilitating heart attacks.")

10. There are a few more minor rules governing the use of the comma.

A. Put a comma before a contrasting phrase:

I expected sympathy, not criticism.
I had some excellent teachers in high school, but also some dogs.

B. When writing the name of a city and state, set the state off with commas.

Kansas City, Kansas, is across the river from Kansas City, Missouri.

Do not put a comma between a state and a zip code; just space twice.

Berkeley, California 94705

C. When writing a date, set off the year with commas.

On July 20, 1969, Neil Armstrong set foot on the moon.

D. Use a comma to separate people's names from their degree or title:

Angela J. Kilton, M.D.
John T. Davis, Ph.D.
Barbara C. Snider, Executive Vice President

E. Use a comma between a declarative clause and an interrogative that follows:

You're not angry, are you?
He did get my letter, didn't he?

A FINAL NOTE

It is better to use too few commas than too many. To see how distracting and irritating unnecessary commas can be, read the following sentences:

Commas, that aren't necessary, only get in the way, of your meaning. Commas, should help your readers, to follow the natural rhythm, of your sentences. You defeat your own purpose, if you slow them down, in the wrong places.

There will be times when you'll be unsure of whether to use a comma or not. When you find yourself in this predicament, it's probably best to follow the advice one of our eighth-grade English teachers passed down to her students: "When in doubt, leave it out."

EXERCISE

Add commas where necessary, but avoid using unnecessary ones:

1. I always finish a semester feeling harrassed exhausted and nearly traumatized and this one is no exception.
2. Wanting to avoid the temptations of television and the telephone Muriel set off for the library.
3. If you know that the Greek prefix *amphi* means "both sides" you may have an easier time remembering the meaning of terms like *amphibian* and *amphitheatre*.
4. In a series of classic experiments Piaget studied the stage-by-stage development of a child's mind.
5. "To know is nothing at all; to imagine is everything" wrote Anatole France who was awarded a Nobel prize three years before his death in 1924.
6. I told the woman who answered the phone exactly what I thought of her her employers and the general ineffectiveness of the human race.
7. The delightful spicy scent of simmering spaghetti sauce beckoned us to the kitchen.
8. Four days before she committed suicide Virginia Woolf wrote in her diary "And now with some pleasure I find that it's seven; and must cook dinner. Haddock and sausage meat. I think it is true that one gains a certain hold on sausage and haddock by writing them down."
9. In 1855 with the help of Sam Houston the Coushatta Indians in Texas tried to make a claim on the land that had been promised them.
10. "Hi there Big Boy" she said.
11. Fitzgerald's unusual first novel *This Side of Paradise* caused a sensation but most readers today consider *The Great Gatsby* which sold far fewer copies at the time it was first released his best work.
12. I stood outside the door reading the name "Marian J. Fisher D.D.S." for several minutes before getting up enough courage to turn the handle.
13. The forecast called for "scattered showers" which is a euphemistic way of saying you'll probably get soaked.
14. "Scattered showers" is a euphemism which weather forecasters use to let you know you'll probably get soaked.
15. Sinclair Lewis' novel *Main Street* for example gives us a fascinating detailed glimpse of small-town America in about 1920.
16. I picked up the test read the first five questions and almost burst into tears.

17. The problem of course continued to plague me the rest of the day even occupying my thoughts as I played tennis and ate dinner with my family.
18. I ordered coffee not a Coke.
19. He was born on July 19 1949 in Everett Washington.
20. You were there weren't you?

Answers:

1. I always finish a semester feeling harassed, exhausted, and nearly traumatized, and this one is no exception. (The comma after "exhausted" is preferred but not required.)
2. Wanting to avoid the temptations of television and the telephone, Muriel set off for the library.
3. If you know that the Greek prefix *amphi* means "both sides," you may have an easier time remembering the meaning of terms like *amphibian* and *amphitheatre.* (Note that the comma comes *before* the quotation marks.)
4. In a series of classic experiments, Piaget studied the stage-by-stage development of a child's mind. (Since the introductory phrase is short, it would also be permissible to write this sentence with no comma. However, the comma makes it a little easier to read.)
5. "To know is nothing at all; to imagine is everything," wrote Anatole France, who was awarded a Nobel prize three years before his death in 1924. (The "who" clause could go in parentheses.)
6. I told the woman who answered the phone exactly what I thought of her, her employers, and the general ineffectiveness of the human race. (The "who" clause in this sentence could *not* go in parentheses. As in Sentence 1, the comma before "and" is optional but preferred.)
7. The delightful, spicy scent of simmering spaghetti sauce beckoned us to the kitchen. (You could say "delightful and spicy" but you coult not say "simmering and spaghetti.")
8. Four days before she committed suicide Virginia Woolf wrote in her diary, "And now with some pleasure I find that it's seven; and must cook dinner. Haddock and sausage meat. I think it is true that one gains a certain hold on sausage and haddock by writing them down." (It would be perfectly correct to put a comma after "suicide," but since another comma is coming up just a few words later, it might seem intrusive. Woolf's use of the semicolon after "seven" is unconventional, but one does not alter the punctuation of a quotation.)

9. In 1855, with the help of Sam Houston, the Coushatta Indians in Texas tried to make a claim on the land that had been promised them.

10. "Hi there, Big Boy," she said.

11. Fitzgerald's unusual first novel, *This Side of Paradise*, caused a sensation, but most readers today consider *The Great Gatsby*, which sold far fewer copies at the time it was first released, his best work.

12. I stood outside the door, reading the name "Marian J. Fisher, D.D.S." for several minutes before getting up enough courage to turn the handle.

13. The forecast called for "scattered showers," which is a euphemistic way of saying you'll probably get soaked. (The *which*-clause could go in parentheses.)

14. "Scattered showers" is a euphemism which weather forecasters use to let you know you'll probably get soaked. (This *which*-clause could *not* go in parentheses; it defines the sort of euphemism we mean.)

15. Sinclair Lewis' novel *Main Street*, for example, gives us a fascinating, detailed glimpse of small-town America in about 1920. (There should be no comma before *Main Street*, since these words identify which novel by Lewis we're talking about.)

16. I picked up the test, read the first five questions, and almost burst into tears.

17. The problem, of course, continued to plague me the rest of the day, even occupying my thoughts as I played tennis and ate dinner with my family.

18. I ordered coffee, not a Coke.

19. He was born on July 19, 1949, in Everett, Washington.

20. You were there, weren't you?

Dash

Used too often and unthinkingly, the dash can make your writing appear abrupt, disconnected, and (you'll excuse the pun) dashed off. But, used with restraint, it can help make your writing more lively and informal. Three kinds of punctuation—commas, parentheses, and dashes—can be used to separate parenthetical or explanatory information from the rest of the sentence:

> My mother, who is inclined to be hot-tempered, once hurled a beer stein at a stray dog who trampled her prized petunia bed.

> My mother (who is inclined to be hot-tempered) once hurled a beer stein at a stray dog who trampled her prized petunia bed.

> My mother—who is inclined to be hot-tempered—once hurled a beer
> stein at a stray dog who trampled her prized petunia bed.

Each kind of punctuation changes the rhythm and emphasis in the sentence. The parentheses play down the words they enclose, while the dashes emphasize them, indicating a break in thought and getting the reader's attention. The commas fall somewhere in between; they're useful when you simply want to include parenthetical material, neither giving it emphasis nor playing it down.

Notice how the dashes break up the following sentences, highlighting the information they set off:

> I remember very little from that summer—the afternoon my brother
> fell out of the cedar tree across the street and broke his arm, the day
> I got my braces taken off, and the night my parents told me they
> had decided to get a divorce.

> Complacency—that is the trait that has tamed many an idealist's passion for truth and change.

> Dwayne has looks, money, brains—and an ego the size of Cleveland.

> Virginia Wade, England's top-ranked tennis player, finally won Wimbledon in 1977—after sixteen years of trying.

The dash is especially useful when you want to interrupt a main clause with a list of some kind:

> Looking at the basic elements of fiction—character, conflict, setting,
> symbol, point of view, and theme—can help us to understand how a
> short story works.

Note that commas would not work in this situation since the list itself contains commas, and parentheses might encourage the reader to skim through the list without paying attention to the elements mentioned.

When typing, make a dash by typing two hyphens with no space on either side.

```
Electron microscopy--which brings into view
infinitesimal worlds invisible to the unaided
eye and even to ordinary microscopes--is a
scientifically and aesthetically fascinating
medium.
```

Ellipses

1. Use ellipses, three spaced periods (. . .) to indicate that you have left out one or more words from something you're quoting. Notice that if you are typing, you should space before and after each period:

Original
"Palm Beach sprawled plump and opulent between the spark- ling sapphire Lake Worth, flawed here and there by house- boats at anchor, and the great turquoise bar of the Atlantic Ocean."

—F. Scott Fitzgerald,
"The Rich Boy"

As You Might Quote It
"Palm Beach sprawled plump and opulent between the spark- ling sapphire Lake Worth . . . and the great turquoise bar of the Atlantic Ocean"

2. In the example, we used ellipses to show that material has been dropped from the *middle* of the quotation. Do not use ellipses before or after what is obviously only *part of a sentence* (". . . clouded haze . . ."). Simply put the words in quotation marks without ellipses:

The "clouded haze" of the environment mirrors the confusion of the protagonist.

Avoid using ellipses *before* a quotation; if you want to begin quoting a sentence midstream, just introduce the quotation with a few words of your own:

Near the end of *A Lost Lady,* Willa Cather explains the secret of Mrs. Forrester's charm: her "power of suggesting things much lovelier than herself, as the perfume of a single flower may call up the whole sweetness of spring."

3. If you want to *drop the end of a sentence* you're quoting and you're afraid that the reader might make the mistake of thinking you've quoted the entire sentence, you need four periods: three ellipsis points and one period. For instance:

Original
"He wondered at his riot of emotions of an hour before. From what had it proceeded? From his aunt's supper, from

As You Might Quote It
"He wondered at his riot of emotions of an hour before. From what had it proceeded? From his aunt's supper, from

his own foolish speech, from the wine and dancing, the merry-making when saying good-night in the hall, the pleasure of the walk along the river in the snow."
—James Joyce, "The Dead"

his own foolish speech, from the wine and dancing. . . ."

Notice in the above example that you do *not* pick up the comma in the original after "wine and dancing" if that is where you want to end your quotation.

If the sentence you're quoting ends with a question mark or an exclamation point rather than a period, use three ellipsis points and a question mark or exclamation point:

"How many hundreds—thousands—of hours have I spent watching sports of all sorts, either at parks or stadiums or over television?
—Joseph Epstein, "Obsessed with Sport"

"How many hundreds—thousands—of hours have I spent watching sports of all sorts . . .?"

4. If you're quoting *poetry* and want to omit one or more lines, include a row of spaced periods. For instance:

Original
This other Eden, demi-paradise,
This fortress built by Nature
  for herself
Against infection and the hand
  of war,
This happy breed of men, this
  little world,
This precious stone set in the
  silver sea,
Which serves it in the office of
  a wall
Or as a moat defensive to a
  house,
Against the envy of less happier
  lands,
This blessed plot, this earth, this
  realm, this England.

As You Might Quote It
This other Eden, demi-paradise,
This fortress built by Nature
  for herself
Against infection and the hand
  of war,
. . . .
This precious stone set in the
  silver sea,
. . . .
This blessed plot, this earth, this
  realm, this England.

—William Shakespeare, *King Richard II*

5. If you're writing *dialogue* and want to show the reader that a speaker's voice is trailing off, use three (not four) spaced periods:

"This isn't goodbye, but . . ."

The Exclamation Point

Exclamation points should be used sparingly, and mostly in dialogue. If you pepper your prose with too many of them, you can sound either hysterical or cutesy. Only if a sentence definitely seems more effective *with* an exclamation point should you put it in.

So, with this caution, here are the times when you may want to wax exclamatory:

1. Use an exclamation point to express strong feeling or emphasis:

I couldn't believe it!
What a mess!
Our team had won!

2. Exclamation points are frequently used in commands, especially if you want to show that the speaker is angry, frightened, or trying to impress someone with the urgency of a situation.

Leave me alone!

But you should not use an exclamation point for a command uttered courteously, calmly, or in a low voice:

"Calm down and start at the beginning," I told him.

Note that if your dialogue ends with an exclamation point, you drop the comma that would otherwise separate the dialogue from your words:

Wrong	*Right*
"Please help me!", I said.	"Please help me!" I said.

Exclamation points can go either inside or outside quotation marks, depending on whether they belong with the quoted material or the sentence as a whole:

He woke up to hear the conductor calling, "Grand Central Station!"
I got an "A"!

The Hyphen

The use of the hyphen illustrates the fact that the English language is still developing. Dozens of words in English made their first appearances as two words, then came to be hyphenated, and are now spelled as one word. For instance:

air plane	air-plane	airplane
brief case	brief-case	briefcase

Other words once hyphenated and now usually spelled as one word include *skyscraper, cooperate,* and *refill.* And today authorities differ as to whether you should write "preelection" or "pre-election," "antiintellectual" or "anti-intellectual."

Some hyphens, then, are a matter of changing fashion or personal preference. But there are some rules you should observe:

1. Hyphenate compound adjectives—that is, two or more words acting as an adjective:

nineteenth-century poetry
stomach-churning ride
a man-made lake
off-campus housing
a two-week vacation
his so-called secretary
a second-rate production
my eight-year-old niece
her third-grade teacher
a let's-put-together-everything-in-the-refrigerator-and-see-what-comes-out casserole

There is only one exception: if a word ends in *-ly*, it is usually not hyphenated:

widely read novelist
sharply angled backhand
highly regarded teacher
clearly stated proposal

2. Hyphenate words beginning with the prefixes *ex-, self-, all-, well-,* and *ill-.*

ex-husband, ex-boss
self-image, self-disciplined
all-knowing, all-inclusive
well-established, well-known
ill-conceived, ill-informed

3. Hyphenate words with prefixes like *anti-*, *pro-*, *pre-*, and *post-* when the next part of the word begins with a capital letter or a number:

anti-American
pro-Carter
pre-World War I
post-1945

4. Hyphenate words with prefixes like *anti-*, *over-*, *post-*, *pre-*, *pro-*, *re-*, *semi-*, and *sub-* when the next letter is the same as the one at the end of the prefix:

over-reaction
pre-empt
re-election
sub-basement
post-test

5. Hyphenate two-digit numbers when you write them out:

twenty-one, thirty-seven, eighty-two

Parentheses and Brackets

PARENTHESES

1. Parentheses are used primarily to set off incidental or explanatory remarks.

Andrew Johnson was the only president to be impeached. (President Nixon resigned before a Bill of Impeachment was formally introduced in the House.)
Andrew Johnson was impeached (although not convicted).

The parentheses tend to play down the material enclosed, so if you want the material to get more, not less, attention, omit the parentheses.

2. Parentheses may also be used to set off dates, references, figures, or examples.

During his brief period in office (January 1961–November 1963), John F. Kennedy captured Americans' imaginations and sparked their self-confidence.

Some recent Presidents may have been more decisive (Truman), have had a more heroic past (Eisenhower), and have been better politicians (Johnson), but none could match Kennedy's style, wit, and casually regal bearing.

Kennedy's potentially apocalyptic antagonism toward Cuba stemmed from (1) his strict adherence to the Monroe Doctrine, which asserts that the United States will not tolerate outside intervention in the Americas, (2) his resolve to be seen as a courageous and decisive world leader, and (3) his personal dislike of Cuban Premier Fidel Castro.

3. When using parentheses with other punctuation marks, be careful to put the other punctuation in the correct place.

    A. Place a punctuation mark *after* the second parenthesis if the punctuation mark applies to the entire sentence and not just to the portion in parentheses.

According to author Jerzy Kosinski, owners of high-performance cars, which often have exciting names (such as Firebird and Charger), may drive irresponsibly and dangerously in order to live up to their car's daring image.

    B. Place the appropriate punctuation mark *within* the second parenthesis if the mark applies only to the material inside the parenthetical section.

I just know I can't live without you. (And I'm not even going to try.)

BRACKETS

1. Brackets are mainly used to set off material added by someone else besides the writer, such as editorial additions or comments.

According to the newspaper report, "The trial [which lasted from April 25 to May 16, 1980] was followed immediately by riots."

2. Brackets are also used to set off parenthetical matter within parenthetical matter.

The books (including Hemingway's *The Sun Also Rises* and *A Farewell to Arms* [*The Old Man and the Sea* was out of stock]) were sent last week by parcel post.

Note: Brackets are seldom used in business and social writing. You may, however, need to use them in term papers and reports of a scholarly or technical nature.

The Period

The period is used in four principal ways.

1. Use a period to end a declarative (regular) or imperative (command) sentence.

> The cockatiel, a poor man's cockatoo, can learn to speak a few words.
> Put the cockatiel back in its cage.

2. Use a period after requests and indirect questions.

> Will you please pass your exams to the front of the room.
> May I hear from you regarding this matter at your earliest convenience.
> He asked us how we managed to pass the exam.

Note that while at first the above look like questions, they are actually polite requests or indirect questions. Actual interrogative sentences would look like this:

> Will you contact me about this matter?
> How did you manage to pass the exam?

3. Use periods after abbreviations and initials.

> John F. Kennedy   Anne B. Wentworth   Mrs.   U.S.A.   Jan.
> a.m.   M.A.   B.S.   Ph.D.   Dr.   Rev.   H.M.S. *Pinafore*

Note that after very common abbreviations the periods are often omitted:

> UNICEF   USA   GOP   UN

The result is called an *acronym.* If you are in doubt regarding a particular abbreviation, check a current dictionary.

4. Use a period to signal omission of words in a quotation. See *Ellipses.*

The Question Mark

The question mark (?) is used after all interrogative sentences, those which ask direct questions.

> Who are you voting for this November?
> Do you remember the name of the dog in *The Thin Man?*

On occasion, question marks are used for special effect. Since they call attention to themselves when so used, employ them sparingly.

1. You may use a question mark after each part of a sentence containing more than one question.

> Are you afraid of my impulsiveness? my strength? my temper?

2. You may use question marks to indicate that a statement is approximate or questionable.

> Calamity Jane (1852?–1903) was a famous frontier markswoman.
> The teacher's good-natured (?) jokes fell flat.

WITH QUOTATIONS

The rules for the punctuation of quotations involving question marks are relatively simple.

1. Place a question mark immediately after a quoted question.

> "Do you know my name?" the amnesia patient asked the doctor.

2. Place the question mark *inside* the quotation marks only if the quotation itself is a question. Otherwise, place the question mark *outside*.

> She asked herself, "Is this the right time, the right place, and the right man?"
> Is this "the time for all good men to come to the aid of their country"?

Quotation Marks

1. Place quotation marks at the beginning and end of any speech you quote directly. If a quotation is interrupted, be sure to put quotation marks around both halves.

> "I have lost any hope of ever buying a house," he said.
> "You may have no hope," she said, "but I do."

Note: Do not put quotation marks around indirect quotations. Indirect quotations paraphrase what someone has said, and they usually begin with the word "that."

> *Direct:*   He said, "I am exhausted."
> *Indirect:*   He said that he was exhausted.

See *Dialogue* for a fuller treatment of the subject.

2. Place quotation marks around all directly quoted material from printed sources.

> While one might assume that the Vice Presidency is a high honor, not all holders of the office have shared that view. John Nance Garner, for instance, observed that "The Vice Presidency isn't worth a pitcher of warm spit."

A. Shorter quotations are introduced with a comma.

> Nixon said, "There can be no whitewash at the White House."

B. Longer, more formal quotations of at least five lines are introduced by a colon, indented 10 typewriter spaces, and single spaced. No quotation marks are used in this case. Shorter quotations are integrated into the paragraph and surrounded by quotation marks, as in number 2 above.

```
      On April 30, 1973, Richard Nixon issued his famous

   "Statement" regarding his role in the Watergate scan-

   dal. He was widely criticized for avoiding the issue

   of Watergate in much of the speech. His attempt to

   shift the audience's attention to other issues is

   obvious:

                    I know that as Attorney General,
                 Elliot Richardson will be both fair
                 and fearless in pursuing this case
                 wherever it leads. I am confident
                 that with him in charge, justice will
                 be done.
                    There is vital work to be done to-
                 ward our goal of a lasting structure
                 of peace in the world--work that can-
                 not wait. Work that I must do.
```

3. Place quotation marks around the titles of short stories, essays, short poems, songs, chapters of books, and reviews.

> The symbolism in Katherine Mansfield's short story "The Garden Party" is obvious.

> My mother's favorite song is "Finlandia."

> T.S. Eliot's famous poems "The Love Song of J. Alfred Prufrock" and The Wasteland are both widely anthologized.

(Note that The Wasteland is a long poem and so is underlined. "Long" usually means that the poem has been published separately.)

(Also see *Titles.*)

4. Place quotation marks around a word, phrase, or sentence that is set off within a sentence.

Many people misspell the word "euphemism."
Slang expressions such as "space cadet" and "with it" fade quickly.
I've always hated psychological jargon, such as the common "Get your head together."

5. Use a single quotation to set off a quotation within a quotation.

"Jim," I gasped, "Why didn't you tell me that I'd misspelled 'euphemism'?"

THE USE OF QUOTATION MARKS WITH
OTHER TYPES OF PUNCTUATION

1. The period and comma always go inside the quotation marks.

"All real Americans love the sting and clash of battle," Patton said.
I replied, "I don't know about you, but I am obviously not a real American."

2. Question marks and exclamation marks go inside the quotation marks when they are part of the quotation. Otherwise, they go outside.

Have you read Faulkner's "Dry September"?
"Of course!" she screamed. "Do you think I'm uneducated?"

3. Colons and semicolons go outside the quotation marks.

For tomorrow, read Faulkner's "Dry September"; come to class prepared to discuss it.

4. Other punctuation marks are used with single quotation marks in the same way as with the double quotation marks.

"I'm sure to mispronounce 'euphemism,'" she cried.
"How in the world am I supposed to say 'euphemism'?"

5. Capitalize the first word in a direct quotation. Do not capitalize the first word in the second half of an interrupted quotation, unless the second half begins a new sentence.

> "I don't know about you," he said, "but I am convinced that I'm a coward."
> "No you aren't!" she insisted. "You're a very sensible man, not a coward."

The Semicolon

1. Use a semicolon [;] to separate two independent clauses (sentences that can stand alone) that are so clearly connected in meaning they don't need a coordinating conjunction (*and, but, for, or, nor, yet, so*) between them.

> I wanted to see the movie; he swore he would never go.
>
> "What they do in heaven we are ignorant of; what they do not we are told expressly...."
> —Jonathan Swift, *Thoughts on Various Subjects*

Note: Semicolons can be used for rhetorical effect, as in the example following:

> "Children begin by loving their parents; after a time, they judge them; rarely, if ever, do they forgive them."
> Oscar Wilde, *A Woman of No Importance*

2. Use a semicolon to separate two independent clauses even when there is a transitional word or phrase present to help make the logical connection between the two parts.

> I wanted to see the movie; however, he swore he would never go.
> The President ordered in the special combat troops; then he informed Congress of his actions.

A. Be careful to recognize sentences that contain *comma splices* (discussed separately in this Usage Manual); that is, watch out for sentences which splice together two independent clauses with only a comma. The transitional expression alone is *not* sufficient to separate the two clauses.

> *Incorrect:*   I wanted to see the movie, however, he swore he would never go.

Correct: I wanted to see the movie; however, he swore he would never go.

       B. You can differentiate coordinating conjunctions (*and, but, for, or, nor, yet, so*) from transitional expressions (*however, in addition, then, therefore, for example,* and so on) by trying to move them around in the sentence. Transitional expressions can be moved around in a sentence; coordinating conjunctions can't.

Correct: The temptation to give up was strong; however, I resisted it.
               The temptation to give up was strong; I, however, resisted it.
               The temptation to give up was strong; I resisted it, however.

Correct: The temptation to give up was strong, but I resisted it.

Ludicrous: The temptation to give up was strong, I resisted it, but.

(See Chapter 8 for more on transitional expressions and coordinating conjunctions.)

       C. Do not misuse the semicolon. You can't use it unless the parts being connected by it can both stand alone, that is, unless both parts are independent clauses. An incorrectly used semicolon creates a punctuation *fragment* (discussed separately in this Usage Manual).

Incorrect: He flatly refused to do some chores; such as ironing his shirts.
Revision: He flatly refused to do some chores, such as ironing his shirts.

Incorrect: He said that he hated to iron; because it took so much time.
Revision: He said that he hated to iron because it took so much time.

The rule is simple: Unless both halves can stand alone, unless a *period* between them would be correct, don't use a semicolon.

    3. In a complicated series, use a semicolon for clarification. If elements in a sentence have other, internal punctuation, you can use

a semicolon to separate them even though they are not grammatically independent.

> On our vacation last summer, we visited Eden, New Mexico; Paradise, Oklahoma; Inferno, Texas; and End-Of-The-Road, Arkansas.

> He decided to take a chance, to run for office, to face the possibility of defeat; but before he could register as a candidate, he was stricken by polio and paralyzed from the neck down.

EXERCISE:

Correct any errors involving semicolons. You may have to add *or* remove them.

1. Although the public TV channel is often pretentious and snobbish; at least commercials do not continually interrupt the programs.
2. Libraries may someday contain no books at all; instead of shelves filled with different-sized, different-colored volumes, patrons would find only tidy, uniform boxes of microfilm.
3. The following officers were elected: Jane Hogue, president, Mary McGrath, vice-president, Alan Suhonen, secretary, Tom McCauley, treasurer, Amy Andamanda, sergeant-at-arms.
4. Sequels to successful movies sometimes are more profitable than the originals, however, they most often fail at the box office.
5. Thornton Wilder's *Our Town* deals with simple values in an idealized American town; a fact which caused some critics to scorn it as simple-minded.

Answers

1. Although the public TV channel is often pretentious and snobbish, at least commercials do not continually interrupt the programs.
2. Libraries may someday contain no books at all; instead of shelves filled with different-sized, different-colored volumes, patrons would find only tidy, uniform boxes of microfilm.
3. The following officers were elected: Jane Hogue, president; Mary McGrath, vice-president; Alan Suhonen, secretary; Tom McCauley, treasurer; Amy Andamanda, sergeant-at-arms.
4. Sequels to successful movies sometimes are more profitable than the originals; however, they most often fail at the box office.
5. Thornton Wilder's *Our Town* deals with simple values in an idealized American town, a fact which caused some critics to scorn it as simple-minded.

Underlining (italics)

Since few typewriters are equipped with italics, underline words that you wish to appear in italics in print. These include:

1. Titles of newspapers, magazines, books, plays, movies, television shows, musical productions, paintings, and sculptures (see "Titles" in this Usage Manual):

> He subscribes to both The Wall Street Journal and Newsweek.

> In senior literature, our high school class read several novels: Great Expectations, The Great Gatsby, Native Son, and One Flew over the Cuckoo's Nest.

> Kramer vs. Kramer was a breakthrough film in that it looked at divorce and childrearing from a man's point of view.

Note: Titles of short stories, magazine and newspaper articles, songs, and poems go in quotation marks.

2. Words, phrases, or sentences you want to emphasize:

> "And what's the matter with you?" my uncle demanded.

> This was 1959 in Des Moines, Iowa—venereal disease was a subject that was simply not discussed.

> Suddenly everything was clear. Colonel Preston was the only one who really benefited from Lady Augusta's death.

Note: Be careful not to overdo underlining for emphasis, since too much of it can make your writing seem hysterical.

> I could not understand what possible pleasure anyone could take in learning about a subject I considered boring and unpleasant beyond belief.

3. Foreign words and phrases:

> In high school, football was my raison d'être.
> The voters passed legislation aimed at ending de facto segregation.
> "Cuando viene el doctor?" I asked the policeman in my schoolboy Spanish.

4. You may underline a letter, number, word or expression you're discussing, or you may put it in quotation marks. Just be consistent:

Correct	Equally Correct
Many people misspell <u>definite</u>, substituting an <u>a</u> for the second <u>i</u>.	Many people misspell "definite," substituting an "a" for the second "i."
The expressions <u>Dutch courage</u> and <u>Dutch treat</u> originated at a time when England and Holland were rivals in imperialism.	The expressions "Dutch courage" and "Dutch treat" originated at a time when England and Holland were rivals in imperialism.

EXERCISE:

Use underlining where necessary in the following sentences. (In Sentence 3, use it to provide emphasis where you feel it's appropriate.)

1. A famous stage direction in the play Auntie Mame refers to a character as "a carnation wearing a man."
2. I read voraciously that summer, devouring Little Women, Treasure Island, The Swiss Family Robinson, and all seven of C.S. Lewis' books about Narnia.
3. "Hey, no way, man," was John's response when the basketball coach first suggested he enroll in a ballet class to improve his balance.
4. My sister likes to think of herself as a budding femme fatale.
5. His handwriting is so sloppy that his 2's look like 7's and the word adolescent comes out looking like ocelot.

Answers

1. Underline <u>Auntie Mame</u>.
2. Underline <u>Little Women</u>, <u>Treasure Island</u>, and <u>The Swiss Family Robinson</u>. (Do not underline "Narnia," since that is not an exact title.)
3. Depending on how you "hear" the sentence, the underlining can appear in different places. For instance, you might underline the "way" in "Hey, no <u>way</u>, man." Or if you wanted to emphasize that John later changed his mind, you might underline "first" later in the sentence.
4. Underline <u>femme fatale</u>.
5. Underline <u>2</u>, <u>7</u>, <u>adolescent</u>, and <u>ocelot</u>, *or* put these words in quotation marks.

FINAL EXERCISES—Punctuation

Use commas, semicolons, dashes, colons, hypens, quotation marks, apostrophes, and parentheses as needed in the following sentences (several of them can be punctuated in more than one way). Sometimes you will have to change punctuation marks that are incorrectly used; other times you will have to add them.

1. On Sunday I went to a quadruple bill of Hitchcock thriller's, that night I had several well plotted nightmares.
2. When you knock on my grandfathers front door the doorbell hasnt worked for years you never know what to expect when he answers.
3. Who said We have nothing to fear but fear itself?
4. He quoted the last lines of Keats' poem Ode on a Grecian Urn Beauty is truth, truth beauty—that is all/Ye know on earth, and all ye need to know.
5. I think of my first apartment a studio with peeling paint and rattling water pipes with much affection and deep gratitude that I no longer live there.
6. Looking out into the garden we saw: roses, sweet peas; delphiniums; bachelor buttons; carnations; and petunias.
7. His parent's gave him money to buy a typewriter instead he invested in a fifteen year old Buick.
8. It was a morning out of heaven a light breeze stirred the delightfully scented privet hedge and white butterflies fluttered over the shaded lawn.
9. When informed that Calvin Coolidge had died Dorothy Parker is said to have asked How could they tell?
10. I remember the girls I had crushes on when I was ten years old Valerie Brown who owned every single one of the Hardy Boys mysteries Joanne Blossom whose name fit her perfectly and Laura Smith whose experiment on the effect of Coca-Cola on rats won a blue ribbon at the Science Fair.
11. As part of the communitys effort to achieve racial integration in the schools first second and third grade children are being bussed to one school from all parts of town.

Answers (Final Exercise on Punctuation):

1. On Sunday I went to a quadruple bill of Hitchcock thrillers; that night I had several well-plotted nightmares. (In place of the semicolon, you might use a dash; you could also split the sentence into two sentences. Commas after "On Sunday" and "that night"

are optional—they are not wrong, but probably slow the sentence down unnecessarily.)

2. When you knock on my grandfather's front door—the doorbell hasn't worked for years—you never know what to expect when he answers. *Or* When you knock on my grandfather's front door (the doorbell hasn't worked for years), you never know what to expect when he answers.

3. Who said, "We have nothing to fear but fear itself"? (It was Franklin D. Roosevelt.)

4. He quoted the last lines of Keats' poem "Ode on a Grecian Urn": "Beauty is truth, truth beauty—that is all/ Ye know on earth, and all ye need to know." (The slash is used to show where the break in the lines comes when they are printed as verse.) The apostrophe appears correctly after the *s* because the poet's name ends in *s* (John Keats).

5. I think of my first apartment, a studio with peeling paint and rattling water pipes, with great affection—and deep gratitude that I no longer live there. (The phrase "a studio with peeling paint and rattling water pipes" could equally well be set in parentheses or between dashes. The dash before "and deep gratitude" is optional—but helps show the shift in the writer's feelings.)

6. Looking out into the garden, we saw roses, sweet peas, delphiniums, bachelor buttons, carnations, and petunias.

7. His parents gave him money to buy a typewriter; instead he invested in a fifteen-year-old Buick. (A dash could appear in place of the semicolon, or you could begin a new sentence with "Instead.")

8. It was a morning out of heaven: a light breeze stirred the delightfully scented privet hedge, and white butterflies fluttered over the shaded lawn. (You could use a dash or semicolon in place of the colon, or the sentence could be split into two.)

9. When informed that Calvin Coolidge had died, Dorothy Parker is said to have asked, "How could they tell?"

10. I remember the girls I had crushes on when I was ten years old: Valerie Brown, who owned every single one of the Hardy Boys mysteries; Joanne Blossom, whose name fit her perfectly; and Laura Smith, whose experiment on the effect of Coca-Cola on rats won a blue ribbon at the Science Fair.

11. As part of the community's effort to achieve racial integration in the schools, first-, second-, and third-grade children are being bussed to one school from all parts of town. (Note that the "loose" prefixes "first" and "second" are hyphenated because, like "third," they form a compound modifier with "grade"; "first-grade, second-grade, and third-grade children" is a bit cumbersome, however.)

REDUNDANCY

The most common type of redundancy occurs when writers merely repeat themselves by using two words with the same meaning. For example, in 1973 President Nixon issued a statement promising that Elliot Richardson, the newly appointed Attorney General, had been directed "to do everything necessary to ensure that the Department of Justice has the confidence and trust of every law-abiding person in the United States." In this context at any rate, "confidence" and "trust" mean virtually the same thing.

Many commonly used phrases are redundant. Avoid them:

[new] innovation	[future] plans
[period of] time	[deliberate] lie
[pair of] twins	[close] proximity
adequate [enough]	consensus [of opinion]
circle [around]	[past] experience
[month of] January	[personal] friend
[year of] 1975	[advance] planning
[state of] Mississippi	[entirely] destroyed
large (or small) [in size]	is [currently]
few (or many) [in number]	was a [former]
[past] history	[convicted] felon

On occasion, a writer will develop a paragraph by redundancy, by stating the *same assertion* in different ways. The way to avoid this error is to check to see that you are being more and more specific, that you are *proving,* not *repeating.* (See Chapter 3, "Methods of Development.")

EXERCISE:

Eliminate the redundancy in the following passages:

1. In the month of January alone the child told three deliberate lies.
2. In my opinion, it seems to me that during the period of time of the 1970s, I think that by and large the majority of people were apathetic and indifferent to the point of not caring about things.
3. Although large in size, this monument is surprisingly and amazingly inviting to the visitor, who may wish to touch and feel its surface and exterior, developing a close intimacy with what might seem to someone else who was not present at the time like just a mere block of granite.
4. Sometime soon, in the not too distant future, today's present energy sources may no longer be sufficiently adequate to meet the

continually ever-increasing, necessary requirements of businesses and individuals.

5. The past experience of many of my personal friends has taught me the lesson of the necessity of advance prior planning to help me in reaching and attaining my future goals.

(Also see "Wordiness" in this Usage Manual.)

Possible Answers

1. In January alone, the child told three lies.
2. I think that during the 1970s the majority of people were apathetic.
3. Although large, this monument is surprisingly inviting to the visitor, who may wish to touch its surface, developing an intimacy with what might seem a mere block of granite.
4. Soon, present energy sources may not be adequate to meet the growing requirements of businesses and individuals.
5. My friends' experiences have taught me the necessity of planning to help attain my goals.

REPETITION

Repetition—of sounds, words, phrases, sentence patterns—can be used to heighten the impact of your writing (see page 204). But since such repetition is effective because it's noticeable, you should use it only consciously and sparingly, lest it annoy rather than impress the reader.

When Martin Luther King delivered his famous "I have a dream" speech, he wanted listeners to notice and even anticipate each repetition of the title throughout his address. When someone writes that a species of wildlife has been "unconscionably and irretrievably" lost through our greed and carelessness, he is using the repeated "-ably" endings to underscore his words.

But when someone writes a passage like the following, he is repeating words and other units carelessly, distracting the reader in the process:

> The Turn of the Screw is a confusing and bemusing work. *The Turn of the Screw* is confusing because its plot is ambiguous. *The Turn of the Screw* is confusing also because Henry James' style is hard for the reader to follow, making it hard for the reader to know what James is saying, let alone what the underlying point of *The Turn of the Screw* might be.

Note the following:

The writer seems to have forgotten about pronouns, repeating the book's title four times in a brief paragraph.

Each sentence begins essentially the same way: "*The Turn of the Screw* is confusing . . ."

The writer has almost comically juxtaposed "confusing and be-musing," which add a jarring rhyme to his sentence. (They also mean essentially the same thing; see "Redundancy" in this Usage Manual.)

"Hard for the reader to follow" and "hard for the reader to know" come gratingly close to each other.

Compare the original with the following revision:

> *The Turn of the Screw* is confusing because its plot is ambiguous and because Henry James' style is difficult to follow, making it hard for the reader to know what James is saying, let alone what the underlying point of the book might be.

Note that the revision is shorter than the original because we've eliminated most of the repetition and used joining devices like verbal phrases to incorporate the writer's ideas into one sentence. You might prefer a couple of shorter sentences to our long one, but in any case you should watch for annoying and time-wasting repetition in your own writing.

EXERCISE

Rewrite the following paragraph, eliminating unnecessary and distracting repetition of sounds, words, phrases, and sentence patterns.

Income tax forms may seem intimidating, but income tax forms are actually fairly easily filled out. Income tax forms are written at a third-grade level and they are written so that they lay out each step clearly. If you lay out your papers—W-2's, receipts, bank statements, etc.—before you start working on the income tax forms themselves, you'll find that the whole process goes much more smoothly when you start working on the income tax forms. If you go through each line of the income tax form one at a time, if you go through each line of the income tax form in order, and if you go through each line according to instructions, you'll find the process perhaps practically painless—unless you're not getting a refund.

Possible Answer

Income tax forms may seem intimidating, but they are actually rather easy to fill out. They are written at a third-grade level, with each step laid out clearly. If you assemble all your papers—W-2's, receipts, bank statements, etc.—before you start working on the forms themselves, you'll find that the whole process goes much more smoothly. By going through each line in order, and according to instructions, you may find the procedure almost painless—unless you're not getting a refund.

RUN-TOGETHER SENTENCES

Run-together sentences are closely related to those with comma splices. And if putting only a comma between two independent clauses is a misdemeanor, then putting nothing at all between the independent clauses is a felony. A run-together occurs when a writer "runs together" two independent clauses without any punctuation or conjunction whatsoever.

>   independent clause   independent clause
> The President first ordered the surprise attack then he informed Congress of his decision to send in troops.
>
> Sometimes it's difficult to work there are constant distractions.
>
> I want to go maybe it's not possible.

As you can see from these examples, run-together sentences are hard to follow. In the second example, for instance, one might misread the sentence at first, thinking the writer means that "Sometimes it's difficult to work *there*" (in a particular location).

Like sentences with comma splices, run-together sentences can be corrected in a variety of ways.

1. Punctuate the independent clauses as separate sentences:

> The President first ordered the surprise attack. Then he informed Congress of his decision to send in troops.
>
> Sometimes it's difficult to work. There are constant distractions.
>
> I want to go. Maybe it's not possible.

2. Use a semicolon to separate the independent clauses:

The President first ordered the surprise attack; then he informed Congress of his decision to send in troops.

Sometimes it's difficult to work; there are constant distractions.

I want to go; maybe it's not possible.

3. Use a coordinating conjunction plus a comma to join the independent clauses:

The President first ordered the surprise attack, and then he informed Congress of his decision to send in troops.

Sometimes it's difficult to work, for there are constant distractions.

I want to go, but maybe it's not possible.

4. Turn one of the independent clauses into a dependent clause:

dependent clause

After the President ordered the surprise attack, he informed Congress

independent clause

of his decision to send in troops.

independent clause   dependent clause

Sometimes it's difficult to work because there are constant distrac-

tions.

dependent clause   independent clause

Although I want to go, maybe it's not possible.

As in sentences with comma splices, methods 3 and 4 of correcting run-togethers are usually preferable because they help cut down on choppiness and show readers the logical relationship between the two clauses.

(See also "Comma Splices" and Chapter 8, "Coordination and Subordination," p. 201.)

EXERCISE

Correct any run-together sentences you find below.

1. Many students have unreal expectations about college life they think it will be relatively easy and always enjoyable.
2. They soon learn, however, that college is difficult in many respects.

3. When you go to Jack in the Box for a Bonus Jack you don't even need to leave your car you just speak into the intercom and order your meal.

4. At the end of McDonald's golden arches there is no pot of gold instead there is plenty of good food for hamburger-loving Americans.

5. In recent months, a number of observers have severely criticized television probably this is because there is growing concern about the effect of TV on children.

Answers

As always, there are several ways to correct the run-together sentence.

1. Many students have unreal expectations about college; they think it will be relatively easy and always enjoyable.

   Many students have unreal expectations about college. They think it will be relatively easy and always enjoyable.

   Students who have unreal expectations about college think it will be relatively easy and always enjoyable.

   Note: Coordination doesn't work well in this sentence, but you might try another way of making one independent clause subordinate, incapable of standing alone. For example, you could use a *verbal:*

   Having unreal expectations about college, many students think that it will be relatively easy and always enjoyable.

2. *Correct.* The group of words coming after the transitional expression "however" cannot stand alone; "that college is difficult in many respects" is a dependent clause.

3. Like sentence 1, sentence 3 can be corrected using all four methods. We prefer to subordinate:

   When you go to Jack in the Box for a Bonus Jack, you don't even need to leave your car, because you can just speak into the intercom and order your meal.

4. Sentence 4 can also be corrected all four ways. The semicolon works well here:

   At the end of McDonald's golden arches there is no pot of gold; instead there is plenty of good food for hamburger-loving Americans.

5. In recent months, a number of observers have severely criticized television, probably because there is growing concern about TV's effect on children.

   Note: We offer only this correction because the others, involving a period and a semicolon, would be unnecessarily wordy. The "this is" is not needed.

SEQUENCE OF TENSES (SEE TENSE SEQUENCE)

SLANG (SEE COLLOQUIALISMS/SLANG)

SPELLING

Interestingly, your ability to spell bears no relationship to your intelligence or verbal ability; some of the world's great writers have been rotten spellers. (The only trait researchers have been able to correlate with spelling ability is visual memory.)

If you have a serious spelling handicap, we encourage you to get one of the many self-help books available (your college bookstore probably carries some) and get to work on your own. You'll find that you can tackle spelling systematically; instead of memorizing every word individually, you can learn them in blocks and relate rules to large numbers of words.

The danger of remaining a poor speller is that people tend to judge (or misjudge) you on the basis of your spelling—they often believe that because they've found one readily visible problem in your writing, it must be flawed in general. Besides, you don't want to go through life chained to a dictionary, painstakingly looking up many of the words you want to use, or worse, avoiding them because you're not sure how to spell them.

If you have trouble spelling only a small percentage of the words you use, then your task is much easier. Here are some techniques to help you learn to spell words you have trouble with.

1. Make flash cards, leaving out the part of the word you tend to misspell. For instance, suppose you (like thousands of others) often misspell *separate.* But you don't mess up the whole word; it's only the "a" in the second syllable that gives you trouble. So write SEP_RATE on one side of the card, and "A" on the other. Go through your accumulated flash cards once a day, and gradually eliminate words you have spelled right several times in a row.

2. Pronounce troublesome words carefully, trying to hear all their sounds. We often slur words like *literature, representative, temperament,* and *mathematics.* Sometimes you have to mentally exaggerate the pronunciation of a word to remember its spelling: thinking of "business" as if it were pronounced "busy-ness" when you're trying to remember how to spell it will help you get the *i* in the right place. Hear the "o" in *sophomore,* the "a" in *boundary.*

3. Divide a long word into syllables to see how it is put together. You'll have an easier time spelling *assimilate* correctly if you

break it into parts, noticing that the *s* is actually pronounced twice: as-sim-i-late. (See our section on "Division" for hints on dividing words into syllables.)

4. Invent your own memory devices. For instance, think of having an iron in your immediate env*iron*ment. The spelling of *weird* (since it goes against the usual "i before *e*" rule) *is* weird. Actually, most of the common words that violate this rule are in the sentence

"Neither leisured foreigner seized the weird height."

5. Become interested in word families. Often you can remember how to spell a longer word if you think of the root it is derived from. If you think of "finite," meaning limited, you'll have an easier time remembering that *definite* ends in *-ite.* You'll remember the *n* in *government* if you think of *govern.*

Coming as it does from several different language sources, English has a rather erratic spelling system—much less phonetic than that of many other languages. (George Bernard Shaw once parodied the irregularity of English spelling by saying that "fish" ought to be spelled "ghoti"—after all, *gh* is pronounced like *f* in *enough; o* is pronounced like short *i* in *women,* and *ti* is pronounced like *sh* in words like *nation.*) But the following rules are reliable enough to be useful:

1. Remember this old jingle?

I before *e*
Except after *c*
Or when said as *a*
As in *neighbor* and *weigh.*

Examples: *I* before *e:* piece, field, believe, handkerchief, pierce
Except after *c:* ceiling, receive, conceit, perceive
Or when said as *a:* eight, veil, beige, reign
Important exceptions: weird, seize, either, neither, leisure, height, foreign

2. Dropping a silent e: A silent *-e* at the end of a word usually functions to make a vowel long. It changes *fat* to *fate, dim* to *dime, hop* to *hope, tub* to *tube.*

But if you are adding a suffix beginning with a *vowel,* the silent *-e* gets dropped:

hope	+	ing	=	hoping
come	+	ing	=	coming

desire	+	able	=	desirable
like	+	able	=	likable
force	+	ibly	=	forcibly
insure	+	ance	=	insurance
adhere	+	ence	=	adherence
rose	+	y	=	rosy
serve	+	ant	=	servant
perspire	+	ation	=	perspiration
true	+	ly	=	truly

Retain the -e when you are adding a suffix beginning with a *consonant:*

advertise	+	ment	=	advertisement
awe	+	some	=	awesome
like	+	ly	=	likely
force	+	ful	=	forceful
trance	+	like	=	trancelike

Exception: Words ending in *-ce* or *-ge* normally retain the *-e* when you add *-able* or *-eous:*

manageable
advantageous
serviceable
peaceable

Important exceptions to these rules: judgment (no *-e* in American spelling), *mileage, aging, acknowledgment, awful, dyeing* (to avoid confusion with *dying*), *singeing* (to avoid confusion with *singing*).

3. Changing *y* to *i:* When a word ends in *-y preceded by a consonant,* the *y* changes to *i* before any suffix except one starting with another *i.*

beauty	+	ful	=	beautiful
marry	+	age	=	marriage
cry	+	ed	=	cried
comply	+	ance	=	compliance
victory	+	ous	=	victorious
weary	+	ness	=	weariness
heavy	+	ly	=	heavily
worry	+	er	=	worrier

Keep the *y* before a suffix beginning with *-ing*:

pry	+	ing	=	prying
marry	+	ing	=	marrying
pity	+	ing	=	pitying

If a word ends in *-y preceded by a vowel,* the *y* usually remains when you add a suffix:

joy	+	ful	=	joyful
pray	+	ed	=	prayed
employ	+	er	=	employer
buy	+	er	=	buyer
betray	+	al	=	betrayal

4. Doubling a Final Consonant: With words of one syllable that end in a *single consonant preceded by a vowel* (*run, stop*), you double the consonant before adding a suffix beginning with a vowel (*running, stopped*). The same is true of words of *more* than one syllable ending in the same combination when they are accented on the last syllable (*occur* becomes *occurred*).

A. Examples of one-syllable words ending in a vowel plus a consonant:

plan	+	ed	=	planned
rag	+	ed	=	ragged
fit	+	ing	=	fitting
red	+	er	=	redder
thin	+	est	=	thinnest
drug	+	ist	=	druggist
rid	+	ance	=	riddance

B. Examples of two-syllable words ending in a vowel plus a consonant and accented on the last syllable:

com-mít	+	ee	=	committee
com-pél	+	ed	=	compelled
be-gín	+	ing	=	beginning
re-fér	+	al	=	referral

C. Examples of similar two-syllable words that are not accented on the last syllable (and so do *not* double the consonant):

óf-fer	+	ed	=	offered
díf-fer	+	ing	=	differing
ó-pen	+	ed	=	opened

D. Note that if the pronunciation is changed by shifting the accent, the spelling changes correspondingly:

préference (the accent is on the first syllable, so the r doesn't double)
preférred   (the accent is on the last syllable of the root word, preférr, so the r does double).

E. If there are *two* vowels before the final consonant, do not double the consonant:

ava*i*l	+	able	=	available
att*ai*n	+	ed	=	attained
awa*i*t	+	ing	=	awaiting

The only exception is with words with *q:* since *q* is always followed by a *u,* the *u* does not really count as a vowel:

| quit | + | ing | = | quitting |
| equip | + | ed | = | equipped |

5. Plurals
   A. Most words in English form a plural simply by adding *-s:*

flower	flowers
tree	trees
paper	papers

B. If a word ends in *-o,* or a sound like *-s, -ch, -x,* or *-z,* the plural is usually *-es:*

mosquito	mosquitoes
tomato	tomatoes
boss	bosses
Jones	Joneses
beach	beaches
wish	wishes
box	boxes
quiz	quizzes

C. If a word ends in *-f,* the plural is usually *-ves* (note the change in pronunciation):

half	halves
calf	calves
shelf	shelves
thief	thieves

(*but* chiefs, handkerchiefs)

D. If a word ends in *-y* preceded by a consonant, the plural is usually *-ies.*

baby	babies
sky	skies
cry	cries
party	parties

Other words ending in *-y* simply require *-s:*

key	keys
day	days

E. For letters, numbers, and typographical signs, add *'s* to show the plural:

A's   t's   7's   ?'s

Note: These rules also hold true for forming the third person singular of present tense verbs:

He bosses everyone around him.
She wishes she had never come.
He stretches his stories.
Jack always cries at movies.
What you just said echoes my own feelings.

EXERCISES

1. Fill in the blanks with *ie* or *ei,* according to the rule:

dec____ve

y ____ld

fr____ght

gr____f

s____ve

rec____pt

r____n

ach____ve

2. Add the suffix we've indicated to each of the following base words, dropping the silent -e where necessary:

write + ing _____

prepare + ation _____

commence + ment _____

culture + al _____

tire + some _____

ice + y _____

structure + al _____

imagine + ative _____

argue + able _____

fame + ous _____

outrage + ous _____

live + ly _____

menace + ing _____

visualize + ation _____

bale + ful _____

trace + able _____

change + able _____

3. Add the suffix we've indicated to each of the following base words, changing the y to i where necessary:

duty + ful _____

ally + ance _____

fry + ed _____

satisfy + ing _____

ceremony + ous _____

certify + ed _____

delay + ed _____

carry + er   _____

pay + able   _____

empty + ness   _____

bounty + ful   _____

convey + or   _____

heavy + er   _____

deny + al _____

ugly + est   _____

4. Add the suffix we've indicated to each of the following base words, doubling the consonant where necessary:

stop + ed   _____

whip + ing   _____

tag + ed   _____

big + est   _____

occur + ence   _____

admit + ance   _____

budget + ed   _____

incur + ed   _____

slip + age   _____

transmit + al   _____

commit + ed   _____

brighten + ing   _____

slug + ish   _____

repel + ant   _____

fog + y   _____

defer + ed   _____

defer + ence   _____

5. Make the following words plural:

potato   _____

berry   _____

tax   _____

princess   _____

wrench   _____

theory   _____

C̲ ____

dish _____

fox   _____

fellow   _____

4̲ ____

sinus   _____

leaf   _____

way   _____

Answers

1. deceive, yield, freight, grief, sieve, receipt, rein, achieve
2. writing, preparation, commencement, cultural, tiresome, icy, structural, imaginative, arguable, famous, outrageous, lively, menacing, visualization, baleful, traceable, changeable
3. dutiful, alliance, fried, satisfying, ceremonious, certified, delayed, carrier, payable, emptiness, bountiful, conveyor, heavier, denial, ugliest
4. stopped, whipping, tagged, biggest, occurrence, admittance, budgeted, incurred, slippage, transmittal, committed, brightening, sluggish, repellant, foggy, deferred, deference
5. potatoes, berries, taxes, princesses, wrenches, theories, C̲'s, dishes, foxes, fellows, 4̲'s, sinuses, leaves, ways

---

SUBJUNCTIVE MOOD

If I <u>were</u> you . . .
I wish my father <u>were</u> here.
We demand that he <u>resign</u> immediately.
If Jane <u>weren't</u> such a lady . . .

These verbs belong to the subjunctive, a vanishing breed of verb forms that were once an important part of the English language but now survive in only a few situations. Although the subjunctive is a technicality you can get through life without understanding, certain uses are still observed by careful writers, and knowing when to use the subjunctive can give your writing some nuances impossible to attain without it.

1. The main purpose of the subjunctive is to show that a circumstance is doubtful or actually contrary to fact. Usually the subjunctive follows *if, as if,* or *as though:*

> He looks as if (or as though) he <u>were</u> ill. (He may not be.)
> If I <u>were</u> that little brat's mother [but I'm not], I'd knock him into the middle of next week.

The subjunctive also follows the verb *wish:*

> I wish it <u>were</u> possible to master astronomy without using complex mathematics. (But it isn't.)

2. The subjunctive is also used in *that* clauses which express formal demands, resolutions, or motions:

> I move that the meeting <u>be adjourned.</u>
> We demand that he <u>stop</u> using these unfair tactics.

3. In most cases, the subjunctive is identical to the usual verb forms. The only forms that are still identifiable as subjunctives are these:

- *were* in the first and third-person singular (*that I were, that she were, that the house were*)
- *be* throughout the present tense (*that I be, that you be, that he be, etc.*)
- third-person verbs without *-s* endings (*that he go, that she leave, that the committee inform*)

4. The subjunctive also survives in certain common expressions left over from earlier times:

> Long live the Queen! (as opposed to "The Queen lives long")
> Heaven forbid! (as opposed to "Heaven forbids")
> as it were . . . (as opposed to "as it was")
> God bless you! (as opposed to "God blesses you")
> Suffice it to say . . . (as opposed to "It suffices to say")
> Be that as it may . . .
> Far be it from me . . .
> Come what may . . .

These idioms don't usually give anyone any trouble, but they are interesting illustrations of how the subjunctive continues to be used occasionally.

EXERCISE

We've left the verb forms blank where the subjunctive is required in the sentences below. Fill in the correct forms:

1. If I _____ you, I'd think the situation over more
     (was, were)
   carefully.

2. I ask that my daughter _____ excused from the examination.
                              (be, is)

3. If only aspirin _____ completely safe!
                     (was, were)

4. They demanded that the coach _____ .
                                    (resign, resigned)

5. George felt as if he _____ about to explode.
                           (was, were)

Answers:

1. were
2. be
3. were
4. resign
5. were

SUBORDINATION, FAULTY

Subordination is a means of joining two sentences and showing the logical connection between them. The process is called subordination because one idea receives more emphasis than the other. Look at the possible ways to join the following sentences.

> Many Americans have little religious faith. Small religious revival groups are on the rise.

A hopeful minister might choose to subordinate the first sentence to the second.

> Although many Americans have little religious faith, small religious revival groups are on the rise.

A confirmed atheist, on the other hand, would probably subordinate the second sentence to the first.

> Many Americans have little religious faith, <u>although</u> small religious revival groups are on the rise.

Sometimes when ideas are joined in this manner, the logic between the ideas goes awry and the resulting sentence doesn't make sense. This misjoining is called *faulty subordination.*

> *Illogical:* He had a limited vocabulary <u>because</u> he used many obscenities.

If you stop to examine the logic of this sentence, you'll see that it doesn't make sense. The fact that a person has a limited vocabulary cannot be caused by his frequent use of obscenities. The writer probably meant something like, "I concluded that he had a limited vocabulary because he used frequent obscenities." Or perhaps he simply subordinated the wrong clause: "Because he had a limited vocabulary, he used many obscenities."

Hint: It's easier to spot a faulty "because" clause if you turn the sentence around and put the "because" clause first:

> Because he used many obscenities, he had a limited vocabulary.

A sentence in which a "because" clause is correctly used will work either way:

> I stayed indoors whenever possible because it was so oppressively hot and humid outside.
> Because it was so oppressively hot and humid outside, I stayed indoors whenever possible.

Faulty subordination can also occur with other conjunctions:

> *Illogical:* Although I like Gothic novels, I like whodunits.

This sentence doesn't work because there is no contrast between the two clauses: liking Gothic novels does not contrast with liking whodunits. One clause has to be changed to create the contrast set up by "Although."

> *Logical:* Although I like Gothic novels, I <u>truly adore</u> whodunits.

Another kind of faulty subordination sometimes crops up with "which" clauses. When you're using prepositions with "which" clauses, be sure to choose the same preposition you would use if the clause were a sentence by itself.

>*Wrong:*   the problem in which I spoke

You would never write, "I spoke *in* a problem"; you would say, "I was speaking *of* or *about* a problem."

>*Correct:*   the problem about which I spoke
>   the problem of which I spoke

or perhaps less awkward:

>   the problem I spoke of
>   the problem I spoke about

(See also adjective clauses, pages 244–245.)

EXERCISE:

Rewrite sentences containing subordination problems to eliminate the errors:

1. Though Americans have always showed themselves equal to a crisis, they should be able to weather our current economic woes.
2. He was a loving father because he uncomplainingly got up in the middle of the night to comfort his daughter whenever she had a nightmare.
3. My uncle is getting older, since his eyesight isn't as good as it used to be.
4. While political cartoonists try above all for humor, serious criticism usually lurks behind every chuckle.
5. I no longer remember the day in which the accident occurred.
6. I often think of the park near which I lived as a child.
7. Great artists often present their ideas in a form in which the public isn't ready for.
8. Even though the election will soon be upon us, my favorite candidate doesn't have a chance of winning.

Suggested Revisions:

1. Since Americans have aways showed themselves equal to a crisis, they should be able to weather our current economic woes.
2. I knew he was a loving father because he uncomplainingly got up

in the middle of the night . . . . Or: Because he was a loving father, he uncomplainingly got up in the middle of the night . . . .

3. Since my uncle is getting older, his eyesight isn't as good as it used to be.

4. Correct

5. I no longer remember the day on which the accident occurred.

6. Correct

7. Great artists often present their ideas in a form [which] the public isn't ready for. ("Which" is optional; "in which" is definitely incorrect.)

8. Even though my favorite candidate is standing for election, he doesn't stand a chance of winning.

TENSE SEQUENCE

In every English sentence, the form of the verb shows the general *time* in the sentence. For instance:

> He is there. (right now)
> He was there. (at some time in the past)
> He will be there. (at some time in the future)

These different forms are called tenses, and there are basically five you need to know about:

> *Present:* she walks, she is walking, she does walk
> *Past:* she walked, she was walking, she did walk
> *Future:* she will walk, she will be walking
> *Present Perfect:* she has walked, she has been walking
> *Past Perfect:* she had walked, she had been walking

It's the two perfect tenses that may occasionally cause problems in your writing, especially when the events in a sentence occur at different times. For instance:

> I suddenly realized that I had forgotten to pick up a birthday present for Aunt Matilda.

You should use the past perfect here because the act of forgetting took place *before* the realization that you had forgotten, and "realized" is already in the past.

> *Wrong:*
> After World War II, thousands of American soldiers returned home to find that the jobs they held before the war were no longer available.

Right:
After World War II, thousands of American soldiers returned home
to find that the jobs they <u>had held</u> before the war were no longer
available.

In general, you use the present perfect tense to show action beginning in the past and continuing up to the present ("I have been wanting to learn French ever since I was ten years old") or for repeated actions in the past ("I have often walked down this street before"). You also need the present perfect tense when you are using the present tense to paraphrase the events in a story:

Toward the end of the play, the father finally <u>discovers</u> that he <u>has
been</u> duped by Tartuffe's sanctimonious posing.

(If you were using the past tense to summarize the events of the play, the second verb would have to be in the past perfect:

Toward the end of the play, the father finally <u>discovered</u> that he <u>had
been</u> duped by Tartuffe's sanctimonious posing.)

Another common mistake involving sequence of tenses is the use of *would have* in an *if*-clause.

Wrong:
If I would have known it would be such a demanding class, I wouldn't
have taken it this semester.

Right:
If I had known it would be such a demanding class, I wouldn't have
taken it this semester.

EXERCISE 1:

Fill in the correct forms of the verb in the blanks in the following sentences:

1. Grandmother told me she _____ to the United States fully ex-
                          (come)
pecting the streets to be paved with gold.

2. Suddenly Jane Eyre understands the meaning of the strange cries

she_____ since her arrival at Thornwood.
   (hear)

3. Many Americans are compulsive credit-card buyers; only when the

bills start to pour in do they realize how much money they_____

_____ paying.

(com-

mit themselves to)

4. Taxpayers _____ their refunds within a few weeks if they file
(receive)
their returns before March.

EXERCISE 2:

Correct any problems in sequence of tenses in the following
sentences. Some may be correct as they stand.

1. I felt that I already demonstrated my ability on several previous
occasions.
2. If he would have told me the truth right away, I wouldn't have
minded so much.
3. The story is told by a stranger, who wonders about Ethan Frome
and gradually pieces together the things that have happened to
make him what he is.
4. Tracy Austin became the youngest winner in the history of the
U.S. Tennis Championships by defeating Chris Evert Lloyd in the
1979 final—even though Lloyd defeated her on most of the occasions they previously played each other.

Answers:

1. 1. had come
    2. has heard
    3. have committed themselves to
    4. will receive
2. 1. I had already demonstrated
    2. If he had told me the truth
    3. *Correct*
    4. Lloyd had defeated her on most of the occasions they had
       previously played each other.

TENSE SHIFT

Throughout a paper, or at least a paragraph, you should stick to the
same verb tense unless you have a specific reason for changing.
        Students tend to run into the most trouble with shifts in tense
when they're *telling a story* or summarizing a plot. While you can
recount a story in either the past or the present (which is usually

better except for first-person narratives), you can't do both simultaneously, as the writer of the following passage attempted to do.

> Nick's first meeting with the fish is after he gets off the train. As he was walking along the stream, he stopped and looked into it. He began to watch a trout and saw it making shadows in the stream, just as Nick has a shadow over him because of all the awful things he was confronted with in the war. The trout tries to go upsteam against the current, and in so doing he tightened his whole body. At this point "Nick's heart tightened as the trout moved. He felt all the old feeling." Nick, who is projecting his inner feelings onto the fish, is barely holding himself together. He got up and began to walk up a steep hill. Like the trout which must make it upstream, Nick must walk up the hill instead of taking an easier route. This was his way of leaving everyone and everything behind him as he walked on the road to rehabilitation.

EXERCISE:

Using the present tense, make the verbs in the following paragraph consistent:

In the movie *Rollercoaster,* George Segal played a safety inspector who was fighting two battles: one against his cigarette habit, the other against a ruthless and coldly clever saboteur, who is played by Timothy Bottoms. Bottoms makes his sinister presence felt at the beginning of the picture, when he callously diverted a rollercoaster car from its tracks, sending passengers plummeting to their deaths. Later, making sure that the executives from whom he is trying to extort money and attention are sure of his power, he started a fire in another amusement park. Throughout all this Segal, who continues to half-heartedly bum cigarettes, gets an increasingly clear picture of the man whose voice and cruelty he comes to recognize. Finally, when Bottoms felt that he had been double-crossed by Segal, he becomes furious and says he would destroy the new rollercoaster at Magic Mountain. In the end, he was stopped by Segal (and a certain amount of luck), and Segal has also conquered his other nemesis, tobacco—at least for the time being.

Possible Revision:

In the movie *Rollercoaster,* George Segal plays a safety inspector who is fighting two battles: one against his cigarette habit, the other against a ruthless and coldly clever saboteur, who is played by Timothy Bottoms. Bottoms makes his sinister presence felt at the beginning of the picture, when he callously <u>diverts</u> a rollercoaster car from its tracks, sending passengers plummeting to their deaths. Later, making sure that the executives from whom he is <u>trying</u> to extort money and attention are sure of his power, he starts a fire in another amusement park. Throughout all this Segal, who <u>continues</u> to half-heartedly bum cigarettes, <u>gets</u> an increasingly clear picture of the man whose voice and cruelty he <u>has come</u> to recognize. Finally, when Bottoms feels that he <u>has been double</u>-crossed by Segal, he <u>becomes</u> furious and says he <u>will destroy</u> the new rollercoaster at Magic Mountain. In the end, <u>he is stopped</u> by Segal (and a certain amount of luck), and Segal <u>has also conquered</u> his other nemesis, tobacco—at least for the time being.

TITLES

1. We punctuate the title of a written work differently depending on whether it names a volume by itself or *part* of a volume. Thus names of books, magazines, and newspapers are underlined (in print they appear in italics) while names of poems, short stories, and articles (which are usually not published alone) appear in quotation marks. For example:

> Margaret Mitchell's best-selling novel about the Old South, <u>Gone With the Wind</u>
>
> "A Good Man Is Hard to Find," one of Flannery O'Connor's most famous short stories
>
> Frost's poem "The Road Not Taken"
>
> Shakespeare's tragedies <u>Hamlet</u> and <u>Macbeth</u>
>
> <u>The New York Times</u>
>
> An article called "Is Inflation Out of Control?" in the March 3, 1980 issue of <u>Newsweek</u>

This rule may seem perverse, but if you've ever done a bibliography for a term paper in which you used magazine articles, you'll see why you need two kinds of punctuation:

> McDowell, Bart. "Behind the Headlines: The Panama Canal Today." <u>National Geographic</u> CLIII, February 1978, pp. 279-94.

If there were only one way to indicate a title, the name of the article would be indistinguishable from the name of the magazine.

2. You also underline titles of plays, movies, television shows, musical productions, operas, paintings, and sculptures:

> Noel Coward is mostly remembered today for his delightful comedies like <u>Hay Fever</u> and <u>Blithe Spirit</u>, but he also wrote serious plays, songs, short stories, and film scripts.
>
> Last weekend we went to see a double bill of disaster movies: <u>Towering Inferno</u> and <u>Airport.</u>
>
> I never enjoyed <u>All in the Family</u> as much after Edith left the show.
>
> For a musical first produced in 1927, <u>Show Boat</u> deals with some rather surprising issues, including racial inequality and miscegenation.
>
> For years I thought Verdi's opera <u>La Traviata</u> was called <u>La Triviata.</u>
>
> Sometimes it's hard to appreciate great art: when you finally get to stand in front of the <u>Mona Lisa</u>, it's hard to separate it from all the cartoons of it you've seen.
>
> Michaelangelo's <u>David</u> represents the Renaissance ideal of the human male.

3. Song titles go in quotation marks:

> From the bathroom came an off-key rendition of "Oh, What a Beautiful Morning."

WHO/WHOM

The distinction between *who* and *whom* is no longer observed as faithfully as it once was. But you should still have at least a general idea of how to use *who* and *whom* correctly. Here is the explanation.

Actually, there are two explanations, both of which lead to the same place. The first approach is grammatical: if you have a good understanding of subjects and objects, you'll understand that *who* is always the subject within a clause, whereas *whom* is an object. For example:

> Many people believe that President Harding, who had trouble with suffixes, was the first to use the word "normalcy"; up until then, the word had been "normality."
>
> ("Who" is the subject of the verb "had.")
>
> Many people believe that President Harding, to whom suffixes were always something of a mystery, was the first to use the word "normalcy."
>
> ("Whom" is the object of the preposition "to"; the subject of the clause is "suffixes.")
>
> President Harding was the first president whom the women's vote helped to elect.
>
> ("Whom" is the object of the verb phrase "helped to elect"; "vote" is the subject of the clause.)

If all this is Greek (or at least Latin) to you, here's another way you can tell whether to use *who* or *whom*. Take the *who/whom* clause out of the sentence and rewrite it as a complete sentence, substituting the appropriate third-person pronoun (*he, she, they, him, her,* or *them*).

> he, she, they   correspond to   who
>
> him, her, them   correspond to   whom

For example:

> I wondered who/whom would be there. (*They* would be there, so *who* is correct.)
>
> A girl who/whom I knew in high school won a Mercedes in a box-top contest.
>
> (I knew *her* in high school, so *whom* is correct.)

Note: In rewriting the *who/whom* clause as a separate sentence, work *only* with the words that are part of that clause. If you look at the rest of the sentence, this method will not work.

Do not be misled by an intervening expression, like "I thought" in the next example:

> It upset me to be betrayed by someone who/whom I thought was my friend.
>
> (I thought *he* was my friend, so *who* is correct.)

EXERCISE: Choose the Correct Form:

1. "May I ask (who/whom) is calling?" asked the aloof secretary.
2. Horace, (who/whom) I dated during my freshman year, is now an undertaker.
3. We expect financial help from those (who/whom) can afford it.
4. The people (who/whom) followed us into the restaurant turned out to be the mayor and her husband.
5. The people (who/whom) we followed into the restaurant were extremely rude to the headwaiter, (who/whom) didn't know quite how to cope with them.
6. We will provide transportation for (whoever/whomever) needs it.
7. Give the message to (whoever/whomever) the agency sends.
8. Give the message to (whoever/whomever) answers the telephone.

Answers:

1. who (he is calling; who is the subject of the verb is calling)
2. whom (I dated him; whom is the object of the verb dated; the subject of the clause is I)
3. who (they can afford it; who is the subject of the verb can afford)
4. who (they followed us; who is the subject of the verb followed)
5. whom (we followed them; whom is the object of the verb followed; the subject of the clause is we); who (he didn't know; who is the subject of the clause)
6. whoever (they need it; whoever is the subject of the verb needs). This was a hard one: you expect to see a whomever after a preposition, and if you tried the substitution method, you might have made the mistake of looking at the whole sentence: "We will provide transportation for them." Don't forget that you work *only with the adjective clause.*
7. whomever (the agency sends her; whomever is the object of the verb sends; the subject of the clause is the agency)
8. whoever (he answers the telephone; whoever is the subject of the verb answers)

WORDINESS

When a writer takes more words than necessary to convey an idea, we say he or she is "wordy." Wordiness stems from a desperate attempt to pad a short paper, from a misguided sense of what sounds elegant, or from carelessness. The remedy for this disease is the knife: cut ruthlessly.

Example: Advice which by its nature is inherently dishonest has no place in counseling.

Revision: Dishonest advice has no place in counseling.

Example: In terms of the tendency toward over-eating during those times when you are unusually busy, a particular degreee of care should be exercised in an effort to resist such a temptation.

Revision: Try not to overeat when you are unusually busy.

Example: Regarding the theory that the occurrence of earthquakes may on some occasions be due to the fact of the gravitational pull of astronomical bodies in the solar system, the majority of seismologists view this concept with a certain amount of skepticism.

Revision: Most seismologists are skeptical of the theory that some earthquakes are caused by the gravitational pull of the moon and planets.

You can avoid wordiness if you avoid the following:

1. empty phrases ("regarding the idea that . . ."; "in our highly technological society," etc).
2. overqualification ("it seems to me that," "in my humble opinion," "there is an appearance of," and so on)
3. piling up of prepositions ("due to the fact that" when you mean "because"; "so as to" instead of "to"; "for the purpose of" instead of "for.")
4. using abstractions instead of cutting straight through to the main subject.
5. unnecessary *which-* or *that*-clauses.

EXERCISE: Eliminate the wordiness in the following passages.

1. She received an "A" due to the fact that she produced fine work.
2. The job by which I earn my living often appears to me to be one involving a great deal of boredom.
3. There seemed to be a certain amount of depression among the majority of the members of the class.
4. In this fast-paced, technological world in which we live, the allocation of funds from the federal sector of the national economy does not appear to be sufficient to permit the maintenance and growth of existing systems of mass public transit and the development of new systems of this nature.

Possible Answers:

1. She received an "A" because she produced fine work.
2. My job is boring.
3. Most of the class seemed depressed.
4. The federal government isn't spending enough on maintaining and developing mass transit systems.

WRONG WORD (also see "Adjective/Adverb Confusion," page 300, and Chapter 10)

The heading here is practically self-explanatory. Usually a wrong-word error is the result of picking a word whose definition is close to the intended meaning but isn't quite right. The writer may have pulled an unfamiliar word out of a thesaurus without checking its meaning in the dictionary. Though a valuable aid, the thesaurus can't be used thoughtlessly with good results. Occasionally a wrong-word error is the result of a mental slip, a confusion between two words that sound alike.

> The taxi pulled into the train *terminal,* slamming on its brakes as a harried passenger emerged.
>
> Everyone *coagulated* on the corner at nine for the car wash.

"Terminal" is not what the writer intended here, though it's close. Undoubtedly the writer confused "terminal" with "depot" because they're both stations from which passengers disembark. "Terminal," however, applies to airplanes whereas "depot" applies to trains. In the second sentence the writer obviously meant to say "congregated" but confused the sound and meaning with "coagulated." When you find a "wrong word" error marked on a paper, look the word up in the dictionary so you can avoid repeating the mistake.

EXERCISE: *Find and correct any misused words in the following sentences.*

1. Yesterday I received 500 fan letters from enthusiastic friends around the world.
2. From the apex of the door hung a delicate Chinese wind chime.
3. The scientist was murdered by cancer, the very disease he was trying to find a cure for.

4. The library was so short of funds it desperately needed donors to work evening hours.
5. There were not enough work forces to cover the weekly work schedule adequately.

Answers:

1. Yesterday I received 500 fan letters from enthusiastic admirers around the world.
2. From the top of the door hung a delicate Chinese wind chime.
3. The scientist was killed by cancer, the very disease he was trying to find a cure for.
4. The library was so short of funds it desperately needed volunteers to work evening hours.
5. There were not enough employees to cover the weekly work schedule adequately.

COMMONLY CONFUSED AND MISUSED WORDS

ADVICE/ADVISE:

Advice is a noun meaning "counsel." *Advise* is a verb meaning "to give counsel."

> The batter followed his coach's advice to bunt.
> He advised me to continue with law school.

Spelling note: If you remember that "advice" rhymes with "rice" and that "advise" rhymes with "rise," you'll avoid confusing the spelling of the two words.

AFFECT/EFFECT:

Affect is a verb with two distinct meanings: it can mean "to influence" or "to imitate in order to impress."

> The polls did not affect my vote in the election.
> Though he was from the Bronx, he affected an English accent.

Effect is a verb meaning "to accomplish" and a noun meaning "consequence" or "result."

> He effected changes in the electoral process.
> These changes have created certain beneficial effects.

A LOT:

A lot is spelled as two words, not one.

ALREADY/ALL READY:

Already means "previously," but *all ready* means that everything or everyone is ready.

> Timothy insisted that he had already done his homework.
> We were all ready to walk out the door at a moment's notice.

ALL RIGHT/ALRIGHT:

All right is sometimes spelled *alright,* though the latter is not considered good usage. Both are found in the dictionary but *all right* is the more accepted spelling.

ALL TOGETHER/ALTOGETHER:

All together means "all in the same place." *Altogether* means "entirely."

> We were all together at Christmas for the first time in five years.
> The electrician was altogether wrong about the power failure in the TV.

AMONG/BETWEEN:

Among is used to discuss a group rather than separate individuals. *Between* is used to discuss two things even though they may be part of a larger group.

> There was little agreement among the members of the committee.

> The referee tried to step between the two fighters.

> We studied the War Between the States for six months.
> (Though the Civil War was between more than two states, each side is thought of as one group.)

AMOUNT/NUMBER:

Amount refers to a quantity of something that can't be counted; *number* refers to things that *can* be counted.

> Limit the amount of sun you expose yourself to in the Mediterranean.

> I can't remember the number of sunburns I've inflicted upon myself there.

CAPITOL/CAPITAL:

Capitol means a "building in which a legislature assembles." *Capital* is used for all other meanings.

The congressman hurriedly left the White House and arrived at the Capitol in time for the briefing session.

Bogota is the capital of Colombia.

Starting that business will require a huge capital investment.

COARSE/COURSE:

Coarse means "rough" or "crude." *Course* means "a path of action or progress, a unit of study, a direction."

The sandpaper is very coarse.
The sailboat lost its course in the rough waters.
The math course I'm taking at school is enough to make me give up education.

COMPLEMENT/COMPLIMENT:

Complement means "something that completes or makes perfect," or, as a verb, "to complete or make perfect."

The sterling silver place setting was the perfect complement to the fine china.

The drapes complemented the rug beautifully.

Compliment means "a flattering remark" or as a verb, "to say something flattering."

I found his compliments superficial and self-serving.
He couldn't help but compliment the speaker on his poise.

CONSCIENCE/CONSCIOUS:

Conscience refers to that part of the mind that makes moral judgments about one's own actions. *Conscious* means "perceiving, comprehending or noticing." (Note that "conscience" ends with an "ns" sound and "conscious" ends with an "s" sound.)

His guilty conscience forced him to return the carrier pigeons he had stolen.

She was barely conscious after the accident.

CONTINUAL/CONTINUOUS:

Continual refers to something that happens frequently and intermittently, whereas *continuous* refers to something uninterrupted.

The stockbroker was <u>continually</u> interrupted by the sound of the tickertape.

Her boyfriend's calls were a <u>continual</u> harrassment throughout the day.

The <u>continuous</u> sound of the air raid siren frightened people more than the bombs.

The ski run went <u>continuously</u> downhill for two miles.

Note: You can remember the difference between these words if you think of the "ous" in continuous as standing for "<u>o</u>ne <u>u</u>ninterrupted <u>s</u>equence."

COUNCILLOR/COUNSELOR:

A *councillor* is a member of a council. A *counselor* is one who gives advice. Both may be spelled with either one or two l's, but the spellings used here are preferred.

One <u>councillor</u> refused to change his vote.
The marriage <u>counselor</u> told the young couple to wait a few months before making the final decision.

CRITERIA/CRITERION:

Criteria is the plural, *criterion* the singular of the same word.

The various <u>criteria</u> the scientists used failed to make the test accurate.
He had only one <u>criterion</u> for his success: financial security.

DISINTERESTED/UNINTERESTED:

Disinterested means "impartial." *Uninterested* means "not interested."

The two scholars continued their <u>disinterested</u> discussion of Keynesian economics.
The young boy was <u>uninterested</u> in the evening news.
You want a judge to be <u>disinterested</u>, but not <u>uninterested</u>.

EVERYDAY/EVERY DAY:

Every day is two words unless used as an adjective.

Muggings occur practically <u>every day</u> in big cities.
Muggings are practically an <u>everyday</u> occurrence in big cities.

EXCEPT/ACCEPT:

Except is a preposition meaning "but" or a verb meaning "to exclude." *Accept* is a verb meaning "to receive with consent."

> He met everybody at the party <u>except</u> the hostess.
> Current members of Congress were <u>excepted</u> from the pay raise.
> Valentino was overjoyed to <u>accept</u> the young woman's invitation to dinner.

FARTHER/FURTHER:

Farther is usually used to designate a physical distance; *further* usually refers to an abstract distance.

> It's <u>farther</u> from the U.S. to Argentina than it is from the U.S. to Europe.
> The <u>further</u> we go into this subject, the less I like it.

FEWER/LESS:

Fewer is used with countable nouns; *less* is used only with things that cannot be counted.

> The <u>fewer</u> days we spend in Palm Springs in midsummer, the better.
> The <u>less</u> time we spend in Palm Springs in midsummer, the better.

HARDLY

Don't use *hardly* with any contraction formed from *not.*

> *Wrong:* I <u>can't hardly</u> wait for Christmas morning.
> *Right:* I <u>can hardly</u> wait for Christmas morning.

> *Wrong:* Because time ran out, the speaker <u>didn't</u> have <u>hardly</u> any time to respond to his opponent.
> *Right:* Because time ran out, the speaker <u>didn't</u> have any time to respond to his opponent.
> *Right:* Because time ran out, the speaker <u>hardly</u> had any time to respond to his opponent.

INFER/IMPLY:

Infer means "to deduce or surmise"; *imply* means "to hint or suggest." The one who speaks or acts *implies*; the one who listens or observes *infers.*

> I <u>inferred</u> from his manner that he was upset with the service at the restaurant.
> By his manner he <u>implied</u> that he was upset with the service at the restaurant.

IN REGARD TO:

In regard to is sometimes incorrectly written "in regards to." Such usage is not considered appropriate in standard English.

ITS/IT'S:

Its shows possession; *it's* is a contraction for *it is,* or *it has.*

> Art is <u>its</u> own reward.
> <u>It's</u> difficult to make a living as an artist.
> <u>It's</u> been years since he sold a painting.

LEAD/LED:

Lead is a noun referring to a heavy metal; *led* is the past tense of the verb *to lead.*

> <u>Lead</u> is a substance the steel industry couldn't do without.
> The Pied Piper <u>led</u> the children out of the city.

LIE/LAY:

Lie means "to recline"; *lay* means "to put or place an object." The confusion between the two verbs comes as much from the various forms they take in different tenses as from their proximity in meaning. The chart below should serve to clarify the confusion.

	Lie	*Lay*
Present	I <u>lie</u> on the bed.	I <u>lay</u> the book on the desk.
Past	I <u>lay</u> on the bed.	I <u>laid</u> the book on the desk.
Perfect	I have <u>lain</u> on the bed.	I have <u>laid</u> the book on the desk.
Progressive	I <u>am</u> <u>lying</u> on the bed.	I <u>am</u> <u>laying</u> the book on the desk.
Future	I <u>will</u> <u>lie</u> on the bed.	I <u>will</u> <u>lay</u> the book on the desk.
Imperative	<u>Lie</u> on the bed.	<u>Lay</u> the book on the desk.

(It may help you to compare *lie* and *lay* with *sit* and *set.*)

LOOSE/LOSE:

Loose is an adjective meaning "not tight"; *lose* is a verb meaning "to miss from one's possession or fail to keep."

> The hangman noticed that the knot was <u>loose.</u>
> To <u>lose</u> one's life is grim, but to <u>lose</u> one's liberty is a disaster.

Note: If you know how to pronounce these words (*loose* rhymes with *goose*) and think about that pronunciation as you write them, you probably won't confuse them.

MEDIA/MEDIUM:

Media is the plural of *medium,* though in speech many use it as a singular. If you are referring to just one medium, use the singular.

> *Plural:*   The various news <u>media</u> have all contributed to making Iran well-known.
>
> *Singular:*   The <u>medium</u> of television has contributed to making Iran well-known.

NO/ANY:

Use *any* with negatives or with any contraction formed with *not.*

> *Incorrect:*   He did<u>n't</u> know <u>nothing</u> about the U.F.O.
>
> *Correct:*   He did<u>n't</u> know <u>anything</u> about the U.F.O.
>
> *Correct:*   He knew <u>nothing</u> about the U.F.O.

OF/HAVE:

Of is a preposition and never used in contractions; *have* is an auxiliary verb which can be used in a shortened form in contractions. Because *of* and *have* are often pronounced the same, they're often confused.

> *Incorrect:*   I could <u>of</u> danced until at least midnight.
>
> *Correct:*   I could <u>have</u> danced until at least midnight.

PASSED/PAST:

Passed is the past tense of the verb *to pass; past* is a noun or an adjective referring to a prior time.

> In the <u>past</u> year he has <u>passed</u> all his contemporaries in emotional maturity.

PHENOMENA/PHENOMENON:

Phenomena is the plural, "phenomenon" the singular of the same word.

> Several strange <u>phenomena</u> made them think the house was haunted. No one could explain the <u>phenomenon</u> of the eerie green light that kept appearing in the dark closet.

PRECEDE/PROCEED:

Precede means "to come before"; *proceed* means "to go forward or to go on."

> The majorette preceded the band by fifty yards.
> The majorette proceeded down the street, oblivious to the band.

PRINCIPAL/PRINCIPLE:

Principal is a noun referring to the head of a school or the money on which interest is calculated. It can also be an adjective meaning "main" or "primary." *Principle* is a noun referring to a law or rule.

> Our school principal was well-liked by all the students.
> They were able to live off the interest their money earned, never touching the principal.
> The principal reason to finish the course is that it's part of the major.
> Einstein's theories now rank among the primary principles of modern physics.

REGARDLESS/IRREGARDLESS:

There is no such word as "irregardless." Use *regardless* instead.

SIT/SET:

Sit is a verb meaning "to occupy a place or seat." *Set* is a verb meaning "to place or put down."

> The museum curator sets the sculpture on the pedestal and then sits fascinated, staring at it.

(Compare lie/lay)

SIGHT/SITE/CITE:

Sight is a noun referring to vision or a guiding device on a gun; *site* means "a place of position"; and *cite* is a verb meaning "to quote, mention, or name."

> His line of sight was obstructed by the herd of elephants.
> The architect spent a year designing the house for that particular site.
> The prosecutor cited a key ruling from a 1968 case that clinched the victory.

THAN/THEN:

Than is used for comparison; *then* means "at that time" or "next."

> The first book I read was better than the second.
> We went to Scoma's for dinner, then on to the play.

THEIR/THERE/THEY'RE:

Their indicates possession, *there* indicates existence or location, and *they're* is a contraction of "they are."

> The parents found their children at the park.
> There is little justification for putting the bookshelves over there.
> They're tired of writing "I will not talk in class" on the chalkboard.

TO/TOO/TWO:

To is a preposition or part of the infinitive form of a verb; *too* is an adverb meaning "also" or "excessively"; *two* stands for the number 2.

> Last weekend we went to the beach.
> He forgot to leave two apples for the trick-or-treaters.
> He was too tired to think about Halloween.

USE/USAGE:

Use is a noun or verb referring to the act of employing something; *usage* is a noun usually referring to a customary practice.

> The backpacker enjoyed the use of his friend's new light-weight tent.
>
> Strict adherence to formal English usage requires the subjunctive in some circumstances.

USED TO:

Used to is an auxiliary verb which requires the "-*d*" ending. Since it is not present tense, it is never spelled "use to."

WEATHER/WHETHER:

Weather is a noun referring to climate; *whether* is a conjunction usually used to express alternatives.

> The stormy weather will not stop us from going on the picnic.
> Whether or not we will enjoy the picnic is another question.

WHOSE/WHO'S:

Whose indicates possession; *who's* is a contraction for "who is" or "who has."

> Whose leotard is that crumpled in the chair?
> I know the gentleman who's being honored at the dinner party to-night.
> "Who's been sleeping in my bed?" I demanded.

YOUR/YOU'RE:

Your indicates possession; *you're* is a contraction of "you are."

> "You're going to read your new book tonight, aren't you?"

The Research Paper

Whether your instructor calls it a research paper, a term paper, a term report, a library paper, or a documented essay, during your years in college you will probably be asked to write at least one fairly long paper based on outside reading. (Most likely, you'll end up doing several.) Writing a research paper will teach you several skills: choosing a suitable topic and narrowing it to something you can explore thoroughly, using a library to locate sources, sifting through material to find what will best suit your purposes, interpreting and condensing what you read, and presenting your findings clearly and logically so that someone can quickly learn what you consider most important about a subject. This training is useful not only for the assignments you'll be given in college, but also for writing, research, and analysis you may someday have to do on a job.

The prospect of writing a research paper can seem overwhelming, but it may help to remember that in many ways producing a research paper is easier than writing an essay because you're not expected to come up with all the ideas yourself. Your job is largely to find and present the best of what other people have said about your topic. Remember also that any complex job becomes easier when you break it down into manageable parts. We suggest the following steps:

1. Set up a schedule.
2. Choose a topic.
3. Narrow your topic.
4. Write a preliminary statement of purpose.
5. Locate your sources.
6. Compile a working bibliography.
7. Take notes on cards.
8. Consider redefining your topic and write out a tentative plan.
9. Organize your notes into a working outline.
10. Write your first draft.
11. Edit your draft.
12. Put your footnotes and bibliography into the proper form.
13. Type or write out the final copy.

Step 1: Set up a Schedule

Even before you've decided what you're writing on, the first step is to set up a reasonable schedule. It's especially important to have a firm date on which you'll begin writing; many students tend to become so involved in the research that they take far more notes than they can possibly use and end up producing a hurried final draft. To make sure that doesn't happen to you, work backwards from your deadline, being generous with your time at the end to allow for unexpected difficulties. If your paper is due on December 15, for instance, aim for having it ready to type by December 1. If you have the whole semester to work on the paper, your schedule might look like this:

By October 1: Be ready to begin research on a specific topic.
From now until then: Decide on a topic. Narrow it to something manageable and write a tentative statement of purpose. [We'll explain what this is later.]
By October 9: Have several books and articles on the topic at hand, with a bibliography card for each.
From October 1 to 9: Locate useable sources, possibly narrowing the topic further depending on what's available. Fill out a bibliography card for each source.
By November 1: Have all research completed.
From October 9 to November 1: Look through sources, locating the most useful sections. Read these carefully, taking notes on cards. Refine the statement of purpose. Write down a preliminary plan [explained later] .
By November 10: Be ready to write.
From November 1 to 10: Go through all note cards. Set aside what doesn't seem useful. Organize what's left and write up a detailed outline.
By December 1: Have completed draft ready to type.
From November 10 to December 1: Write the paper. Transform the outline into a rough draft and revise the rough draft into a polished one.
December 15: Hand in the paper.

If you have less than a full semester to work on your project, use the same steps, but fit them into the time you have. (For example, with a month to complete the paper, you might give yourself four days to decide on a topic, two weeks for the entire research, and so on.)

Step 2: Choose a Topic

There are two kinds of research papers. In some papers, the writer's job is just to gather information about a topic and present these findings as accurately and clearly as possible. In others, the writer uses research to develop a *position* on a topic. These research papers have a thesis: their purpose is to convey the writer's opinion and persuade the reader to accept it. *Make sure that you understand which kind of research paper your instructor wants you to write* and that you pick a topic appropriate to the assignment. For instance, it would be difficult to form a thesis on "The History of the Modern Deck of Playing Cards," but a topic like "Methods of Treating Parents Who Abuse Children" encourages you to take a stand, to show which methods seem to work best and why.

If you've been assigned a specific topic or have already chosen one for yourself, skip the rest of this section and go on to Step 3, page 441. But if you're still undecided, read on.

Frequently, instructors give students a list of topics to choose from. With luck, there will be one that particularly interests you and that you would enjoy reading about. However, if none of them looks particularly inviting, there are a few ways you can choose one:

Pick a topic you think you can easily find material on (you might ask the reference librarian to go over the list with you and suggest a topic for which you can find good sources).

Pick a topic you already know something about.

Show the suggested topics to a friend and talk over the possibilities; he or she may be able to give you ideas to pursue.

Pick a topic you know nothing about and challenge yourself to learn something new.

You may be told to come up with a topic that relates to the course, without being given a list of choices. If your textbook has touched upon a subject you'd like to know more about, or if your instructor has mentioned something in class that you'd like to study more deeply, you may have a topic right there. Otherwise, you may be able to make your outside interests part of a topic relating to your course. For example, if you were assigned a paper for a basic physics course and knew you wanted to be a teacher, you might write on "Teaching Simple Concepts of Physics in the Elementary School." (*To be certain* that your topic will be acceptable, clear it with your instructor before you begin your research.)

Occasionally, the assignment is to write a research paper on any subject you choose. The ideal topic is something you're interested in and would like to learn more about. Maybe you were intrigued to hear that many nursery rhymes—"Old King Cole" and "Mary Mary Quite Contrary," for instance—actually had their origins in political happenings of their day, and you want to find out more about them. But if you have no idea what to write about, try browsing in the library under some general subjects you're interested in: biology or music or history. You might also check out books on display in different sections of the library, since these may suggest a topic you wouldn't have thought of.

Sometimes a topic begins as a question:

How did American educators first react to the invention of the television?

How is bone china made?

What is the history of Halloween?

To what extent does the incidence of heart attacks (or ulcers) correlate with the level of a person's job?

Why do leaves of some trees turn red or brown and drop off trees in the autumn?

How did the Roman gods and goddesses differ from those of the Greeks?

When and how did women get the vote in the major countries of Europe?

What was Freud's childhood like, and what effect might it have had on the development of his psychological theories?

Or your topic might begin with a name or a term you've heard of but know nothing about:

Bay of Pigs	Disraeli
Free Speech Movement	House Committee on Un-
Dadaism	American Activities
Piaget	Martin Luther
Stanislavski	Transcendentalism
Sappho	Copernicus
Buddha	Clarence Darrow
Bluebeard	Microfiche

If you still don't have a topic, here's a list of general subjects that might give you an idea:

People:	Writers, artists, scientists, historical leaders, inventors, philosophers, religious leaders, sports figures
Movements:	Political, literary, philosophical, religious, artistic
Literature:	Writers, works, movements
Creative Arts:	Music, painting, dance, theatre, sculpture, film, architecture
Psychology:	Theories, significant figures, history, methods of therapy, animal psychology
Business and Economics:	Leaders, theories, marketing, transportation, banking, real estate, personnel and industrial relations

Medicine:	Breakthroughs, famous doctors or nurses, history of the treatment of an illness
Technology:	Computers, inventions, everyday household objects

For other ideas on choosing a topic to write on, refer to pages 86–88 in Chapter 5.

Finally, we present some warnings:

1. Beware of a topic so technical that only a specialist in the field could treat it adequately. You don't want to get bogged down in material you won't be able to understand.

2. Even if you happen to know a lot about a technical subject—linear accelerators, for instance—remember your audience. A physics instructor would probably be able to understand a technical discussion while your English instructor might not. When in doubt, ask your instructor whether your choice of topic is appropriate.

3. Avoid a topic that won't lead you to a fair range of source materials. For example, there may not be much to find on last week week's international crisis. (On the other hand, tracing the steps that *led* to that crisis over the last few years would lead you to a variety of sources.)

Step 3: Narrow Your Topic

Once you've found your topic, you need to make sure you can treat it thoroughly in the number of pages you've been assigned. Often you'll have to narrow your first choice drastically to reduce it to manageable size, and the sooner you make that decision, the more time you'll save. For example, you could not hope to cover a topic as broad as "black-white relations in the South" in a twenty-page paper (or even a much longer one, for that matter). To do justice to this topic, you'd have to pick a particular aspect of it:

The Underground Railroad
The Ku Klux Klan
School Segregation
Busing
Martin Luther King
Famous Slave-Owners and Their Slaves

Even this first narrowing probably won't be enough. The topics we've just listed are still too broad; they embrace many different subtopics, most of which would be suitable for whole papers in themselves. If you were to choose the Ku Klux Klan as your topic, for instance, you'd find yourself reading about its leaders, its atrocities, its philosophy, its historical development, and its periods of greatest activity, just to name a few of the possibilities. From these you could devise a topic that you could research well and write up thoroughly and responsibly, something as specific as "times when the KKK has been the most active."

To help yourself narrow your topic, do some preliminary reading on it. Look at the table of contents in a couple of books on your subject to see how the authors have broken it down. You'll probably find particular sections or chapters that seem more interesting to you than others: one of these might become your topic.

However you go about choosing a topic, don't regard your choice as final, since you may decide you need to refine it further as you get into the research.

Step 4: Write a Preliminary Statement of Purpose

You won't know exactly what you want to say about your topic, of course, until you've done a fair amount of reading on it. But you'll have an easier time focusing this reading if you have a sense of purpose. What is it you're looking for? For example, you might be looking for reasons behind the Ku Klux Klan's intense activity during certain periods. You can easily convert your *sense* of purpose into a *statement* of purpose: "In this paper I plan to explain why the Ku Klux Klan is more active at some times than at others." This sentence may or may not find its way into your final paper, but it will certainly help you concentrate on gathering useful material. (Remember to regard your statement of purpose as tentative: you may decide to modify it as your paper begins to take shape.)

Step 5: Locate Your Sources

For most term papers, you will collect information on your topic by reading books, articles, and reports written by experts. The library is the best place to begin your search for materials. To discover what is available, you need to familiarize yourself with some basic references: the card catalog, indexes to magazines and newspapers, abstracts, and general reference books. Remember too that the reference librarian can explain how your library is organized and can suggest other places to look for information. It's also wise to check any source you have in hand to see if it will lead you to other materials. For instance, if you locate a book on your subject, check to see if it contains a bibliography listing other books or articles that look promising. When you start your research, make a list of places to check, and add to that list as you go along.

As you locate possible sources of information, you need to

evaluate them and decide which are the most useful, informative, and authoritative. The best research paper is the one based on the best sources. Because you may not be familiar with the most respected sources in a given field, you should ask yourself these questions about any book or article.

1. Is the source up-to-date? Scholars are continually revising and adding to our knowledge, so you naturally want to find the most current presentation, as long as it is sound and not merely "new." A research paper based upon material disproved or modified twenty years ago is clearly not worth much.

2. Is the source complete? Magazines often offer brief summaries of complex issues and subjects, but such condensations are seldom complete enough to be accurate. Try instead to find the source from which the brief article was taken.

3. Does the source seem factual and unbiased? Especially on controversial topics, try to spot unsubstantiated opinion.

4. Is your source *primary* or *secondary*? A primary source is the original or first-hand record of an event or fact. A secondary source is produced by another writer who comments on the primary material. For example, if you're writing about Lincoln's "Gettysburg Address," the address itself is a primary source, but any book or article about it is a secondary one. There is nothing wrong with good secondary sources, and you will rely heavily on them. But whenever possible, return to the primary source and judge it for yourself.

5. Has this source been mentioned anywhere else? One way to become familiar with the best works and authors in any field is to note those names that turn up repeatedly in bibliographies, in reference books, in classroom discussions, and so on.

A word of caution about one commonly used source of information on almost any subject, the encyclopedia. The encyclopedia is often useful in providing you with a broad overview of your subject. But it is not designed to provide the depth and accuracy of treatment a research paper calls for. An encyclopedia is a summary of other summaries, and as such it takes you too far away from primary sources.

THE LIBRARY CARD CATALOG

For most projects, the library card catalog is your best resource. By checking the card catalog, you can discover which books your library owns or has access to. The card catalog is cross-indexed, with items listed under three headings: author, subject, and title. Begin your search by going to the relevant subject heading, whether it is "animal communication," "novelists," or "Peru." (Often, libraries have two separate catalogs, one with author and title cards, and the other with subject cards.) Also remember that there may be synonyms for your subject heading. If you are looking under the heading "EYE," also check the heading "OPHTHALMOLOGY." Or if you are looking under "PRISONS," check "CRIME," "PUNISHMENT," and "RE-FORMATORIES," too.

The card catalog is not intimidating once you have learned how to interpret its codes. So learn how to read a card: from it you can obtain all sorts of useful information, such as how recent a book is, how long it is, and whether it contains special helpful information like a bibliography. These facts may save you time and steps by helping you decide whether or not you want to lay your hands on the book itself.

To become familiar with the way the card catalog works, examine these sample cards.

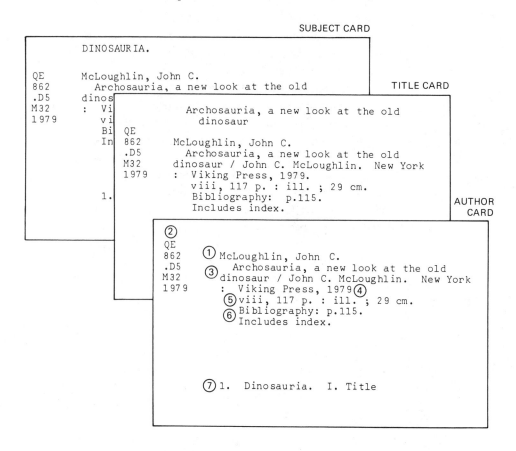

1. Author's name, last name first
2. Call number, telling you where in the library the book is shelved
3. Title of book
4. Publication information, including number of edition, place of publication, name of the publisher, and date of publication
5. Description of the book, including such information as the number of introductory pages (usually in roman numerals), the num-

ber of pages in the text, illustrations, and height of the book in centimeters

6. Note by cataloger about contents of the book (especially important is mention of a bibliography)

7. Cross references to other listings in the card catalog, telling other places to look for this card and cards for related books

INDEXES

An index is a catalog of articles in magazines, journals, anthologies, newspapers, and other collections. Periodical indexes are to articles what the card catalog is to books in the library. Like the card catalog, indexes are rich sources of information, often leading you to material you can find nowhere else. An index can, for example, help you find articles on a subject so recent that there hasn't been time for a book on it to be published yet. Most often, the entries in an index are listed alphabetically by both subject and author.

The most useful index for general purposes is the *Readers' Guide to Periodical Literature* (1900–present), which lists articles printed in over 135 popular magazines. To familiarize yourself with this index, study the sample page reproduced below.

CARRIAGES
  See also
  Coaches and coaching
CARRIERA, Joanne
  College commuter. Seventeen 38:38 Ag '79
CARRIERS, Aircraft. See Aircraft carriers
CARRIERS, Flower. See Flower holders
CARRIERS, Picnic. See Picnics—Equipment and supplies
CARRIERS of infection
  See also
  Animals as carriers of infection
  Mosquitoes as carriers of infection
① CARRIGAN, Charles R. and Gubbins, David
  Source of the earth's magnetic field; with biographical sketches. il Sci Am 240:14, 118-28+ bibl(p 168) F '79
CARRIKER, Melbourne R. and Palmer, R. E.
  New mineralized layer in the hinge of the oyster. bibl il Science 206:691-3 N 9 '79
CARRINGTON, Betty Watts, and Bush, Freda
  Mother-to-be, baby-to-be. bibl il Essence 10:84-7+ My '79
CARRINGTON, Peter Alexander Rupert Carington, 6th Baron
  Carrington on Rhodesia; excerpts from interview by F. Melville. por Time 115:79 Ja 7 '80

     about
  Britain's pragmatic patrician. por Time 114:63 N 26 '79 •
  Carrington's feat. D. Butler and A. Collings. il por Newsweek 94:62+ D 17 '79 •
  Man in the middle in Zimbabwe-Rhodesia is Britain's Kissinger—Lord Carrington. F. Hauptfuhrer. il pors People 12:42-4 O 22 '79 •
  On the brink of peace. il por Time 114:47 D 17 '79 •
CARRINGTON, Terri Lyne
  Profile. R. Brown. il por Down Beat 46:32-4 Mr 22 '79 •
CARRIÓN, Alejandro
  Modern Colombian novel. il Américas 31:45-6 Mr '79
CARRO, Geraldine
  Mothering. See issues of Ladies' home journal
CARROLL, Charles
  Mount Clare. M. F. Trostel. bibl il Antiques 115:342-51 F '79 •
CARROLL, Constance
  Young, gifted and black, she heads California college. il pors Ebony 34:76-8+ Je '79 •
CARROLL, Diahann
  Diahann Carroll; interview by C. L. Sanders. il pors Ebony 35:164-6+ N '79

     about
  On their own. A. Ebert. il por Essence 10:84+ O '79 •
CARROLL, Jane
  On falling in love; it's maddening and it hurts so good. Glamour 77:75+ F '79

CARRUTHERS, Jeff
  Very complicated way south. il map Macleans 92:34 N 12 '79
CARS (automobiles) See Automobiles
The CARS (rock group) See Rock groups ④
CARS, Railroad. See Railroads—Cars
CARSON, D. A.
  Church that does all the right things, but. . . por Chr Today 23:28-31 Je 29 '79
CARSON, Gerald
  Fences. il Blair & Ketchums 6:78-86 O '79
  Glorious bird. il Natur Hist 88:30-2+ Je '79
  Great enumeration. il Am Heritage 31:6-17 D '79
CARSON, Joanna (Ulrich)
  Johnny and I; a talk with Joanna Carson; interview by M. Funt; excerpt from Are you anybody; conversations with wives of celebrities. il pors Good H 189:119+ Ag '79
CARSON, Johnny
  Johnny Carson; interview by T. White. il pors Roll Stone p38-48+ Mr 22 '79

     about
  Ed McMahon; my 20 years with Johnny. B. Von ② Furstenberg. il pors Good H 189:118-19+ Ag '79 •
  Family feud. pors Time 114:86 S 24 '79 •
  Friars and friends try to roast a not-so-lame duck named Johnny Carson. J. Kessler and J. Seymore. il pors People 11:36-41 My 21 '79 •
  Great Carsoni. R. Ebert. il por Film Comment 15:58-9 Jl '79 •
  I call on Johnny Carson. P. Martin. il pors Sat Eve Post 251:74-9+ My '79 •
  NBC fights to keep its peacock from singing his swan song. il pors People 12:52+ D 24 '79 •
  Where's Johnny? H. F. Waters and M. Kasindorf. por Newsweek 93:65 Ap 30 '79 •
  Why Johnny can't leave. M. Kitman. New Leader 62:26-7 My 21 '79 •
CARSON, Johnny L. and others
  Ciliary membrane alterations occurring in experimental mycoplasma pneumoniae infection. bibl il Science 206:349-51 O 19 '79
CARSON, Lettie Gay
  She's been workin' on the railroad. E. Broudy. il pors Blair & Ketchums 6:73-9 Ap '79 •
CARSON, Mary
  How to get more married each day. il U.S. Cath 44:6-11 Je '79
CARSTENS, Karl
  Unpopular vote. Time 13:48 Mr 19 '79

     about
  Tumb president. D. Binder. New Repub 180:16-18 Je 16 '79 •
CARTAGENA, Colombia
  Cartagena; centuries of sunlight. A. J. Lowe ③ and E. V. Byleveld. il Américas 32:33-8 Ja '80

As you can see, there are four main types of entries for you to check:

1. Entries by authors
2. Entries about a person
3. Entries about a subject
4. Cross-indexing by subject, title, and author (references which lead you to entries located under other headings)

You may discover that as useful as it is, the *Readers' Guide* is just a starting place, since it lists only articles in popular magazines, not more specialized magazines and journals. There are many specialized indexes, covering almost every topic imaginable. Your reference librarian is your best resource for finding these indexes, but just to get an idea of what is available, look over this list:

General
Nineteenth Century Readers' Guide (1890-99)
Readers' Guide to Periodical Literature (1900-present)
International Index (1907-65)
    Succeeded by Social Sciences and Humanities Index (1965-1975)
    Succeeded by Social Sciences Index (1974-present) and
                Humanities Index (1974-present)
New York Times Index (1913-present) (This is a useful resource for finding information about recent public events and issues covered in the *Times* and often available on microfilm.)

Special
Applied Science and Technology Index (1913-present)
Art Index (1929-present)
Biography Index (1946-present)
Book Review Digest (1905-present) (This is another very valuable resource, since you can look up a book you are interested in, see how it was reviewed, and decide whether it will be useful to you.)
Education Index (1929-present)
Engineering Index (1884-present)
Monthly Catalog of United States Governments Publications (1895-present)
Music Index (1949-present)
Public Affairs Information Service (1915-present)

ABSTRACTS

Like an index, an abstract leads you to materials. It also provides a brief *description* of what the article, book, monograph, or report is about. The descriptions range from a single sentence to several hundred words, and can help you determine whether you want to read the entire work. Like indexes, abstracts cover a diversity of subjects, especially in the sciences. Of the hundreds of abstracts available, here are a few of the most often used:

Abstracts of English Studies	Metallurgical Abstracts
Biographical Abstracts	Physics Abstracts
Chemical Abstracts	Psychological Abstracts
Forestry Abstracts	Sociological Abstracts
Geoscience Abstracts	

OTHER REFERENCE BOOKS

So much information is now available that there are hundreds of reference books that tell you how to find material on a given subject. For example, in Constance Winchell's *Guide to Reference Books,* 8th edition (1967), you can look up your field of interest, find out which reference works are important, and discover indexes and bibliographies more specialized than those in our brief list.

The following lists contain the most commonly used and important reference books. Remember that these lists provide only a starting place in your search; consult the reference librarian for more suggestions on particular topics.

General Encyclopedias
Collier's Encyclopedia, 24 vols. (1965)
Encyclopedia Britannica, 15th ed., 30 vols. (1974)
World Book Encyclopedia

Dictionaries
Sir William A. Craigie and James R. Hulbert, eds., *A Dictionary of American English,* 4 vols. (1938–44)
A New English Dictionary on Historical Principles (also called the *Oxford English Dictionary*), 12 vols. and suppl. (1888-1933)
Webster's New Dictionary of Synonyms (1973)

Biography
Current Biography (1940–present)
Dictionary of American Biography, 22 vols. (1928-58)
Albert M. Hyamson, *A Dictionary of Universal Biography of All Ages and of All Peoples,* 2nd ed. (1951)
Who's Who in America (1899–present)
Who's Who in the World, rev. ed. (1973)

Quotations
John Bartlett and E. M. Beck, *Familiar Quotations,* 14th ed. (1968)
Bergen Evans, *Dictionary of Quotations* (1968)
Oxford Dictionary of Quotations, 2nd ed. (1953)

Almanacs, Yearbooks and Other Collections of Facts

The American Annual (1923–present)

Facts on File (1940–present)

Information Please Almanac (1947–present)

Statistical Abstract of the United States (1878–present)

The World Almanac and Book of Facts (1868–present)

Step 6: Compile a Working Bibliography

A bibliography is a list of the references you've consulted in preparing a research paper. It appears at the end of your paper (see pp. 494–495 for an example).

Whenever you discover a source that looks at all promising, immediately fill out a bibliography card for it. You can make out your card even before you locate the work by taking down the relevant information from the card catalog or periodical index you're using.

You'll save time and headaches later on if you take the trouble to fill out the card *in the exact form* you'll use in your finished bibliography. Then when you type up the final bibliography you can just alphabetize and copy over the cards for the works you actually used. There are several forms for both footnotes and bibliographies in use today, and your instructor may ask you to use a certain style that differs from the one we present here. Ours is the form used by the Modern Language Association, which you can take as your model anytime you're not instructed otherwise.

Sample cards follow for a book and for an article on the topic of the paper we've included at the end of this section, "The Death of the Dinosaurs." Note that you can comment on what looks useful

Ostrom, John H. "A New Look at Dinosaurs," *National Geographic*, August, 1978, pp. 152–185.

> Colbert, Edwin H. *Dinosaurs: Their Discovery and Their World.* NY: E.P. Dutton & Co., Inc., 1961.
>
> Seems to treat subject thoroughly. Looks scholarly yet easy to read.

about a work. (If you find more sources than you have time to go through, these comments can help you decide later which ones to concentrate on.) Correct forms for other kinds of bibliographic entries (books with more than one author, articles by an anonymous author, anthologies, etc.) appear on pp. 462–469.

Step 7: Take Notes on Cards

Use your note cards to

- summarize what you've read
- record important names, dates, and facts
- store quotations you may want to use
- jot down ideas that occur to you as you read
- remind yourself of where you've found particular information and how you think it might fit into your paper.

As you take notes, be careful to record on every card the source of the information so that you'll be able to footnote your findings accurately. Since you've already recorded all the publication data about the works you're consulting on bibliography cards, there's no need to do it again. Simply indicate on your note card the author and page number from which you've taken the quotation, fact, or summary you're recording: "Arnold, p. 91." (If you're using more than one book by the same author, you'll also need an abbreviated title: "Rodriguez, *History*, p. 319" or "Rodriguez, *Guide*, p. 243.")

It will also save you time later if you put a brief phrase at the top of each note card to indicate what the note is about. These phrases can save you time at the next step: organizing your cards by grouping related notes together.

Beware of the impulse to copy down too much. You can often boil an author's words down to a few lines. For instance, you could summarize the quotation below as briefly as we've done on the sample note card that follows:

> There can be no doubt about it. All the dinosaurs, along with various other Cretaceous reptiles, became extinct at the end of that period of geologic history. Not one of them survived into a later geologic age, as is amply proved by the fact that during almost a century and a half of paleontological exploration, the wide world over, no trace of a dinosaur bone or tooth has ever been found in any post-Cretaceous rocks, not even in the earliest of them. The proof of the geologic record on this score is irrefutable.

> *Background*
>
> No doubt that dinosaurs totally extinct by end of Cretacious period — not one bone found later.
>
> Colbert, p. 249

Sometimes, of course, you'll want to take down an exact quotation. If so, copy it accurately, being careful not to change a single word or even any punctuation. (If there are quotation marks in a passage you're quoting, change them to single quotation marks.) If you come across an obvious printing error, copy it as it appears, adding the word *sic* (Latin for *so*) in brackets after the error to show that it isn't *your* mistake:

> "All of the dinosaur [*sic*] on the planet suddenly became extinct after 165 million years."

If you want to leave out part of a sentence you're quoting, and can do so without distorting the author's meaning, insert ellipses (. . .)

to replace the missing word(s). If you're leaving out the end of a quoted sentence, include a fourth dot for the period. (See "Ellipses" on page 380 of the Usage Manual for more information on ellipses.)

Often you may find it useful to add a note about how you might use the quotation:

> *Cooling of Climate Theory*
> "The evidence shows that any such changes certainly took place slowly. There was a gradual replacement of world-wide tropical and subtropical environment by zoned temperature belts such as typify our world today...."   Colbert, pp. 153-54
> Use this to refute idea that dinosaurs froze to death.

Many of the cards you fill out will be hybrids, containing both an author's words and your own. Sometimes you'll need to alter a quotation slightly to make it fit the syntax of your sentence: indicate a word you've changed by putting brackets around it. Again, make sure that you're not changing the author's meaning. For instance, rather than copying out the whole quotation on the last card, you might have recorded it this way:

> *Cooling of Climate Theory*
> Slowly and gradually the climate cooled, replacing "world-wide tropical and subtropical environment [with] zoned temperature belts" like ones today.
>   Colbert, pp. 253-54

Accurate notes will help you to avoid the problem of plagiarism, the use of the words or ideas of another person as if they were your own. Plagiarism is a serious offense, punishable by expulsion at many colleges. So be scrupulous about putting an author's exact words in quotation marks, even if you're only copying a phrase from a sentence. Otherwise you may pick up a card two weeks and ten articles later with the uncomfortable feeling that some of what you've written down is someone else's wording, and you won't know how much you have to alter it to make it your own.

There is one last kind of note card we should mention: the "idea card." Sometimes in the course of your research, you'll begin to see how the paper may come together. If you get a good idea, write it down so you won't forget it:

Idea

Possible way to conclude paper: show how "greenhouse effect" theory could apply not just to dinosaurs but to man.

A few last suggestions on taking notes:

1. If a quotation is long, Xerox it, being sure to note the source and page number, and tape it to a card or sheet of paper.
2. Skim what you're reading before you begin taking notes; otherwise you may waste time taking too many. Looking through an article or chapter in advance will help you focus on the most relevant sections.
3. If you write on only one side of a card, you may be able to save time later by stapling the card to your rough draft. If your notes go onto a second card, be sure to label the second card carefully in case it gets separated from the first one.

Step 8: Consider Redefining Your Topic and Write Out a Tentative Plan

As you're going through your references taking notes, you may find that you have to narrow your topic further to leave yourself enough room to explore it thoroughly. Writing on the role of minor political parties during the 1930s, for example, you may decide to narrow your topic to the role of the Socialist party, or even to Norman Thomas, its Presidential candidate. Occasionally, you'll discover you have to make your topic *broader* because you can't find enough information on it. Changing your topic also means rephrasing your statement of purpose. Don't fight to hang on to your original notion of the paper. Even if you've spent some time taking notes you're now unable to use, you'll be better off if you cut your losses and change to a topic you can manage.

As you do your research and perhaps redefine your topic, you'll also be making changes in your bibliography. You'll discard references that don't turn out to be worthwhile and add new ones that turn up in your reading.

If you're writing a research paper that requires you to take a stand on the subject, this is also the time for you to work out a trial thesis; you'll have an easier time focusing your research if you have an idea of what you're trying to prove. For instance, the writer of a paper on the history of the Ku Klux Klan might at this stage be ready to hypothesize that the Klan has been strongest at times when white Southerners were feeling politically and economically threatened. Or the writer of a paper on possible reasons why dinosaurs became extinct might now favor one theory over the others.

Your next step is to begin thinking of how your paper will shape up. As you do your research, keep a list of possible section headings for your paper. For instance, if you were writing about the British psychologist Havelock Ellis, a pioneer in the study of human sexuality, some of your categories might be:

1. His life
    childhood
    education
    career
2. His publications
    early reactions to them
    what people have said about them more recently
3. How he became interested in studying sexuality
4. His beliefs about sex
5. His research
6. His contributions to the field

You may later decide to drop some of these categories and add others, but having this tentative plan in front of you will help you work more efficiently as you take notes. To help you fit the notes on your cards into their proper positions in the paper, you can also put abbreviations of these headings ("Life," "Contributions," "Publications—Recent Response") at the top of your cards.

Note that you probably haven't bothered to figure out an order for your categories yet; that will come next.

Step 9: Organize Your Notes Into a Working Outline

The titles on your cards and the categories you've listed on your tentative plan will help you to organize your note cards. Go through the cards, sorting them into the categories on your plan and setting aside those that don't seem to fit anywhere. Then arrange the cards in each stack in a sequence that seems logical, grouping related cards together. Put rubber bands around each sorted pile and then arrange the piles in what seems to be the most effective order, at least for now.

You'll probably discover that some of your stacks are much thicker than others, a fact indicating that you have more information for some parts of the paper than for others. That is to be expected, since you almost certainly won't be giving equal emphasis to each part of the paper. But now is the time to think about *proportion:* how much space you want to devote to each main category on your plan. If a stack seems too thin, you'll need either to do more research on that aspect of your topic or to leave it out of the paper, depending on how important you decide it is. If a stack seems disproportionately fat, weed out the more expendable cards (saving them in case you later decide some ought to go back in).

Also look through the "miscellaneous" cards you set aside, the ones that didn't fit anywhere else on your plan. If any of them are important enough to be worked in, you may need to add one or more categories. But don't feel you have to include something just because you've gone to the trouble of copying it down; leave it out unless it contributes in some essential way to your purpose in writing the paper. (Sometimes facts or quotations that don't seem to belong in the body of a paper can be used in the introduction or conclusion: see Chapter 6 for help with those parts of your paper.) Again, don't throw out any of your cards, no matter how unusable they may seem, until you're finished with the paper.

Now you're ready to write up a working outline, remembering that you can still make changes in it during the actual writing of the paper. But the more definite and detailed you can make your outline at this stage, the easier you'll find the first draft. There are two kinds of outlines: topic outlines, with phrases as entries, and sentence outlines, with complete sentences. Perhaps your instructor will ask you to submit one kind or the other; otherwise it's up to you. The advantage of a topic outline is that you can get it down quickly; the advantage of a sentence outline is that it forces you to define for yourself exactly what you want to say at every step, leaving you less to do as you draft your paper.

The following is the topic outline for the sample research paper on the extinction of dinosaurs at the end of this appendix. If you're not sure how an outline works, match up each notation on the outline with the corresponding part of the paper.

Outline

I. Introduction
    A. Dinosaurs successful for 165 million years
        1. Diversity of types
        2. Mammals by contrast insignificant
    B. Suddenness of dinosaur's extinction
        1. No large animals for millions of years after dinosaurs
    C. Scientists' curiosity about reasons for extinction
        1. *Chemistry* Magazine quote about inadequacy of present theories
        2. Statement of purpose: "I intend to examine these theories, as well as several others, in the hope of finding a generally acceptable explanation."
II. Early Theories Now Disregarded
    A. God's Mistake
        1. Since dinosaurs disappeared, God must have been unhappy with them—replaced them with man
        2. Refutation
            a. Darwin's theory of evolution
            b. Dinosaurs thrived for 165 million years—man around only 60 million
    B. Racial Senility
        1. Dinosaurs became too big and specialized to survive
        2. Refutation—specialization *enabled* them to survive
            a. Ceratopsian "collars" anchored jaws
            b. Hadrosaurs' crests increased sense of smell
III. Older Theories Still Respected
    A. Cooling of Climate
        1. Dinosaurs long believed to be cold-blooded lizards who froze when climate cooled
        2. Refutation
            a. New evidence that dinosaurs actually were warm-blooded
                i.   Large surface-to-volume ratio helped them retain heat
                ii. Dinosaurs speedy over land
                iii. Low percentage of predatory dinosaurs

        b. Climate cooled too gradually to kill dinosaurs so suddenly

           i. Laramide Revolution gradual—some would have adapted

    B. Change in Food Resources

      1. Cooler climate led to different sort of vegetation that dinosaurs couldn't digest

      2. Refutation—change of vegetation also very gradual

    C. Food shortage

      1. Disruption of photosynthesis process in plants caused massive food shortage

      2. Strength—would explain why only the biggest animal—the dinosaur—died out

      3. Weakness—McLoughlin argues less light reached earth, causing photosynthesis problem, but can't explain for sure why this happened

IV. More Recent Theories

    A. Supernova

      1. Supernova exploded near earth, bombarding planet with ultraviolet radiation

      2. Weakness—"scientifically glib" theory since there's no way to prove or disprove supernova explosion

    B. Radiation Poisoning

      1. Wobbles caused by Laramide Revolution allowed ultraviolet radiation to penetrate earth's magnetic field, poisoning dinosaurs either:

        a. directly—they had nowhere to hide—or

        b. indirectly—via mutations (eggshells too tough to crack)

      2. Refutation—not all dinosaurs large; many as small as mammals

    C. Plant Poisoning

      1. During Cretaceous period, flowering plants became dominant; these contained alkaloids which dinosaurs couldn't taste

      2. Apparent support—dinosaurs found in contorted positions, as if killed by poison

      3. Refutation

        a. Alkaloid plants developed over 50 million years—wouldn't explain suddenness of extinction

        b. Contorted positions caused by drying out of long neck muscles

    D. Lime Starvation

      1. In moist areas, soil's lime deposits washed away, depriving dinosaurs of lime necessary for bones and properly calcified eggshells

       2. Apparent support—cache of dinosaur eggs found with very thin shells

       3. Refutation

          a. Theory based on Eliseyev's observations in Congo—no way to prove dinosaurs' environment was similar

          b. Cache of eggs found may not be representative

V. Greenhouse Theory

    A. Define greenhouse effect—whereby carbon dioxide in the atmosphere traps heat and warms the earth's surface

    B. Cooling of climate was followed by brief warming trend

       1. Proof—increased carbon levels found in fossils beneath ocean's floors reflect increased carbon dioxide in atmosphere. Greenhouse theory would account for this.

    C. Increased temperatures could kill off dinosaurs two ways

       1. Directly—dinosaurs too large to release excess heat

       2. Indirectly—

          a. Heat kills sperm—so dinosaurs became sterile

          b. Heat caused thinning of eggshells and thus prevented hatching of strong young dinosaurs (analogy with birds, dinosaurs' closest living relative)

VI. Conclusion

    A. Best theory is one with fewest weaknesses

    B. Brief summaries of weaknesses of several theories

    C. Evidence for Greenhouse Theory seems substantial

       1. Accounts for extinction of a large animal while smaller ones survived

       2. Accounts for the suddenness of the extinction

    D. Greenhouse Theory especially important because it may provide information about survival of another dominant species—man

       1. End with long McLean quotation

       2. Despite many differences between dinosaurs and man, we would still be susceptible to a sustained greenhouse effect—so our survival might someday be threatened

Step 10: Write Your First Draft

Comfortably ahead of the day your paper is due, you should force yourself to stop doing research and begin writing up what you've found. (If you finish with time to spare, you can always go back and expand parts of the paper, but you will probably find that you have more than enough information already. Also, you'll have a much better idea of which sections of the paper could stand some filling out after you have a rough draft.)

With the combination of your outline and your note cards, you may actually find this an easier paper to draft than an ordinary essay for which you've done much less detailed planning. You have all your raw material at hand; you just need to put it together. Here are some suggestions that should help:

1. Try to keep a sense of proportion as you write. If you expect the paper to be 15 pages long, for instance, estimate how many pages you think you'll need to devote to each major section on your outline. Keep tabs on yourself as you work on the rough draft, and force yourself to stop working on a particular section if you've gone much over your estimate. This should help you keep the parts of the paper in proper balance, so that you don't end up with a paper that spends too long on background and then rushes its conclusions (a common fault). Remember too that there is nothing wrong with changing your outline as you write if you find that you have much more to say on a particular section than you'd expected. Perhaps you can narrow the topic so that you can leave out some of the other sections you'd originally planned to include.

2. Double-space your first draft and leave generous margins. Write on only one side of the paper so that you can cut and paste if you decide to rearrange the paper.

3. For now, put the footnotes in the text, setting them off from the rest of your writing with slashes. (If you list them on a separate piece of paper, it's easy to lose track of where they belong, especially since the numbering will probably change as you make insertions or deletions.) For example:

> The extinction probably took as little as a million years, "an instant in geographical time." / McLoughlin, p. 101 /

Since most of the ideas in a research paper come directly or indirectly from outside sources, students are often unsure of what needs footnoting. In general, footnote *all quotations* and any idea which comes specifically from a certain source and is not a matter of general agreement. For instance, reading about the extinction of dinosaurs, you would find in several sources the fact that dinosaurs had disappeared by the end of the Cretaceous period, so there is no need to footnote that. On the other hand, if you were summarizing Eliseyev's theory that the dinosaurs died off because of lime starvation, you would need to footnote that information. If you spend a whole paragraph summarizing information from the same source, just put a footnote at the end of it. But if you have more than one quotation in a paragraph, even if they're from the same source, you must footnote each one separately.

4. Your instructor doesn't want to read a paper full of quotations strung together by occasional words of your own; he or she wants to read what *you* have to say. Although it's impossible to prescribe a proportion right for every situation, quotations should gen-

erally amount to less than a quarter of your paper. Make sure you have a specific reason for including every quotation in your final draft: usually that it's especially well-phrased or provides needed support for an important point. (For instance, you will often want to quote the exact words of a recognized expert in the field.) Where you can, summarize quotations in your own words, making sure they are different enough from those of the original not to leave you open to charges of plagiarism.

5. As you're writing, you may want to save time by not copying out whole quotations. You can staple your card to the page or even just put "Burton quote" with a circle around it. But when you get ready to edit your draft, you should make sure that all quotations are inserted where they belong, for only then will you be able to see how your paper reads.

6. Concentrate on integrating quotations smoothly into the writing. You should usually give the name of the person you're quoting, and identify him or her if readers are likely to be unfamiliar with the name. For instance:

According to Dale Russell of the National Museums of Canada,

" ___ ."

As Winston Churchill put it, " ___ ."

" ___ ," writes Freud, " ___ ."

In the words of Carolyn Heilbrun, a professor of English at Columbia University, " ___ ."

Sometimes the way you introduce a quotation will help you signal the reader about what to expect from the quotation:

John Kenneth Galbraith has a different explanation: " ___ ."
Ann Faraday, a British psychologist who has published two books on dream interpretation, suggests that the answer is not so simple:

" ___ ."

Or your introductory words can let the reader know what *you* think of the quotation:

A more plausible theory comes from Lewis Thomas: " ___ ."

Remember that you can alter quotations to fit your sentence, as long as you do not distort the author's meaning:

Original quotation: "Both time and distance in the old sense have been annihilated." (George B. Leonard, *Education and Ecstasy*)

How you might fit it into your sentence:

> George B. Leonard refers to the annihilation of "both time and distance in the old sense."

7. Give your readers clear signals to help them follow the turns in your presentation or argument. Remember the transitions we looked at in Chapter 8:

therefore	first, second, third
in particular	in addition, also
however	in fact
for example, for instance	instead
in other words	on the other hand
nevertheless	finally
but, yet	thus, so

Sometimes, of course, you'll need more:

> Despite these advantages,
>
> Although many scientists agree,
>
> But before we can fully understand the problem,

Also remember to use clear topic sentences to show your reader what your paragraphs are about:

> "There are three reasons for . . .,"
> "Experts in the field disagree sharply about the causes of . . .,"
> "The solution will not be simple."

Step 11: Edit Your Draft

If you can, set your rough draft aside for a few days (or at least overnight) once you've completed it. You'll be able to see it much more clearly if you get away from it for a while.

As you read over your draft, try to hear how it sounds. "Listening" to your prose will alert you to such problems as choppiness, awkward phrasing, abrupt or missing transitions, and errors in grammar or punctuation. If something sounds bad, put an "X" in the margin and read on so that you don't lose your sense of the paper as a whole. Then go back and work on the passages you "X"-ed.

If possible, ask a friend to read the paper and to let you know where he or she has trouble following your ideas or has questions about what you're saying.

See pages 251–276 for other ideas on editing your paper.

Step 12: Put Your Footnotes and Bibliography Into the Proper Form

FOOTNOTES

Since the term paper is based upon information gathered from a variety of authorities, it is essential that you give these sources credit. Footnotes are the standard means by which we cite references to outside materials.

SOME GENERAL PRINCIPLES OF FOOTNOTE FORM

- Number footnotes consecutively throughout the paper.
- In the body of the paper, place the footnote number slightly above the line and immediately after the material it refers to.
- It is now generally accepted for footnote references to go on a separate sheet at the end of the paper. The only notes that should really go at the bottom of the page are those in which you offer an explanatory comment or aside, since a reader is unlikely to bother flipping to the end of the paper to read it. For this kind of footnote, use an asterisk instead of a number. Footnotes at the foot of the page should be single-spaced.*
- Footnotes at the end of the paper should be double-spaced. The first line should be indented five spaces from the margin. The second line should be flush with the margin.
- The basic information contained in your first reference to a work is as follows:
  Author
  Title
  Publishing Information (place of publication, publisher, date of publication)
  Page cited
- A simplified footnote form is used for subsequent references to a work.

THE BIBLIOGRAPHY

The bibliography is a list of all works consulted for the term paper, whether you have quoted directly from them or not.

- Bibliography entries are made alphabetically, according to the author's last name.

---

*This is the form to use. Type a line of fifteen spaces, then double-space, indent the asterisk, and single-space your note.

- Bibliography entries begin at the left-hand margin. The second line should be indented five spaces.
- As with footnotes, it is generally preferred that bibliography entries be double-spaced.

NOTATION

The following section provides examples of typical footnote and bibliography entries. Follow exactly the order in which the information is given and the punctuation used here.

Books

1. A book with a single author

Footnote:

Gary Zukav, The Dancing Wu Li Masters: An Overview of the New Physics (New York: Bantam Books, 1979), p. 133.

Bibliography:

Zukav, Gary. The Dancing Wu Li Masters: An Overview of the New Physics. New York: Bantam Books, 1979.

2. A book with two or more authors

Footnote:

Sandra M. Gilbert and Susan Gubar, The Madwoman in the Attic: The Woman Writer and the 19th Century Literary Imagination (New Haven: Yale University Press, 1979), p. 263.

Bibliography:

Gilbert, Sandra M. and Susan Gubar. The Madwoman in the Attic: The Woman Writer and the 19th Century Literary Imagination. New Haven: Yale University Press, 1979.

3. A book with more than three authors
Footnote:

John Tibbetts, et al., <u>Teaching in the</u>

<u>Developing Nations: A Guide for Educators</u>

(Belmont, California: Wadsworth Publishers,

Inc., 1968), p. 43.

Bibliography:

Tibbetts, John, et al. <u>Teaching in the</u>

<u>Developing Nations: A Guide for</u>

<u>Educators</u>. Belmont, California:

Wadsworth Publishers, Inc., 1968.

4. A book with an anonymous author
Footnote:

<u>Understanding Solid State Electronics</u>

(Dallas, Texas: Texas Instruments, Inc.,

1978), p. 79.

Bibliography:

<u>Understanding Solid State Electronics</u>.

Dallas, Texas: Texas Instruments,

Inc., 1978.

5. A book with organizational authorship
Footnote:

President's Commission on Higher Educa-

tion, <u>Higher Education for American Democ-</u>

<u>racy</u> (Washington, D.C.: Government Printing

Office, 1947), I, 26.

Bibliography:

President's Commission on Higher Education.

<u>Higher Education for American Democ-</u>

<u>racy</u>. Washington, D.C.: Government

Printing Office, 1947.

6. A previously published book in a new edition

Footnote:

      Pertti J. Pelto and Gretel H. Pelto, <u>Anthropological Research: The Structure of Inquiry</u>, 2nd ed. (Cambridge, England: Cambridge University Press, 1978), p. 89.

Bibliography:

Pelto, Pertti J. and Gretel H. Pelto. <u>Anthropological Research: The Structure of Inquiry</u>, 2nd ed. Cambridge, England: Cambridge University Press, 1978.

7. A work in a collection of pieces by different authors with an editor or editors

Footnote:

      Joseph F. Kett, "Adolescence and Youth in 19th Century America." In <u>Education in American History</u>, ed. Michael B. Katz (New York: Praeger Publishers, 1973), p. 55.

Bibliography:

Kett, Joseph F. "Adolescence and Youth in 19th Century America." In <u>Education in American History</u>. Ed. Michael B. Katz. New York: Praeger Publishers, 1973.

8. A work in two or more volumes

Footnote:

      Vernon Louis Parrington, <u>Main Currents in American Thought</u> (New York: Harcourt, Brace and Co., 1954), II, 410.

Bibliography:

Parrington, Vernon Louis. <u>Main Currents in</u>

<u>American Thought</u>. Vol. II. New York:

Harcourt, Brace and Co., 1954.

9. A work in translation

Footnote:

Fyodor Dostoyevski, <u>The Brothers</u>

<u>Karamazov</u>, trans. Constance Garnett (New

York: Modern Library, 1950), p. 557.

Bibliography:

Dostoyevski, Fyodor. <u>The Brothers</u>

<u>Karamazov</u>. Trans. Constance Garnett.

New York: Modern Library, 1950.

10. A work in a series

Footnote:

Jean E. Kennard, <u>The Literature of the</u>

<u>Absurd</u>. Harper Studies in Language and

Literature (New York: Harper and Row, 1975),

p. 34.

Bibliography:

Kennard, Jean E. <u>The Literature of the</u>

<u>Absurd</u>. Harper Studies in Language

and Literature. New York: Harper and

Row, 1975.

11. The introduction to a work

Footnote:

Richard Shaull, "Foreword," <u>Pedagogy of</u>

<u>the Oppressed</u> by Paulo Freire (New York:

The Seabury Press, 1968), p. 14.

Bibliography:

Freire, Paulo.   Pedagogy of the Oppressed.

New York: The Seabury Press, 1968.

(*Note:* In the bibliography, a book is referred to as a whole and so is noted according to its author. In the footnote, the specific part of the book is referred to.)

12. The editor's introduction (or preface or foreword)
Footnote:

Thomas L. Ashton, ed., "Introduction."

Ten Short Novels (Lexington, Mass: D. C.

Heath and Co., 1978), p. 2.
Bibliography:
Ashton, Thomas L., ed.   "Introduction," Ten

Short Novels.   Lexington, Mass: D. C.

Heath and Co., 1978.

Magazines, Newspapers

13. A signed article in a magazine
Footnote:

James Baldwin, "Dark Days," Esquire,

October, 1980, p. 43.
Bibliography:
Baldwin, James.   "Dark Days."   Esquire,

October, 1980, pp. 43-46.

14. An unsigned article in a magazine
Footnote:

"Search and Destroy--the War on Drugs,"

Time, 4 September 1972, p. 24.
Bibliography:

"Search and Destroy--the War on Drugs."

Time, 4 September 1972, pp. 22-31.

15. A signed article in a newspaper
Footnote:

Richard Burl and Bernard Gwertzman,

"How the U.S. Came to a Key Decision," San

Francisco Chronicle, 15 October 1980, Sec.

1, p. 22, col. 1.

Bibliography:

Burl, Richard and Bernard Gwertzman. "How

the U.S. Came to a Key Decision." San

Francisco Chronicle, 15 October 1980,

Sec. 1, p. 22, cols. 1-2.

16. An unsigned article in a newspaper

Footnote:

"Iran, Iraq to give U.N. Council a

Try," San Francisco Chronicle, 15 October

1980, Sec. 1, p. 21, col. 2.

Bibliography:

"Iran, Iraq to give U.N. Council a Try."

San Francisco Chronicle, 15 October

1980, Sec. 1, p. 22, cols. 1-3.

17. An editorial

Footnote:

Editorial, New York Times, 23 January

1979, Sec. A, p. 23, col. 1.

Bibliography:

Editorial. New York Times, 23 January 1979,

Sec. A, p. 23, cols. 1-2.

18. An article in a journal

Footnote:

Stephen B. Hulley, M.D., et al.,

"Epidemiology as a Guide to Clinical

Decisions," New England Journal of

Medicine, Vol. 302, No. 24 (June, 1980),

1384.

Bibliography:

Hulley, Stephen B., M.D., et al.

"Epidemiology as a Guide to Clinical

Decisions." New England Journal of

Medicine, Vol. 302, No. 24 (June

1980), 1384-88.

19. A signed article from a general encyclopedia
Footnote:

Nicola Abdo Ziadeh, "Bourbon, House

of," Encyclopaedia Britannica: Macropaedia

Knowledge in Depth, Vol. III, p. 79, 1975

ed.

Note: In a work that is alphabetically arranged, volume and
page number must be given only if the citation is to one page
of a multi-page article.)

Bibliography:

Ziadeh, Nicola Abdo. "Bourbon, House of."

Encyclopaedia Britannica: Macropaedia

Knowledge in Depth. 1975 ed.

20. An unsigned article from a general encyclopedia
Footnote:

"Habersham, James," Encyclopedia Ameri-

cana, 1980 ed.

Bibliography:

"Habersham, James." Encyclopedia Americana.

1980 ed.

21. A signed article from a special encyclopedia
Footnote:

James L. Rau, "Steel Manufacture,"

McGraw-Hill Encyclopedia of Science and

Technology, Vol. XIII, p. 103, 1977 ed.

Bibliography:
Rau, James L.   "Steel Manufacture."

<u>McGraw-Hill Encyclopedia of Science</u>

<u>and Technology</u>.   1977 ed.

SUBSEQUENT FOOTNOTES

After you have cited a reference in a footnote the first time, you may refer to the same source again using a shortened form. Usually, just the name of the author and the page number is sufficient:

Baldwin, p. 45

If you are using more than one work by the same author, include the title of the work you are citing:

Baldwin, *The Fire Next Time,* p. 77.

If you should consult a source not illustrated here, two standard manuals to consult are:

MLA Handbook for Writers of Research Papers, Theses, and Dissertations. New York: Modern Language Association, 1977.
Turabian, Kate. *A Manual for Writers of Term Papers, Theses, and Dissertations,* Fourth Edition. Chicago: University of Chicago Press, 1973.

Step 13: Type or Write Out the Final Copy

Your instructor may give you certain specifications for how your final manuscript should look. If so, follow them. Otherwise, observe these general guidelines:

- Double-space throughout the paper, except as noted below.
- Leave a 1½″ margin at the top and on the left, a 1″ margin on the right, and a 1″ margin at the bottom of each page.
- On the first page, repeat your title in capital letters a third of the way down the page. Then triple-space and begin your text. Center "-1-" at the bottom of the page. (See the first page of our sample research paper.)
- For the rest of the paper, put each page number at the top of the page, either at the center or in the right-hand corner.
- Indent and *single-space* a long quotation (anything over four lines). Don't use quotation marks at beginning or end of the passage; the

fact that it's indented shows it's a quotation. (See p. 19 in the sample paper for an example.) Keep double quotation marks *within* the passage, of course.

- Prepare a title page, following our sample.
- Make all corrections neatly; redo a page on which you have more than one or two visible errors. Proofread the paper with even more care than usual.

THE DEATH OF THE DINOSAURS:

WHY DID THEY BECOME EXTINCT?

by

Sylvia Q. Student

Course Number
Instructor's Name
Date

THE DEATH OF THE DINOSAURS:

WHY DID THEY BECOME EXTINCT?

For more than 165 million years dinosaurs were
the dominant form of life on earth. They were ex-
ceedingly diverse in size and shape, ranging from
Archaeopteryx, a pigeon-sized dinosaur, to the massive
Brontosaurus, a beast fifteen times as large as a bull
elephant. Some were peaceful herbivores, like the
horned Triceratops, which consumed tons of greenery
each day, and some were predatory carnivores like the
huge Tyrannosaurus, which ripped its prey apart with
sharp talons and massive jaws. So successful and so
numerous were the dinosaurs that our ancestors, the
mammals, were by comparison insignificant, tiny creatures hiding in nooks and crannies to escape the
notice of the dominant dinosaurs.

Some 70 million years ago, at the end of the Creta-

ceous period, all the dinosaurs suddenly died off.
This mass extinction is one of the great unsolved
mysteries of our planet. After successfully growing
and adapting for 165 million years, the dinosaurs disappeared. Scientists will probably never know how
much time passed before this mass extinction was complete, but they postulate that it occurred with what
is phenomenal speed for geological time. The extinction probably took as little as a million years, "an
instant in geological time."[1]

After the disappearance of the dinosaurs, there
exists no trace in the fossil record of the earth's
rocks of a large land animal for millions of years.
Then gradually, the mammals began to creep in, expanding to fill the role played by the dinosaurs.

Man's curiosity about the dinosaurs' end has yet
to be satisfied, although piles of books have been
written offering one theory after another to account
for their extinction. A recent article in Chemistry
magazine about the extinction of the dinosaurs said
that "none of the host of previous theories including
cooling of the climate, change in food resources, . . .
intensified cosmic radiation, or rivalry of mammals
has been generally accepted as a comprehensive explanation."[2] I intend to examine these theories, as

well as several others, in the hope of finding a
generally acceptable explanation.

In the mid-1800s, as soon as scientists had enough
proof that giant creatures had once dominated the earth
and then disappeared from it, people argued that surely
dinosaurs were one of God's mistakes. According to this
theory, He then corrected His mistake by wiping out the
entire dinosaur population before going on to work on
mammals and ultimately the "perfect" creature, man.
This "mistake" theory lost ground as more and more people came to accept the theories of Charles Darwin, who
argued that all forms of life evolve gradually, following natural laws that dictate the rise and fall of
various kinds of animal life. Today scientists would
find it very difficult to call a class of creatures
that thrived for 165 million years a "mistake," especially since man himself has been around for only some
60 million years.[3]

Another early theory postulated that dinosaurs became extinct because their genes became "senile."
Adherents to this theory argue that dinosaurs got too
big, too unwieldy, and too specialized to survive.
They see the odd bony frills and crests on the heads
of many types of dinosaurs as proof that their genes
had deteriorated and produced these wild forms. This

early theory also lost ground as scientists researching dinosaurian remains came to see just how useful
these supposedly unnecessary "frills" were. Actually,
it seems, these specializations were just what enabled
dinosaurs to survive for so many million years. For
instance, the large "collars" framing the heads of the
Ceratopsian dinosaurs acted as anchors for the enormous muscles needed to support their equally enormous
jaws.[4] The crests on hadrosaurs seem to have been
hollow, which allowed extra nasal capacity and greatly
increased their sense of smell, which in turn helped
them detect and escape from predators.[5]

Once scientists ascertained that dinosaurs were
very successful and efficient creatures, they began
to look elsewhere for the cause of their sudden disappearance. The geologic record reveals that at about
the time dinosaurs were vanishing, the earth's climate
cooled off considerably, due to various geologic and
atmospheric changes, not all of which have been adequately explained. Having long held the belief that
dinosaurs were cold-blooded reptiles (indeed, the name
"dinosaur" means "terrible lizard"), scientists thought
that the colder temperatures explained the dinosaurs'
death. Since reptiles can't control their own body
temperatures, they must rely on a steady external

source of heat, the sun, to stay alive. If, during

this climatic shift, some type of cloud cover prevented

the sun's full warmth from reaching the earth, the

dinosaurs would have grown colder and more sluggish,

until they literally slowed down and froze to death.

This theory that a colder climate killed the cold-

blooded dinosaurs has been rejected for a couple of

decades by scientists who claim that much evidence

supports the idea that dinosaurs were warm-blooded,

not cold-blooded as was originally thought. These

scientists believe that dinosaurs were likely to be

warm-blooded for three reasons. First, most dinosaurs

were so large that their surface-to-volume ratio

allowed for a great deal of heat retention. While

they might not have been like mammals, who generate

their own heat internally, dinosaurs could have stored

whatever heat was available for long periods in the

vast bulk which kept their body temperatures relatively

stable. Second, the speed of some dinosaurs over land

has been estimated at up to 80 kph (faster than a race-

horse runs). If they had been cold-blooded, dinosaurs

could have moved only one-tenth that fast. Third, the

percentage of dinosaurs that were predatory was very

low. Research on other animals indicates that in a

cold-blooded community 25 per cent of the population

are carnivores (meat-eaters) but that less than five
per cent are carnivores in a warm-blooded group. Scientists have estimated that only 2.0 to 3.3 per cent
of the dinosaurs were carnivores, which seems to suggest that they fall into the warm-blooded category.[6]

If, as the most recent findings seem to indicate,
the dinosaurs were in fact warm-blooded, the cooler
climate should not have suddenly killed them off. For
one thing, the Laramide Revolution (that "sequence of
earth forces that gave rise to our modern great systems of mountains"[7]), which very possibly was responsible for the change in temperature, occurred very
gradually. The climate cooled slowly, replacing
"world-wide tropical and subtropical environments
[with] zoned temperate belts" like the ones the earth
has today.[8] The change would have been too gradual
to have wiped out all the dinosaurs. Some should have
adapted to or endured the cooler weather, especially
the smaller, mammal-sized ones, which could seek shelter from the elements.[9]

Even if the colder climate did not kill off the
dinosaurs directly, it might have done so indirectly,
some scientists argue, by changing the earth's food
resources. Simply put, this theory states that the
tender vegetation the dinosaurs had been eating was

replaced by coarser vegetation, which the dinosaurs couldn't digest.[10] Since this shift in plant types must also have occurred very gradually, this theory seems weak and is open to the same criticism as the cooling climate theory, namely that it doesn't account for the rapid demise of the dinosaurs.

One scientist, John McLoughlin, has postulated that a change in food resources was in fact the cause of the dinosaurs' death, but he argues for a sudden decrease in food resources, not a gradual shift from one form of plant life to another. McLoughlin notes that any theory correctly accounting for the death of the dinosaurs must account for the fact that while dinosaurs and many forms of marine plankton vanished (as the geologic record proves), mammals and reptiles survived. He theorizes that something disrupted the process of photosynthesis in plants, causing a massive food shortage. The plant-eating huge dinosaurs, the life form requiring the most energy in the form of many tons of plants per day, would be the hardest hit. In turn, if these herbivores died out, the carnivores wouldn't have them to prey on and they too would die out. The marine dinosaurs, used to consuming vast numbers of plankton in the oceans, would also starve. But the reptiles, which could go for longer

periods on less food and even hibernate, would survive,
as would the small mammals, which also needed less food
and either could hibernate or were small enough and
mobile enough to get at the earth's remaining food.[11]

McLoughlin's theory seems sound in that it does
account for the fact that only dinosaurs died out.
But it is still an unproven and rather sketchy theory
because McLoughlin can't explain why the mass food
shortage occurred. (And he doesn't even mention the
disappearance of the small, mammal-sized dinosaurs,
which it would seem should have survived just like the
mammals.) McLoughlin argues that the plants' and
planktons' photosynthesis processes could have been
disrupted, even for a relatively short time, if less
light reached earth due to some sort of massive cloud
cover caused by a meteorite or supernova explosion.
But there is no way of proving that such an event did
occur.

This idea of McLoughlin's, that a supernova exploded near the earth, has been advanced by other
scientists, including Dale Russell of the National
Museums of Canada. But unlike McLoughlin, Russell
feels that the dinosaurs were killed off by radiation,
not starvation. His scenario reads this way: Close
to our own solar system, a supernova occurred. A

supernova is a rare astronomical phenomenon in which
most of the material in a star explodes, creating an
incredibly brilliant but short-lived object and producing vast amounts of energy in the form of radiation.
This supernova explosion in turn, Russell argues, dam-
aged the earth's ozone layer and bombarded the planet
with ultraviolet radiation. According to Russell, the
dinosaurs were especially susceptible to the radiation
poisoning because of their huge size.[12] A creature
weighing many tons could hardly burrow underground to
escape the radiation, even if it had known it was
poisonous.

One strong objection to the supernova theory is
that there is no way to prove that such an event occurred. Even many scientists who think that radiation
probably was the cause of the mass extinction reject
the supernova explanation, calling it "scientifically
glib."[13] These scientists, among them D. Cohen, pro-
pose another cause of the large doses of radiation
that they think killed the dinosaurs: wobbles in the
earth's rotation. According to Cohen, much of the
earth's protection from the continual normal barrage
of ultraviolet radiation from space is provided by
the earth's magnetic field. Wobbles in the earth's
rotation cause fluctuations in that field. Cohen feels

that the likelihood of such wobbles is excellent if we consider the geologic events of the period, namely the Laramide Revolution mentioned earlier, which gave rise to our mountain systems and broke up the earth's major land masses.[14]

Even though they can't be proven conclusively, both of the radiation theories are attractive, mainly because radiation has such widespread effects. We greatly fear radiation because we know it can kill both directly (as the world witnessed in the horrifying events following the dropping of the atom bomb on Hiroshima in World War II) and indirectly, by causing mutations. According to scientist H. K. Erben of Bonn University, lethal mutations could have caused dinosaur eggs to develop very tough shells, so tough that the babies could not crack them to get out.[15] Or other radiation-induced mutations could have very adversely affected the already highly specialized dinosaurs, making them less capable of adapting to their world.[16]

Our own fears about the effects of radiation should not, however, keep us from questioning the likelihood that radiation poisoning did kill the dinosaurs. There are several considerations that the radiation theory does account for, but one main one that it does not: the fact that mammals and reptiles survived. The

radiation poisoning theory does seem plausible in the
case of large land dinosaurs. And while the large
marine dinosaurs could escape by remaining under water
(water blocks radiation), the masses of plankton these
marine dinosaurs fed on would have been wiped out by
radiation, leaving them with no food source. But it
is only the extinction of the large dinosaurs that the
radiation theory accounts for. The theory doesn't explain why mammals and reptiles survived but small dinosaurs didn't. If we argue that the mammals and
reptiles could burrow into the earth or hide under
rocks to escape the poisoning, we must ask why the
smaller dinosaurs--and there were many types of small
dinosaurs--didn't also do the same thing and so survive
too.

Another intriguing theory is advanced by Tony Swain
of the Royal Botanic Gardens in Kew, England. He pro-
poses that the dinosaurs were poisoned by eating plants
that had a high alkaloid content. His proof runs as
follows: During the Mesozoic era, a new type of vegetation, flowering plants, came into prominence and
provided much of the vegetation dinosaurs fed on.
These flowering plants contained alkaloids, a substance
dinosaurs couldn't taste. Consequently, as the dinosaurs ate increasing numbers of these flowering plants,

they ingested massive amounts of **alkaloids** and so poisoned themselves. It happens that alkaloids cause a violent death, with much the same symptoms as strychnine poisoning. Tony Swain notes that dinosaurs are often unearthed lying on their backs, in painfully contorted positions which suggest death by poison. Coincidentally, it also happens that alkaloids, like DDT, can cause thinning of the eggshell. So it is possible that the flowering alkaloid plants killed off the dinosaurs indirectly, by causing them to lay eggs with shells so thin they broke instead of harboring the dinosaur young.[17]

While Swain's theory is ingenious, there are several weaknesses in it. The rise of the alkaloid plants took 50 million years, all during which the dinosaurs consumed them and flourished. Why, after 50 million years on this diet, would the dinosaurs suddenly become extinct with startling rapidity? Moreover, the geologic record indicates that the flowering plants were well-established and dominant **before** the period of greatest diversification and domination of the dinosaurs.[18] It is unlikely that dinosaurs would have flourished and expanded their **dominion** if they were being poisoned off. In addition, the presence of alkaloid plants wouldn't account for the fact that marine dinosaurs

and carnivorous dinosaurs, including small ones that
probably fed on reptiles and mammals, also died out.
Swain's observation about the contorted death positions
of dinosaurs can be accounted for by the fact that as
the dinosaurs' neck muscles dried out after death, they
contracted, causing the odd contortions. This phenomenon is common among birds--the dinosaur's only living
relative--today.[19]

A Russian geologist named Vasily Eliseyev has
advanced still another intriguing but doubtful theory.
While visiting the Congo, Eliseyev noticed that all of
the animals were undersized (he saw hippos about five
feet long and gazelles "the size of hares"[20]) and immediately realized that the cause of this change in
entire populations could easily have led to the mass
extinction of the dinosaurs some 60 million years ago.
Eliseyev argued that the external cause was low levels
of lime in the soil. In very moist areas, the soil's
lime deposits are washed away; this process, which
takes place today in the Congo, was likely to have
happened during the Cretaceous period, Eliseyev believes. Since animals need lime for their bones (and
for calcified eggshells), this lime starvation can
cause serious problems; the total symptoms, says
Eliseyev, probably resembled those caused by rickets.

These symptoms included collapse of bones and convulsions, along with the weakening of eggshells already mentioned. It should be noted, however, that Eliseyev feels this lime starvation affected only the large dinosaurs; the small ones, he argues (as do others), were killed off by competition with mammals of a similar size.[21]

Like all the theories advanced, Eliseyev's has weak spots. First of all, he is making a comparison between conditions in the Congo and conditions all over the world during the late Cretaceous period, and there is no way to prove that the conditions were similar. Moreover, he supports his theory by referring to a large cache of dinosaur eggs, found in southern France, that have very thin shells. Other scientists are quick to point out that it is not safe to generalize or to assert that dinosaurs everywhere were laying thin-shelled eggs just because one cache of eggs in one location exhibits this symptom. The southern France cache may not represent conditions elsewhere, and there is no proof from other egg caches to support Eliseyev's conjectures.[22]

By far the most elegant theory is that of scientist Dewey McLean, who believes the dinosaurs were killed by the greenhouse effect. Greenhouse effect is a term used to describe the phenomenon whereby carbon dioxide in the atmosphere traps infrared radiation (heat) and warms the earth's surface. In short, McLean believes that a "greenhouse" was created on the earth, and the resulting rise in temperature killed all the dinosaurs.[23] This description sounds simple enough, but it is much too sketchy to show McLean's depth of proof or the solidity of his theory, which deserves examination in detail.

The most important aspect of McLean's proof is his explanation of how the greenhouse effect got started, especially in light of the widely accepted evidence mentioned earlier of a cooling trend on earth during the late Cretaceous period, not a warming trend. Until recently, the geologic record has indicated that such a cooling of the earth's temperature occurred during the Mesozoic era. But now scientists have accumulated evidence which suggests that this cooling trend was interrupted by a brief warming trend, lasting as little as a million years. The very complicated proof involves increased carbon levels found in fossils taken from beneath the ocean's floors. McLean postulates that this increased fossil carbon level reflects a warming trend during the late Cretaceous period, when the dinosaurs disappeared, and he explains the way the warming trend

began as follows: A vast number of flowers, the coccolithophorids, are known to have become extinct at
this period of geologic history. One function of plant
life is to take in the CO_2 (carbon dioxide) expelled
by living organisms and turn it into oxygen and car-
bohydrates, thereby reducing the amount of CO_2 in the
atmosphere. There were so many of these coccolithophorids that their disappearance could have easily caused
a rise in the atmospheric level of CO_2. According to
McLean, solubility of CO_2 is inversely related to temperature; therefore, the slight rise in CO_2 caused by
the disappearance of the coccolithophorids would cause
a slight rise in temperature, which in turn would
cause a further rise in the level of CO_2 in the air.
Greater CO_2 concentration would raise the temperature
further, which in turn would allow the release of even
more CO_2 from the oceans, and so on.[24]

Having established the warming trend, McLean then
explains how this rise in temperature killed off millions of dinosaurs. McLean cites evidence that a rise
of as little as three degrees Celsius could have caused
the death of many of them, for several reasons. (The
great beauty of his theory is that the argument is the
same whether the animals were warm-blooded or cold-
blooded.) In general, the dinosaurs faced several

problems. One of these is that the dinosaurs, with their very low surface-to-volume ratios, would have had quite a bit of trouble releasing excess heat. Smaller animals have larger surface-to-volume ratios and therefore don't have this problem. The warming trend becomes especially significant in light of the fact that the rise in temperature need only be a fraction of what is required to cause immediate death, because heat kills sperm. Dinosaurs, who were not scrotal, could have become sterile due to a rise in temperature much less than the greenhouse effect is capable of causing. The possibility of male sterility is supported by an unusual number of unhatched eggs found in the most recent fossil layers of the Cretaceous period. There are several interesting side effects of the heat: high temperatures cause thinning of the eggshell in most birds; chickens in atmospheres of five per cent CO_2 laid eggs with thin shells after only a few hours' exposure; and thin eggshells lead to weak bones.[25] Scientists have used research carried out with birds largely because the small bird is the only living descendant of the dinosaur. It is quite likely that the heat and CO_2 affected the dinosaurs just as they affect the dinosaur's modern relative. Thus, the warming trend could have caused the extinction of the dinosaurs by causing infertility or by causing the production of weak eggs that didn't allow for strong young to be hatched.

All the theories discussed here have been formulated, presented, supported, and argued over endlessly by eminent scientists. It is not possible to judge their acceptability by the measure of the individual scientist's personal prestige. Rather, these theories must be judged by their plausibility, by how many coincidences or unclear causes they include. Clearly, a theory that relies on accident, a theory that is "scientifically glib," is not likely to be as acceptable as one which seems supported by other scientific data.

Some theories have obvious weaknesses: the cooling of the climate took place over a long period, much too long to cause the sudden extinction of the dinosaurs. Likewise, the change in vegetation should not have caused so sudden an event. We cannot prove that a supernova occurred, or that dinosaurs poisoned themselves. Finally, the theory of lime starvation does not itself account for an extremely rapid extinction, nor can it be proven by the geologic record that the earth during this period was deprived of lime.

Thus, we are left with McLean's greenhouse theory. If McLean and other scientists are right about a brief

warming trend caused by the greenhouse effect in the
late Cretaceous period, they can account for the extinction of dinosaurs but the survival of all other
forms of life. McLean's research is especially important to us today, since it may tell us something about
the survival of another dominant species--man. Scientists are worried now that modern man may soon confront
a greenhouse effect like that experienced by the dinosaurs. As McLean warns, the temperature is going up.

> Thus, the combined negative thermal effects on
> animal life and flooding associated with melting
> of the polar ice caps signal potential catastrophe
> ahead if the increasing atmospheric content of
> human generated CO_2 is not brought under control.
> A critical problem for humans is to avoid arriv-
> ing inadvertently at a critical threshold that
> might trigger an abrupt accelerated warming of
> the climate beyond their capacity to control, or
> adapt to it. The duration of such a "greenhouse"
> would, in human terms, last an interminable period,
> and its impact on life would be incalculable.[26]

The urgency is unmistakable. It is precisely this
urgency that makes McLean's theory so hard to ignore.
While man is not encumbered by the bulk that made
dinosaurs so susceptible to a rise in temperature, and
while man has mechanisms for releasing heat that dinosaurs lacked, if the greenhouse effect lasted long
enough and became severe enough, even man's great ability to adapt and survive might be threatened, and still
another "mass extinction" would be left in the geologic
record for some far distant life form to ponder.

End Notes

1. John C. McLoughlin, Archosauria: A New Look at the Old Dinosaur (New York: The Viking Press, 1979), p. 101.

2. "Rickety Dinosaurs," Chemistry, July, 1977, p. 3.

3. McLoughlin, p. 101.

4. McLoughlin, p. 85.

5. McLoughlin, p. 80.

6. "What Did In the Dinosaurs: Warm Blood or Soft Eggs?" Science News, 22 July 1972, p. 53.

7. Edwin H. Colbert, Dinosaurs: Their Discovery and Their World (New York: E. P. Dutton & Co., Inc., 1961), pp. 252-53.

8. Colbert, p. 254.

9. McLoughlin, p. 104.

10. Isaac Asimov, "Where Did All the Dinosaurs Go?" Science Digest, June, 1970, pp. 79-80.

11. McLoughlin, pp. 104-105.

12. Peter Gwynne and Susan Begley, "Second Thoughts about Dinosaurs," Newsweek, 15 May 1978, p. 98.

13. Daniel Cohen, "The Great Dinosaur Disaster," Science Digest, March, 1969, pp. 45-52.

14. Cohen, pp. 45-52.

15. Asimov, pp. 79-80.

16. Asimov, pp. 79-80.

17. Mark C. Blazek, "What Killed the Dinosaurs?" Science Digest, April, 1976, p. 24.

18. Adrian J. Desmond, The Hot-Blooded Dinosaurs: A Revolution in Paleontology (New York: The Dial Press/James Wade, 1976), p. 187.

19. McLoughlin, p. 103.

20. "Rickety Dinosaurs," p. 3.

21. "Rickety Dinosaurs," p. 3.

22. Colbert, p. 256.

23. Dewey M. McLean, "A Terminal Mesozoic 'Greenhouse': Lessons from the Past," Science, 4 August 1978, p. 405.

24. McLean, pp. 401-406.

25. McLean, pp. 403-406.

26. McLean, p. 406.

Bibliography

Asimov, Isaac. "Where Did All the Dinosaurs Go?"

Science Digest, June, 1970, pp. 79-80.

Blazek, Mark C. "What Killed the Dinosaurs?" Science

Digest, April, 1976, p. 24.

Cohen, Daniel. "The Great Dinosaur Disaster." Science

Digest, March, 1969, pp. 45-52.

Colbert, Edwin H. Dinosaurs: Their Discovery and

Their World. New York: E. P. Dutton & Co., Inc.,

1961.

Desmond, Adrian J. The Hot-Blooded Dinosaurs: A

Revolution in Paleontology. New York: The Dial

Press/James Wade, 1976.

Gwynne, Peter, and Susan Begley. "Second Thoughts

about Dinosaurs." Newsweek, 15 May 1978, pp. 96-

98.

McLean, Dewey M. "A Terminal Mesozoic 'Greenhouse':

Lessons from the Past." Science, 4 August 1978,

pp. 401-406.

McLoughlin, John C. Archosauria: A New Look at the

Old Dinosaur. New York: The Viking Press, 1979.

Ostrom, John H. "A New Look at Dinosaurs." National

Geographic, August, 1978, pp. 152-185.

"Rickety Dinosaurs." Chemistry, July, 1977, p. 3.

Thomas, Roger D. K., and Everett C. Olson, eds. <u>A</u>

   <u>Cold Look at the Warm-Blooded Dinosaurs</u>. Boulder,

   Colorado: Westview Press for the American Asso-

   ciation for the Advancement of Science, 1980.

"What Did In the Dinosaurs: Warm Blood or Soft Eggs?"

   <u>Science News</u>, 22 July 1972, p. 53.

Index

Note: Page numbers in italics refer to the Usage Manual.

Commonly Used Correction Symbols

ab	Improper abbreviation
ac	Adjective clause error
agr/pro	Pronoun and antecedent do not agree
agr/s-v	Subject and verb do not agree
cap	Use a capital letter
choppy	Choppy passage; sentences should be joined
cliché	Find a fresh phrase
f comp	Faulty comparison
inc. comp	Incomplete comparison
f coord	Faulty coordination
cs	Comma splice
dev	Paragraph development needed
dm	Dangling modifier
empty	Passage lacks substance; says nothing
euph	Inappropriate euphemism
focus	Sentence or passage is poorly focused
frag	Sentence fragment
gr	Grammar error such as wrong pronoun case; incorrect use of articles; incorrect verb form; adjective used for adverb or vice-versa; *like* or *as* misused
id	Error in idiom; wrong preposition used
jargon	Inappropriate use of jargon
lc	Use a lower case letter
logic	Illogical
mm	Misplaced modifier